W9-BZU-050

Fodor's EXPLORING

South Africa

FODOR'S TRAVEL PUBLICATIONS

NEW YORK • TORONTO • LONDON • SYDNEY • AUCKLAND

WWW.FODORS.COM

© Automobile Association Developments Limited 2006 (registered office: Fanum House, Basing View, Basingstoke, RG21 4EA, UK. Registered number 1878835).

Published in the United States by Fodor's Travel Publications, a unit of Fodors LLC, a subsidiary of Random House, Inc., and simultaneously in Canada by Random House of Canada Limited, Toronto.

Fodor's and Fodor's Exploring are registered trademarks of Random House, Inc.

Published in the United Kingdom by AA Publishing

ISBN: 1-4000-1624-X
ISBN-13: 978-1-4000-1624-2

Fifth Edition

Fodor's Exploring South Africa

Author: **Melissa Shales**
Joint Series Editor: **Josephine Perry**
Cartography: **The Automobile Association**
Cover Design: **Tigist Getachew, Fabrizio La Rocca**
Front Cover Silhouette: **Nik Wheeler**

A02413

Printed and bound in Italy by Printer Trento S.r.l.
10 9 8 7 6 5 4 3 2 1

How to use this book

ORGANIZATION

South Africa Is,
South Africa Was
Discusses aspects of life and culture in contemporary South Africa and explores significant periods in its history.

A–Z
Breaks down the country into regional chapters, and covers places to visit, including walks and drives. In addition, Focus On articles consider a variety of topics in greater detail.

Travel Facts
Contains the strictly practical information vital for a successful trip.

Hotels and
Restaurants
Lists recommended establishments throughout South Africa, giving a brief summary of their attractions.

Safari Guide
Rounds up South Africa's most common birds and animals and describes how to recognize them.

ADMISSION CHARGES
Standard admission charges are categorized in this book as: expensive (over R30), moderate (R15–R30) or inexpensive (under R15).

ABOUT THE RATINGS
Most places described in this book have been given a rating:

 ▶▶▶   Do not miss

▶▶   Highly recommended

▶   Worth seeing

MAP REFERENCES
To help you locate a particular place, every main entry has a map reference to the right of its name. This is made up of a number, followed by a letter, followed by another number, such as 54A2. The first number (54) refers to the page on which the map can be found. The letter (A) and the second number (2) pinpoint the square in which the place is located. The maps on the inside front cover and inside back cover are referred to as IFC and IBC, respectively. A red square denotes a place of interest.

Contents

How to use this book 4

Contents pages 5–7

My South Africa 8

SOUTH AFRICA IS 9–22
Heaven and hell 10–11
The toe of Africa 12–13
The powerhouse of Africa 14–15
The Rainbow Nation 16–17
Urban 18–19
Rural 20–21
Liberal 22

SOUTH AFRICA WAS 23–44
Prehistoric 24–25
The Cape of Good Hope 26–27
The early colonists 28–29
The Mfecane 30–31
The Great Trek 32–33
The British Empire 34–35
The Randlords 36–37
The Anglo-Boer Wars 38–39
Apartheid 40–41
The Struggle 42–43
Freedom 44

A–Z

Western Cape 45–101
Introduction 46–49
Cape Town 50–67
Cape Town environs 68–73
The Breede River Valley area 76–77
Groot-Karoo 78
Klein-Karoo 79–81
Overberg and South Coast 82–83
West Coast and Cederberg 84–85
Winelands 86–93

Focus On
Coloureds and Cape
  Muslims 64–65
Flora 74–75
Wine 88–89
Walks
Historic Cape Town 66–67
Stellenbosch 90–91
Drives and tours
The Cape of Good Hope 71–73
The wineries 92–93
Swellendam to Cape Agulhas 94–95
The Garden Route 96–101

Eastern Cape 102–121
Introduction 103–105
The Karoo 112–113
Nelson Mandela Bay 116–118
The Wild Coast 119
Focus On
Cape architecture 114–115
The Nguni 120–121
Tour
The 1820 Settler Towns 110–111

Free State, Northern Cape and North-West Province 122–145
  Introduction 122–125
  Free State 126–127
  Eastern Highlands 128–131
  Northern Cape 134–143
  Kimberley 137–139
  North-West Province 144–145

Focus On
The San 132–133
Diamonds 140–141
Tour
Diamond drive 142–143

Gauteng 146–173
  Introduction 147
  Johannesburg 148–157
  Johannesburg environs 157–159
  Pretoria (Tshwane) 162–169
  Pretoria environs 170–171
  Focus On
  Gold 160–161
  South African art 172–173
  Walk
  Central Pretoria 168–169

Mpumalanga and Limpopo Province 174–187
  Introduction 174–177
  Limpopo Province 178–180
  Mpumalanga 181–187
  Drive
  Rim of the escarpment 184–185

KwaZulu-Natal 188–215
  Introduction 188–191
  Durban 192–197
  Durban environs 200–201
  Battlefields 202–207

The Drakensberg 208–209
Pietermaritzburg and the Natal
  Midlands 210–211
Zululand 212–213
Northern KwaZulu 214–215
Focus On
Sports 198–199
Tour
The Disputed Territory 204–207

Beyond South Africa 216–224
  Introduction 216–217
  Lesotho 218
  Swaziland 219
  Zimbabwe 220–221
  Botswana 222
  Namibia 223
  Mozambique 224

Practicalities 225–240

TRAVEL FACTS 241–256

**HOTELS AND
RESTAURANTS** 257–265

Safari Guide 266–284

Index 285–288

Maps and Plans
South Africa: regions and
  three-star sights IFC–IBC
Western Cape 48–49
Cape Town 51
Cape Town environs 52
Drive: The Cape of Good Hope 72
Walk: Stellenbosch 90
Tour: The wineries 92
Drive: Swellendam to
  Cape Agulhas 94
Drive: The Garden Route 96–97
Eastern Cape 102
Tour: The 1820 Settler towns 110
Free State, Northern Cape, and
  North-West Province 124–125
Gauteng 146
Johannesburg environs 149
Johannesburg 150–151
Pretoria (Tshwane) 163
Mpumalanga and
  Limpopo Province 174
Drive: Rim of the escarpment 184
Kruger National Park 187
KwaZulu-Natal 188
Durban 192–193
Tour: The Disputed Territory 204
Beyond South Africa 216

Brought up in Zimbabwe, Melissa Shales has spent many years revisiting Africa, writing guides to South Africa, Zimbabwe and Kenya, as well as many articles on countries such as Mozambique, Botswana, Malawi, Namibia, Tanzania and Zanzibar. She has also written books about places as far afield as Paris, Marrakech, Turkey, India and Italy, and has edited over 100 travel guides.

My South Africa

When I researched the first edition of this book in 1995, Nelson Mandela had been in power for less than a year and the world was watching as a euphoric South Africa partied. Over three months and 16,000km (10,000 miles), I travelled by boat, plane, car, bus and helicopter. I stayed in guesthouses, game lodges, historic homes, business hotels and tents. I watched whales tumbling in Hermanus Bay, sat breathlessly still as an overly playful elephant tickled the back of my neck, and ate crocodile and ostrich, washed down with ambrosial wines. I played tourist under indigo skies and a blazing sun, in sandstorms and heaven-splitting thunderstorms, gossiped to kindly Afrikaner ladies, saw Cape Dutch mansions, Zulu huts and elegant Victorian town houses. Everywhere I went, I was overwhelmed by kindness and generous hospitality; it seemed an almost perfect holiday destination, a long, long way from the horrors of the apartheid years. All seemed possible.

I have been back to South Africa many times since then. My familiarity with the country has sometimes made it hard to spot the changes. South Africa has moved firmly onto the world stage, both as an economic and political tour de force and as one of the world's most popular tourist destinations. The towns are gradually turning more 'African', and community-based tourism is really taking foreign currency to the people who need it most. Yet there are still huge problems. Although political violence has effectively ended, there is still far too much violent crime in the cities. Rumours about high-level corruption are rife, and a horrifically high percentage of the working population is HIV positive. The economy is suprisingly buoyant, bouncing back after being badly knocked by word events. And there is still the seemingly endless task of raising all South Africa's people from below the poverty line to an acceptable standard of living, health care and education.

My latest trip was with my sister, who was returning for the first time since 1975. She was almost in tears at the seismic shifts for the better—the sense of optimism, hope, and promise that she felt all around her, and the immense pride in their country shown by all South Africans. For all its problems, this magical country has a lot to teach the West.

Melissa Shales

South Africa Is

Dismayed by horrific films of squatter camps and township violence, of police brutality and children lying dead in the dust, many tourists stayed away from South Africa until the 1994 elections. Now they are arriving in droves in search of the New South Africa; by 2003, visitor numbers had risen to over 6.5 million (1.95 million from outside Africa).

10

THE EUROPEAN IMAGE At first glance, South Africa looks like an affluent suburb superimposed on the African bush—exactly the impression its former rulers, middle-class urban whites, tried so hard to create. If it seems a little old-fashioned in some ways, it is also superficially comfortable, familiar, well tended and non-threatening.

South Africans used to pride themselves on clinging to the old virtues by which everyone went to church on Sunday, women stayed at home to look after their families, and the niceties of afternoon tea were strictly observed. It was a squeaky clean image based on the biggest conjuring trick in history—nearly 40 million people were made to vanish. The

Above: Sprawling Soweto shanties
Below: The Dutch Reformed church is the social hub of most small Afrikaner communities

harsh laws of apartheid kept Africa and poverty out of sight in huge settlements of corrugated iron and cardboard that appeared on no map or signpost. Black people were allowed into view only if they were smiling and subservient. Most towns were as European as possible, filled with chintz and antiques, trendy boutiques and coffee shops.

Tourism, designed largely for the South African home market, traditionally concentrated on the coast, whites-only game parks and cool, green uplands where golf courses stretch amid the pine plantations.

THE NEW SOUTH AFRICA Of course, this image of rich white/poor black, good black/bad white is as simplistic and unrealistic as any other cultural stereotype. The truth is far more complicated. South Africa has a population of about 44 million, with 11 official languages and cultural

traditions from across Europe, Asia and Africa. There has been violence and oppression, the non-whites have been shamefully used, and the townships are a sin against humanity, but today luxury dwellings and run-down shanties stand side by side on the same street. Tribal chiefs and traditional healers live and work alongside pinstriped politicians and orthodox medical professionals. There are black millionaires and professors, white taxi drivers, waiters and beggars, and even, astonishingly, black people who mourn the passing of apartheid.

The New South Africa is a mindbending paradox: A sunny land of apparent peace and harmony with a boiling undercurrent of violent crime in its centres. Voices of doom mutter about chaos and corruption or talk of

Below: Fruit stalls are affordable and accessible. Right: Middle-class suburbia lives behind tight security

betrayal. A surprisingly large number of people embraced the Government of National Unity's call for 'Masakhane' (Working together for a better future). Most people, of whatever colour, are optimistic that the changes are for better.

It was inevitably going to take some time for people to be rehoused, for

11

economic as well as political power to shift, for the richness of African culture to emerge from the townships and villages, for the history books and museums to be revised, and for a people used to being invisible to take possession of their true heritage. Ten years on, there are noticeable signs of improvement, although there is still a long way to go. Meanwhile, tourists still live largely in a luxurious and almost totally white world, withonly a quick tour of black South Africa. The difference is that they can now wander the lush gardens, swim in limpid pools and quaff fine wines without the slightest twinge of conscience.

Most Eurocentric world maps give little idea of how large South Africa actually is. With an area of 1,228,376sq km (474,153sq-miles), it is five times the size of the UK and one-eighth the area of the US. Kruger National Park alone is as big as Wales, and the distance between Johannesburg and Cape Town is the same as from London to Rome. The country has 2,954km (1,831 miles) of coastline bordering the Atlantic and Indian oceans.

12

BOUNDARIES South Africa has land borders with Mozambique, Swaziland, Zimbabwe, Botswana and Namibia, and totally surrounds the enclave of Lesotho. Since the 1994 elections, the country has been redivided into nine provinces, along roughly tribal lines—Western Cape, Eastern Cape, Northern Cape, North-West Province, Gauteng, Limpopo Province, Mpumalanga, the Free State and KwaZulu-Natal. At the time of writing, it still has three capitals, a legacy from the Second Anglo-Boer War. The legislature is in Cape Town (the former British capital); the administration is in Pretoria (Tshwane, capital of the old Transvaal); and the judiciary is in Bloemfontein (capital of the Orange Free State). Everyone seems happy with the status quo at the moment.

GEOGRAPHY The terrain ranges in altitude from sea level to South Africa's highest peak, Injasuti (3,408m/11,178ft), in the Drakensberg, near the Lesotho border, and covers ecosystems from tropical forest to desert dunes. Almost every crop known

❏ Cape Town is at about the same latitude as Sydney in Australia and Rio de Janeiro in Brazil. If folded into the northern hemisphere, it would be level with Cyprus or Los Angeles, while the Kalahari Desert would fit neatly into the Sahara. ❏

to humanity can find a natural home somewhere in the country.

The Western Cape, cut off from the hinterland by the mountains of the Cederberg, Hex River, and Swartberg, has a distinct Mediterranean climate with cool, grey, wet and windy winters and warmer, sunny summers. It is ideal for wine and deciduous fruits. The more northerly KwaZulu-Natal coast, also cut off by the vast wall of the Drakensberg, is subtropical, hot, and humid, clipped by the south-west monsoon. Here, the main crops are tropical fruits, such as bananas (the country's most profitable product), pineapples and sugarcane.

Beyond the mountains is the Karoo, a dramatic semidesert capable of supporting only sheep, ostriches and, increasingly, antelope, while in the west blow the barren red sands of the Kalahari. In the middle, the land climbs onto the high, flat central plateau, to the cattle and corn prairies of the Free State and, most importantly, the diamond and gold deposits of Kimberley and the Witwatersrand (see pages 137 and 160–161).

Finally, in the northeast, the high-veld drops off a dramatic escarpment in a flurry of mountains where tea and avocados, cherries and bananas, eucalyptus and pine all flourish cheek by jowl. Below, the lowveld provides a hot, dry habitat for baobabs, acacias, elephants and lions.

WATER South Africa is a land of plenty, rich in agriculture, industry and minerals, but there are only two

*From the roads across the Free State to the Kalahari and the fruit farms of the Cape,
distances are vast and the horizons endless*

major rivers, the Vaal and the Orange
(Gariep). The whole subcontinent is
regularly gripped by drought, the
population is rising steadily, and
with the change in government came
long-overdue schemes for creating
proper water supplies, plumbing and
drains in all the black towns and
villages. The demands on the water
supply continue to increase sharply
and, in spite of careful water
management and the occasional

season of magnificent rains, the
water table is dropping below the
level of the boreholes, and the desert
is expanding. In some areas, people
have already been forced off the
land, while the government is trying
to implement massive projects to
bring water down from the mountains of Lesotho and even from as far
north as the Zambezi (despite the fact
that Zimbabwe has its own serious
water problems to contend with).

South Africa is wealthy, ranking at 20 among the world's top trading nations and one of the largest producers of many minerals, notably gold. It accounts on its own for 15 per cent of the GNP of the African continent, but it also has Third-World slums, horrendous unemployment, homelessness and high crime levels. Vast problems must be overcome if the country's two societies are ever to merge without the entire economic structure collapsing.

SANCTIONS During the last years of apartheid, sanctions were enforced officially by the UN. However, South Africa was situated strategically across the Cape sea route and was a major supplier of vital minerals such as uranium and chromium. Most developed countries continued to trade under the counter, while neighbouring black countries were totally reliant on South Africa's ports. The economy was battered, but survived; turning inwards, it became broad-based and self-sufficient.

THE NEW WORLD Since the 1994 elections, when South Africa was welcomed back into the global fold, the economy has been pulled in many conflicting directions. Exports have risen rapidly; the wine industry has doubled production; and there are now five times as many foreign tourists, with numbers still rising. The government policy of affirmative action is providing fast track promotion for black managerial candidates. Multinational companies are lining up and the government welcomes anyone prepared to invest.

On the downside, new imports have damaged the balance of trade, while union demands for improvements for black wages to meet those of white workers, for a shorter working week, better conditions, and housing, has exacted a heavy toll on profits; the gold price dropped and the world-wide recession of the late 1990s hit hard. Nervous white workers left in droves, creating a brain drain, before there were enough well-qualified and experienced black workers to take their place. Strikes, lockouts and other industrial actions crippled some industries, while wage demands pushed prices up sharply.

The move from the land to the cities has been less a drift than a deluge; the black market or 'informal sector' runs most small businesses in the townships; and, as a final complication, an estimated 4 million illegal immigrants from elsewhere in Africa have flooded the job market.

❏ South Africa is the world's leading supplier of gold (15.7 per cent), aluminosilicates (36.9 per cent), chromium (49.5 per cent), platinum (65.9 per cent), vermiculite (43.9 per cent), and zirconium (46.7 per cent). It ranks second for titanium, vanadium and manganese; third for fluorspar and antimony; and is high among world rankings for diamonds and coal. It also has significant uranium iron, lead, silver, zinc, nickel and copper deposits. ❏

REDEVELOPMENT The main economic focus of the government is the implementation of the Reconstruction and Development Programme (RDP), a nationwide scheme to provide a proper infrastructure, including housing, water, drainage, electricity, schools and clinics for all black townships and villages. Large amounts of money are needed, with global aid pouring into the void alongside every

available scrap of tax revenue. The fledgling welfare system is stretched beyond its limits; inessentials and luxuries are being stripped away. With the honeymoon over, the black community is waiting impatiently for its slice of the cake.

So far, the government has steered a skilful route along this narrow, potentially treacherous divide, preaching self-help, patience, sustainable and environmentally friendly development, the expansion of legal business, equal opportunities, and capital investment. If they can convince their electorate and the international business community to back them with hard cash, South Africa could become an economic Utopia—manufacturing now makes up 25 per cent of all exports. Growth is at a healthy 4 per cent and inflation stable at 3–6 per cent. However, debt accounts for 37 per cent of the GDP and unemployment is still over 30 per cent. The rand and investment has recovered post 9/11 but with evidence of high-level corruption. President Mbeki has serious work to do to keep the country's progress on track.

Top: Downtown Johannesburg
Below: The Rand Club, still a focus for Gauteng's financiers

'Let us be channels of love, of peace, of reconciliation. Let us declare that we have been made for togetherness, we have been made for family, that, yes, now we are free, all of us, black and white together, we, the Rainbow People of God!' Archbishop Desmond Tutu.

The new South Africa has adopted Archbishop Desmond Tutu's catchy phrase as the slogan of its quest for racial harmony. It is singularly apt, given the country's complicated population mix. Of its estimated 44.5 million people, 75.2 per cent are black, 13.6 per cent white, 8.6 per cent mixed race and 2.6 per cent Indian.

The black population is subdivided into nine main tribal groupings based on language. Zulu (23 per cent of the population) and Xhosa (18 per cent) are the largest groups. Ndebele, Northern Sotho, Southern Sotho, Swati, Tsonga, Tswana and Venda are first languages for more than 1 million people, and each is further divided into local tribal groups. Minorities include the all-but-extinct San (Bushmen) and Khoikhoi (Hottentots), the aboriginal inhabitants of the country, and the Cape Malays, whose ancestors were slaves from the Dutch East Indies in the 18th century.

The 'coloureds' are mixed-race people, the result of early black-white or Khoi-San-Malay contact, although since the 19th century they have largely married among themselves, creating a distinct cultural group. The Indians, brought in to work the Natal

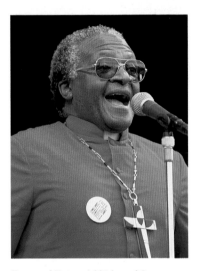

Desmond Tutu, archbishop of Cape Town during the years of struggle

cane fields and lumped together ethnically under apartheid, came mainly from the south, but most of India's 65 main 'tribes' are represented.

Most whites are Afrikaner (of Dutch extraction) or English. However, the 17th century saw significant immigration of Germans and French Huguenots fleeing religious persecution. Later additions include Greeks, Italians and Portuguese, as well as immigrants from every other nation in Africa and Europe. Finally, there is a substantial Jewish community.

LANGUAGE Afrikaans is the first language of around 15 per cent of the population, including many of the coloureds, and English of 9 per cent. These and the nine main black

South Africa's 'coloured' community has a distinctive and vibrant culture

16

❏ The Zulu, Xhosa and Ndebele all belong to a related racial group, the Nguni. Though similar in language and culture, they have been responsible for some of South Africa's most persistent conflicts: 19th-century frontier wars between the Zulus and Xhosa; traditional conflicts between the Xhosa and their offshoot tribe, the Mfengu; the Zulus' attempted slaughter of the renegade Ndebele in the early 19th century; and the vicious township wars of the late 20th century between the largely Xhosa-run ANC and the mainly Zulu Inkatha Freedom Party (IFP). ❏

survived even the darkest years of apartheid. The nearest thing to a state church has been the Protestant Dutch Reformed Church, the most influential of the myriad Christian churches.

Other important Christian denominations include the Church of England, the Roman Catholics, the Methodists and the thriving Church of Zion. There are also significant numbers of Hindus, Muslims and Jewish people, while many people still follow traditional African religions—often in tandem with Christianity.

Whatever their faith, South Africans are a fairly religious people, and many of them are deeply shocked by so-called Western liberalism and the upsurge in pornography since censorship was abolished. Most are also conservative (with a small 'c') when it comes to women's rights in the home or workplace. Though more women work today, few so far have risen higher than junior management.

languages are now all official languages of the country. English is used as the main language of government and business, and each province uses English, Afrikaans and whichever African language predominates. Most people speak fluent English and/or Afrikaans as well as their home tongue. The television news is presented in different languages on different evenings, and many broadcasts are multilingual.

THE CONSERVATIVE MAJORITY

South Africa has always been a secular state that allowed freedom of religion—a liberal policy that

Right: Ndebele woman
Top: Traditional bead work

From the time in 1652 when Jan van Riebeeck laid out his kitchen garden in the settlement that was to become Cape Town, to the emergence of Johannesburg's dramatic skyline from the squalor of a mining camp, South Africa's towns and cities have been carefully planned.

GRACIOUS LIVING Most towns were built on a grid layout, with Dutch-style squares and English-style parks to give a feeling of space, and broad streets lined with ornamental trees. Official buildings became ever larger and grander, culminating in Sir Herbert Baker's (see page 166) superb Union Buildings in Pretoria. Until the early 20th century, the towns were relatively multiracial, with areas like Cape Town's District Six and Johannesburg's Sophiatown as vibrant cultural melting pots. They produced innovative art, music and dance and created pockets of bohemian life beneath the stern noses of the Dutch Reformed pastors.

From the turn of the 20th century onwards, South Africa experienced an explosion of immigration from Europe. While suburbs of mock-Tudor houses cocooned in cool green

Above: Jacarandas shade many of Pretoria's streets. Below: Some of Soweto's better housing

gardens sprouted across the hills, the urban centres became crowded. The whites were increasingly anxious to enjoy their idyll untroubled by signs of poverty or race. A series of forced 'slum clearances' began as distraught non-whites were dumped far out of town. As soon as they were gone, their properties were bulldozed and the land redeveloped.

TOWNSHIPS Satellite townships grew up rapidly around every city. Few were marked on the maps or street signs, even though many were soon larger than their white neighbours. Some had family dwellings, serried rows of tiny tin-roofed houses. Others consisted of squalid, barrack-style hostels for male workers living three to a room and sharing a basic kitchen and bathroom among 12. Wives and families remained in the villages, seeing their men only once or twice a year. A very few of the larger townships like Soweto—already the size of a

18

major city—developed small middle-class areas with good houses and suitable facilities. On the whole, however, there were few real shops, the only food available sold from tiny market stalls. Clinics and schools were scarce and many of the latter were boycotted by children refusing to learn in Afrikaans. A boycott of the white alcohol trade led to the growth of shebeens, illegal drinking haunts. By the 1980s, shanty towns began to grow up around the official townships, vast seas of plastic, corrugated iron and cardboard. With the repeal of the Pass Laws in 1986, the situation became even worse as families flocked to the city to join their men, where they lived three families to a room or built new shanties.

DEVELOPMENT The government now has to sort out the mess. Most of the townships have been incorporated within the municipal boundaries of the white towns and money is being poured into development. Since 1994, the Reconstruction and Development Program has provided about 1.8 million new homes across the country. In some areas, the authorities are simply building streets, drains and lavatories. Families are allocated a plot with a lavatory and it is up to them to build their house around it. As black stallholders take their wares to the streets of the white cities,

Market stalls in Peddie—a lively, and essentially African, small town

specially built markets offer them new opportunities. Outside Johannesburg, few black families have moved into the white suburbs.

Levels of violent crime are finally dropping but are still high, and tourists should be cautious in cities, especially Johannesburg. White people visiting any black township are strongly recommended to take a black friend or guide to escort them.

❑ Official figures show that 60 per cent of the population live in towns. Today, however, the figure is probably closer to 80 per cent as women and children leave the villages to join their menfolk. ❑

Most of South Africa's large population is clustered in a few key cities. Much of the rest of the country seems almost empty. Large tracts of the Kalahari are virtually uninhabitable, with settlements spread sparsely along the few watercourses, while farms in the Free State and Karoo stretch over vast areas.

20

THE REMOTE LIFE The commercial farmers are still almost all white, many the descendants of trekboers who set out into the unknown in order to shake off the constraints of civilization. Today they pride themselves on being rugged individualists, living self-contained lives, mixing only with their families and a small handful of neighbours within driving distance. Water comes from boreholes run by windmills; many have their own electricity generators, although the national electricity grid is spreading. The arrival of TV satellite dishes, video recorders and fax machines has given them their first access to daily news and entertainment. All shopping is done by mail or on rare sorties into the nearest market town. Even these can be remote. Upington in the Northern Cape is 800km (496 miles) from its nearest city, Kimberley. Those who can afford it run small planes and plan their rare shopping trips to the city like a military campaign.

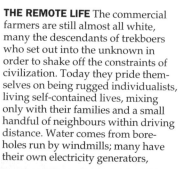

FROM SHEEP TO ANTELOPE The huge farms of the Free State and Karoo run half-wild cattle across virgin bush, or grow vast prairies of wheat and corn. In the Karoo, ostrich farming is making a triumphant return and many farmers are restocking the land with game shot out by their ancestors. Some are breeding antelope for the table, but more deal in live animals to sell to other farmers; others hope to set up lucrative private game reserves. Many are creating hunting concessions for the foreign market.

THE GOOD LIFE Near the coast, the landscape changes. In KwaZulu-Natal, there are still huge plantations of pineapple,

Top: Picking onions in Ceres
Above left: Venda village
Left: Farming in the Transkei

sugarcane and bananas, but most are within a few hours' drive of Durban and the resort towns on the coast. People here have far more contact with the outside world, while in the Western Cape, farmers are wealthy. The area specializes in intensive farming of high-yield fruit crops and, above all, wine. The valleys are patterned by small, neatly combed vineyards, and life is far more sociable, with everyone within easy reach. Because of the international nature of the wine trade, the strong French Huguenot influence and the proximity of Cape Town, the winelands are a remarkably sophisticated area with some of the classiest hotels and restaurants in the country. They also have some of the finest architecture—the white Cape Dutch houses built by the early settlers.

BLACK LIFE Outside those areas once designated as tribal homelands, there is virtually no independent black rural life. All non-whites were removed from any usable land. Some remained on the white farms, each of which has a thriving village housing the farm workers and their families.

Grapes are one of South Africa's most important crops

The work is hard and the pay is poor, but in other ways life is not all bad. Apartheid was always prepared to be paternal to those who toed the line and asked for little. Workers' houses are very basic, too small but hygienic; rudimentary medical care and schooling are provided; the pay often includes a ration of basic foodstuffs; and the farmer's wife usually runs a general store selling everything from canned foods to medicines, pens to beer. Some even provide staff and retirees with small plots on which to grow produce for themselves.

The traditional villages have all but disintegrated. The men have long worked away from home while the women brought up the children and took what work they could find locally. Some of the villages have grown into towns in all but name; others have been left to the old while the youngsters flock to the city. Hardly anywhere do you see the tiny patches and tethered goats of traditional rural life in Africa.

South Africa's constitution is one of the most liberal ever written, with a bill of rights guaranteeing equality for men and women of all races, creeds and colour, with freedom of speech and expression.

South Africa is now a republic within the Commonwealth, with two houses of parliament, the National Assembly and a National Council of Provinces. Until 1996, under a temporary power-sharing constitution, which allowed any party with over 5 per cent of the vote

Thabo Mbeki, who succeeded to the presidency after Nelson Mandela stepped down in 1999

to elect a vice president, Vice President Thabo Mbeki from the ANC (African National Congress) and former President F. W. de Klerk from the National Party acted as deputies to Nelson Mandela as president.

In 1996, shortly before the new permanent constitution came into effect, de Klerk resigned and the National Party withdrew from the Government of National Unity to become the main parliamentary opposition. In 1999, Nelson Mandela stepped down as president amid global celebrations of his achievement and Thabo Mbeki became executive president. The ANC took over 69 per cent of the vote at the last election.

The nine provinces all have a high degree of regional autonomy. Even in KwaZulu-Natal, where the IFP (Inkatha Freedom Party) led by Chief Mangosuthu Buthelezi was campaigning for further autonomy as a Zulu kingdom, things have now settled down and there is little of the violence between the ANC and Inkatha that characterized much of the 1980s and 1990s, with battles now fought in parliament and the courts instead of the streets. The small but persistent demand for an all-white Afrikaaner Volkstaat, led by Vryheidsfront (Freedom Front), the largely discredited AWB and several other small ultra-right wing parties, can be ignored.

Today, the main problems facing the government are the all too familiar global ones of housing, health, education, crime and corruption as the government battles to maintain white confidence and economic stability against the urgent needs of the rural villages, townships and squatter camps and the over-ambitions of the suddenly rich and powerful.

South Africa Was

One of the great debates of all time hovers over a single question: What are the origins of humankind? Charles Darwin was convinced that Africa held the clue, though his contemporaries ridiculed that idea. Man, they thought, was too grand for the dark continent.

It seems that Darwin may have been right after all. With each new find, it becomes more certain that Africa was the cradle of mankind. Research in the 20th century seems to have established that the emergence of the forerunner of modern man from ape-like prehuman forms took place in East Africa about 6 million years ago. More recent attention has been focused on the Leakey family's discoveries in the Rift Valley, at such sites as Olduvai Gorge and Koobi Fora, but some of the earliest discoveries that helped create the timetable of evolution were made in South Africa.

THE BIRTH OF HUMANITY The earliest of the protohumans were the australopithecines (literally 'southern apes'). The first discovery came in 1924 when a fossilized skull of an infant *Australopithecus africanus* (the 'Taung baby') was found in a limestone quarry at Taung in the Northern Cape. Its canine teeth, like those of man, were small, and from the shape of the skull its brain showed humanoid features. In 1936, Dr. Robert Broom unearthed the first adult cranium in the Sterkfontein Caves, near Johannesburg (see page 157). Exposed after 2.5 million years, the species was triumphantly hailed as the 'missing link' between ape and man. In 1998, an almost complete 3.3 million-year-old skeleton was also discovered at Sterkfontein. In 1945 came definitive proof that the species walked on two legs.

Australopithecus africanus lived between 1 and 3 million years ago.

Further discoveries have since identified several other species (or possibly subspecies) in Africa: *Australopithecus robustus*, and the even earlier *Australopithecus boisei* and *Australopithecus afarensis*, thought to date back around 5.5 million years.

From about 2 million years ago, a new species emerges. *Homo habilis* ('handy man') walked upright with an awkward gait and dramatically outsplayed feet, and probably lived partially in trees. He had a brain with less than half the capacity of that of a modern human, but his hands were flexible and capable of fashioning crude stone tools for hunting.

Top: Reconstruction of Australopithecus africanus. *Right: Fossil bones give clues to early man*

An artist's impression of
Australopithecus africanus

UPRIGHT MAN *Homo erectus*, the first of the protohumans to be fully adapted to standing and walking upright, with leg bones barely distinguishable from those of modern man, lived 1.5 million–250,000 years ago. His brain was smaller than ours, but it is thought that he could speak, and his hands were free to develop the most crucial of human skills: The ability to make and to use tools. He was also the first to kindle a fire, and the first to have wandered beyond the African continent—*Homo erectus* bones have been found in China and Java. Some of the earliest remains were excavated in 1948 at Swartkrans, near Krugersdorp.

HOMO SAPIENS Modern man is still a babe in arms in this time frame.

The earliest *Homo sapiens* and Neanderthal subspecies are believed to have emerged about 100,000 years ago. By about 40,000BC, *Homo sapiens* (modern man) was dominant and spreading fast, with a varied array of cultures. Southern Africa was inhabited by the San (Bushmen) whose lives as nomadic hunters remained relatively unvaried until the arrival of black tribes from the north and white tribes from the sea.

The story has not ended, however. Each new find adds another piece to the puzzle. In 1995, some foot bones from Sterkfontein, lying forgotten in a museum, were re-examined. They belong to an australopithecine nicknamed 'Littlefoot', have a slightly divergent big toe and weight-bearing arch, are extraordinarily early (dating from 3.3 million years ago), and have overturned all existing theories on how man came to walk upright.

The history of the Cape of Good Hope is inextricably linked with the search for and defence of a sea route to India. It is a history of rivalry between the Portuguese, the English, the Dutch and, to a lesser degree, the French.

26

PORTUGUESE EXPLORERS The earliest recorded voyage around the Cape was made in 1488 by the Portuguese navigator Bartolomeu Dias. Dias failed to discover the long-searched-for route to India, but a decade later one of his countrymen, Vasco da Gama, succeeded. Da Gama triumphantly rounded the Cape in 1488, then went on to reach the Indian subcontinent before returning to Europe in 1499. At last the route to the Indies had been found, and the trade potential was enormous. The Portuguese moved quickly to consolidate and protect the route, claiming the right to overlordship of the Indian Ocean and domination of its trade.

Early expeditions all called into southern Africa as they passed, to collect water or barter with the Khoikhoi for fresh meat, but no efforts were made to set up a permanent outpost. Table Bay itself was not explored until 1503, when Admiral Antonio de Saldanha climbed Table Mountain and visited Robben Island. Later that century, the Portuguese lost their dominant trading position to the Netherlands and England, who both set about finding routes to the East.

DUTCH SETTLEMENT In 1580, Sir Francis Drake rounded the Cape, and by 1591 the first English expedition bound for the Indies had left Plymouth. By 1594 the Dutch were on their way. Early in the 17th century, national efforts were controlled by the British East India Company and the Dutch East India Company respectively. It was the Netherlands, with its larger merchant fleet, that dominated trade. The Dutch East India Company established a victualling station at the Cape, and in 1652 Jan van Riebeeck was dispatched to run it. His job was to provide fresh water, vegetables and meat for passing Company mariners—who suffered all kinds of deprivation on the long voyage from Europe—as well as to repair their vessels.

A STRATEGIC BASE Dutch rule came to an end with the first British invasion in 1795 as part of the military strategy of the Napoleonic Wars. The colony was

Top: Table Mountain
Left: A 16th-century view of Africa

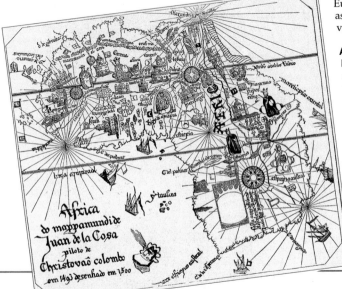

handed back in 1803, only to be invaded in 1806 when Napoleon again became a danger. This time, the Congress of Vienna (1815) confirmed the British occupation and the Cape colony was ceded to the British Crown. The aim was strategic, as by then, the Cape had become a naval base on the sea route to India and the Far East.

The Cape became an important focus of

communication—a vital link between the motherland and far-flung territories. The Royal Navy set up its local headquarters in Simon's Town, and many thousands of eager white immigrants landed here, ready to make their fortunes in the diamond and gold fields. The 1890s was a decade of almost unparalleled growth as South Africa's economy boomed. During World War I the route became strategically important, as

merchant shipping that might otherwise have used the Suez Canal was diverted south. After the war, the route was no longer profitable and trade dwindled until the fresh outbreak of war in 1939, when history repeated itself.

DECLINE AND RECOVERY The Egypt–Israeli war of 1967, which closed the Suez Canal, again focused attention on the Cape. In the 1980s, trade sanctions were imposed on South Africa and traffic tailed off until the Cape's most frequent visitors were bulky supertankers simply too big to pass through the Suez Canal. Regular passenger transport declined; the last mail-ship voyage took place in October 1977. Today, with South Africa back at the helm of the continent's economy, freighters and cruise ships are lining up to get into its ports, and the future is looking hopeful.

Left: Jan van Riebeeck
Below: Cape Town in the 17th century

27

The arrival of the first Dutch settlers in the Cape in the 1650s was to have far-reaching consequences, not only for the locals, but for the very survival of stable African societies throughout the entire subcontinent.

EARLY LINKS The Khoikhoi (called Hottentots by the early Dutch colonists) were mainly gentle pastoralists who were happy to barter sheep and cattle for iron and other metals. It was a trade that became vitally important to the survival of European mariners on their months-long voyage to the East.

For centuries, the sailors came, looked, traded and went away again. A few stayed awhile on dry land. The Portuguese, who pioneered the route to India, were sometimes shipwrecked, having to stay on the shores of Table Bay until rescued by the next passing fleet. In 1615, the British left a small party of convicts, but they retreated to Robben Island until rescued. Then, in 1647, the crew of a wrecked Dutch East Indiaman, the *Haerlem*, built a fort during their year-long stay.

FOUNDING OF THE CAPE COLONY It was only in 1652, when the Dutch East India Company established the Cape refreshment station for the scurvy-ridden crews of passing ships (see page 26), that a settled white community came into existence, with a set policy and continuity of command. The local Khoikhoi welcomed the Dutch settlers at first, conducting trade as usual. Jan van Riebeeck, the first commander of the new Cape Colony, successfully gained their trust, all the while claiming the Cape Peninsula and adjacent land for the VOC (Verenigde Oost-Indische Compagnie—Dutch East India Company, see box below). Contact with the Khoikhoi was at first restricted by the Company. As a result, a small number of Company employees—particularly those free burghers the Company had released from its service, and to whom it had granted land—were unable to find local labour, and imported slaves from the East Indies.

By the 1680s, the settlers were moving out from the embryonic Cape Town and were successfully raising their own cattle. The Khoikhoi lost not only their barter livelihood, but also, gradually, their grazing land and water rights as the Europeans annexed the lush, well-watered valleys. The Khoikhoi society began to disintegrate. In 1713 smallpox decimated the people of the south-western Cape, and by the 1740s the remaining few were working as labourers for the colonists, many in conditions of dreadful servitude.

EXPANSION In the early years settler numbers increased slowly. The majority were Dutch, members of the Dutch Reformed Church, but their numbers were augmented by Germans and French Huguenots escaping from persecution in their homelands. Many of these settlers

❑ In 1602, the Dutch East India Company received a charter to conduct all Dutch trade between the Cape of Good Hope and the Strait of Magellan. With its headquarters in Batavia (Jakarta), it acted more like a nation than a trading company, conquering and ruling huge territories and fighting off all competition. The profits were enormous in the 17th century, but trailed off over the next hundred years until, by 1799, with corrupt officials, it was nearly bankrupt. The company was dissolved and its possessions and debts were taken over by the Dutch state. ❑

An ox wagon, a major form of transportation, approaching a Boer farm

brought to Africa a tradition of dissent and a legacy of resentment against Europe.

As the settlement expanded, borders were extended. When the burghers sought to beat the Company's often draconian rules by quitting areas under their control, the authorities simply extended their influence into the newly formed districts.

By the 1770s many settlers had drifted well beyond the confines of van Riebeeck's original territory, heading northwards as far as the Orange River and eastwards towards the Great Fish River. The more determined were farmers driven by a ruthless quest for land, larger herds and, above all, total independence. They drew European control far into the hinterland, eventually coming into conflict with more warlike people—such as the Xhosa on the Eastern Frontier—who found themselves having to defend their territory against the gun.

29

Governor Willem van der Stel at his farm, Vergelegen

Mfecane *(literally 'crushing')* is a word used by the Zulus to describe the ripple effect of early 19th-century Zulu expansion and empire-building in what is now KwaZulu-Natal. *The keys to these events were a need for land and the vengeful bloodlust of Shaka.*

Among the often warlike Nguni societies of the 18th century (see page 17), chiefdoms expanded, spilling over into ever more virgin territory. Consequently, by the beginning of the 19th century there was a land shortage, aggravated by a devastating drought, overgrazing, serious soil erosion and the ever closer presence of the white Voortrekkers (see pages 32–33). A scramble for power and influence ensued, forcing many smaller chiefdoms into defensive alliances against land-hungry foes. This led to larger groupings, such as the southern Mthethwa. Their ruler (from about 1809) was Dingiswayo, considered to be the first of the great Zulu kings. Another such group included the northern Ngwane who, under Sobhuza, were to flee inland, defeating smaller Sotho and Nguni clans they met on the way and eventually amalgamating them into what became the Swazi nation.

SHAKA In 1815, Dingiswayo was murdered by a rival clan, the Ndwandwe. Shaka emerged as the new king. Born in 1787, the son of a minor Zulu chief, he grew up in Dingiswayo's court and became a military commander. One of his first acts was to change the name of the ruling tribe and all the conquered clans to that of his clan, the Zulus. Shaka was a military genius and totally ruthless. From the moment he took power, he set about expanding his army, turning it into one of the deadliest fighting forces in Africa. He invented the hugely effective, short stabbing *assegai* to replace the traditional javelin-style throwing spear, allowing the army to reuse their weapons. He also developed brutally efficient new tactics, such as the terrifying *impi* with the warriors attacking in a curved 'bull-and-horns' formation. In this, the main army advanced on the enemy from the front, while units of the fastest runners created diversions down the opposition's flanks, and troops from the rear moved around outside the horns to close the circle. By the end of his reign, Shaka had subjugated most of the smaller, weaker clans and controlled a vast area of land, left vacant by the flight of those who refused to submit to his authority. Murdered in 1828 by his half-

British Lieutenant Farewell negotiates with Shaka

❏ A second word, *Difaqane*, also describes this period of black South African history. A Sotho word, it is used for the intertribal wars west of the Drakensberg that followed invasions of peoples fleeing the Mfecane wars farther east. Of all the conquered and dispossessed tribes, the Sotho were the most affected, and their word has connotations of defeat and loss. ❏

brothers, Dingane and Mhlangane, he remains one of the greatest heroes of the Zulu nation.

THE BATTLE FOR LAND It was the ripple effect caused by the refugees from Zulu might that created such widespread upheaval. As terrified peoples moved north, they collided and clashed with other inhabitants who had settled in a wide arc which spread from what is now Swaziland to the highveld and Lesotho. In turn, the new arrivals displaced the former settlers as they secured land on which they could graze their cattle and grow their crops.

The events of this period gave rise to an enduring myth: The land into which the Voortrekkers and other early pioneers stepped in the 19th century was empty country, depopulated by the Mfecane. The reality was quite different. In fact, this was a land where people had gathered in places of safety and were desperately endeavouring to re-establish order in their shattered societies. The presence of the settlers—with their guns, wagons and horses—only exacerbated an already unpleasant situation, eventually leading to appalling violence and some of the most tragic episodes in South Africa's history, among them the horrifying Battle of Blood River (see page 204).

Boers charge Dingane's army

The Great Trek signalled the determination of Dutch-speaking farmers (Boers) to find a 'Promised Land' where they would be beyond the limits of British control. This led briefly to the establishment of several independent Boer republics. The Great Trek is a landmark in the history of South Africa, heralding an era of expansionism, bloodshed and land seizure.

INTO THE INTERIOR The Trek began in 1835, when the first of many groups of bitter Voortrekkers left Grahamstown, Uitenhage and Graaff-Reinet and headed for the largely unknown interior. The Eastern Cape was a particularly tense region, being the frontier between Xhosa territory and the Cape Colony and a focus for refugees who had fled the rise of the Zulu state. The Boers were unhappy about having to fight the Xhosa for land or submit to British rule. They felt that the colonial government had failed to provide them with sufficient protection against the Xhosa, while the abolition of slavery in 1834 had robbed them of valued possessions.

That year, reconnaissance expeditions claimed that Natal was fertile and largely uninhabited. In fact, the Africans had only moved away temporarily in the wake of the Mfecane and were soon to return, only to find themselves ousted by Boer intruders (see page 31).

During the following decade, thousands more Boers migrated, many of them the so-called 'trekboers', semi-nomadic pastoral farmers; others were cattle ranchers or sheep farmers. Each group of Voortrekkers had its own leader but they all followed much the same route through 'Transorangia' (the highveld), only splitting when some went into Natal while others continued north.

VOORTREKKER LIFE A family might have more than one wagon carrying all its worldly goods. Drawn by oxen, the wagons could hold a surprising amount—furniture, bedding, clothes, food, agricultural implements, weapons and shot, even fruit trees. They were narrow and designed to put as little weight as possible onto the oxen. In the evenings the wagons were drawn into a protective circle (*laager*), the gaps and space under the wheels filled with thorn branches. The *laager* became an instant fort for the Voortrekkers, who would hide behind the wagons and shoot at any attackers. The livestock were herded into a *kraal* (corral) in the middle. People would gather around a fire to sing, pray, chat and even dance.

Top: Tapestry homage to the Voortrekkers, Pretoria. Left: Statue of Piet Retief, Pietermaritzburg

THE BOER REPUBLICS The varied terrain the Voortrekkers covered, at a rate of about 10km (6 miles) a day, was treacherous. Not only was the topography often difficult, but they ran the risk of encounters with wild animals, the tsetse fly, and the malarial mosquito. The courage they displayed is still a key feature of Afrikaner folklore. They also ran into strong local resistance. Small parties of trekboers, missionaries and adventurers had preceded them, so the Africans were not completely unused to the white man, but this was the largest group they had ever seen. In 1838 a party led by Piet Retief was massacred by Dingane. Desire for revenge led to the Battle of Blood River (see page 204) and eventually to Dingane's death and the creation of the Boer Republic of Natalia (1838), which was promptly annexed by Britain. The Boers then trekked north, and in 1860 formed the South African Republic (ZAR) in Transvaal. Another party proclaimed the Orange Free State (1854) beyond the Vaal and Orange rivers. Others headed for Delagoa Bay and were annihilated by the Tsonga, while a party led by Louis Trichardt ended up in Lourenço Marques, where most died of tropical diseases.

Voortrekkers crossing the Transvaal

The British ruled this corner of Africa for most of the 19th century. Their initial occupation of the Cape in 1795 had little impact, and it was only from 1814 onwards, eight years after they had wrested the Cape Colony from the Dutch for the second time, that they started to develop the Cape's potential for settlement and trade. This African subcontinent, Britain finally realized, would be an excellent source of labour and raw materials and a market for manufactured goods.

British rule in the 19th century was characterized by certain key events now regarded as milestones in South Africa's history. It started with the mass immigration in 1820 of settlers from Britain. This resulted in exhausting conflict with the Xhosa on the eastern frontier, and the gradual settling by whites of what is now called KwaZulu-Natal, following the Great Trek. In 1843, Natal was annexed by Britain as a second colony. Subsequent bloody clashes between Zulu, Boer and Briton punctuated the following decades.

BOERS VERSUS BRITAIN In 1852 and 1854, Britain recognized the independence of two new Boer republics, the fledgling South African Republic (ZAR) in the Transvaal and the Orange Free State. Then, in 1877, it annexed the Transvaal in the first attempt to create a federation in southern Africa. In 1880, the Boers, led by Paul Kruger, revolted against their new government. Within a few weeks they had won the first Anglo-Boer War, enjoying a crushing victory at the Battle of Majuba (1881). Kruger became president of the ZAR, while William Gladstone's government agreed to withdraw the British force and restore self-government to the Boers. Kruger grudgingly accepted this arrangement, which

Top: A model soldier in Talana Museum, Dundee
Left: The Battle of Majuba— a crushing defeat for the British

Above: Cape Prime Minister Cecil Rhodes. Right: ZAR President Paul Kruger

was formalized by the Convention of Pretoria in 1881.

The empire-builders were far from content. They had visions of controlling territories in Africa from the Cape in the south to Cairo in the north, and although Britain still claimed status as the paramount power in South Africa and reserved ultimate control over the Transvaal's foreign affairs, it could not now claim the republic as a colony. Many resented this, among them the multimillionaire diamond magnate, Cecil John Rhodes (prime minister of the Cape in the 1890s).

The discovery of gold in 1886 made the Transvaal the richest and most powerful nation in southern Africa— and that made Britain nervous. It also made millionaires Cecil Rhodes and Alfred Beit a second fortune, and brought Boer and *uitlander* (foreigner) into conflict. The wealth of the Witwatersrand proved too alluring a prize. In 1895, Rhodes and others conspired to take over the Transvaal and install a British administration by means of the ill-fated Jameson Raid

(see page 37). The raid was a disaster, but it indicated British intentions to Kruger. The Second Anglo-Boer War was not long in coming (see pages 38–39). The victorious British granted limited self-government to former Boer republics, but from then on, they effectively controlled the whole of modern South Africa and all its mineral wealth.

UNION After the war, the colonial government began the process of reconstruction. The mines were put back into operation and, by 1907, the former republics were given representative government. In 1910 the Cape, Natal, the Orange Free State and the ZAR were bound into a single national entity, the Union of South Africa. The local black Africans were not consulted. Voter franchise—or the lack of it—was the most negative outcome. Only whites could be elected to parliament, and English and Dutch became the official languages. By excluding blacks, the Act of Union sowed the seeds of discontent resolved only with the freeing of Nelson Mandela in 1990.

In the last quarter of the 19th century, the discovery of diamonds in Kimberley, followed by the first gold diggings on the Witwatersrand, transformed the landscape, population and history of South Africa. Almost overnight, what had been a poor and little-known country became rich, famous and powerful.

Fortune-hunters rushed to the arid zones of discovery from every corner of the globe. They included some two dozen men, most of them immigrants from England, Holland and Germany, who staked claims but also started auxiliary services. They opened hotels, set up dealerships, and even ran the elevators that gave the men access to their diggings. They also built alliances, fed feuds and appetites, and, in the 1870s and 1880s, went on to take control of the diamond fields. From 1886 onwards, they moved north to finance and run the gold mines. Nicknamed the Randlords by the British press, they acquired immense wealth, power and influence.

WEALTH AND POWER Supreme among the Randlords was Cecil John Rhodes—diamond magnate, gold-mine owner, politician and empire-builder extraordinaire. His chief rival for control of the diamond fields was showman Barney Barnato, who combined financial wizardry and cabaret. Other high fliers in this mixed bunch were Lionel Phillips, Alfred Beit, Joseph Robinson, Julius Wernher, Solly Joel and Samuel Marks. Later, Ernest Oppenheimer founded the dynasty that still controls the world's diamond market.

The Randlords' lives were colourful and controversial. Their ostentatious wealth contrasted dramatically with the increasing poverty of the rural poor, both white and black. Only the feather barons in Oudtshoorn (see page 80) came anywhere near matching their flamboyant lifestyle. They built large, showy mansions in and around fledgling Johannesburg as well as in fashionable parts of London. They collected art, much of which forms the

Top: The diamond diggings at Kimberley
Above left: The powerful Oppenheimer family in 1933
Left: Showman millionaire Barney Barnato

36

Prospectors used simple methods to find gold in 1900

core of major national galleries in Cape Town and Johannesburg, sponsored foundations, and set up scholarships. But this immense wealth brought with it a lust for power—those who controlled the gold controlled the country.

Photo: *Mr. G. T. Ferneyhough*
PROSPECTING FOR GOLD ON THE RAND.

THE SHAPING OF MODERN SOUTH AFRICA

The Randlords' most enduring legacy is to the economy of South Africa. The discovery of gold and of diamonds contributed hugely to South Africa's regional power base and gave it a crucial standing in the world economy. Mining has affected the lives of every one of the social and ethnic groups in the country. One of the first pieces of discriminatory legislation to be passed on the way to apartheid was designed to oust black miners from their diamond claims, make sure that claim ownership was white, and reduce the blacks on the diamond fields to a cheap, compliant labour pool. Gold was vital to the subcontinent and cheap labour was vital to gold if profit margins were to be kept high on international sales. The Randlords were easily persuaded to ally with many of the worst racial excesses of the republican and, later, the South African governments.

THE JAMESON RAID

The struggle for control finally toppled into intrigue and war. Rhodes, as prime minister of the Cape Colony, wanted to oust Paul Kruger, leader of the Transvaal Boers, and set up a British-ruled Federation of South Africa. With his sights on yet another personal fortune, he was convinced that only Britain possessed the know-how to exploit the region's immeasurable riches. The deeply religious Kruger not only regarded the discovery of gold as a mixed blessing, but was hostile to the presence of the British and other *uitlanders*. In 1895, Dr Leander Jameson, a close associate of Rhodes, led a raiding party into the Transvaal aiming to cause an insurrection and remove Kruger. The Jameson Raid not only ended in ignominious defeat and finished Rhodes' political career in South Africa, it also sowed the seeds for the Second Anglo-Boer War.

In 1870, the British annexed a small hill on the Orange Free State border, which turned out to be the Kimberley diamond pipe; then gold was discovered, and in 1877 they annexed the South African Republic (ZAR). The furious Boers fought for their independence and won, at the Battle of Majuba in 1881.

THE PATH TO WAR The ZAR was officially given its independence again in 1884, but by then its gold was attracting great interest from scores of foreign prospectors. British imperialists, goaded on by the huge wealth being engendered, instigated the Jameson Raid in 1895 (see page 37), hoping to ignite an uprising that would lead to the installation of a British administration in the ZAR. It was a disaster, and subsequent events led President Kruger to demand that Britain withdraw the troops massed on his border. Ignored, he invaded Natal in 1899, and so began the Second Anglo-Boer War.

Kruger's commandos were in essence a 'people's army', wearing civilian clothes. But they had a distinct advantage over the regular British troops because they knew the countryside and climate and were excellent horsemen. Before the war was over, Britain had committed 448,715 troops—outnumbering the Boers by nearly five to one.

THE SIEGE OF LADYSMITH The Boers started out well, as they beat the British at Talana Hill and routed them at Nicholson's Nek. But their four-month siege of Ladysmith in northwest Natal was ill-timed and ended in disaster. The Boers' original aim was to advance into Natal and the Cape to stem the influx of British troops, but the siege lasted too long. Even though it tied up four-fifths of the British army, the road to Durban was left virtually open, and the Boers—aside from attacks at Weenen, Estcourt and Mooi River—remained far too cautious. The British had time to bring up fresh troops via Durban, the Boers lost their advantage—and ultimately lost the war.

Various unsuccessful attempts were made to relieve Ladysmith, such as the disastrous Battle of Colenso, but it was not until after such famous battles as Spienkop and Paardeberg that the siege was lifted.

Top: The Battle of Majuba, 1881. Left: Jameson captured by the Boers in 1895

Le Petit Journal

SUPPLÉMENT ILLUSTRÉ

Huit pages / CINQ centimes

DIMANCHE 19 JANVIER 1896

AU TRANSVAAL

Le docteur Jameson prisonnier des Boers

CONCENTRATION CAMPS In 1900, Pretoria and then Johannesburg surrendered, but the war was not yet over. A rural guerilla war began as Boer commandos split up, continuing the fight in smaller, more mobile bands in an effort to deny the British control of the countryside. Retribution was swift and terrible. For every belligerent act, every sabotage of railway lines, the British reacted with twice the force. They burned farmhouses, instituting a devastating scorched-earth policy. Anything that might sustain the guerillas was flushed out of the countryside, and that included horses, cattle, sheep, women and children. Boer women and children—so-called refugees— were dumped into huge camps, located near the railways and run along military lines—the world's first concentration camps. Neglect of elementary precautions led to epidemics of typhoid and dysentery. By the end of the war, 136,000 Afrikaners were imprisoned in 50 camps; over 26,000 women and children had died of disease and neglect. The horror of the camps was brought to light by an English philanthropist, Emily Hobhouse, and these revelations helped bring about the Peace of Vereeniging (1902). There is a memorial to the Afrikaner dead in Bloemfontein (see page 127).

❑ Whites were not the only inmates of the concentration camps. Entire populations of black locations or mission stations were uprooted and transferred to sites adjoining the Boer camps. It is believed that by the end of the war, there were some 115,700 Africans living in 66 camps. Unlike the whites, they were used as a labour force for the British army, and were not fed, as they were expected to be self-sufficient. More than 14,000 deaths are recorded; there were undoubtedly many others. There is no memorial to the African dead. ❑

Boers hold their position against the Grenadier Guards, 1900

'Apartheid' means the segregation and separate development of the races. Though its roots go back to the slave-owning colonists and to economic and political developments in the 19th century, much of the legislation that made up the core of apartheid policy was, in fact, born of 20th-century British policies.

FIRST STEPS Basing their thinking on the teachings of John Ruskin, the British colonial administrators came up with an ideal of separate development, by which the 'superior' (i.e. white) race assisted the other races towards an eventual goal of equality and reintegration. Meanwhile, they would be given tasks suitable to their abilities and progress (i.e. menial). It was, of course, in the interests of the dominant whites to ensure that progress was not too swift. The ultra-right-wing Afrikaner Broederbond (Brotherhood), founded in 1918, took the notion much further.

It was Jan Smuts' Native Affairs Act of 1920 that took the first step towards real political segregation, establishing the principle that African political activity should be divorced from 'white' South Africa. It ushered in a period of intense debate on 'native policy', during which state ideology was refined and clarified.

APARTHEID LEGISLATION Nearly 30 years later, in 1948, the Afrikaner National Party under Hendrik Verwoerd and D. F. Malan coined the word 'apartheid', and fought and won the election on a ticket of oppression. The new government immediately adopted apartheid as a national political scheme, bringing in many new laws. What is called 'petty' apartheid was instituted: separate public benches, building entrances and public lavatories. These regulations were united under the Separate Amenities Act. Sex outside marriage between races was already banned, but the 1949 Mixed Marriages Act and the Immorality Act banned any sex between the races. The Population Registration Act of 1950 legislated for a national register according to racial classification, with every citizen to be issued with documents stating their racial group. Race was identified by physical attributes, 'measurable' in ways that defy belief, for example, if an official stuck a pencil in your hair and it stayed fast, you were black, not coloured (mixed race).

Laws allowing Africans into urban areas were redefined; Africans had to carry a pass with them at all times. Failure to do so was a criminal offence. This effectively made Africans aliens in their own land. 'Group Areas' defined as White, Black, Indian or Coloured made physical separation absolute. You lived where the state told you to. If you tried to resist, you were forcibly removed. On the crucial issue of land, the Prevention of Illegal Squatting Act (1951) gave the government power to move African tenants from privately or publicly owned land.

Top: Apartheid even led to separate beaches
Left: Hendrik Verwoerd, architect of apartheid

More and more demonstrators braved the police

All this was only the completion of legislation begun under Cecil John Rhodes as prime minister of the Cape Colony from 1890 to 1895. The exclusively Afrikaner Nationalist politicians justified the ruthless apartheid system as the only alternative to segregation and the end of white South Africa.

THE DEATH OF APARTHEID For 30 years the National Party government wrestled with the implementation of apartheid, an unwieldy, contradictory, and deeply unsavoury policy. There was heavy media censorship, a total lack of freedom of speech, and increasing violence, with torture, poorly explained deaths, disappearances and attendant horrors. But the level of protest, at home and abroad, grew steadily and bravely until white South Africa was an international pariah.

Under the force and effect of economic sanctions and diplomatic pressure, President F. W. de Klerk announced that he would repeal discriminatory laws. Seizing the political initiative, he surprised his supporters by unbanning the African National Congress (ANC), the Pan African Congress (PAC) and the Communist Party—and releasing from jail the popular hero Nelson Mandela. The government, bowing to the inevitable, finally abandoned the indefensible apartheid policy, explaining it away as an experiment that foundered and did not work.

The roots of the Struggle are nearly as deep as those of the oppression. By the end of the 19th century, a feeling of African nationality was emerging among the Christian-educated blacks. At first this focused around religion, with the foundation of many African churches, but political movements were not far behind.

FIRST STIRRINGS In 1912, a handful of mission-educated black men in the Eastern Cape and Natal founded the South African Native National Congress (SANNC), the country's first black political party. Four years later, the University of Fort Hare opened, giving blacks a first chance at higher education. Around the same time, a young Indian lawyer, Mohindas Karamchand Gandhi, began the first of his many non-violent protests on behalf of the Natal Indians. In the 1920s, the mainly Zulu Inkatha Movement was founded, also in Natal. Any small political successes were met with a massive right-wing backlash.

In 1923, the SANNC became the African National Congress (ANC),

which in 1928 began to work with the Communist Party. The war years saw the creation of the African Miners' Union and the ANC Youth League, the first mass protests in the townships, bus boycotts, squatter camps and black-run strikes in the mines. All were crushed violently by the police. The outcome was the Nationalist victory in the 1948 elections, and the official implementation of apartheid.

Below and opposite: Violence and death dogged the fight for freedom
Right: Steve Biko

PROTEST AND SUPPRESSION In 1959, the more militant Pan African Congress (PAC) was formed by breakaway members of the ANC, led by Robert Sobukwe. In 1960 Sobukwe persuaded thousands to burn their pass books (see page 40). In Sharpeville, south of Johannesburg, the police panicked and fired on a crowd, killing over 200 people. The government declared a state of emergency, arrested Sobukwe, and banned the PAC and ANC. Both organizations went underground and formed military wings, the PAC's *Poqo* and the ANC's *Umkhonto we Sizwe*.

Oliver Tambo and several other key leaders fled into exile. In 1962 many remaining ANC leaders, including Nelson Mandela and Walter Sisulu, were charged with treason and sabotage in the Rivonia Treason Trial, and sentenced to life imprisonment—most on Robben Island. Effective protest was over for nearly a decade.

TOWNSHIP VIOLENCE By the early 1970s, a new generation of young, bright and committed activists was ready to take up the Struggle. The most charismatic and famous was Steve Biko, leader of the Black Consciousness movement. Speaking to black and white students, he aimed to raise black awareness and pride. Biko was to die under dubious circumstances in a police cell in 1977.

Meanwhile, the schoolchildren of Soweto took to the streets. The police responded brutally and many hundreds were killed, injured or arrested, while others fled to ANC camps outside the country. By 1980 violence on the township streets was commonplace. The media was heavily censored, but pictures of singing children facing armed police and attack dogs were being daily flashed onto TV

sets across the globe. There was a permanent state of emergency, with tens of thousands detained without trial to face torture, police brutality and inexplicable deaths in custody. Zulu Chief Mangostho Buthelezi, who had revitalized Inkatha, was not prepared to play second fiddle to the ANC. Horrific factional violence broke out in the townships and workers' hostels between supporters of the various political parties and tribal groups. So-called traitors were burned

alive, with a car tyre filled with gas hung around their necks.

In 1986, international sanctions were imposed and the first cracks were seen in the apartheid armour. The pass laws were repealed, the Indians and coloureds were given a limited franchise, and many of the petty rules of apartheid were abolished. The real drama was still to come.

The road to freedom was finally opened in 1990, when President F. W. de Klerk made a momentous speech in parliament, repudiating apartheid, repealing the laws that upheld discrimination, and unbanning organizations such as the ANC. He withdrew the South African army from Angola, gave Namibia its independence, and pledged to work towards a truly democratic society.

But the greatest indication that freedom was here to stay came with the release of Nelson Mandela from his 27-year imprisonment on Robben Island. He would accept his own freedom only when all South Africans had theirs. Over 100,000 people waited for hours on the old Parade Ground in the heart of Cape Town before Mandela stepped out onto the balcony of City Hall to give his first public address.

❑ 'We have, at last, achieved our political emancipation. We pledge ourselves to liberate all our people from the continuing bondage of poverty, deprivation, suffering, gender and other discrimination.

Never, never and never again shall it be that this beautiful land will again experience the oppression of one by another…The sun shall never set on so glorious a human achievement.

Let freedom reign. God bless Africa!'

Nelson Mandela, Presidential Inaugural Address, quoted in *The Long Walk to Freedom*, 1994 ❑

Talks now began in earnest between the government and the various opposition parties. To the astonishment of the world, a referendum held in 1992 among white South Africans resulted in an overwhelming vote to end apartheid. The violence continued unabated until the last moment,

with massacres at Boipatong south of Johannesburg and Bisho in former Ciskei, and has still not died away completely, with sporadic trouble in the townships. In 1994, however, the country held its first truly democratic elections, and Nelson Mandela and F. W. de Klerk jointly accepted the Nobel Peace Prize. On 10 May, with the eyes of the world watching, Nelson Mandela took office as President of the New South Africa.

Top: Nelson Mandela and F. W. de Klerk Below: ANC election poster

A-Z Western Cape

▶▶▶ REGION HIGHLIGHTS

Company's Garden and Government Avenue
pages 66–67

Drive: The Garden Route
pages 96–101

Kirstenbosch National Botanical Gardens
page 69

Oudtshoorn
pages 80–81

Table Mountain and Cableway *page 62*

Touring the wineries
pages 92–93

Victoria and Alfred Waterfront *page 63*

Walk: Stellenbosch
pages 90–91

Western Cape

WHAT'S IN A NAME
Bartolomeu Dias rounded Cape Point in bad weather and called it 'Cabo Tormentoso' (Cape of Storms). The name that actually stuck, however, thanks to Sir Francis Drake, was the Cape of Good Hope. When Drake sailed around the point in benign sunshine in 1577, he was moved to describe it as 'the fairest Cape we saw in the circumference of the world.'

FIRST INTENTIONS
'It is apt to be forgotten that the Cape was not occupied with the view to the establishment of a European colony in our present sense of the word. The Dutch took it that they might plant a cabbage garden: the English took it that they might have a naval station and half-way house to India.'
James Bryce, *Impressions of South Africa*, 1897

PATCHWORK LAND The Western Cape's plump, roughly L-shaped body borders the Indian and Atlantic oceans. At its heart, where the two oceans meet, is Cape Town, a life-line to sailors and a magnet to tourists. The city is the single biggest tourist attraction in South Africa, with around 800,000 foreign visitors a year. Yet the authorities are aiming for many more, with new hotels opening all the time; a convention centre at the V&A Waterfront; Century City, a whole new district with a major theme park, Ratanga Junction (see page 63) and Africa's largest shopping area and entertainment complex; and the lavish Grand West Casino complex at Goodwood.

The founding fathers chose well when they colonized the coastal strip. The climate is moderate and pleasant, the land fertile and well-watered, and the scenery superb. As might be expected when a colony is founded by a gardener, the first farms were up and running within a very few years. With the planting of the first vines only three years after Jan van Riebeeck's arrival in 1652, the Cape had found its true vocation. The surrounding area is as steeped in wine as Bordeaux—and has its roots in the same place. The arrival of the French Huguenots from 1685 spurred the industry into something more than the occasional flagon of cheap wine, while the German contingent provided the fruity tones, redolent of the Mosel, that characterize so much of the best South African white wine. Today, the industry is up with the best, and

for the connoisseur or the tippler, a dozen wine routes offer an extraordinary range of tasting opportunities.

Beyond these tidy, whitewashed valleys lies a jagged line of craggy mountains—the Cederberg, the Hex River Mountains and the Swartberg. The south faces, slapped by ocean clouds, are thick with forest or powerfully scented by the Cape's unique herbal *fynbos* (see page 74). On the dry far side, the picture is very different. People either love or hate the Karoo. It is rocky, dry and dusty, twisted at times into fantastic rock formations. From a distance its scrubby vegetation looks unimpressive, but if you look closely and carefully it is magnificent, and when the spring flowers are in bloom it is an artwork worthy of Jackson Pollock. The inhabitants of this tough land are as rugged as their surroundings. Their ancestors headed into the unknown with nothing more than a flimsy wagon and a few cooking pots to escape the ordered urban life with all its rules and regulations. These communities are hospitable, but introverted. Most are more concerned with physical survival than metaphysics, but the desert has sometimes borne extraordinary blooms in powerful writers or artists such as Laurens van der Post, Olive Schreiner and Helen Martins (see page 113).

Then there is the coast itself, a delightful playground of rocky headlands and golden beaches, where whales and surfers alike frolic in the crashing waves. A major road, the N2, runs along the coast, linking the numerous small

Above: The lush Breede Valley is perfect for growing fruit

Below: Weird rock formations, including the 'Sewing Machine', crown the Cederberg

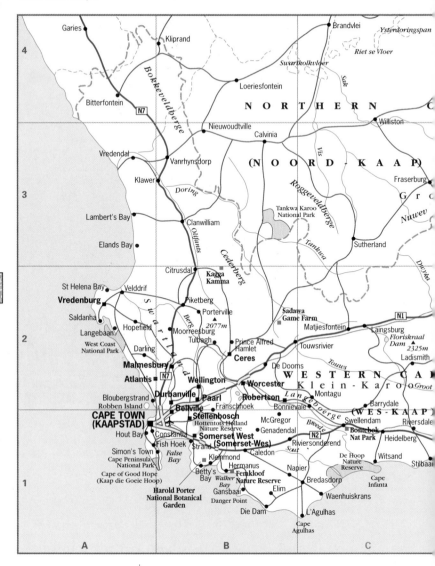

towns of the Garden Route, so called because of its rampantly green forests. A popular holiday destination for white South Africans, the area has inevitably become crowded, with bungalows and holiday homes stretching along the dunes to link many of the towns in a continuous ribbon development. At the same time, the forest has been pushed a little farther away and the coast has lost a little of its beauty, but at least there are now facilities and entertainment for the many thousands who flock here each year. And there are still plenty of isolated coves and deserted dunes for those who care to seek them out.

This is a patchwork land, the ideal holiday destination with something for everyone, and all within a reasonable distance. It may not be 'real' Africa, but the Western Cape has a magic all its own.

TOURIST INFORMATION
Cape Town Tourism, The
Pinnacle, corner of Burg
and Castle streets, Cape
Town 8000 (tel: 021-426
4260, fax: 021-426 4266,
www.tourismcapetown.
co.za).

Vosburg

Britstown

Brak

De Aar

N12

N10

Carnarvon

Hanover

A P E

N1

Victoria West

Richmond

Loxton

Sneeuberge

Murraysburg

ot - K a r o o

eldberge

Nelspoort

1966m

Karoo
National
Park

Graaff-Reinet

Leeu

Beaufort West
(Beaufort-Wes)

Aberdeen

Sundays

N9

Leeu-Gamka

E A S T E R N   C A P E
(O O S - K A A P)

Prince Albert
Road

N12

Grootrivierberge
Groot

Gamka

Prince
Albert

Klaarstroom

Willowmore

Steytlerville

Swartberg
Pass

Swartberg
Cango
Caves

Meiringspoort Pass

De Rust

Baviaanskloofberge

Calitzdorp

Olifants

Uniondale

Kouga

E Oudtshoorn

Cango
Wildlife Ranch

Joubertina

Kareedouw

Robinson
Pass

N9

Wilderness
National
Park

Outeniekwaberge

George

Plettenberg Bay
Plettenbergbaai

N2

Sedgefield

Knysna

Cape
Seal

Tsitsikamma
Forest National
Park

Mosselbaai

Albertinia

Mossel Bay
(Mosselbaai)

Ystervarkpunt

0	50	100	150 km
0	50		100 miles

D

E

*Bright beach huts stand
sentinel at Muizenberg*

TOURIST INFORMATION
Cape Town Tourism, The Pinnacle, corner of Castle and Burg streets, Cape Town 8000
(tel: 021-426 4260, fax: 021-426 4266, www.cape-town.org.za).
Open Mon–Fri 8–6, Sat 8.30–2, Sun 9–1 (summer); Mon–Fri 8–5, Sat 8–1.30, Sun 9–1 (winter). In addition to the Cape Town information centre, this building houses tourist information for the whole Western Cape, and has limited information on the rest of South Africa. Reservations are handled free of charge. There is also a cybercafé in the building.

50

Windsurfers enjoy spectacular views in Table Bay

Cape Town

Even before Vasco da Gama first rounded the Cape in 1498, sailors kept a lookout for Table Mountain, visible from 150km (93 miles) out to sea. The Phoenicians and Arabs thought it was filled with magnetism that could draw a ship in to its doom, while the massive mythical bird, the roc, nested on the slopes and a race of dwarves called the Wac-wac lived in the bay area. When later sailors actually stepped ashore, they discovered good fresh water and the cattle-farming Khoikhoi, who were willing to trade fresh meat and milk. Table Bay became a regular revictualling stop, but it was 150 years before any Europeans came to stay, although several nationalities made abortive and short-lived attempts.

FOUNDATIONS In 1652 the Dutch East India Company sent a small fleet of three ships to the bay, commanded by Jan van Riebeeck. Their mission was to provide fresh produce for passing ships. Van Riebeeck laid out the 18ha (45-acre) Company's Garden as a market garden, built a fort in which to live, founded a small hospital, and made a safe area for ship repairs, and thus the foundations of modern Cape Town had been laid. Since then the much-loved city has grown from strength to strength, acquiring numerous nicknames, ranging from the 'Mother City' to the 'Tavern of the Seas'.

Today, this is one of the world's prettiest cities, cocooned in a shallow bay by the looming bulk of Table Mountain, its tiny central area neat and elegant. If it can be compared to anywhere else, Cape Town is most akin to San Francisco. Like that city, it owes its existence to a

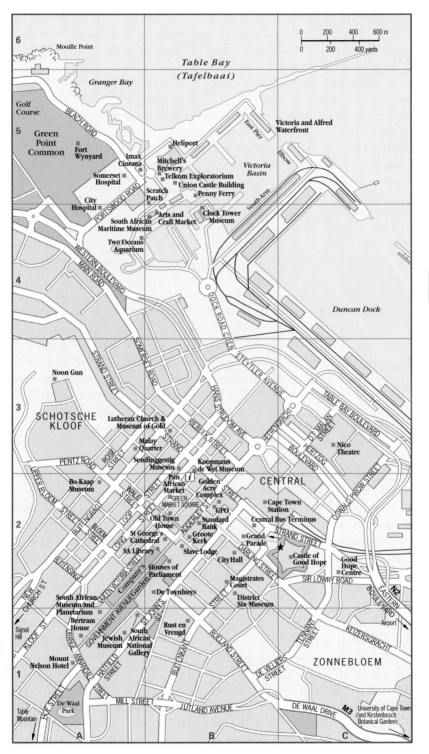

Table Bay
(Tafelbaai)

Granger Bay

Mouille Point

Golf
Course

Green
Point
Common

Fort
Wynyard

Heliport

Imax
Cinema

Mitchell's
Brewery

Telkom Exploratorium

Union Castle Building

Penny Ferry

Scratch
Patch

Somerset
Hospital

City
Hospital

South African
Maritime Museum

Arts and
Craft Market

Clock Tower
Museum

Two Oceans
Aquarium

Victoria and Alfred
Waterfront

East Pier

Elbow

Victoria
Basin

South Arm

Duncan Dock

BEACH ROAD

PORTSWOOD ROAD

WESTERN BOULEVARD

MAIN ROAD

SOMERSET ROAD

STRAND STREET

DOCK ROAD

COEN STEYTLER AVENUE

HERTZOG BOULEVARD

TABLE BAY BOULEVARD

DF MALAN STREET

HERTZOG

Noon Gun

SCHOTSCHE
KLOOF

Lutheran Church &
Museum of Gold

Malay
Quarter

Sendinggestig
Museum

Koopmans
de Wet Museum

Nico
Theatre

CENTRAL

PENTZ ROAD

ROSE STREET

RIEBEEK STREET

HANS STRIJDOM AVE

BUREN STREET

OSWALD PIROW STREET

Bo-Kaap
Museum

Pan
African
Market

GREEN
MARKET SQUARE

Golden
Acre
Complex

Cape Town
Station

Central Bus Terminus

UPPER BLOEM STREET

BUITENGRACHT

BLOEM STREET

LONG STREET

LOOP STREET

WALE STREET

STRAND STREET

Old Town
House

Standard
Bank

GPO

St George's
Cathedral

Groote
Kerk

Grand
Parade

SA Library

Slave Lodge

City Hall

Castle of
Good Hope

Good
Hope
Centre

BUITENSINGEL

QUEEN VICTORIA STREET

ADDERLEY STREET

PLEIN STREET

DARLING STREET

STRAND STREET

SIR LOWRY ROAD

Houses of
Parliament

Company's Garden

De Tuynhuys

Magistrates
Court

District
Six Museum

NEW CHURCH ST

GOVERNMENT AVENUE

ST JOHN'S STREET

ROELAND STREET

TENNANT STREET

EASTERN BOULEVARD

N2

Airport

South African
Museum and
Planetarium

Bertram
House

Jewish
Museum

South
African
National
Gallery

Rust en
Vreugd

KEIZERSGRACHT

Signal
Hill

KLOOF ST

ANNANDALE STREET

HATFIELD STREET

GOVERNMENT AVENUE

BUITENKANT

DE VILLIERS STREET

ZONNEBLOEM

Mount
Nelson Hotel

De Waal
Park

Table
Mountain

HOF STREET

FRANCE

MILL STREET

JUTLAND AVENUE

DE WAAL DRIVE

M3

University of Cape Town
and Kirstenbosch
Botanical Gardens

THE PERFECT GARDEN

When Jan van Riebeeck laid out his market garden in 1652, the first things he planted were Turkish and broad beans, peanuts, aniseed, fennel, medlar, quince, Spanish oranges, cucumber, pumpkin, onions, watermelon, endives and beets. The following year, the gardens were enlarged, adding parsnips, chives, artichokes, pimpernel, rosemary, gooseberries, blackberries, apricots, and plums. The 18ha (45-acre) garden was tended by 300 slaves. Mr. and Mrs. van Riebeeck picked the first oranges in 1661.

sweeping bay and natural harbour. It lives on the edge of the Winelands and has the same mix of old, pretty buildings, a lively waterfront and serious business, in this case as the legislative capital of South Africa and one of the country's most important business hubs. Publishing, the arts and the gay community all flourish, and the city prides itself on being liberal, although until recently this approach extended only as far as the boundaries of the white community.

Kirstenbosch National Botanical Gardens

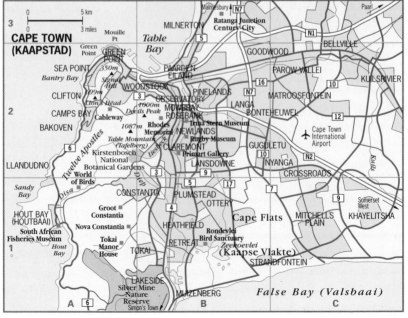

EUROPEAN STYLE Cape Town does not seem like part of Africa. The climate is Mediterranean, the buildings European and many of the faces you see around you are light-skinned. Nevertheless, it has real magic and charm, providing plenty of mellow history, fascinating museums, good shopping and enchanting gardens, such as the superb Kirstenbosch National Botanical Gardens. You can take gentle strolls around town or embark on more serious hikes on the mountain, where you also find some of the world's most dramatic views and spectacular sunsets. There are great beaches and countryside and wineries and wine cellars, where wine tasting is all part of the experience. In season, whale-watching is within easy day-trip distance. At night, there is superb food and drink from haute cuisine to sumptuous seafood, live music (particularly jazz), theatre and dancing. For the moment, it is even relatively safe, although you should be careful after dark. The only blot on the landscape is the city's sometimes changeable and bad-tempered weather. When good, it is superb, but it can blanket the city in grey cloud on a whim, send bitter winds whistling through the winter streets, and drop dank rain for days on end.

Around the gentle urban centre, Greater Cape Town is vast. Leafy white suburbs stretch up the slopes, around the mountain and along the coast to merge almost imperceptibly into the commuter towns of the peninsula. To the east, on the Cape Flats, the black townships and squatter camps spread as far as the eye can see, an ocean of corrugated iron and cardboard, plastic bags and wooden boxes. Local population estimates range at anything from 2.5 to 3.5 million. Even the census-takers have no clear idea. For tours, see pages 58 and 238.

Suburban Cape Town under the Lion's Head

NOT SO LIBERAL
Cape Town has always prided itself on being sophisticated, liberal and cosmopolitan—the one place in South Africa where the races could mingle freely. Yet it is the site of the very first forced clearance. This took place in 1901, long before the official start of apartheid and while the colony was still under British rule. Whole communities have been forced from their homes no fewer than 46 times in the city's history.

ANTON ANREITH

The sculptor Anton Anreith (1754–1821) was, together with Louis Thibault, responsible for revitalizing Cape architecture. Born in southwest Germany, he served his apprenticeship under a rococo sculptor—which led to what has been called his high baroque style—then came to the Cape where, first a carpenter, he went on to become a master sculptor. His best work can be seen in the Groote Kerk, the Lutheran Church (see page 57), on the Castle's Kat Balcony, and on the pediment of Groot Constantia's Wine Cellar (see page 68).

Anton Anreith's Kat Balcony in the Castle of Good Hope

▶ **Bertram House** 51A1

Company's Gardens, top of Orange Street
(tel: 021-424 9381)
Open: Tue–Thu 10–4.30. Admission: inexpensive
This beautifully proportioned red-brick house was built in 1830 for an English lawyer, John Barker, and is now a rare example of early 19th-century Cape British domestic architecture. Its Regency-style rooms are rich with furniture, ceramics and silver illustrating the lifestyle of a well-to-do English family in the Cape.

▶▶ **Bo-Kaap** 51A2

Bounded by Rose, Wale, Chiappini and Shortmarket streets
For tours of the area, contact Grassroute Tours
(tel: 021-706 1006, www.grassroutetours.co.za)
Built in the late 18th and early 19th centuries for European artisans, the little cube houses of Bo-Kaap were taken over by the Muslim Cape Malays (see pages 64–65), whose community survived as the only non-whites in central Cape Town. These days the steep streets are once more bright with colour and life.

The **Bo-Kaap Museum** (71 Wale Street, tel: 021-424 3846. *Open* Mon–Sat 9.30–4.30. *Admission: free*), in one of the finest surviving houses, offers a fascinating glimpse into late 19th-century Muslim life and the contribution of Islam to South African history, culture, food and the Afrikaans language.

▶▶ **Castle of Good Hope** 51C2

Castle Street (tel: 021-787 1249, www.castleofgoodhope.co.za)
Open: daily 9–4. Conducted tours 11, noon, 2
Changing of the Guard, noon; no unaccompanied sightseeing.
Admission: free
Founded by Simon van der Stel as the headquarters of the VOC (Dutch East India Company), this solid pentagonal fort is the oldest European building in South Africa (1666–79). Five bastions surround utilitarian structures from dingy, graffiti-covered cells to armouries. From 1691, several officers' houses were built onto a massive defensive wall, the Kat. The Secunde's House, home of the deputy-governor (1695), has rooms furnished in 17th-, 18th- and early 19th-century styles. The Governor's Residence, best known for Anton

Anreith's magnificent baroque Kat Balcony (*c*1785), is furnished in grand style with military and maritime objects and part of the William Fehr Collection of furniture, paintings, china and glass with an African theme. Look for the many paintings of Cape Town through the ages, and for paintings by Thomas Baines.

▶ **City Hall and the Grand Parade** see page 66

▶▶▶ **Company's Garden and Government Avenue** see pages 66–67

▶ **District Six** 51B2

This began life as a cosmopolitan port area where some 60,000 people of a dozen races and every colour mingled to create a vibrant community. In 1966, it was declared whites-only and all other races were shipped off to townships; in 1979, the area was bulldozed and the rubble used to build the new harbour. Since then, protests have been so vociferous that the land has remained empty. Today, a fascinating **Museum** (Buitenkant Methodist Church, 25a Buitenkant Street, tel: 021-461 8745. *Open* Mon–Sat 9–4. Sun by appointment. *Admission: moderate*) displays photos and recollections of the district and its street signs, saved from the bulldozers. Past inhabitants all sign a cloth (now over 68m/225ft long) and write down memories on a huge floor map.

Former residents re-create their bulldozed homes in the District Six Museum

▶ **Greenmarket Square** 51B2

The second-oldest square in Cape Town, built in 1710 as a market, is still home to one of the city's liveliest and most popular flea markets. It also contains the city's first civic building—the Old Town House (see page 58).

▶ **Groote Kerk** 51B2

Adderley Street, entrance in Church Square, off Parliament Street (tel: 021-461 7044)
Open: Mon–Fri 10–2. Admission: free

Until a wood and thatch church was commissioned by Governor Willem Adriaan van der Stel in 1678 and consecrated in 1704, services were held on Van Riebeeck's ship, the *Dromedaris*. The original church was replaced by this rather drab, but much larger building in 1841. Only the pretty clock tower belongs to the first edifice.

Inside, the huge room has sturdy box pews and a magnificent wooden pulpit, carved by Anton Anreith in 1788. The organ is the largest in the southern hemisphere, with 6,000 pipes and 32 foot pedals. This is the mother church of the Dutch Reformed Faith.

A VENERABLE PEAR
The oldest tree in Company's Garden is a saffron pear that stands near the café. It is believed to have been imported from Holland in the time of Jan van Riebeeck and to have provided fruit for 17th-century sailors. The tree needs careful treatment but still produces edible fruit each year, most of which is pickled.

COMMERCIAL ART GALLERIES

The art scene has exploded in Cape Town, with new galleries opening every month. The quality, of course, varies hugely, but a number have exciting, constantly changing exhibits that showcase the best in South African art. Among the best are: the Association for Visual Arts (AVA), 35 Church Street (tel: 021-424 7436); João Ferreira Gallery, 80 Hout Street (tel: 021-423 5403); and Rose Korber Art Consultancy, 48 Sedgemoor Road, Camps Bay (tel: 021-438 9152). The tourist office publishes an excellent arts and crafts map with listings of many other galleries.

▶ Houses of Parliament 51B2

Parliament Street and Government Avenue
(tel: 021-403 3683)
Enter via Parliament Street gate. Tickets available for parliamentary sessions (Jan–Jun) on presentation of passport at Room V12, Old Assembly Wing.
Guided tours must be booked two weeks in advance (Mon–Fri 9–12).
Jacket and tie required during parliamentary sessions
Admission: free

Cape Town's imposing brick and stucco Houses of Parliament (1884) are the seat of the country's legislative government. Inside, the enthusiasm and jazzy African dress of the new multiracial parliamentarians is breathing new life into the gloomy old building.

Next door, De Tuynhuys (1700) is the office of the state president (see page 67).

▶ Irma Stern Museum 52B2

The Firs, Cecil Road, Rosebank (tel: 021-685 5686)
Open: Tue–Sat 10–5
Admission: inexpensive

Once the home of South Africa's best-known artist, Irma Stern (1894–1966), this little museum contains an excellent collection of the artist's own work and the souvenirs of her travels, from Zairi masks to oriental ceramics and old furniture. A follower of the German Expressionist movement, Irma Stern painted South African people and landscapes.

Powerful studies still crowd the walls of Irma Stern's studio

▶ Jewish Museum 51A1

88 Hatfield Street, Gardens
(tel: 021-465 1546,
www.sajewishmuseum.co.za)
Open: Sun–Thu 10–5, Fri 10–2. Admission: expensive

This fascinating and modern museum depicts Jewish life in South Africa, from the immigrants' origins (depicted by a Lithuanian *shtetl*—a small Jewish town or village formerly found throughout Eastern Europe) to the strong role they have played in the country's history and cultural life, in a series of permanent and temporary exhibitions. It also incorporates South Africa's oldest synagogue, built in 1863, and has a shop and kosher café.

Next door, the **Holocaust Centre**, 88 Hatfield Street (tel: 021-462 5553. *Open* Sun–Thu 10–5, Fri 10–1. *Admission: free*), uses photographs, exhibits, survivors' testimonies and audio-visuals in a moving tribute to the victims of Nazi genocide.

▶▶ Koopmans de Wet House 51B3

35 Strand Street (tel: 021-481 3935)
Open: by appointment only. Admission: inexpensive

This charming Georgian town house (now a museum) was built in 1701, and much altered by later owners. The pink-and-white pilastered façade has been attributed (without proof) to Louis Thibault and Anton Anreith. Its name comes from its most famous inhabitant, Maria Koopmans de Wet (1834–1906) who, as well as being a noted hostess and art collector, was also an enthusiastic advocate of the Afrikaans language.

The spacious rooms, decorated in European style with *trompe-l'oeil* pilasters, swags and friezes, are elaborately furnished in the late 18th-century manner. Behind the courtyard, in contrast, are the slave quarters.

▶ **Long Street**   *51A2*

Laid out in the 18th century, Long Street runs right through the heart of town, from sea to mountain. Wander through the place slowly, craning upwards at the delightful architectural details or peering under the shadowed balconies at the extraordinary shops. There are churches, mosques, banks, offices, apartment buildings, cafés, restaurants and clubs, art deco shopfronts, curly cast iron, double-tiered verandas on elaborate Victorian houses and exuberant neoclassical buildings awash with brightly painted decorative plasterwork; the roofline is a profusion of turrets, gables and minarets.

The street's oldest inhabitants could pack a theatre on tales of former residents: retired pirates, drag queens, exotic dancers…

More restrained, but still lively, Long Street now offers anything from Zulu beads to 1970s nostalgia clothes, second-hand books, vintage wine, plumbers' fittings or 18th-century Cape Dutch furniture. This is the ideal opportunity to kit yourself out with a Madiba shirt at the **Pan African Market** at number 76 (tel: 021-426 4478. *Open* Mon–Fri 9–5, Sat 9–3) or have a sauna at the **Turkish Baths** (*Open* 7–7 daily, women only 10–4 daily. *Admission: inexpensive*).

▶ **Lutheran Church** *51B3*

96 Strand Street
(tel: 021-421 5854)
Open: Wed 9 and 12,
Sun 10.15
Admission: free
Until 1771, Lutherans and other denominations were forced to worship in the Dutch Reformed church. This, the country's first Lutheran church, was built in 1774 by a wealthy merchant, Martin Melck (see page 58). Anton Anreith carved its magnificent wooden pulpit, and it so impressed the council of the Dutch Reformed church that they wanted one, too (see page 55).

LONE SURVIVOR
Although many 18th-century houses on Long Street are undoubtedly entombed within later shells, only one (No. 185, now the Palm Tree Mosque) survives intact. It was converted into a mosque in 1805 by a freed Malay slave, Jan van Boughies, who planted the two palms that gave the building its name.

57

Office buildings dwarf Koopman de Wet House, a delicate relic

TOURING CAPE TOWN

Topless Tours (tel: 021-511 1784) runs guided tours of the city on an open-topped bus, as well as day-trips to the peninsula. **Legend Tours** (tel: 021-697 4056/7) operates day tours of ethnic Cape Town, visiting Bo-Kaap, District Six, the townships, Cape Flats and Robben Island. They also run tours of the peninsula and Winelands. For city walking tours, contact **Cape Town on Foot** (tel: 021-426 4260). Cultural tours are offered by **Grassroute Tours** (tel: 021-706 1006, www. grassroutetours.co.za), **Thuthuka Tours** (tel: 021-433 2429, www.township crawling.co.za) and **Cape Town Calling** (tel: 083-404 4433). For extreme sports, including abseiling, shark diving and sky diving, contact **Adventure Village**, 229 Long Street (tel: 021-424 1580, www. adventurevillage.co.za). For city helicopter flights, try **Sport Helicopters** (tel: 021-419 5907/8) or **Civair** (tel: 021-419 5182). **Waterfront Boat Trips** (tel: 021-419 3122) runs cruises and sailing excursions from the V&A Waterfront.

The grandiose Rhodes Memorial

▶▶ Gold of Africa Museum 52B3

96 Strand Street (tel: 021-405 1540, www.goldofafrica.com).
Open: Mon–Sat 10–5. Admission: moderate
The Martin Melck House is one of Cape Town's oldest houses and a rare example of a building with a *dakkamer*—a room in the roof with windows facing the sea. This fine old parsonage has now been transformed into a scene of utter opulence, a small but beautifully displayed collection of African gold, much of it magnificent royal and ceremonial regalia from West Africa. Allow plenty of time to see past the initial dazzle to the incredible detail of the workmanship.

▶▶ Old Town House 51B2

Greenmarket Square (tel: 021-481 3933)
Open: Mon–Fri 10–5, Sat 10–4. Admission: free
By the 18th century, the Burgher Watch, responsible both for law and order and fighting fires, patrolled the city nightly from its base in Old Town House (1755). The bell in the tower summoned citizens to listen to proclamations read from the balcony. The building later became the town hall. It is now an art gallery housing the Michaelis Collection of 17th-century Dutch and Flemish works.

▶ Rhodes Memorial 52B2

Off Rhodes Drive, Rondenbosch (tel: 021-689 9151)
Open access (tea garden closed Mon)
Cecil Rhodes (1853–1902) became a multimillionaire businessman and scholar, founded several British colonies, and built most of southern Africa's railways. He also found time to be prime minister of the Cape Colony. This memorial, with fine views, stands near the university and Rhodes' former home, Groote Schuur. It is now the president's main residence.

▶▶ Rust en Vreugd 51B1

78 Buitenkant Street (tel: 021-465 3628)
Open: Mon–Fri 9–4. Admission: free
The name of this 18th-century house means 'rest and joy'. One of the finest domestic buildings in the Cape, it was

once the home of the state prosecutor and had a splendid view of the bay. Now it is tucked away inland behind the ugly foreshore.

Inside is part of the William Fehr Collection of Africana (see also Castle of Good Hope, page 55), with fine watercolours by Thomas Baines, lithographs, engravings and paintings of the early Cape, plus extraordinary cartoons by George Cruickshank.

▶ St. George's Cathedral   51B2
Wale Street (tel: 021-424 7360)
Open: Sun–Fri 6.30–6, Sat 6.30–12. Admission: free
Consecrated in 1834, the first Anglican Cathedral of St. George the Martyr was thought to look like an average English parish church, not nearly grand enough for the Mother City. In 1901, architect Sir Herbert Baker was let loose, adding considerably to the length and grandeur of the building and replacing the neoclassical entrance with his favourite grey stone neo-Gothic design.

The cathedral is much bigger now, but still looks like a large, welcoming parish church. The vaulted interior is more imposing than the outside. The highlights are a series of modern stained-glass windows by Gabriel Loire. The eight along the nave depict the Creation; the Christ in Majesty above the transept is dedicated to Lord Louis Mountbatten. This was the seat of Cape Town's flamboyant archbishop, Desmond Tutu. It also hosted events such as the memorial service for Joe Slovo, the communist, atheist, ex-Jewish Minister of Housing in the Government of National Unity, who died in December 1994.

▶ Sendinggestig Museum   51B3
40 Long Street (tel: 021-423 6755). Open: Mon–Fri 9–4,
Sat, school holidays 9–12. Admission: donation
This charmingly decorative, apricot-and-white mission church was built by the South African Missionary Society in 1804, and used both for worship and the education of slaves and non-Christians. It now houses a museum of mission work in South Africa.

ARCHBISHOP DESMOND TUTU
Archbishop Desmond Mpilo Tutu was born on 7 October 1931. Ordained in 1961, he became Anglican Dean of Johannesburg (1975–76), Bishop of Lesotho (1976–78), and the first black secretary-general of the South African Council of Churches (1979), representing around 12 million Christians. In 1984, he became the first black bishop of Johannesburg and was awarded the Nobel Peace Prize. In 1986, he was elected the first black Anglican archbishop of Cape Town. An outspoken advocate of nonviolent reform and black nationalism, he nevertheless avoided imprisonment and won the hearts of South Africans of all colours. He resigned as archbishop in 1996, but continues to play an active role in the rebuilding of South Africa.

BIG BANG

Just below Signal Hill, the Noonday Gun shatters the air on the dot of noon every day except Sunday. It was instituted to help ships in the bay correct their chronometers and, after 1918, to mark a two-minute pause in honour of South Africa's war dead.

▶ **Signal Hill**   52A2

Off Kloof's Nek, or reached on foot via Bo-Kaap and Longmarket Street

Forming one arm of Table Bay, Signal Hill is far smaller than Table Mountain but has easy access, no lines and superb views, particularly dramatic at sunset and at night, when a vast field of lights spreads below. At the summit are picnic tables and short, pleasant (if windy) strolls. Nearby is the tomb of the Saudi saint, Tuan Sayeed Alawie, incarcerated on Robben Island for 11 years.

▶▶ **Slave Lodge**   51B2

49 Adderley Street (tel: 021-460 8242)
Open: Mon–Fri 10–4.30, Sat 9–1.
Admission: inexpensive, free Sat

For 130 years, this long, low house (built in 1685) was used to house slaves working in Company's Garden. After the second British occupation in 1811, Louis Thibault converted it into government offices. Today it is one of the finest museums in the country, with beautifully displayed exhibits from Greek and Roman amphorae to ferocious throwing knives of the Sudan. The second half of the museum is dedicated to South Africa, with coins, weapons, ceramics, stamps and textiles, excellent collections of furniture and objets d'art (particularly silver) from white South Africa, and tribal art and utensils from the black community. Take a look at the roughly engraved postal stones found in Table Bay near the Versse River (see panel opposite).

The National Gallery graces the end of Government Avenue

▶ **South African Library**   51B2

Queen Victoria Street (tel: 021-424 6320)
Open: Mon–Fri 9–6, Sat 9–1. Admission: free

Founded in 1818, this national copyright and preservation library is the oldest cultural institution in South Africa and one of the world's first free libraries. Regular exhibitions include the 5,000-volume private collection of former governor Sir George Grey, which has more than 100 medieval illuminated manuscripts. Among them are the oldest book in South Africa, a gospel dating to AD900 and a First Folio Shakespeare.

▶ **South African Maritime Museum**   51B4

Dock Road, V&A Waterfront (tel: 021-405–2880)
Open: daily 10–5. Admission: moderate. Children under 12 must be accompanied by an adult to visit the ships

The Cape of Good Hope has produced some fascinating maritime history. Here you can learn about it *in situ*: The frequent shipwrecks, Table Bay Harbour, shipping lines and maritime archaeology, with models, a shipwright's workshop and SAS *Somerset*, which is the world's only surviving boom defence vessel. It also houses the *Alwyn Vincent*, built in 1959 and the only steam tug still in use in the southern hemisphere.

▶ **South African Museum and**   *51A1*
Planetarium

25 Queen Victoria Street (tel: 021-481 3800)
Open: daily 10–5. Planetarium shows Mon–Fri 2, Tue 8pm,
Sat 2.30; children's shows Sat–Sun 12
Admission: inexpensive; museum free on Wed

This stately building is South Africa's oldest museum, dating from 1825. The anthropology hall specializes in southern African tribal culture and includes rock paintings and several dioramas of San and Khoikhoi life. Other sections include white South African furniture, silver and objets d'art, geology (with replica dinosaurs) and marine life in the Southern Ocean, with a 20.5m (67ft) skeleton of a blue whale. The Planetarium gives a delightful explanation of the southern hemisphere's night sky and presents audio-visual shows about Robben Island.

▶▶ **South African National Gallery**   *51A1*

Government Avenue, Company's Garden (tel: 021-467 4660)
Open: Tue–Sun 10–5
Admission: moderate, free Sun

Although the gallery originally exhibited mainstream European art with a number of fine oils and sporting pictures by such painters as Stubbs and Munnings, sanctions and the collapse of the rand forced the curators to buy locally. It now shows good contemporary South African art, an increasing amount of traditional tribal art, from decorated knobkerries to beadwork, and exciting work by modern black artists in both traditional and ultramodern styles. Travelling exhibitions include foreign work, photography and experimental and ethnic art.

POSTAL STONES
In the early days of the Cape Sea Route, sailors could be away for years on end. To send news home and make contact with other ships in their fleet, they would leave letters under a rock engraved clearly with the name of the ship from which it had come and for whom it was intended. The stones were also sometimes used to pass on personal letters, delivered by ships newly arrived from Europe or on their last leg home.

61

View from Signal Hill. The hill was once used to watch for the arrival of ships to Table Bay

THE TABLECLOTH

Table Mountain is all too frequently covered by a swirling layer of white cloud that fits comfortably over the top like a cloth. Some say that each summer the retired pirate, Van Hunks, has a pipe-smoking contest with the Devil (the rheumatic old man cannot climb in winter, so the mountain remains clear). In reality, the Cape's summer south-easterly prevailing wind (known as the Cape Doctor) sweeps into the bay, gets trapped, and deposits its moisture neatly over the mountain.

Cableway at Table Mountain, Cape Town

▶▶▶ Table Mountain and Cableway 52A2

Lower Cable Station, Tafelberg Road, off Kloof's Nek (tel: 021-424 8181, www.tablemountain.net)
Cableway runs daily, weather permitting (not in cloud or high wind), Dec–end Jan 8am–8pm; Feb–end Apr 8.30–7.30; May–end Nov 8.30–5. Check locally. Admission: expensive

Guarded by Lion's Head and Signal Hill and Devil's Peak, Table Mountain towers 1,087m (3,565ft) above Cape Town. Its sloping pedestal, covered with *fynbos* (see page 74) and forest, leads to a 500m (1,640ft) high sheer-sided slab of bare sandstone marking the northern end of a ridge stretching 50km (31 miles) to Cape Point.

The mountain started to form some 700 million years ago when mud and sand deposits were laid deep on the seabed; 600 million years ago, they were pushed upwards and molten granite poured in around them. After 200 million years of erosion, a shallow sea returned, leaving mud, ripple marks and marine fossils, before the whole of southern Gondwanaland (a huge ancient continent) was covered in heavy sheet ice. Some 160–300 million years ago, shifting tectonic plates lifted the mountains clear of the water and Gondwanaland began to break up into the modern continents. About 70 million years ago, further upward movement re-exposed Table Mountain to the winds and rain.

A spectacular revolving cable car affords easy access to the viewing platforms. The weather can be treacherous, so get a guide if you're planning to walk up the steep but easy path or to go any distance on the top. During peak season, reserve in advance for the cable car and check the weather. Tickets are available from Waterfront Information Centre (tel: 021-418 2369) and Lower Cable Station. For walking tours, contact Due South Hikes (tel: 083-258 4824, www.hikesandtours.co.za); to abseil or cycle down the mountain, contact DownhillAdventures (tel: 021-422 0388, www.downhilladventures.com) or Adventure Village (tel: 021-424 1580, www.adventure-village.co.za).

▶▶ Two Oceans Aquarium 51A4

Dock Road, V&A Waterfront (tel: 021-418 3823,
www.aquarium.co.za)
Open: daily 9.30–6
Admission: expensive

This beautiful aquarium concentrates on the species
found in and around the Cape Peninsula, from both the
Indian and Atlantic oceans and from the mountain lakes
and streams inland. There are 4,000 fish of 300 species in
several large set pieces, including a kelp forest, an open
ocean pool, a tropical tank and seal and penguin pools, a
tidal tank showing life above and below the watermark,
and an ecosystem following the progress of river life from
mountain stream to estuary. Smaller tanks show sections
of reef and water management, and children can examine
creatures such as anemones and starfish in the touch pool.
Experienced divers may dive in the shark tanks.

▶▶▶ Victoria and Alfred Waterfront 51C5

Victoria and Alfred Basins, Table Bay Harbour
(tel: 021-408 7600, www.waterfront.co.za). Open: all hours.
Admission: free. Satellite tourist information office at the
entrance and a regular shuttle bus to Adderley Street

In 1860, Queen Victoria's second son, Alfred, tipped the
first rock for the construction of the Victoria Basin. A
century later, Cape Town's old harbour was left virtually
derelict by the advent of the container port. Given a new
lease of life in one of the world's most successful urban
reclamation projects, it now hums as the heartland of the
city. Working fishing boats, yachts and harbour cruise
boats skim the water, while wooden walkways hold
brightly lit shopping malls, the largest crafts market in
South Africa, restaurants and a fascinating maritime
museum (see page 60) and aquarium (see above).

Other attractions include an **Imax Cinema** (tel: 021-419
7365) with a five-floor screen, the **Telkom Exploratorium**
(tel: 021-419 5957. *Open:* Tue–Sun 9–6), a hands-on science
exhibit and harbour cruises (see page 58). The striking
Shimansky Collection is the first diamond musem to open
in Cape Town (check with tourist office for details).

The Victoria and Alfred
Waterfront is a popular
evening playground

RATANGA JUNCTION
Take the Sable Road exit
off the N1, 10km (6 miles)
from Cape Town, tel:
0861-200 300.
www.ratanga.co.za. *Open*
daily 11–7. Closed May,
Aug–end Nov. *Admission:
expensive (includes all
rides).*
  Africa's first full-scale
theme park provides an
entertaining day out with
rides for all, from toddler-
friendly trains to thrilling
waterslides and a grue-
some rollercoaster. The
theme is Africa, from non-
specific souks (market-
places) to the mines and
bushveld safaris.
  Next door, **Century City**
is a whole new suburb
built around **Canal Walk**
(tel: 021-555 4433), the
largest shopping mall in
Africa. There are 400
stores, 40 restaurants,
17 cinema screens, plus
live entertainment, canal
walks and cruises and
more. In addition, there's
the huge interactive MTN
ScienCentre (tel: 021-529
8100, www.mtnscien
centre.org.za. *Open*
Mon–Thu 9.30–6, Fri–Sat
9.30–8, Sun 10–6.
Admission: expensive) and
Intaka Island wetlands
reserve.

Under the old regime, there was a distinct hierarchy. First came the northern European whites, then the Latins, followed by the Japanese, Chinese, Cape Malays, Indians, Cape coloureds and blacks. Each had a different level of housing, education and social status. The communities, particularly those imported from the East, retained their own cultural traditions.

THE SACRED CIRCLE

In 1693, Sheikh Yusuf, who claimed descent from Mohammed, was banished to the Cape, where he and his followers continued to live and worship much as before. On his death in 1699, his tomb became a centre of pilgrimage, while the 25 holy men who followed him were buried in Constantia, Oudekraal, on Signal Hill, on the slopes of Table Mountain or on Robben Island. Their tombs (or *karamats*) form a 'sacred circle' around Cape Town, and are said to provide the city with spiritual protection against natural disasters.

SAFE JOURNEY

The most famous of Sheikh Yusuf's disciples was Paay Schaapie, a freed slave responsible for the establishment of Islam in South Africa. He was recognized as a saint while still living, and after his death it became the practice among his followers to take soil from his tomb when going on a journey. It is said he loved the Tana Baru, the burial ground at the top of the Bo-Kaap, so intensely that he would not allow the soil to remain away too long, and thus a safe journey was ensured.

'Coloureds' There are about 1.4 million 'coloureds' of mixed race. Some originate from the offspring of black servants and their white masters, some from the integration of the San and Khoikhoi (see page 132) to form the KhoiSan. Some of these women then had children by white men, some intermarried with black tribes from farther north and east. Historically, in Europe and America, anyone with any black ancestry is considered part of the black culture. This is not the case in South Africa; the coloureds were isolated, accepted socially by neither black nor white communities, while their only true heritage, the San culture, was destroyed by urban living.

By the late 19th century, there were sufficient numbers for them to form a distinct cultural group. They were mainly Christian, Afrikaans-speaking and worked as skilled manual labourers, particularly on the railways.

Cape Malays There is a large Islamic presence in the Cape region, drawn from Indian, Far Eastern, black and coloured communities. The Cape Malays are a much smaller group of about 12,000 people, largely confined to the tiny Bo-Kaap district of Cape Town (see page 54). Virtually none has Malay ancestry, most having been imported as slaves from Singapore, Sri Lanka, Madagascar and, above all, Indonesia by early Dutch settlers. The name comes from the Malayal language used as a lingua franca among traders across the Dutch East Indies. The community calls itself either Cape Muslim or Indo-African.

Unlike most people from slave nations, these were highly educated and skilled people, prized as builders and carpenters as well as household servants. They brought with them Sufism (the mystical branch of the Islamic faith), holy men and teachers and a strong cultural identity. Relatively few have intermarried with other ethnic groups and they are proud to have kept their nationhood and traditions, many of which have died out elsewhere.

Their language and history were officially banned during centuries of repression, but were kept alive by underground classes and texts written in Arabic script, known to all good Muslims but totally indecipherable to the Afrikaners. People do still speak Malayal today, but most commonly use Afrikaans. In fact, the first book in Afrikaans is said to have been written in Bo-Kaap, and the language was taught formally for the first time at the Auwal Mosque in Dorp Street, one of the oldest mosques in Cape Town (1804).

The holy men did their best to buy up the slaves and free them, but it was not until slavery was banned throughout the British Empire in 1834 that the newly freed Muslims moved into Bo-Kaap. There are now 11 mosques scattered among the small, square, vividly painted houses that crawl up the side of Signal Hill. In 1966, the area was declared a slum and the Muslims were ordered out. Some went, but many more remained and eventually the authorities lost interest and left them alone, the only non-white community to survive in central Cape Town. Many of the houses were even rebuilt to the original design. Today, the area is a unique, fascinating testament to the old city, vibrant with noisy street life, as women in traditional *burkhas* (headscarves) and men in *kufias* (robes) gather on the corners to chat.

Yet the community is under threat once more, a victim of its success. Young, trendy Capetonians have recognized the charm of the district and the fascination of the architecture and are snapping up houses, driving prices way out of the reach of locals.

The houses in Bo-Kaap are rapidly becoming some of Cape Town's most sought-after real estate

CARNIVAL TIME
For two days a year (1 and 2 January) the coloured community erupts onto the streets of Cape Town in a blaze of colour and noise. Their exuberant Carnival began as a thanksgiving for the abolition of slavery and, almost incidentally, welcomes in the new year. Preparations are intense and often competitive as district troops are formed. They spend several months creating spectacular original costumes, music and dance.

Walk

Historic Cape Town
(see map, page 51)

The old centre of Cape Town is surprisingly small; much of it is built on reclaimed land and the harbour water used to lap the castle walls. This gentle stroll takes in most of the main attractions. Allow one to two hours, or a full day if you plan to visit the many sights en route. Start beside the **Castle of Good Hope** (see page 54).

Walk across into the **Grand Parade**, usually less than grand with a noisy mix of cars parking, taxis cruising for business and a lively flea market full of buckets of flowers and bolts of cloth. Carefully positioned in front of Table Mountain, the positively imperial **City Hall** (Darling Street, tel: 021-400 2230. *Open* during business hours and for concerts. *Admission: free*) was built in 1905 in a blend of Italian Renaissance and British colonial styles. It has been carefully restored and is now the home of the Cape Town Symphony Orchestra, which holds regular concerts there. After Nelson Mandela's release from jail in February 1990, a crowd of 100,000 people waited for up to seven hours to hear his first speech from the balcony. It began: *'Amandla! Iafrika! Mayibuye!'* (Power to the people!).

Walk along Darling Street until you come to Adderley Street. To your right is the **Heerengracht**, a dull area of 1960s concrete apartment houses. One of the few mixed-race areas of Cape Town was demolished to create this monstrosity. Turn left up **Adderley Street**, the city's main shopping street. It has several charming small arcades and grand colonial and art deco buildings. The **Standard Bank** is on the left; peer inside at the magnificent 19th-century banking hall used by Cecil Rhodes and other luminaries of the time.

Also on the left, near the top of the street, are the sombre, plain grey **Groote Kerk** (see page 55) and the Cape Dutch **Slave Lodge** (see page 60), in front of which stands a statue of Jan Smuts in battle dress. To the right, by Government Avenue, is **St. George's Cathedral** (see page 59). From here, walk up leafy, pedestrian **Government Avenue►►►**, where squirrels play under the trees. A little way up on the left are the red-brick-and-white-stucco **Houses of Parliament** (see page 56). To the right is the **South African Library** (see page 60).

Just beyond is the entrance to **Company's Garden►►►** (top of Adderley Street. *Open* daily 7–dusk. *Admission:*

Well-shaded Government Avenue is the historic heart of Cape Town

Above: Company's Garden began as a market garden
Right: De Tuynhuys is now home to the office of the state president

free). In 1652, Jan van Riebeeck and the Dutch East India Company laid out an 18ha (45-acre) vegetable garden to supply merchant ships with fresh fruit and vegetables. Only 3.2ha (8 acres) of South Africa's first market garden survive, transformed by Sir Herbert Baker into a lush English park with lawns, shady trees, elegant walkways and manicured flower beds. Opposite the entrance, **De Tuynhuys** was built in 1700 as a Company Guest House to accommodate any overflow of dignitaries from the castle. Altered over the centuries, it has been restored to its 1795 Regency appearance and is now the office of the state president.

At the top of the garden is an open plaza. On your left are the **South African National Gallery** (see page 61) and South Africa's oldest **Synagogue**, its first service held in 1841. Directly ahead is the **South African Museum and Planetarium** (see page 61). Continue to the top of Government Avenue, where you will see **Bertram House** (see page 54) on your right. Cross the street and walk under the pillars up Hof Street to reach the strawberry-pink **Mount Nelson Hotel**. This is the oldest and plushest hotel in central Cape Town (see page 259), where you can indulge in tea with smoked salmon sandwiches while you rest your aching feet.

If you wish, browse the shops along **Long Street** (see page 57), eventually reaching **Greenmarket Square** (see page 55) for some serious haggling, or intellectual stimulation at the **Old Town House** (see page 58).

Cape Town environs

▶ Cape Flats
52B1

*For township tours contact Township Tours
(tel: 083-310 6454); Legend Tours (tel: 021-697 4056/7);
Grassroute Tours (tel: 021-706 1006); Thuthuka Tours (tel:
021-433 2429); Cape Town Calling (tel: 083-4044433)
Admission: expensive*

The wide, marshy plain of the Cape Flats—site of Cape Town's townships—lies inland from Table Mountain. The first township in South Africa was founded 5km (3 miles) from Cape Town in 1901. It was later moved because it was considered to be too close to the middle of town, and the people were resettled in **Langa**, which survives today. The infamous **Crossroads** now has regular streets and drains, but for many years it was a massive squatter camp where residents lived under the daily threat of the bulldozers. The most astounding of the three main townships in the area is **Khayelitsha**, which sprang from nothing to become a shanty city of over 1 million people in the space of a very few years. Serious efforts are being made to provide better conditions, but steady urban drift ensures that as soon as one area is sorted out, another squatter camp springs up to replace it.

Shanties on the Cape Flats show a very different view of Cape Town

DIVINE WINE
Napoleon is said to have demanded nothing but Constantia wine during his exile on St. Helena; Bismarck was a patron; Jane Austen recommends its 'healing powers on a disappointed heart'; and King Louis Philippe of France liked it so much that he bought the whole vintage in 1833.
 Constantia Vineyards, Buitenverwachting (tel: 021-794 3522). For cellar tours in range of venues in Constantia contact Constantia Valley Publicity and Tourism (082-953 7067, www.constantia valley.com).

▶ Groot Constantia
52A1

*Groot Constantia Road, about 15km (9 miles) south of the city centre
Museum (tel: 021-795 5128, www.grootconstantia.co.za)
Open: daily. Cellar tours on the hour every hour until 4;
tastings Mon–Fri 9–6. Admission: moderate*

One of the oldest estates in South Africa, founded in 1685, this was the home of Governor Simon van der Stel. A century later, it was taken over by the Cloete family, who created a range of world-famous dessert wines, Constantia Frontignac, Pontac and Steen. Sadly, the grand age ended with the phylloxera outbreak in the 1860s and the estate was sold to the nation in 1885 by a near-bankrupt family. Since then, it has been used as an experimental station and museum. However, from 1975 onwards, there has been much replanting and Constantia wine is regaining both quality and reputation.
 At the entrance a small museum shows the history of the manor. The elegant Cape Dutch house itself, designed by Louis Thibault, was destroyed by fire in 1925, but has

been carefully restored to the original plans, with high walls, flagged floor, heavy wooden ceilings and dark green shutters. It is beautifully furnished in sturdy, late 18th-century style. Behind it, the old cellars, with their magnificent pediment by Anton Anreith (1791), contain a fascinating small museum of wine. The modern cellars include a cellar tour, wine tasting and a shop, while the Jonkershuis (old stables) houses an excellent restaurant.

▶▶▶ Kirstenbosch National Botanical Gardens   52A2

Rhodes Drive, Newlands
(tel: 021-799 8800, www.nbi.ac.za).
About 10km (6 miles) from the city centre
Open: Apr–Aug daily 8–6, Sep–Mar daily 8–7
Admission: inexpensive. Guided walks on the hour (tel: 012-762 912. Pre-booking essential)

In 1895, Cecil John Rhodes bought this estate and bequeathed it to the nation. In 1913, Henry Harold Welch Pearson, Professor of Botany at the University of South Africa, founded the National Botanical Gardens. They grew rapidly to become one of the world's most important botanical collections. Most of the 530ha (1,310-acre) estate, stretching up the eastern flank of Table Mountain, is local *fynbos* and coastal forest, but there are 36ha (89 acres) of delightful formal gardens. These have rich collections of flowers and trees, a fragrance garden and Braille trail, a pond, a herb garden and specialist collections of pelargoniums, restios, proteas, cycads and ericas. Concentrating on the indigenous flora of southern Africa, the gardens contain some 6,000 of South Africa's 22,000 plant species, while a further 900 grow in the wild areas. Several walking trails, lasting from 45 minutes to 6 hours, lead into the woods and up the mountain. A strong educational and scientific programme concentrates on the conservation of many rare and endangered species. The restaurant serves tea, coffee and lunches and a garden shop sells plants, souvenirs and books. Concerts are held in the gardens every Sunday during the summer. Allow at least half a day to explore.

GREEN HISTORY
The Kirstenbosch Gardens contain a living history of the Cape region, starting with the remains of a wild almond hedge planted by Jan van Riebeeck in 1660 to protect the cattle from marauding Khoikhoi. There is an avenue of fig and camphor trees (from China and Japan) planted by Rhodes during his tenure, and Professor Pearson, founder of the gardens, is buried among his first collection, in the Cycad Amphitheatre.

69

Anton Anreith's magnificent carving adorns the old cellars at Groot Constantia

CONVICT ISLAND
The first-ever European attempt to colonize the Cape Peninsula was in 1615, when eight British convicts were left on the shore. They crossed to Robben Island and remained there until rescued by a passing ship some months later. With the arrival of the Dutch 40 years later, Robben Island became a high-security prison, which it remained for nearly 350 years.

Below: Splendid Victoriana along the main road in Simon's Town.
Bottom: African penguins strut for the tourists at Boulders Beach

►►► Robben Island   48A2

9km (6 miles) off the Green Point coast
Robben Island Cruises (tel: 021-419 1300, www.robben-island.org.za)
Departures on the hour every hour between 9 and 3, from Nelson Mandela Gateway, just beside the Clock Tower. The tour lasts 3.5 hours and includes a bus tour of the island and a prison tour led by a former inmate. Admission: expensive

Measuring only 2 by 3.5km (1.25 by 2 miles), Robben Island takes its name from *robbe*, the Dutch word for seals. It still has colonies of Cape fur seals and penguins, but the island is far more infamous for its past inhabitants: high-ranking exiles, Islamic holy men, political dissidents, robbers, pirates and murderers. In the 19th century, it held black leaders captured during the Frontier Wars; from the 1960s inmates included high-profile political detainees such as Nelson Mandela, who spent 27 years here. The last prisoners left in May 1991, leaving the island a wildlife sanctuary and place of pilgrimage for South African nationalism.

►► Simon's Town   48A1

40km (25 miles) south of Cape Town
Tourist Information, Main Road (tel: 021-786 2436)

Named after Simon van der Stel, governor of the Cape from 1691 to 1699, this little port became the Royal Navy headquarters in 1814 and was taken over by the SA Navy in 1957. It is now a seaside town with charming Victorian houses. The governor's residence (built 1777), later a court and prison, is now the delightful **Simon's Town Museum** (Court Road, tel: 021-786 3046. *Open* Mon–Fri 9–4, Sat 10–4. *Admission: inexpensive*). Other places to visit are the **South African Naval Museum** (St. George's Street, tel: 021-787 4635. *Open* daily 10–4); and the **Warrior Toy Museum** (St. George's Street, tel: 021-786 1395. *Open* daily 10–4. *Admission: inexpensive*). At **Boulders Beach** (Seaforth Road, tel: 021-786 2329. *Open* daily 8–5. *Admission: moderate*) is a colony of African penguins, one of only two on the African mainland.

Kalk Bay, one of many small towns with delightful beaches along the Cape Peninsula

The Cape of Good Hope

A spiny ridge of mountains tails south along the Cape Peninsula to tumble into the sea in a riotous confusion of rocks at Cape Point. The scenery is spectacular, the beaches idyllic, and many of the charming small towns offer an enticing blend of good food, interesting shops and plentiful history. Allow at least one full day.

Cape Town to Muizenberg From the city centre, take the M3 (De Waal Road) to Muizenberg. There are turn-offs en route for **Kirstenbosch** and **Groot Constantia** (see pages 68–69).

Herbert Baker once wielded his architect's pencil in trendy **Muizenberg** (Tourist Information, The Pavilion, Beach Road, tel: 021-788 6193, fax: 021-788 6208, www.tourism capetown.co.za), the favourite resort of the Randlords. Numerous fine houses include the cottage in which Cecil Rhodes died in 1902, kept as a museum/shrine (Main Road, tel: 021-788 1816. *Open* Tue–Sun 10–1, 2–5). Now the town is a bit tired and shabby, but nothing can spoil its lovely, safe, shallow beach, lined by rows of highly painted changing booths. The Venetian-style **Natale Labia Museum** (192 Main Road, tel: 021-788 4106. *Open* Tue–Sun 10–5) is a pleasant art gallery; also visit the **South Africa Police Museum** (186 Main Road, tel: 021-788 7035. *Open* Mon–Fri 8–3.30, Sat 9–1, Sun 2–5) and the **Toy Museum** (8 Beach Road, tel: 021-788 1569. *Open* Tue–Sun 10–4).

Kalk Bay to Cape Point A little farther down the coast, **Kalk Bay** ('lime bay') was named after the kilns in which shells were burned to produce lime. It is a busy fishing port. The main road has antiques and junk stores, crafts shops and eateries. Soak up the atmosphere, climb up to the deep caves pitting the mountain slopes or try surfing on **Danger Beach**.

Continue south along the coast-hugging M4 to **Fish Hoek**, a resort that has the distinction of being the only teetotal town in the country—a stipulation laid down by Lord Charles Somerset in 1818. He also declared free fishing rights for all.

Peers Cave, a rock shelter nearby, is named after the man who discovered the 15,000-year-old skeleton called 'Fish Hoek Man'. This is the best place on the peninsula to see whales.

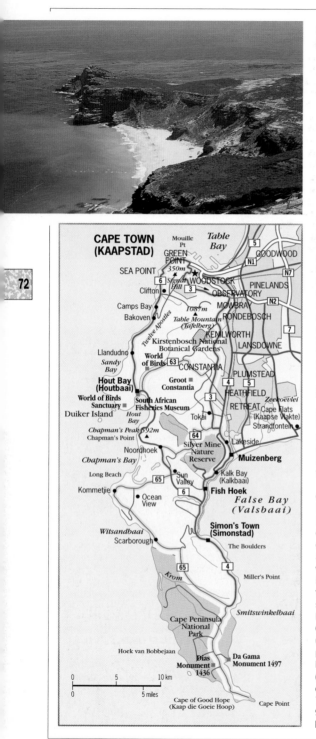

*Cape Point divides
two oceans*

Continue through **Simon's Town** (see page 70) to the farthest tip of the peninsula and the bleak, beautiful **Cape Point**, part of the Table Mountain National Park (tel: 021-780 9204, www.tmnp. co.za. *Open* daily 7–6. *Admission: moderate*). It is the accepted meeting place of the Atlantic and Indian oceans and also the psychological if not physical end of Africa (the most southerly point is actually Cape Agulhas, see page 94). There are drives, places to picnic, walk and swim, plus magnificent flora and small game. The east coast cliffs sheer abruptly into the warm waters of the Indian Ocean's **False Bay**; to the west the land slopes downward more gently to the Atlantic. The visitor centre has a funicular up to the viewing point and a good restaurant. For walks, contact park staff (tel: 021-780 9010; www.capepoint.co.za).

Chapman's Peak Drive
Heading north, take the M65 along the Atlantic coast to **Kommetjie**, a quiet seaside village with a good surfing beach. The water, famously, is freezing, but a shallow, warmer tidal pool provides safe swimming for children. From here, the beautiful 6km (4 miles) **Long Beach**, unsafe for swimming but popular with horse-riders, leads up to **Noordhoek** (Tourist Information, just off Main Road, tel: 021-789 2812. *Open* daily 9.30–5.30). **Chapman's Peak Drive** to Hout Bay,

72

built between 1915 and 1922, is a winding 10km (6 miles) feat of engineering, that is unfortunately closed for reconstruction after landslides. Instead, head north via the M63/M3 through Constantia to reach Hout Bay.

Hout Bay to the city Dominated by the towering peak of The Sentinel, little **Hout Bay** (Tourist Information, Andrews Road, tel: 021-790 1264. *Open* Mon–Fri 9–5, Sat–Sun 10–1) was named after the wood (*hout*) harvested for shipbuilding. Traditionally a bade for crayfish and *snoek* (barracuda) fishing, it is a lively seaside town filled with vacation cottages, fishermen, a thriving marina and several popular restaurants. The local **museum** (4 Andrews Road, tel: 021-790 3270. *Open* Mon–Fr 8.30–4. *Admission: inexpensive*) has an excellent display of *strandloper* (beachcomber) culture, while the **South African Fisheries Museum** (Hout Bay Harbour, tel: 021-790 7268. *Open* Tue–Sun 10–4) has fascinating models, audiovisuals and other fishing displays. From the harbour, Drumboat Charters (tel: 021-438 9208) runs boat trips to the seal colony and seabird sanctuary on **Duiker Island**. In the summer you can see thousands of Cape fur seals here. Nearby, the **World of Birds Sanctuary** (Valley Road, tel: 021-790 2730. *Open* daily 9–5. *Admission: moderate*) is one of the largest bird sanctuaries in South Africa, with over 3,000 birds from around 450 varieties flying free in walk-through aviaries.

Beyond Hout Bay, the coastline becomes one long ribbon development, with houses clustering ever more thickly as you head back into the city. Lovely undeveloped **Sandy Bay** is the local nudist beach. **Bakoven**, named after a large cave shaped like a baker's oven, has two small beaches and is safe for children and popular with snorkellers. Trendy **Camps Bay**, tucked in at the base of the Twelve Apostles, has a wide beach with lawns and a good selection of affordable restaurants. The sea here is very cold with a strong undertow. Surfers use Glen Beach in the adjoining cove. **Clifton** is *the* place to be and be seen. Although the water is freezing, people flock to its four overcrowded beaches. **Sea Point** is closer to the heart of the city and not quite so fashionable, but is lively and trendy with a slightly bohemian tinge.

73

Camps Bay and the Twelve Apostles on the Atlantic Coast

The world is divided into six 'floral kingdoms', distinct botanical habitats from tropical rain forest to tundra. The smallest (90,000sqkm/ 35,000sq-miles) and, for its size, the richest, is the Cape, which stretches from the Cederberg in the Western Cape to Port Elizabeth in the east.

SMALL IS BEAUTIFUL
The largest of the floral kingdoms, the Boreal, stretches much of the way across the northern hemisphere and covers 42 per cent of the earth's land surface. The Cape kingdom covers just 0.04 per cent—a mere 90,000sq km (35,000sq miles).

74

*Top: Proteas in bloom at Kirstenbosch
Below: Quiver trees in the Karoo*

Within the Cape kingdom are a staggering 8,500 species of plants (42.5 per cent of the total for southern Africa), of which 6,000 are endemic. There are more indigenous plant species on Table Mountain (1,470) than in the whole of the British Isles (1,443). Many more are found in the spectacular spring displays of the Karoo and Namaqualand on the far side of the mountains.

Fynbos This magical array of Cape plants and flowers is known overall as *fynbos* (literally 'fine bush'), a group of evergreen, fine-leafed plants that thrive in poor, sandy soil and harsh conditions, with hot dry summers and cold wet winters. From a distance, this heathland vegetation seems less than inspiring, with low, scrubby plants rolling on across the hills, few bushes standing higher than a person's knee. It is only when you look closely that you begin to see the enormous variation in species. Three-quarters are found nowhere else and many are so specialized that they survive in only one valley.

Fynbos is made up of three main plant families—reeds, proteas and ericas—along with several smaller groups of legumes and bulbs. The most common are the wind-

pollinated reeds (*restios*) that here replace grass as general ground cover. Hardy and unpleasant grazing, they survive the weather and wildlife, but are harvested by locals for thatching. Proteas (*proteaceae*) are the national flower of South Africa. Most familiar are the king proteas, with their heavy, furry black-and-pink heads, but there are an infinite number of species, ranging from spiky red flowers to a great mass of minute florets and even inconspicuous, low-lying pincushions. Ericas (*ericaceae*), related to the European heathers, are the only true *fynbos* plant to translate happily to the gardens of the world, although other local species, such as freesias, pelargoniums, campanulas, lobelias and the subtropical gladioli and strelizias have become popular with gardeners and florists alike.

Orange-breasted sunbird in a blooming Protea pityphla

Spring colour Mesembryanthemums and daisies (*asteraceae*) dot the mountains and coast with colour, but really come into their own in Namaqualand, where spring sees magnificent sheets of vibrant pinks, oranges and purples cloaking the landscape for great distances. The Karoo also flowers in spring, but here there is a more subtle cover with tiny yellow and purple flowers gently tinting the soft grey of rock and shale.

Subtropical forest Until about 3 million years ago, the Cape is thought to have had a milder climate and to have been covered by lush, subtropical woodland. This survives a little farther north, along the hills of the Garden Route (Knysna Forest and Tsitsikamma National Park, see pages 100–101) and through into KwaZulu-Natal. Here, the mountains foster a totally different range of species, the most dramatic are the huge, hard yellow-woods and stinkwoods, from which most Cape Dutch furniture is made. Lurking in the undergrowth below these giants are some of the most extraordinary plants in South Africa, the cycads, said to be unchanged since the Jurassic period (150–200 million years ago), when dinosaurs roamed the earth.

FLOWER HUNTING
No one has yet attempted to produce a layman's guide to Cape flora, although there are many huge tomes on specialist aspects, such as proteas. The Kirstenbosch Gardens (see page 69) are an essential first stop, but to see the mass of flowers in all their glory, visit in winter (July/August) for *fynbos* and spring (September/October) for the desert flowers. Most of the desert plants are heliotropic (keep their faces turned towards the sun), so are best seen in the midday heat, with your back to the light. Expect long traffic jams at the height of the season. A telephone hotline, MTN Flowerline (tel: 083-910 1028), operates between June and October.

75

EARTHQUAKE

On 29 September 1969, a massive earthquake measuring 6.5 on the Richter scale reduced much of Tulbagh to ruins. Many early buildings, such as Thibault's Drostdy (1806), were totally destroyed. One of the biggest restoration agendas ever undertaken in South Africa swung into action. Over the years buildings had been altered and extended, windows blocked up and gables rearranged. The earthquake-shattered plasterwork allowed the Tulbagh Restoration Committee to reconstruct the original pattern of building. In Church Street alone, 32 small whitewashed, gabled homesteads have been carefully restored. The results are remarkable.

The Oude Kerk Volksmuseum, Tulbagh, restored after a disastrous earthquake

The Breede River Valley area

▶ Ceres   48B2

130km (80 miles) northeast of Cape Town, off the N1
Tourist Information, John Steyn Library, corner Voortrekker and Owen streets (tel/fax: 023-316 1287, www.ceres.org.za)
Named after the Roman goddess of fertility, Ceres is all about fruit. Tour the huge **Ceres Fruit Growers and Ceres Fruit Juices Co-operative** (tel: 023-316 1287) to see fruit dried, processed and packaged, or pick your own at the **Klondyke Cherry Farm** (tel: 023-312 1521. *Open* Nov–Jan).

In early days the town was often cut off by winter snow, but in 1848, Andrew Geddes Bain built Mitchell's Pass, after which it became an important stop en route to the diamond fields. The **Transport Riders Museum** (8 Orange Street, tel: 023-312 2045. *Open* Mon–Fri 9–1, 2–5, Sat 9–12, on request in winter. *Admission: inexpensive*) traces the transport riders' part in local history.

About 80km (50 miles) north (gravel road), **Kagga Kamma** (PO Box 7143, North Paarl 7623, tel: 021-872 4343, www.kaggakamma.co.za) is a private game reserve, home to some of South Africa's last traditional Bushmen (San). It is famous not only for its strange rock formations but for the paintings of the San, some over 6,000 years old.

▶ Tulbagh   48B2

About 160km (100 miles) north of Cape Town. Tourist Information, 14 Church Street (tel: 023-230 1348, www.tulbagh.com).
Open: Mon–Fri 9–4.30, Sat 10–4, Sun 11–4
Parts of rural Tulbagh seem to be an almost perfect 18th-century town. Church Street is particularly charming, and the old church is the focal point of the **Oude Kerk Volksmuseum** (4 Church Street, tel: 023-230 1041. *Open* Summer Mon–Fri 9–5, Sat 9–4, Sun 11–4. *Admission:*

inexpensive). The four restored buildings houses a collection of furniture and costumes, and displays on the 1969 earthquake (see panel opposite). The **Monbijou Stately House** (36 Church Street, tel: 083-366 6978. *Open* daily Sat–Tue 11 and 3 for tours or by appointement. *Admission: moderate*) is one of the finest of the town's old mansions.

The **Oude Drostdy** (4km/2.5 miles from Tulbagh, tel: 023-230 0203. *Open* Mon–Sat 10–1, 2–4, Sun 2.30–5. *Admission: inexpensive*) is now a museum, housing an unexpected collection of early gramophones as well as the usual Cape Dutch furniture. Free wine tours and tastings.

▶▶ **Worcester** 48B2

105km (65 miles) northeast of Cape Town
Breede River Valley Tourist Information, Kleinplasie Museum Complex, Worcester (tel: 023-347 6411, fax: 023-347 1115, www.breederivervalley.co.za). Worcester Tourist Information, 23 Baring Street (tel: 023-348 2795, fax: 023-347 4678). Open: Mon–Fri 8–5, Sat 8.30–12.30

This sprawling, modern market town is 'capital' of the biggest wine-producing district (see pages 86–87, 92–93). It is also home to the vast **KWV Brandy Cellars** (Church Street, tel: 023-342 0255. Guided tours Mon–Sat at 10 (Afrikaans) and 2 (English); German by appointment. Open for sales Mon–Fri 8–5, Sat 9–4. *Admission: moderate*), where 120 copper kettles distill the famous KWV 10- and 20-year-old brandies.

Allow plenty of time to visit the open-air **Kleinplasie Museum▶** (off Robertson Road, tel: 023-342 2225. *Open* Mon–Sat 9–4.30. *Admission: moderate*), where reconstructed dwellings and farm buildings with accurate furnishings from 1690 to 1900 depict the life and times of pioneer farmers. The area hums with traditional activities, from tobacco rolling to distilling *witblitz*, the local firewater (tastings and sales in the museum).

Next door is the **Kleinplasie Reptile World** (off Robertson Road, tel: 023-342 6480. *Open* daily 9–5. *Admission: moderate*), with over 80 species of snakes, lizards, turtles and crocodiles. Three more museums are the Cape Dutch **Beck House** (1841), furnished as a late 19th-century town house and **Stofberg House** (1920s), which covers the history of Worcester, are both on Baring Street (*Open* Mon–Fri 8.30–1, 1.30–4.30. *Admission: donation*). **Hugo Naudé House** (Russell Street, tel: 023-342 5802. *Open* Mon–Fri 8.30–4.30, Sat 9–12. *Admission: donation*), the former studio of the South African pioneer painter, now houses the municipal art collection.

The **Karoo National Botanical Garden** (Roux Street, tel: 023-347 0785. *Open* daily 8–5. *Admission: moderate*) has 144ha (355 acres) of natural semidesert vegetation, landscaped gardens of quiver trees, aloes and vygies and greenhouses of extraordinary stone plants.

Rolling tobacco at the Kleinplasie Open Air Museum, Worcester

OTHER STOPS
The Breede River valley is an important fruit- and wine-producing area, prolifically fertile and festooned with orchards, vineyards and wheatlands. It has small reserves of plants and birds, and successions of pools, rapids and waterfalls are ideal for trout anglers, canoeists, mountaineers and nature lovers. Several other towns in the region repay a stop. They include Robertson (renowned for its Muscatel grapes and wines and a good base for climbs into the Langeberg range), McGregor, Rawsonville, Bonnievale, Ashton and the spa towns of Montagu and Goudini. Most have a small museum and a wine route.

The vast empty plains of the Great Karoo

THE KAROO

Aptly named 'the land of thirst' by the Khoikhoi, the Karoo is a vast, arid wilderness peppered with flat-topped *koppies* of hard doleritic rock trapping thousands of fossils, from enormous trees to strange amphibious creatures with mammalian features. Its hardy little desert plants curl unnoticed into the greyish dust, bursting into life in spring when their magnificent blossom splashes the landscape with pure colour. The desert is divided into the markedly more fertile Little Karoo, around Oudtshoorn, separated from the sea by the Langeberg and Outeniqua Mountains, and the vast expanse of the Great Karoo beyond the Swartberg to the north (see also page 112).

Groot- (Great) Karoo

▶ Beaufort West 49D3

47km (29 miles) northeast of Cape Town
Central Karoo Tourist Information, D.C. Office,
Church Street, Beaufort West (tel: 023-415 1488)
This is the Karoo's largest town, with streets shaded by pear trees, and three small **museums** (Donkin Street. *Open* Mon–Fri 8.30–12.45, 1.45–4.45, Sat 9–12. *Admission: inexpensive*). One has exhibits on Dr Christian Barnaard, the first man to perform a heart transplant, and one is a history museum.

Karoo National Park (off the N1, tel: 023-415 2828; central reservations tel: 012-428 9111, fax: 012-343 0905, www.sanparks.org for reservations. *Open* daily 5.30am–8pm. *Admission: moderate*), 4km (2.5 miles) south of Beaufort West, encompasses 46,119ha (113,913 acres) of virgin Karoo veld and the Nuweveldberge. Remarkably fecund for a semidesert, it has 64 mammal species, including mountain zebra, black rhino and springbok; 194 bird species, and 59 reptile species. There is a restaurant, basic accommodation, hiking and 4WD trails.

▶▶ The Swartberg 49D2

High and gnarled, the Swartberg (Black Mountains), known as the Cango (Water) Mountains, formed an almost impenetrable 200km (125 miles) barrier to the interior until the arrival of the great Victorian road builders.

Of the seven passes in the area, the most dramatic is the 24km (15-mile) **Swartberg Pass**, built by Thomas Bain using convict labour (1881–88). It has wide panoramas on the southern slopes, but the northern face plunges into a ravine, ending in a cauldron of rock at Eerstewater, near the village of Prince Albert. At the top is a remote valley, Gamkaskloof (once called 'Hell'), settled for nearly 200 years by a group of farmers who were totally isolated before the arrival of the road in 1962. Also worth driving along is the shorter **Meiringspoort Pass**, on the road from De Rust to Beaufort West.

Klein- (Little) Karoo

►► Cango Caves 49D2

29km (18 miles) north of Oudtshoorn on the R328
(tel: 044-272 7410,
www.cangocaves.co.za)
Open: daily 9–4. Access to
caves on guided tours only,
every hour on the hour
Admission: moderate/expen-
sive. Reservations essential
The San lived in the
entrance to this huge
limestone system under
the Swartberg Mountains,
but they never penetrated
far inside. A local farmer,
Jacobus van Zyl, led
the first expedition into
the heart of the caves in
1780, discovering the first
of three sequences of

caverns adorned with stalactites and all manner of fantas-
tical dripstone formations. The largest of the chambers is
a stunning 107m (350ft) across and 16m (53ft) high. The
entire system remains at an even temperature of 18°C
(64°F). Three levels of tours are available: easy half-hour
strolls that take you through two of the caverns; more
comprehensive 1-hour tours into eight chambers; and
full-scale adventure tours, requiring you to wriggle
through narrow passages and climb steep pipes; you
should be reasonably fit for this but do not need any
previous experience.

Cango Caves' dramatic
dripstone formations

► Cango Wildlife Ranch 49D2

About 10km (6 miles) north of Oudtshoorn, on the Cango
Caves road, R328 (tel: 044-272 5593, www.cango.co.za)
Open: daily 8–6 (restaurant open until late)
Admission: expensive
Operating mainly as a breeding centre for rare species,
this farm has over 400 crocodiles, a snake park, lions,
cheetahs (some of which are tame and over-16s can pet),
jaguars and Bengal tigers; comical pygmy hippos; minia-
ture horses and goats; and a deer park. Nearby are the
Cango Ostrich Farm (see page 81) and the **Cango Angora
Rabbit Farm** (tel: 044-279 1259. *Open daily 7–5*).

► Matjiesfontein 48C2

About 260km (160 miles) east of Cape Town
James Logan (see panel) found the dry, crisp Karoo air
good for his weak chest. In the late 19th century, he
founded Matjiesfontein as a resort and health spa,
attracting similarly afflicted guests including Lord
Randolph Churchill and the Sultan of Zanzibar. During
the Boer War, it became the headquarters of the Cape
Command, then a military hospital. Not much has
changed in the last 100 years. Now called the Lord Milner
Hotel (see page 260), it is a monument to Victoriana
and is said to be haunted by armies of jolly, party-
loving ghosts. The old station has a private museum of
Victorian objects.

LOGAN'S LUCK
James Logan arrived from
Scotland in 1877, eventu-
ally settling in the Karoo
where he bought a farm,
Tweedside, and gradually
added land until he
owned over 50,000ha
(123,500 acres). A model
and prosperous farmer,
Logan had the first private
residence with electricity
in South Africa, pioneered
water and sewage treat-
ment, and made a second
fortune from his hotel and
restaurants. His third
fortune came from selling
water to the rail compa-
nies—a locomotive
consumed 250,000 litres
(55,000gal) of water in
crossing the Karoo and
therefore any dependable
supply was invaluable. He
died in Matjiesfontein on
30 July 1920.

Oudtshoorn's ostrich feather millionaires built themselves fantastically palatial homes

PEAR POWER

In 1916, a Karoo farmer invented a new alternative to petrol (gas), brewed from prickly pears. To prove it worked, he invited writer Lawrence Green to accompany him on a drive from Cape Town to Bulawayo (described in Green's book, *Karoo*). Sadly, the venture failed when the farmer inhaled poisonous fumes from the fuel and died. Karoo farmers went back to turning prickly pears into a potent liqueur, which they say is particularly good poured over ice cream!

▶▶▶ Oudtshoorn 49D2

506km (314 miles) east of Cape Town
Klein Karoo and Oudtshoorn Tourist Information,
Baron van Rheede Street
(tel: 044-279 2532, fax: 044-272 8226, www.oudtshoorn.com,
email: info@oudtshoorninfo.com.)
Open: Mon–Fri 8–5, Sat 9–1

Diamonds may have been the treasure of Kimberley, but ostrich feathers were the wealth of the Little Karoo. From the 1880s, sweeping ostrich plumes and feather boas were the height of ladies' fashion. Designers could not get enough, and the arid Karoo proved to be perfect breeding territory. In 1905, the feathers plucked from just six birds fetched R12,000. By the time the railway arrived in 1913, the district was awash with millionaires. Ordinary little Oudtshoorn was transformed into a boomtown filled with spectacular mansions. Oudtshoorn's 'feather palaces' were large, ornate and lavish beyond your wildest dreams. Most were swirling sandstone art nouveau, with circular turrets, iron railings and—the colonial variation—corrugated-iron roofs. The ceilings and cornices were embossed papier-mâché, while the walls and windows were bright with stained glass and vividly glazed tiles.

With World War I the market crashed and for a time Oudtshoorn was in decline. In the late 1930s, however, ostriches again came to the rescue; the first show farm was opened and the tourists arrived. Today the trade is thriving, but this time feathers, though still valuable, are not the crucial product. International demand for low-fat, almost cholesterol-free ostrich meat is soaring. Supple ostrich leather is increasingly popular for expensive designer shoes, bags, belts and accessories. Even the eggs fetch a good market price, both for eating and—halved or carved—as souvenirs.

The town has two excellent museums. Don't miss the **C. P. Nel Museum** (3 Baron van Rheede Street, tel: 044-272 7306. *Open* Mon–Sat 9–5. *Admission: inexpensive*), which occupies the old Boys' High School, a building designed in 1907 by leading 'feather' architect Charles Bullock. The core of the compelling collection was donated in 1953 by C. P. Nel, a prominent local businessman. It tells the history of Oudtshoorn, ostriches and the feather trade. **Le Roux Townhouse** (146 High Street, tel: 044-272 3676. *Open* Mon–Fri 9–1, 2–5. *Admission: free*) is a carefully restored offshoot of the C. P. Nel Museum. Built by Charles Bullock for J. H. J. Le Roux in 1909, it is one of the finest of the 'feather mansions'. Lavishly appointed, it still contains most of its original furnishings.

There are several ostrich show farms in Oudtshoorn offering a full range of tours and facilities. **Highgate** (off the Mossel Bay Road, the R328, 10km/6 miles from town, tel: 044-272 7115, www.highgate.co.za. *Open* daily 7.30–5, tours last up to 2 hours. *Admission: expensive*) was one of the first ostrich farms in the valley (1887). It was also the first to turn ostriches into a tourist attraction in 1937, setting the agenda for all tours. There you can still investigate every aspect of the birds' life—see them being born, reared and plucked, handle a baby, sit or ride on an adult, and watch an ostrich Derby, with 'professional' jockeys on board; buy the eggs, eat the fillet and wear the shoes.

At the **Safari Ostrich Farm** (off the R328 Mossel Bay Road, 5km/3 miles from Oudtshoorn, tel: 044-272 7311, www.safariostrich.co.za. *Open* daily 8–5.30. *Admission: moderate*) there is a restored feather baron's mansion, Welgeluk (1910), and the tour explains how products from feather dusters to handbags are made. The **Cango Ostrich Farm** (about 15km/9 miles north on the R328 Cango Caves road, tel: 044-272 4623, www.cangoostrich. co.za. *Open* school holidays 8–5; out of season daily 8–4.30. *Admission: moderate*) is smaller and simpler than the other two but has a wine cellar and butterfly farm.

OSTRICHES
South Africa now has around 560 ostrich farms producing about 300,000 ostriches a year, over half of them in Klein-Karoo. The female lays up to 15 eggs per clutch, each weighing the equivalent to 24 hen's eggs. They take six weeks to hatch. The young are fawn, while adult males are black and white and the females chocolate brown. They take two years to reach maturity, when they weigh about 100kg (220lb). The birds run in herds of 100–150 and are plucked every nine months, each bird losing 1kg (2lb) of feathers at a time. For all you need to know about ostriches: www.ostrichesonline.com.

The victory lap in an ostrich race

82

Whales and tourists dominate daily life in Hermanus

The Overberg and South Coast

The Overberg ('over the mountain') is the end of Africa, the segment of the south coast on the far side of the Hottentots Holland Mountains from Cape Town. It was one of the first areas beyond the bay to be colonized. Cut off by the mountains, the isolated Overbergers developed their own distinctive food, language and a strong sense of independence, heavily influenced by missionaries at **Genadendal** (which has an excellent mission museum in Herrnhut House), Elim and Zuurbraak.

Several pleasant resorts include: **Gansbaai**, an unspoiled fishing village with safe swimming—for shark diving off the coast, contact Shark Lady Adventures (tel: 083-746 8985, www.sharklady.co.za); **Betty's Bay**, backed by magnificent mountains and site of the superb **Harold Porter National Botanical Garden▶** (tel: 028-272 9311. *Open* daily 8–6. *Admission: inexpensive*); and **Kleinmond** (tel: 028-271 5657, www.hanzklipkleinmondtourism.co.za) between Hermanus and Betty's Bay, where you can find within a 5km (3 mile) radius every type of Western Cape natural habitat, from beach dunes to *fynbos*.

▶ **Cape Agulhas and environs** see pages 94–95

▶ **Hermanus** 48B1
100km (62 miles) east of Cape Town
Tourist Information, 105 Main Road (tel: 028-312 2629,
fax: 028-313 0305, email: infoburo@hermanus.co.za)
Open: Mon–Sat 9–5, Sun 11–5
Fashionable Hermanus was founded early in the 19th century by Hermanus Pieters, who earmarked its green cliffs and freshwater stream as excellent summer grazing. But it was fishermen who settled it in the 1850s, and since the 1900s it has been a popular summer resort.

There are several fine beaches nearby, but the real draw is the whales. Hermanus is the only town in the world with an official 'whale crier' (MTN Whale Hotline, tel: 083-910 1028) who wanders the streets with a sandwich board and kelp horn. There are good viewing points for whales from the cliffs and the Old Harbour. The harbour was the focal point of the early village; now it is the hub of

a tourist town, part of a 'living' **Old Harbour Museum** (Marine Drive, tel: 028-312 1475. *Open* Mon–Sat 9–1, 2–4. *Admission: inexpensive*), with exhibitions on local fishing and whaling. A sonar buoy catches the whales' song and transmits it live into the museum hall. In the square above is a lively crafts market, while the Old School House is an annex to the museum with fascinating old photographs. Hiking trails include one through the mountain and coastal *fynbos* of the **Fernkloof Nature Reserve**.

▶▶ Swellendam   48C1

220km (134 miles) from Cape Town
Tourist Information, Voortrek Street
(tel/fax: 028-514 2770, email: infoswd@sdm.dorea.co.za,
www.swellendamtourism.co.za)
Open: Mon–Fri 8–1, 2–5, Sat 9–12.30

The well-watered area around Swellendam, now rich in wheat fields, cows and fruit trees, once attracted great quantities of game, which in turn attracted the Hessekwa Khoikhoi. The first Europeans arrived in the 1740s, carving out farms along the Breede River. Many of their original homesteads still exist. By the early 19th century, Swellendam was a gung-ho eastern frontier village on the pioneering Kaapse Wapad (Cape wagon road). Named after Governor Swellengrebel and his wife, Helena ten Damme, Swellendam flirted briefly with independence before becoming a charming town with oak-lined streets, pristine Cape Dutch and Victorian houses and a fine Dutch Reformed church.

The **Drostdy Museum** (18 Swellengrebel Street, tel: 028-514 1138. *Open* Mon–Fri 9–4.45, Sat–Sun 10–3.45. *Admission: moderate*) is in the former seat of the *landdrost* (governor's representative). One of the finest such buildings in the country, it dates from 1747 and incorporated a courtroom and an office. It now displays a fine collection of 18th- and 19th-century Cape furniture as well as art. The museum also includes the old jail and two houses: Mayville (built in 1853), an impeccable Victorian house with delightful cottage garden, and the Auld House. **Bontebok National Park** (entrance 6km/4 miles south of Swellendam, tel: 028-514 2735. *Open* daily 8–7) is home to the once rare antelope that gives the park its name. To the north, the **Marloth Nature Reserve** climbs a flank of the Langeberg Mountains.

HOME SWEET HOME
When the earliest European cattle traders climbed into the lush green mountains east of Cape Town for the first time, they found a band of the Khoikhoi Chainoukwa clan, who proclaimed that this was the best place in the world. The homesick explorers promptly named the range the Hottentots Holland Mountains. In 1672, the Chainoukwa sold the mountains to the Dutch East India Company and left the area, much of which ended up as the personal property of the Van der Stel family, even though Company officials were forbidden to own any land.

Swellendam's magnificent Dutch Reformed church

83

Try the Cederberg for wilderness walking and dramatic views

The West Coast and Cederberg

▶▶ Cederberg
48B2/B3

About 220km (137 miles) north of Cape Town.
Cederberg/Olifants River Valley Publicity Association, Old Jail Building, Main Street, Clanwilliam (tel: 027-482 2024, fax: 027-482 2361, www.clanwilliam.info)
Open: Mon–Fri 8.30–5, Sat 8.30–12.30

The 100km (62-mile) long, north–south Cederberg take their name from the endangered Clanwilliam cedar tree (*Widdringtonia cedarbergensis*), which grows uniquely in these mountains at an altitude of 1,000–1,500m (3,280–4,920ft). The vast protected wilderness area offers great hiking, walking, climbing and riding, with magnificent views and sandstone formations such as the dramatic Wolfberg Arch. There are clear river pools for swimming and San rock paintings up to 6,000 years old. Rare and wonderful flora and fauna includes the snowball protea, the Clanwilliam yellowfish and a mass of colourful bird life, plus a healthy leopard population. Pick up hiking permits, maps and information about the area from the Algeria Forestry Station, or write ahead to the Cederberg Publicity Association (see panel, left and above).

The two nearest towns are **Clanwilliam** (Tourist Information, see above) and **Citrusdal** (Tourist Information, Sandveldhuisie Country Shop, Church Street, tel/fax: 022-921 3210, www.citrusdal.info. *Open* Oct–Jul Mon–Fri 9–4.30, Sat 9–12; Aug–Sep daily 9–4.30). Clanwilliam is famous for its health-giving rooibos tea (see panel), Citrusdal for its oranges. The area between was named Olifants River Valley by early explorers because of the herds of elephant roaming it. Today it is all very different, with neat citrus groves and well-kept vineyards.

TOURS AND HIKING
For specialist tours of the region, contact Cederberg Travel, PO Box 25, Clanwilliam 8135 (tel: 027-482 2444). Obtain hiking permits and information from Algeria Forestry Station, Private Bag XI, Citrusdal 7340 (tel: 027-482 2812). For Dwarsrivier (tel: 027-482 2825; for Kromriver (027-482 2807).

▶▶ West Coast and Swartland 48A2/A3

West Coast Publicity Association, Plein Street, Moorreesburg (tel/fax: 022-433 1072, www.touismmoorreesburg.co.za.
Open: Mon–Fri 9–5, Sat 9–12
Greater Vredenburg Tourism Bureau, Hugo and Hugo Toyota, corner of Main and Veldrift roads, Vredenburg (tel/fax: 022-715 1142, www.sawestcoast.com).
Open: Mon–Fri 9–5

Dominated by the icy, plankton-rich Benguela Current, the Atlantic West Coast is a region of huge kelp beds and abundant sealife, seabirds and seals. Known as the 'Lobster Coast', after the prolific Cape rock lobster (*Jasus lalandi*) found along these shores, the area was once a key whaling station. It is still a crucial commercial fishing ground, although it is struggling against overfishing.

Although the water is bitterly cold, the dry climate, cool sea breeze and easy access from Cape Town make this a popular vacation area, focused around **Langebaan** (Tourist Information, Library, tel: 022-772 1515. *Open* Mon–Fri 9.30–4.30, Sat 9–12), where water sports on the sheltered lagoon are the main attraction. The lagoon is part of the huge **West Coast National Park** (tel: 022-772 2144. *Open* daily 7–7), famous wetlands whose offshore islands offer predator-proof nesting sites for an estimated three-quarters of a million seabirds of 200 different species, including Cape gannets, crowned cormorants, and other waders and small colonies of African penguins. In spring, the whales arrive.

Also nearby, at Langebaanweg, is the **West Coast Fossil Park** (tel: 022-766 1606, www.museums.org.za. *Open* daily, phone for tour times as booking essential), a fossil-rich site within a phosphate mine.

Saldanha Bay (Tourist Information, see above) is named after the 16th-century Portuguese Admiral Antonio de Saldanha. The huge natural harbour is famous for its mussels and as a major port, processing iron ore from mines 860km (534 miles) inland.

St. Helena Bay and **Elands Bay** (Tourist Information, Church Street, tel: 022-972 1640) have world-famous surf.

A little way inland, **Darling** (Tourist Information in the museum, tel: 022-492 3361, fax: 022-492 2935. *Open* daily 9–4) marks the start of the flower lands, a blaze of colour in spring (see pages 74–75). The **Darling Museum** (Pastorie Street, tel: 022-492 3361. *Open* daily 9–1, 2–4) has numerous butter-making utensils. This is also the home of comedian Pieter Dirk Uys' seminal character, Mrs. Evita Bezuidenhout, who holds court at Evita Se Perron (tel: 022-492 2831). The Moravians, Catholics and Dutch Reformed Church were active in the area in the early 19th century, and several local villages, including Ebenhaeser, Goedverwacht, Rietpoort, Vergenoeg and Wupperthal, began life as missions.

ROOIBOS

Rooibos ("red bush', *Aspalanthus linearis*) is an indigenous plant of the Cederberg. The coloured population were the first to drink it as a tea, but by the mid-19th century it was being drunk more widely. In 1904, Benjamin Ginsberg started trading seriously, and by 1930 full-scale cultivation was under way, based around Clanwilliam. Now common throughout South Africa, with small quantities exported, it is brewed and presented like ordinary tea, looks a dark, reddish brown—and is terribly healthy. It is free of tannin and stimulants, rich in vitamin C, relaxing and contains antiallergenic agents. There are several farm and factory tours around Clanwilliam; ask the tourist office for details.

85

Saldanha Bay survives largely on Atlantic deep-sea fishing

The Winelands

▶▶ Franschhoek 48B2

80km (50 miles) northeast of Cape Town
Tourist Information, 28a Huguenot Road (tel: 021-876 3603,
fax: 021-876 2768, email: info@franschhoek.org.za,
www.franschhoek.org.za)
Open: Oct–Apr Mon–Fri 9–6, Sat 9–5, Sun 10–5; May–Sep
Mon–Fri 9–5, Sat 9.30–1, Sun 10–5

In 1688, Governor Simon van der Stel granted the valley to a small group of Huguenots (see panel). The French tradition lives on in the sea of vines, in farms with names such as La Provence, Bourgogne and Mont Rochelle, in the French surnames of current Afrikaans-speaking residents and in the exceptional number of good restaurants.

Today, Franschhoek is basically all about wine (see pages 92–93), but also visit the **Huguenot Museum** (Lambrecht Street, tel: 021-876 2532. *Open* Mon–Sat 9–5, Sun 2–5. *Admission: inexpensive*). Housed in the curious Saasveld, a replica of a Cape Town house built by Louis Thibault in 1791, it contains a fascinating collection of Huguenot memorabilia.

Next door is the **Huguenot Memorial**, by Coert Steynberg, erected in 1938 to celebrate the 250th anniversary of the Huguenots' arrival. Above the town, is the winding **Helshoogte** (Hell's Heights) **Pass** with lovely views.

THE HUGUENOTS
Like other early Protestants, French Huguenots were persecuted by the Catholic church, their darkest moment coming on St. Bartholomew's Day, 1572, when 10,000 were massacred in Paris. Shortly afterwards, Henry of Navarre took the throne. While he was forced to convert to Catholicism, he remained sympathetic and signed the Edict of Nantes allowing religious freedom. It was revoked by Louis XIV in 1685 and thousands of Huguenots fled France. Most were skilled artisans and were of real benefit to their host countries, creating a range of industries from tapestry to wine, while France went into a long period of industrial decline.

86

Coert Steynberg's Huguenot Memorial, Franschhoek

▶ Paarl 48B2

55km (34 miles) north of Cape Town on the N1
Tourist Information, 216 Main Street (tel: 021-872 3829, www.paarlonline.com).
Open: Mon–Fri 9–5, Sat 9–1, Sun 10–1

Paarl gets its name from the nearby Paarl Rocks, three huge, granite domes, 500 million years old. They are said to glisten like pearls after rain, but the mountain was known more aptly to the Khoikhoi as Skilpad (Tortoise Mountain). The surrounding area is a nature reserve with walks and scenic drives. On the hilltop is the **Taal Monument** (1975), a huge sculptural homage to the Afrikaans language by Ian van Wyk (tel: 021-863 2800. *Open* daily 9–5. *Admission: free*).

Paarl is the uncrowned capital of the Cape Winelands

In town, be prepared for a hike; Main Street is over 12km (7 miles) long, but a short stretch near the tourist office includes many of the finest historic buildings. A walking guide is available. The **Paarl Museum** (303 Main Street, tel: 021-872 2651. *Open* Mon–Fri 9–5, Sat 9–1. *Admission: inexpensive*) is in a Cape Dutch house and former Dutch Reformed parsonage (1787). The rooms have embroidered Victorian fashions, silver, ceramics and furniture, and a full history of Paarl with documents and photographs, and a display on the Group Areas Act. For the **KWV Wine Cellars** and winery tours, see page 93. Displays in the **Afrikaans Language Museum** (Pastorie Avenue, tel: 021-872 3441. *Open* Mon–Fri 9–5. *Admission: inexpensive*) include the printing press of the first Afrikaans newspaper, *Die Afrikaase Patriot*. **Le Bonheur Crocodile Farm** (Babylonstoren Road, 7km/4 miles from Paarl, tel: 021-863 1142. *Open* daily 9–5. *Admission: moderate*) features crocs live, on the plate, and as fashion accessories. A short distance from town on the Malmesbury Road, **Die Vonds Snake Park** (tel: 021-869 8309. *Open* Mon–Sat 9.30–5.30. *Admission: moderate)* has over 40 species of snake, as well as tortoises, lizards, leguaans and other reptiles.

▶▶▶ Stellenbosch see pages 90–91

▶ Wellington 48B2

8km (5 miles) north of Paarl
Tourist Information, 104 Main Road (tel: 021-873 4604, fax: 021-873 4607, email: welltour@mweb.co.za, www.visitwellington.com). Open: Mon–Fri 9–4.30, Sat 10–12

Originally named Wagenmakersvallei (Wagon Maker's Valley), little Wellington was the northernmost of the early Cape settlements, where people transferred their goods to wagons for the trek north. Its name was changed in 1840, in honour of the British Duke of Wellington. It has a wine route, fine historic houses and a small **museum** (Church Street, tel: 021-873 1410. *Open* Mon–Sat 9–1, 2–5. *Admission: free*) containing early Dutch tools and Egyptian objects.

AFRIKAANS
The earliest European settlers in South Africa were Dutch. Over the years, their language evolved into Afrikaans, soaking up a number of French, German and English words from later settlers, Malay terms from the slaves and a little smattering of local African languages. It was recognized as an official language in its own right in 1925. Afrikaans and Dutch are still very closely related; the Dutch understand it easily but say it is comparable to an English person listening to a simple form of Shakespearean English.

South Africa is making a name for itself as a producer of excellent 'New World' wines. In fact it has the oldest wine making industry outside Europe and the Mediterranean, and new wines are coming onto the market all the time.

Sudden international acceptance and marketing possibilities in the mid-1990s launched a frenzy of activity, with over 400 new wines hitting the shelves in 1995 alone. It also created problems, as the vineyards were unable to satisfy demand. In 1995, some sold their entire vintage within three weeks, leaving disgruntled locals to complain as popular wines simply disappeared into more lucrative foreign markets. Since then, production and exports have grown massively.The country is currently the world's eighth largest wine producer, with about 12.5 per cent of the global market. There are around 4,340 vineyards, covering about 108,000ha (266,760 acres) throughout the Western Cape, producing wabout 834 million litres (183.4 million gallons) of wine as well as table grapes, raisins, grape juice, fortified wines, spirits and industrial alcohol. The industry supports 345,500 jobs.

The Winelands There are increasing numbers of vineyards in the Orange River valley (Northern Cape) and the Limpopo Province, but most are concentrated in a small area of the Western Cape, from the Swartland in the west to the Overberg in the east. There are 50 official growing regions, of which the most important include Constantia, Stellenbosch, Paarl, Worcester and the Klein-Karoo.

Together they make up the Winelands— soaring, rugged mountains and steep-sided valleys combed with razor-straight lines of vines, embellished with thickets of oak and gracious, white-washed Cape Dutch homesteads.

The grapes The whites include global favourites such as Chenin Blanc (Steen, which alone accounts for 31 per cent of all planting), Chardonnay and Sauvignon Blanc, as well as the more specialist Muscatels or Moscadels (also known to local wine-growers as Hanepoot), Colombard, Gewürztraminer and Bukettraube. Look for the two unrelated Rieslings (European Weisser Riesling and local Cape Riesling). Among the reds are Cabernet Sauvignon, Merlot, Gamay, Pinot Noir, Shiraz, Cinsault (also known as Hermitage) and a local hybrid grape called Pinotage (Pinot Noir and Cinsault).

Top: The year begins for the winegrowers with the grape harvest
Above: Elegantly carved show casks displayed in the KWV cellars

The wines Much of the production is handled by a series of growers' co-operatives, all of which are members of the giant KWV, which handles 70 per cent of overseas sales. The results include many unexceptional, pleasant table

Vines cover most of the land around Stellenbosch

Boschendal, founded in 1685, is one of the oldest wineries in South Africa

wines, but tastes and methods are getting more sophisticated and are now rivalling some of the world's finest. The real gems are the tiny estate-bottled vintages (known as estate or boutique wines) that are extremely difficult to find outside South Africa. Many of these are superb—full-bodied, slightly smoky reds and lightly scented, fruity whites. For foreigners unfamiliar with the names and, in some cases, the grape varietals, exploring the wine list becomes an intensely pleasurable adventure. Even French vintners are having to admit, reluctantly, that South Africa's white wines are superb.

The vineyards The larger vineyards produce at least half a dozen wines including white, red, sparkling, dessert and fortified wines. Stellenbosch's Rustenberg estate has been producing wine for 300 years, while exceptional Sauvignon Blanc comes from the restored Klein Constantia vineyards, which produced some of the earliest and most famous wines in the Cape. Meerlust, between Cape Town and Stellenbosch, has been in the Myburgh family for seven generations; it specializes in Pinot Noir and the Bordeaux-style Rubicon. Boschendal is known for Pinot Noir and Sauvignon Blanc, Backsberg for Pinotage and Chardonnay, Villiera for Merlot, and L'Ormarins for Shiraz. Most estates offer tastings, though some charge a small fee (see pages 92–93).

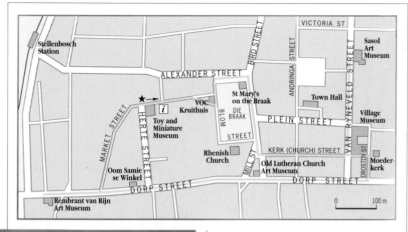

Walk

Stellenbosch

Governor Simon van der Stel was not a modest man. In November 1679, he visited the Eerste River valley and founded the Cape Colony's second town, naming it Stellenbosch after himself (he is also responsible for Simon's Town on the peninsula). Although it is now home to a major university and is one of the bases of the wine industry, Stellenbosch remains a picture-perfect town of whitewashed Cape Dutch cottages and elegant Georgian and Victorian town houses, with oak-lined avenues

set around a village green. Some of it is an illusion, as careful reconstruction and restoration has repaired the ravages of three major fires, and the suburbs contain their fair share of hideous 1950s garages and supermarkets. The heart of town is delightful but full to the brim with tourists. The best way to see the town is on foot. This walk marks the high points; the tourist office publishes a walking tour guide giving details of the many old buildings you will see en route.

Start at the tourist office, housed in an old Cape Dutch rectory that also contains a small **Toy and Miniature Museum** (corner of Market and Herte streets, tel: 021-886 7888. *Open* Mon–Sat 9.30–5, Sun 2–5. *Admission: inexpensive*). Walk up Market Street. At the top, the **VOC Kruithuis**, the Dutch East India Company arsenal (1777), has a military museum (Blom Street, tel: 021-887 2902. *Open* Mon–Fri 9.30–1, 1.30–5. *Admission: inexpensive*).
 Nearby is the Rhenish church, built in 1823 (and enlarged in 1840) as a project to train local coloured people and former slaves in a profession.
 Straight ahead, **Die Braak** (meaning 'fallow land') was once a military parade ground but is now a combination village common and parking area. In the northeast corner is the pretty Anglican church of **St. Mary's on the Braak** (1852). A bevy of delightful

Stellenbosch has many of South Africa's finest Cape Dutch houses

Shopping at Oom Samie's is a step back in time

Georgian and Victorian houses surrounds it. Walk across the common and turn up Church Street to reach the jewel in the crown of Stellenbosch.

A whole block has been included in the **Village Museum** (18 Van Ryneveld Street, tel: 021-887 2902. *Open* Mon–Sat 9.30–5, Sun 2–5. *Admission: moderate*), with four period houses restored and furnished to illustrate architectural and fashion changes between 1709, 1780, 1800–1820 and the 1850s. The detail is impeccable, down to the cottage gardens, and the progression from wooden furniture and flagged floors to fustian Victoriana is fascinating. Turn right out of the museum. On the next block is the **Sasol Art Museum** (52 Ryneveld Street, tel: 021-808 3693. *Open* Tue–Fri 9–4, Sat 9–5, Sun 2–5), with an important collection of 19th- to 20th-century works and prehistoric San rock art.

Retrace your steps to Drostdy Street, then right along **Dorp Street**, one of the longest streets of old houses surviving in the country.

Everything is here, from Dutch gables to Georgian pediments.

Towards the bottom is **Oom Samie se Winkel** (82–84 Dorp Street, tel: 021-887 0797. *Open* daily 9–5.30). It is not often that a store becomes a tourist attraction in its own right, but the architecture, layout and stock of this glorious Victorian shop appear not to have changed for 100 years. Some of its delights include African masks, toys, spices and dried fruit. There is an atmospheric wine shop that specializes in rare vintages and a tea garden, while the oak-beamed De Akkerpub next door is the country's third oldest.

Farther along the road, the Cape Dutch house, Libertas Parva, contains the **Rembrandt van Rijn Art Museum** (Dorp Street and Aan-De-Wagenweg, tel: 021-886 4340).

Retrace your steps and turn left onto Market Street to reach the tourist office.

❏ Stellenbosch is 48km (30 miles) east of Cape Town. Tourist Information, 36 Market Street, Stellenbosch 7600 (tel: 021-883 3584, fax: 021-883 8017, www.stellenbosch.org.za). *Open* Sep–May Mon–Fri 8–5.30, Sat 9–5, Sun 9.30–4.30; Jun–Aug Mon–Fri 9–5, Sat 9.30–4.30, Sun 10–4. Guided tours leave from the tourist office Mon–Fri at 10 and 3, Sat 3, Sun 10. *Admission: expensive*. For guided walking tours, including ghost and twilight tours, tel: 021-887 9150. ❏

Touring
the wineries

Fruits of the vine

No fewer than 12 districts of the Western Cape have wine routes, totaling literally hundreds of properties. These pages cannot provide a comprehensive guide, or even a coherent route. Instead, a few of the most rewarding visits have been included, whether for the quality of the wine or the tour, or for the setting and architecture of the vineyard. Every property listed offers tastings and sales; most also have restaurants, tea gardens or picnic baskets. For organized tours, contact Vineyard Ventures (tel: 021-434 8888, email: vinven@iafrica.com).

Backsberg (Klapmuts/Simondium Road, Paarl, off the R45, tel: 021-875 5141. *Open* Mon–Fri 8.30–5, Sat 8.30–1). A famous estate, owned by the Back family, specializing in classic reds; there is a small museum of early winemaking equipment and an audio-visual self-guided tour of the cellars.

Boschendal (Priel Road/R310, Groot Drakenstein, tel: 021-870 4200, www.boschendal.co.za Tastings: Mon–Fri 8.30–4.30, Sat 8.30–12.30; Dec–Jan, also Sun 9.30–12.30.

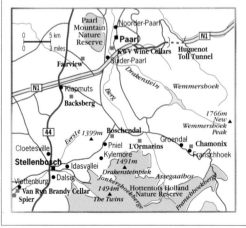

> ❏ **Tasting** You may be offered up to a dozen different wines at a tasting. Start with the dry whites and work through to the heavier reds, leaving fortified wines and spirits till last. Sniff the bouquet, take a small mouthful, swill it around your mouth, and—if you are strong-willed—spit it out. Rinse your glass and mouth with water between each wine. Appoint a nondrinking driver and pace yourself or you will be seriously light-headed by the end of the visit. Most vineyards are happy to provide soft drinks for drivers and minors. ❏

Manor house: *Open* daily 9.30–5. Cellar tours by appointment). This is among the area's oldest wineries (1685), and has become one of South Africa's preeminent producers of red wines. Combine a vineyard tour with a trip around the superbly restored Cape Dutch manor, which is filled with magnificent 17th- and 18th-century furniture, Ming porcelain and Dutch East Indies Company glass. The estate also has a fine restaurant and café, and will provide picnic hampers in summer (booking essential).

Chamonix (Uitkyk Street, off the R45 to Cape Town, Franschhoek, tel: 021-876 2494, www.chamonix.co.za. *Open* daily 9–5). There is a restaurant and guest cottages. Originally part of La Cotte, one of the early Huguenot estates, this has been a separate property only since 1990, but has already produced several highly acclaimed wines. It also bottles its own spring water and breeds American pinto horses.

Fairview (Suider-Agter Road, Paarl, off the R101, tel: 021-863 2450. *Open* Mon–Fri 8–5.30, Sat 8–1). Owned by the Back family, this fine but less illustrious vineyard is a good family outing. Additional attractions are a herd of 500 Saanen goats, some of which live in a tower,

Boschendal manor is home to one of the country's finest wines

and a thriving cheese-making operation. Milking is at 4pm daily, except in kidding season (Jul–Sep).

L'Ormarins (on the R45, Groot Drakenstein, tel: 021-874 1026, www.lormarins.co.za. Tastings: Mon–Fri, 9–4.30, Sat 9–12. Cellar tours: by appointment) was the very first wine estate in the Franschhoek Valley, the property of a Huguenot settler, Jean Roi. In 1969, the estate was bought by the multimillionaire philanthropist Anton Rupert. Since then it has leapted to prominence, producing some of the country's finest wines. It has a truly magnificent Cape Dutch homestead.

KWV Wine Emporium (Kohler Street, Paarl, tel: 021-807 3007, www. kwv-international.com. *Open* daily 9–4.30. Tours: 10, 10.15 [German], 10.30, 2.15). This formidable cellar is not only the heart of the Cape industry but is also the largest winery in the world. It can store up to 2.3 million litres (500,000gal) of wine and 33,000 hectolitres (75,000gal) of fortified wine at any one time, and has the five largest vats in the world.

KWV was set up to handle South Africa's surplus wine. This vast cooperative, with around 5,000 members, now controls virtually all wine production and, with affiliates, the sale of about 80 per cent of all alcohol (except beer) in South Africa. The KWV label is reserved almost exclusively for wine sold abroad, much of which is mass-produced from the 'wine lake'.

Spier (between Cape Town and Stellenbosch, on the R310, tel: 021-881 3321, www.spier.co.za. *Open* daily with sections open 9.30am–11.30pm. Cellar tours: Mon–Fri 10, 12, 3. *Admission: moderate*). This beautiful Cape Dutch complex is one of the Cape's oldest farms (1652). Now a thriving entertainment complex, it has a winery offering tours and tastings, a shop stocking all the best Cape wines, a farm stand selling excellent foods (including picnics), a gift shop, an open-air amphitheatre with a lively selection of arts events, and a vintage train that runs from the V&A Waterfront.

There are also three good restaurant/cafés, a cheetah park, an equestrian facility and an haute-cuisine cookery school.

Van Ryn Brandy Cellar (Vlottenburg, near Stellenbosch, tel: 021-881 3875. Tours: Mon–Fri 10, 11, 3; Sat 10, 11.30. *Admission: moderate*). Attractions are: an audiovisual presentation on brandymaking, tours of the distillery, cellar and cooperage, and of course, a tasting.

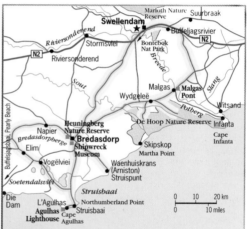

Drive

Swellendam to Cape Agulhas

Known as the Suidpunt (South Point), this area is famous for its wild flowers, calm, sandy beaches and treacherous underwater rocks, holiday homes and historic missions. Distances are not huge, but the route involves some backtracking and gravel roads. Allow 1 to 2 days.

Leave Swellendam on the N2 towards Cape Town, then turn left for **Bredasdorp** (Cape Agulhas Tourism Bureau, Dr Jansen Street, tel: 028-424 2584, fax: 028-425 2731, www.capeagulhas.info). This sleepy little town, founded in 1838, is the 'capital' of a region almost totally dependent on wheat and sheep farming. The **Shipwreck Museum** (Independent Street, tel: 028-424 1240. *Open* Mon–Fri 9–4.45, Sat–Sun 11–3.45. *Admission: inexpensive*) catalogues the history of maritime disasters in the area, displaying figure-heads, coins and furniture salvaged from vessels wrecked off the coast. On the edge of town, the **Heuningberg Nature Reserve** produces spectacular displays of fiery Bredasdorp lilies in April and May.

The Cape Agulhas lighthouse marks the southernmost point in Africa

❑ On 30 May, 1815, the *Arniston*, a British troop carrier sailing from India to England, was forced onto the rocks at Waenhuiskrans and broke up; six of its 378 passengers survived. Among the dead were four boys on their way back to school. A memorial erected by their parents stands on the clifftop, and the ship itself can some-times be spotted at low tide. It is one of more than 400 wrecks strewn along the Cape coast. ❑

Take the road through Napier and turn left for **Elim**, an almost forgotten, coloured village that grew up around a 19th-century Moravian mission (1824). The architecture has been left intact, with whole streets of thatched 'Karoo' cottages. The villagers' main income is from dried flowers, cut in the local *fynbos;* you can visit the drying sheds.

Leaving Elim, head for Struisbaai and L'Agulhas. Named the 'Cape of Needles' after its murderous rocks, **Cape Agulhas▶**, 46km (29 miles) south of Bredasdorp, is the southern-most tip of Africa, now protected as a national park (tel: 028-435 6078, www.sanparks.org.za). It is marked by a small plaque, where a compass needle points due north with no magnetic variation. The real drama is out to sea, where 124 wrecks lie within an 80km (50 miles) radius, their crews drowned between 1673 and 1990 in what Rudyard Kipling called the 'dread Agulhas roll'.

L'Agulhas is one of a series of beach resorts stretching from Pearly Beach in the west, through Buffelsjagsbaai and Die Dam to Struisbaai in the east. The swimming is safe and the angling excellent. Between July nd November, there are great concentrations of Southern right whales.

Agulhas Lighthouse, built in 1849 and modelled on the Pharos lighthouse of Alexandria in Egypt, is the second oldest in the country and the most southerly in Africa. Its beam reaches 50km (30 miles) out to sea. It still works and houses a **museum** (Main Road, tel: 028-435 6078. *Open* daily 9–4.30. *Admission: inexpensive*).

Head back to Bredasdorp, then turn back to the coast for **Arniston** (25km/ 15 miles south of Bredasdorp), officially called Waenhuiskrans—'wagon house cliff'—after an enormous cave nearby, said to be large enough to turn an ox wagon around inside. You can explore the cave at low tide, and there are numerous other caves, cliffs and rock formations in the area. The village is named after a ship that foundered here in 1815 (see box opposite page). Today it is an attractive resort, with holiday homes and excellent fishing, and delightful 19th-century fishermen's cottages.

Fishing boats drawn up on the beach at Arniston

Return to Bredasdorp and head for the **De Hoop Nature Reserve** (50km/30miles east of Bredasdorp, tel: 028-542 1126. *Open* daily 7–6; overnight visitors should arrive before 4). Stretching 5km (3 miles) out to sea, this is an important 36,000ha (88,920-acre) conservation area incorporating rare lowland *fynbos*, dunes and wetlands. It is home to 86 species of mammal, including the Cape mountain zebra, grey rhebok and leopard, and over 250 species of birds, among them the last breeding colony in the region of the rare Cape vulture. You'll find basic accommodation, trails, walks and drives.

Leaving the park, go north, crossing the Breede River on the **Malgas Pont** (a hand-operated pontoon bridge, the only one left in South Africa), through Bontebok National Park to Swellendam.

❏ The right whale, *Eubalaena australis*, was so named because it was thought to be the right whale to catch—large, slow-moving, and rich in oil. It is estimated that about 4,000 are still alive today. Up to 18m (59ft) long and 80 tonnes in weight, they have a smooth, rounded, mainly black body, with occasional white markings on the back and belly, and no dorsal fin. The white, cauliflower-like callosities (knobbly dollops of tough skin) on the head and jaw are as distinctive as fingerprints. Right whales live on plankton and krill filtered from the water. ❏

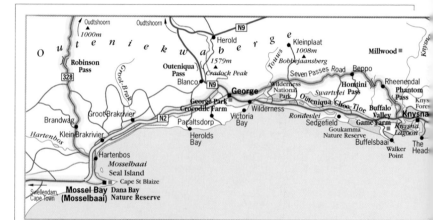

Drive

The Garden Route

One of South Africa's most popular destinations is the Garden Route, named for its landscape of green forests and fertile meadows. Officially it is the strip of the south coast from Mossel Bay in the west to Plettenberg Bay in the east, ranging inland to the Outeniqua Mountains. In practice, Captour includes the whole coast from Cape Town to Port Elizabeth in its marketing campaigns. This is one of the busiest resort areas in the country and the forests and gardens are giving way to roads, golf courses, hotels, holiday homes and campsites. Accommodation is plentiful, but sells out in peak season, so book in advance. Allow at least two days.

The route is easily followed, with the main N2 running the full length and on to Durban. Any stops are clearly signposted. If you have the time, take the more picturesque old roads, which wind through the forests and villages, often on gravel. For the Overberg coast, from Cape Town to Swellendam, see pages 82 and 94.
Swellendam to Mossel Bay. This section runs through several small villages (see map pages 48–49).
Heidelberg (Tourist Information, tel: 028-722 1917, fax: 028-722

1157) was the site of the southernmost battle of the Anglo-Boer War.
Riversdale (Tourist Information, tel: 028-713 2418, fax: 028-713 3146) is home to the **Julius Gordon Africana Museum**, Langstraat (*Open* Mon–Fri 8–12, or by arrangement), which has a fine collection of paintings by many top South African artists. Nearby, a turn-off to the right (B323) leads to **Stilbaai** (Tourist Information, Palinggat, tel: 028-754 2602, fax: 028-754 2549), a coastal resort with good fishing, boating and swimming. Its highlights are the prehistoric (but still working) fish traps, and the town's fountain, full of tame eels. Watch them being fed at 11am Mon–Sat. Back on the N2, **Albertinia** (Tourist Information, Main Street, tel: 028-735 1000, fax: 028-735 2055) is a mining community producing yellow ochre, silica quartzite and kaolin. It also has an aloe factory extracting sap for use in cosmetics and medicines (for tours, tel: 028-735 1454), and is the world's largest producer of thatching reed. About 14km (9 miles) beyond the town there is **bungee jumping** off the Gourits River Bridge (tel/fax: 044-697 7001, www.faceadrenalin.com).

The whole section runs through fairly dull farmland, with wide, rolling wheat fields. Consider taking the mountainous inland route along the R62 through the Karoo villages of Barrydale, Ladismith and Calitzdorp to Oudtshoorn before heading south on the R328 over Robinson Pass to **Mossel Bay** (Tourist Information, Market Street, tel/fax: 044-691 2202,

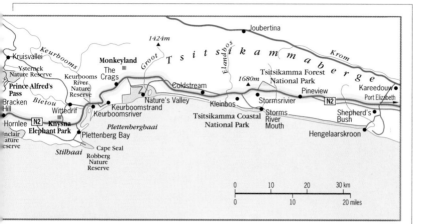

www.gardenroute.co.za *Open* Mon–Fri 9–5, Sat 9–1). This is South Africa's fifth largest port, with industry fuelled by the oil and gas fields off the coast.

The first European to show up here was Bartolomeu Dias in 1488. In 1500, a ship's captain left a letter under a local giant milkwood tree; a year later it was found by the commander of the Third East India fleet. For the next 400 years, the tree became a post office for all passing sailors, and it now forms the heart of the **Bartolomeu Dias Museum Complex** (Market Street, tel: 044-691 1067. *Open* Mon–Fri 9–1, 2–4.45; Maritime Museum Mon–Fri 4–4.45, Sat–Sun 10–4. *Admission: moderate*). The complex has collections of local and maritime history, with a life-size replica of Dias' caravel, a shell museum, a Malay graveyard, Khoi objects and the Fountain, a spring used by Dias. A stone cross, the Padrao, donated by the Portuguese government, commemorates Vasco da Gama's visit in 1497. Other museums nearby include the **Aquarium** (tel: 044-691 1067) and the **Model Shipyard** (Ochre Barn, Market Street, tel: 044-691 1531, www.shipyard.co.za). Walks weave through the **Dana Bay Nature Reserve** to the St. Blaize Lighthouse and Bat Cave, used by early KhoiSan inhabitants, boats run to Seal Island (tel: 044-690 3101), and you can try shark diving (tel: 082-455 2438/234 6333).

The Portuguese explorer Bartolomeu Dias (c1450–1500)

Around the bay to Knysna Follow the old coast road around the bay to **Hartenbos**, where the **Museum** (tel: 044-695 2183. *Open* Mon–Fri 9–4, Sat 10–12.30. *Admission: inexpensive*) covers everything from wagon building to Zulu *impis,* entertainment and the role of women in Boer society.

Rejoin the N2 for about 33km (20 miles), then branch left (N12) for 10km (6 miles) to **George** (Tourist Information, 124 York Street, tel: 044-801 9295, fax: 044-873 5228, www.georgetourism.co.za. *Open* Mon–Fri 8–5, Sat 9–1). Founded in 1788 as a forestry outpost at the foot of the Outeniqua Mountains, George—named after King George III of England—became a town in 1811. It grew up as an administrative centre, living off the timber trade and hops. The huge **Dutch Reformed church** (corner of Meade and Courtenay streets) has a magnificent yellowwood ceiling and pillars and a pulpit that took two men a year to carve. By contrast, the Anglican **Cathedral of St. Mark** (York Street), built eight years later, is tiny. The former **Drostdy** was a private house and hotel before it became the local **museum** (corner of Courtenay and York streets, tel: 044-873 5343. *Open* Mon–Fri 9–4.30, Sat 9–12.30. *Admission: donation*), with local history and art, a display of the area's indigenous woods and timber industry, mechanical musical instruments, plus selected gifts presented to the ex-president P. W. Botha. The

The scenic Outeniqua Choo-Tjoe railway in full steam

massive Slave Tree, in front of the information office, has an old chain and lock embedded in the trunk. Once the site of slave auctions, it is now said to be the biggest oak in the southern hemisphere.

Nearby are two small beach resorts, **Herolds Bay** and **Victoria Bay**; the **George Park Crocodile Farm** (York Street, tel: 044-873 4302. *Open* daily 9–5, feeding at 3. *Admission: moderate*); as well as the wonderful steam railway (see page 235), which runs between George and Knysna through the beautiful Wilderness National Park. Head north from here on a sidetrip to Oudtshoorn and the Klein-Karoo (see pages 79–81).

Return to the N2 and continue for another 8km (5 miles) to **Wilderness** (Tourist Information, Leila's Lane, tel/fax: 044-877 0045, www.wildernessinfo.co.za). In 1877, the legend goes, a young Cape Town man, George Bennett, was allowed to marry as long as he took his bride to live in the wilderness. He bought a farm, named it Wilderness, and triumphantly brought his bride home. Today this is one of the prettiest towns on the Garden Route, tucked behind high dunes along the Touws River estuary. The swimming and beaches are excellent and you can canoe, windsurf and fish on the lakes (tel: 044-877 0179, email: edenadventures@mweb.co.za).

Between Wilderness and Sedge-field, the **Wilderness National Park** (tel: 044-877 1197, fax: 044-877 0366, www.sanparks.org) protects a sensitive wetlands area from encroaching development. It contains 5 rivers, 4 lakes, 2 estuaries and 28km (17 miles) of coastline, and it is surrounded by a further 10,000ha (24,700 acres) of lakes. This is a good area for birdwatchers, anglers and hikers, and home to 79 of South Africa's 95 species of waterfowl, as well as the elusive Knysna loerie and many kingfisher species.

The next stop along the N2 is **Knysna** (Tourist Information, 40 Main Street, tel: 044-382 5510, fax: 044-382 1646, www.knysna-info.co.za),

the largest and most beautiful of the coastal resorts, curled around the hilly shores of a huge (13sqkm/5sq-mile) lagoon. Its narrow access to the sea is guarded by The Heads, two large sandstone cliffs (200m/656ft and 116m/380ft high), and a coral reef. The lagoon is perfect for water sports, while several companies run boat trips, fishing charters and diving on both wrecks and nearby coral reefs (ask the tourist office for details). In addition, the lagoon is home to 200 species of fish, including a rare seahorse, provides excellent fishing and is a major source of oysters.

Plettenberg Bay, a gentle curve of tawny sand

Knysna to Tsitsikamma Forest National Park The **Knysna Museum** (Queen Street, tel: 044-382 1638. *Open* Mon–Fri 9.30–4.30, Sat 9.30–1. *Admission: donation*) is made up of four houses: **Millwood House** (ca 1880) and **Parkes Cottage** (1890) both have displays on the history of Knysna, including memorabilia of its founder, George Rex; the corrugated iron **Parkes Shop** (1890) deals with the Knysna timber industry; the **Old Gaol** (1858) was the first public building. It housed convict labourers on their way to Prince Alfred's Pass. Its bell was used both as a fire alarm and to signal the arrival of the mail. It now has angling and maritime museums and an art gallery. The **Knysna Oyster Company** (Long Street, tel: 044-382 6941, www.knysnaoysters.co.za. *Open* Mon–Fri 8–5, Sat–Sun 9–3) gives farm tours and tastings of oysters and mussels. There is a small **aquarium** (*Open* daily 9–6) at Knysna Heads, and harbour cruises from Thesen's Jetty.

Knysna Forest South Africa's largest expanse of indigenous high forest is home to rare reserves of yellowwood, ironwood and stinkwood trees, some up to 800 years old. It is a dark, eerie world where antelope and birds flit through the undergrowth and monkeys trapeze across giant hardwood trees.

The late 1990s saw the tragic demise of a herd of elephants that used to roam the entire south coast.

The **Knysna Elephant Park** (24km/15 miles east of Knysna, off the N2, tel: 044-532 7732, www.knysnaelephantpark.co.za. *Open* daily 8.30–4.30. *Admission: moderate*) has three young, tame elephants for an up-close encounter, and also guided forest walks (booking essential). The **Buffalo Hills Game Farm** (20km/12 miles southwest, tel: 044-535 9739. *Open* off season, Mon–Sat 11–3, Sun 9–5. *Admission: moderate*) has a wide variety of plains animals, antelope and birds. **Millwood** (32km/20 miles from

Storms River mouth in the Tsitsikamma Forest National Park

Knysna) is a ghost town, based on the abandoned Bendigo gold mine. There are hiking trails nearby.

It is 32km (20 miles) from Knysna to **Plettenberg Bay** (Tourist Information, Melville's Corner Centre, Main Street tel: 044-533 4065, fax: 044-533 4066, www.plettenbergbay.co.za. *Open* Mon–Fri 8–5, Sat 9–1), one of South Africa's most fashionable beach resorts. Named Baia Formosa ('beautiful bay') by the 16th-century Portuguese mariner Manuel da Perestrello, this little town is set on a gently curving sandy bay backed by mountains. The governor of the Cape, Baron Joachim von Plettenberg, renamed it after himself in 1779. The tip of the peninsula is now the **Robberg (Cape Seal) Nature Reserve**, with walks and caves, while the cliffs are excellent for whale- or dolphin-watching. Species seen along here include southern right, humpback, Brydes, minke and killer whales (information tel: 083-910 1028, www.cape-whaleroute.co.za).

On the N2 16km (10 miles) east of 'Plett' is **Monkeyland** (tel: 044-534 8906, www.monkeyland.co.za. *Open* daily 8–6. *Admission: expensive*), an excellent sanctuary for all sorts of primates, from lemurs to South American squirrel monkeys. East again is the start of the beautiful **Tsitsikamma Forest National Park►** (tel: 042-281 1606, www.sanparks. org), whose Khoikhoi name means 'place of sparkling waters'. Dedicated in 1964, it stretches 65km (40 miles) along the coast and 5.5km (3.5 miles) out to sea, covering an extraordinarily rich variety of ecosystems, flora and fauna. Inland there is coastal forest, part of the great Knysna Forest belt, where ancient yellowwoods grow up to 50m (164ft) high. For tours of the forest canopy, contact Tree Top Tours (tel: 042-281 1836, www.storms river.com). On the coast, freshwater wetlands give way to dunes, crashing waves, coral reefs and deep waters. At **Storms River mouth** you can swim and snorkel, and a restaurant and shop. For hikers, the Otter Trail (see page 237) runs right through the park.

▶▶▶ REGION HIGHLIGHTS

Addo Elephant National Park *page 117*

Graaff-Reinet *pages 112–113*

Grahamstown *pages 108–109*

Tour: The 1820 Settler Towns *pages 110–111*

The Wild Coast *page 119*

TOURISM INFORMATION
For information on the whole Eastern Cape, contact the state tourist board, Eastern Cape Tourism Board on the corner of Longfellow and Aquarius, Quigney, East London (PO Box 18373, Quigney, East London 5211, tel: 043-701 9600, fax: 043-701 9649, www.ectb.co.za).

A NEW BEGINNING The Eastern Cape is made up of numerous disparate cultures and ecosystems. It came into being only when the provincial boundaries were rearranged in 1994 (see page 12). Until then, most of the area was simply an extension of the Western Cape, both geographically and politically.

In the far west, the Tsitsikamma Forest (see page 101) gives way to rolling scrub, while to the north are the eastern reaches of the Great Karoo. Around Grahamstown are lush green farmlands and montane forest. In the far east, the Wild Coast lives up to its name as one of South Africa's last undeveloped stretches of coast, the ragged cliffs and towering dunes broken by trailing river mouths and hidden coves of silver sand.

HISTORY This was a frontier land, inhabited initially by the Khoikhoi in the southwest, the Xhosa in the southeast and the San to the north. The Great Trek took the Afrikaners along the coast to the Fish River and ever farther out into the Karoo. They dispossessed the San and Khoikhoi, but left the more warlike Xhosa alone until 1780, when the Cape government extended its authority to the river and forced the two groups into direct conflict

Eastern Cape

Previous pages: The marina at Port Alfred

HUMAN PAWNS

The 1820 Settlers were moved into the region (known as Albany) by the ruthless governor, Lord Charles Somerset, chiefly as a way of breaking an expensive and irritating deadlock in the Frontier Wars. The sudden influx of 5,000 people was sufficient to force the hand of the Xhosa. Each settler family was allocated only 40ha (100 acres) of land, scarcely enough to survive on. The settlers had a rough time for the first 50 years and many gave up farming, retreating to the towns.

Xhosa women selling vegetables in Peddie

in the first of a series of nine bloody Frontier Wars that lasted until the mid-19th century. Meantime, in 1806, the British took control of the Cape, and in 1820, 5,000 British settlers arrived in the Grahamstown area. The Xhosa, who were already fighting not only the Boers but also the Zulus and their own offshoot tribe, the Mfengu, had to fight them, too. Inevitably, the British, with their superior firepower, won the day, and the whole area became part of the Cape Colony.

The dramas continued, however. Owing to the intensity of missionary activity in the area, the black population gained a higher level of education than was the norm elsewhere, and in 1916 the black University of Fort Hare was founded. The area became one of the most politically active in South Africa, providing the nationalist cause with many of its greatest leaders, including Mandela, Sisulu and Biko of the ANC, and Robert Sobukwe, founder of the hardline PAC. During the apartheid years, two black homelands were formed in the province's eastern section: the technically independent Xhosa territory of Transkei and the satellite Mfengu homeland of Ciskei.

A BRIGHT FUTURE Today, most of the region's towns look like toys. The Karoo is dotted with sparklingly clean Afrikaner villages, the coast lined with neat, Disneyesque waterfront estates. Bisho, once capital of Transkei and now state capital of the Eastern Cape, looks as though it is made of Lego, and, from a distance, even the tiny pastel-painted houses of the Xhosa hill villages appear to have just been taken out of the box. Come close, however and noisy street markets and blaring music, battered

Above: Hardwood forest still coats much of the Hogsback. Left: Stone leopards guard the main square of Bisho

Coca-Cola billboards and lines of minibus taxis return you to Africa.

Though much less known than the Western Cape or KwaZulu-Natal, the Eastern Cape is just as rich in possibilities for the tourist. Almost every inlet along the Wild Coast has a small hideaway resort tucked unobtrusively along its banks, but as yet there are few towns and ribbon development of holiday homes is slow, with most people deterred by the bumpy, dusty roads that lead down to the coast. Yet the beaches here are probably the best in South Africa and the real estate agents' billboards are moving ever closer. This is the hot new area, partly because wealthy whites can now safely buy property in the former homelands.

The Garden Route extension to Port Elizabeth is strongly marketed, with the added bonus of the only good game parks in the south. At the same time, a whole new tourism industry is dedicated to following in the footsteps of Nelson Mandela and other nationalist heroes. The future for this fledgling province seems bright.

A PROVINCE DIVIDED
The Eastern Cape is now divided into six regions, taking their names either from traditional local placernames or heroes of the freedom struggle. In the northeast, centred on Kokstad, Alfred Nzo District is a cool high, sparsely populated region on the boarders with Lesotho and KwaZulu Natal. Amathole District takes in miuch more of the popular 'Settler Country'. Formerly the Western District, Cacadu District covers the rural western areas. The Chris Hani District, in the heart of the province, is large semi-desert Karoo. The Nelson Mandela Metropole covers Port Elizabeth and its surrounding satellite towns. A sharp contrast, Oliver Tambo District includes the remote, spectacular Wild Coast and Pondoland. The Ukahlamba District, forms the northern border with the Free State.

THE COELACANTH

Over 350 million years old and thought to have been extinct for 65 million years, the coelacanth (*Latimeria chalumnae*) was rediscovered in 1938 when an East London fisherman landed one in his nets and showed it to museum curator Marjorie Courtenay-Latimer. It was about 1.5m (5ft) long, weighed 57kg (125lb), and was covered in deep-blue scales. Several other specimens have been caught since, and underwater photographs were taken in 1987.

This strange, predaceous fish has a deep, stocky body and rounded, lobe-like fins. The first spine of the dorsal fin is hollow (the name means 'hollow spine' in Greek). Because of the structure of the fins it is thought to be a 'missing link' in the evolution of land animals.

Below: The coelacanth
Bottom: Fishing off the rocks near East London

▶ **East London (Greater Buffalo City)**   *102B1*

Tourism Buffalo City, Shops 1 and 2, King's Entertainment Centre, Esplanade, East London (tel: 043-722 6015, fax: 043-743 5091 www.eastlondontourism.co.za)
Open: Mon–Fri 8.15–4.30, Sat 9–12
Eastern Cape Tourism Board, corner Longfellow and Aquarius streets, Quigney, East London (tel: 043-701 96001, fax: 043-701 9649, www.ectb.co.za)

East London on the Buffalo River was founded in 1847. There are some fine individual buildings such as the City Hall and St. Peter's church and it is a popular resort with magnificent golden beaches stretching 40km (25 miles) along the coast in either direction. **Nahoon** and **Eastern Beaches** have some of the finest surf in South Africa. The old **Lock Street Gaol** (South Africa's first women's prison) is now a shopping mall, while the former fishing harbour is a mini waterfront development called **Latimer's Landing** (where the coelacanth—see panel—was landed in 1938).

The **Anne Bryant Art Gallery** (St. Mark's Road, tel: 043-722 4044. *Open* Mon–Fri 9–5, Sat 9.30–12. *Admission: free*) is an imposing Edwardian mansion containing a fair collection of South African art from the 1880s onward. **Gately House Museum** (1 Park Gates Road, tel: 043-722 2141. *Open* Tue–Thu 10–1, 2–5, Fri 10–1, Sat–Sun 3–5. *Admission: inexpensive*), once home of East London's first mayor, has fine Cape furniture. The impressive **East London Museum** (Oxford Street, entrance in Dawson Road, tel: 043-743 0686. *Open* Mon–Fri 9.30–5, Sat 2.30–5, Sun 11–4. *Admission: inexpensive*) has Xhosa culture, shells and stuffed animals. Star attractions are the world's only dodo egg and a stuffed coelacanth. If you prefer live animals, visit the **aquarium** (Esplanade, tel: 043-705 2637. *Open* daily 9–5; fish feeding at 10.30 and 3, seal shows 11.30, 3.30. *Admission: moderate*) and the **Zoo** (Queen's Park, tel: 043-722 1171. *Open* daily 9–5. *Admission: moderate*). The **Calgary Transport Museum** (Macleantown Road, tel: 043-730 7244. *Open* daily 9–4. *Admission: inexpensive*), 13km (8 miles) from town, has horse-drawn vehicles.

▶ Alice   102B1

About 85km (53 miles) northeast of Grahamstown

Alice's claim to fame is **Fort Hare University**, the first black university in South Africa, founded in 1916 out of the mission-run Lovedale College. Nelson Mandela and many other nationalist leaders studied here. On campus, the **De Beer Centenary Art Gallery** (tel: 040-602 2011. *Open* Mon, Wed, Fri 9–12, Tue, Thu 1–2. *Admission: free*) has an excellent collection of contemporary black art. The **FS Malan Museum** (*Open* Mon–Fri 9–1, 2–5. *Admission: inexpensive*) features collections of traditional beadwork, wood carvings and dress.

▶▶ Hogsback   102B1

144km (90 miles) northwest of East London
Tourist Information, Stormhaven Crafts, Main Road
(tel: 045-962 1024. www.hogsbackinfo.co.za)

In the Amatola Mountains (Amatola means calf—the hills are said to look like a row of calves), Hogsback is a hill station, set in cool green forests with planted pine and eucalyptus on the high ground and virgin hardwood forest on the lower slopes. It is perfectly designed for leisure, with tumbling waterfalls, intimate fireside bars, walking, riding and trout fishing.

▶▶ King William's Town   102B1

60km (37 miles) west of East London. Tourist Information, Library, Ayliff Street (tel: 043-642 3391). Open: Mon–Fri 8.30–5.30, Sat 8.30–1

The birth- and burial-place of Steve Biko, this Settler town was an important base in the Frontier Wars. It has 19th-century churches and colonial architecture. The **Amathole Museum** (3 Albert Road, tel: 043-642 4506. *Open* Mon–Fri 9–1, 1.45–4.30, Sat 10–12.30. *Admission: inexpensive*) covers natural history and Xhosa culture. The satellite **Missionary Museum** (Berkeley Street, tel: 043-642 4506. *Open* Mon–Fri 9–1, 2–5) explains missions' work in the development of South Africa. **Bisho** was a satellite township to King William's Town before becoming the capital of Ciskei, then the Eastern Cape. The fledgling city consists of a sprawl of small grid housing, one vast, pink cement office and shopping building, overlooked by stern stone leopards, and a casino. The Steve Biko Garden of Remembrance is just out of town on the Port Elizabeth Road.

King William's Town is rich in ornate Victorian architecture

▶▶▶ **Grahamstown**   *102B1*

130km (80 miles) northeast of Port Elizabeth; 58km (36 miles) from the coast
Tourist Information, 63 High Street (tel: 046-622 3241, fax: 046-622 3266, www.grahamstown.co.za)
Open: Mon–Fri 8.30–1, 2–5, 2–4, Sat 8.30–12

Founded by Colonel John Graham in 1812, Grahamstown began as the military headquarters of the Cape Colony's eastern frontier, commanding a chain of small forts along the Fish River. After many of the 1820 Settlers had abandoned their unprofitable little farms for the security of urban life, the town took off and flourished, becoming for a time the second city of the colony. In the late 19th century, however, inhabitants were lured north by the prospect of instant wealth in the diamond and gold fields, and the city withered. Today, it is a pleasant country town, with many delightful old buildings and several educational establishments, notably the prestigious Rhodes University, which has about 4,000 students.

Buildings of note The broad, tree-lined streets are filled with imposing public buildings and pleasing Victorian shops and houses. The heart of the town is triangular **Church Square**, originally the military parade ground between Colonel Graham's house and the officers' mess. In the centre rises the spire of the Anglican **Cathedral of St. Michael and St. George**, which was built as a parish church in 1824 and became a bishopric in 1852. The Lady Chapel was finally completed in 1952. The Gothic Revival Methodist **Commemoration Church** was dedicated in 1850 in thanks for the settlers' triumph after 25 gruelling years. It has a fine organ and stained-glass windows. The **Drostdy Gate** was designed for military purposes in 1835 by Major Selwyn and built by the Royal Engineers in 1841 on the site of the old Drostdy. It now forms the pedestrian entrance to Rhodes University. There are fine restored buildings in Hill and MacDonald streets and in Artificers Square (corner of Bartholomew and Cross streets), the artisan quarter where craft workers were given plots to set up workshops.

Memorials The **Settler Memorial Tower**, now part of the City Hall, was built in 1870 to commemorate the 50th anniversary of the arrival of the 1820 Settlers. Work on the main City Hall began in 1877. Overlooking the town on Gunfire Hill is the **1820 Settlers Monument** (tel: 046-622 7155), an arts centre opened in 1974, and home of the Grahamstown Festival (see panel). The **Bible Monument** (Bedford Road) marks an occasion

in 1837 when local British settlers presented a Bible to passing Voortrekkers as a token of friendship for the Dutch community. The **War Memorial** (Church Square) has an inscription specially written by Rudyard Kipling.

Museums The **Albany Museum** (Somerset Street, tel: 046-622 2312 for all sections. *Open* Mon–Fri 9, 2–5, Sat–Sun 2–5. *Admission: inexpensive*), founded in 1855, has several distinct sections. The **History Museum** specializes in the history of the British settlers of 1820 and later, with a good cultural history collection of domestic utensils, furniture and applied arts, and a large collection of 18th- and 19th-century South African art. It also has an excellent display on Xhosa traditions. The **Natural Sciences Museum** deals both with animals and early humans in southern Africa. The **South African Institute for Aquatic Biodiversity** (*Open* Mon–Fri 8–1, 2–5) is a fish museum, with pride of place given to the coelacanth (see page 106). Away from Somerset Street are **Fort Selwyn** (Gunfire Hill), built in 1836, which saw several battles against Xhosa forces, the **Provost Prison** (Lucas Avenue. *Open* Mon–Sat 10–5), and the **Observatory Museum** (Bathurst Street. *Open* Mon–Fri 9.30–1, 2–5, Sat 9–1. *Admission: inexpensive*), with displays on Victorian South Africa and the early diamond industry, and a working camera obscura on the roof.

Left: A statue in the grounds of the Settler's Memorial, Grahamstown
Above: Grahamstown Cathedral

MARIMBAS AND MBIRAS
The International Library of African Music (Prince Alfred Street, tel: 046-603 8557. *Open* Mon–Fri 8.30–12.45, 2–5 by appointment. *Admission: donation*) displays more than 200 traditional, working African musical instruments, and there's a large tape library.

The 1820 Settler towns

Grahamstown is surrounded by a circle of small market towns founded by the early settlers from Britain. Together they make a very pleasant one- or two-day tour. The route forms a basic figure of eight with Grahamstown at the middle. You can do a longer loop northwards over the Hogsback to include Balfour, Seymour, Cathcart, Stutterheim, Bisho and King William's Town (see page 107).

Southern loop Leave Grahamstown on the A67, heading south to Port Alfred. The first stop, after 41km (25 miles), is **Bathurst▶**, named after the British colonial secretary in 1820. Several monuments here include the Anglican and Wesleyan churches, Bradshaw's water-driven wool mill and the Settler fort. There is also an excellent

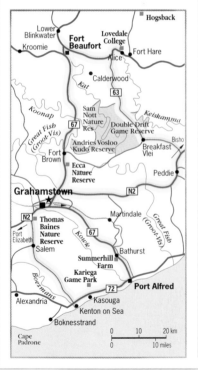

Agricultural Museum (Trappes Street, tel: 046-625 0853. *Open* Tue–Fri 9–4, Sat 9–12, Sun 9–1. *Admission: inexpensive*).

The Bathurst pineapple is an unlikely but highly visible landmark

On the top of Baillie's Beacon, 2km (1 mile) from the town, a toposcope marks the spot from which the settlers staked out their farms. The most obvious attraction is the 16m (53ft) pineapple, which you can climb. There are farm tours with audiovisuals about pineapples, the area's biggest crop. **Summerhill Estate Hotel** (tel: 046-624 0825) also has a Xhosa village, hiking and 4WD trails and canoeing. The **Pig and Whistle Inn** (1831) is one of the country's oldest hostelries.

Port Alfred (Tourist Information, The Causeway, tel: 046-624 1235), 10km (6 miles) on, is a tidy resort on the Kowie River estuary with cruises, canoe trips and fishing charters. The **Kowie Museum** (Pascoe Crescent, East Bank, tel: 046-624 4713. *Open* Mon–Sat 9.30–12.30. *Admission: free*) has personal files on all the 1820 Settlers. Just off the coast is one of South Africa's most colourful reefs (contact Kowie Dive School, tel: 046-624 2213).

From here, take the A72 west for 22km (13 miles) to the pleasant resort of **Kenton on Sea** (Tourist Information, Municipality Building, tel: 046-648 2418), with good beaches and safe swimming. The **Kariega Game Park** (14km/9 miles from Kenton on Sea, on the Grahamstown road, tel: 046-636 7904, fax: 046-636 2288, www.kariega.co.za) is a Big Five game lodge on a 5,000ha (12,350 acres). Take the A72 back toward Port Alfred and turn left for Grahamstown, via the village of **Salem** and the **Thomas Baines Nature Reserve**.

Northern loop Leave Grahamstown on the N2 heading toward Bisho, and turn left after 6km (4 miles), via the **Ecca Nature Reserve**. **Fort Beaufort** is 69km (43 miles) farther on, beside the Kat River. It has a **local history museum** and a Martello Tower of 1847; the officers' mess now houses a small **Military History Museum** (Durban Street. *Open* Mon–Sat 9–5),

with paintings by local hero, Thomas Baines. Nearby **Lovedale College** (1841) has educated many of South Africa's great nationalist leaders, including Nelson Mandela, Oliver Tambo and Mangosuthu Buthelezi.

Take the A63 east for 22km (14 miles) to **Alice** and **Fort Hare** (see page 107). The road south from here leads through the **Double Drift Game Reserve** (tel: 040-635 2115), part of a formidable wildlife preserve on a magnificent looping gorge of the Great Fish River. At the intersection with the N2, turn right. **Peddie**, named after Colonel John Peddie, was built in 1835 as an earth fort. In May 1846 the town, defended by a small white contingent and friendly Mfengu tribesmen, was attacked by 9,000 Xhosa warriors. From the mid-19th century a town developed around the fort (no longer extant). It is now a lively, largely black community, with music and market stalls. Grahamstown is 58km (36 miles) west on the N2.

❑ Born 18 July 1918 at Qunu, near Umtata, Nelson Rolihlahla Mandela graduated in law from the University of the Witwatersrand and started South Africa's first black law practice, in partnership with Oliver Tambo. In the 1950s, he became active in the emerging ANC, holding various offices including Commander-in-Chief of the militant wing, *Umkhonto we Sizwe* (Spear of the Nation). In 1963, he was sentenced to life imprisonment on Robben Island. Released unconditionally on 11 February 1990, he headed the ANC delegation in talks leading to South Africa's first truly democratic elections. Later he and F. W. de Klerk were awarded the Nobel Peace Prize for their success in dismantling apartheid. From 10 May 1994, until 1999, Mandela was President of the Government of National Unity. ❑

MINOR MUSEUMS
In addition to those listed, many small towns in the province have museums. For collections of domestic furniture, ceramics, silverware and glassware visit Adelaide (*Open* Mon–Fri 8–1, 2–5); Aliwal North, the Kerkplein Museum (*Open* Mon–Sat 9–12); Cathcart, the CM Van Coller Museum (*Open* Mon, Tue, Thu, Fri 10–12, Wed 2–4); and Dordrecht, the Anderson Museum (*Open* Mon–Fri 9–12). For war displays visit Barkly East Museum (*Open* Mon–Fri 9–12, 3–4.30). The Burgersdorp Cultural Historical Museum is housed in two typical Karoo houses (*Open* Mon–Fri 8–4) and the Humansdorp Museum (*Open* Mon–Fri 10–1, 2–4) displays domestic items and has a restored water mill. The Somerset East Museum (*Open* Mon–Fri 8–1, 2–5) boasts Victorian herb and rose gardens and a blacksmith's shop.

Beyond the Valley of Desolation stretch the Plains of Kamdeboo

The Karoo

▶ Cradock — 102B2

240km (150 miles) north of Port Elizabeth
Tourist Information, Civic Centre, Market Square
(tel: 048-881 2383, fax: 048-881 1421)
This quaint Karoo town in the upper Fish River valley was founded in 1813. The incongruous 1867 **Groote Kerk** (great church) on Stockenstroom Street, was modelled on London's St.-Martin-in-the-Fields. Local author Olive Schreiner (*The Story of an African Farm*, published 1883) lived here as a child; the **Schreiner House** (Cross Street, tel: 048-881 5251. *Open* Mon–Fri 8–12.45, 2–4.30. *Admission free*) is now a museum. The **Great Fish River Museum** (High Street, tel: 048-881 4509. *Open* Tue–Fri 8–1, 2–4, Sat 8–noon. *Admission: inexpensive*) has displays of local pioneer life. **Die Tuishuise Hotel** (see page 260) comprises nearly a whole street of impeccably restored and furnished houses.

▶▶▶ Graaff-Reinet — 102A2

251km (156 miles) northeast of Port Elizabeth
Tourist Information Centre, Old Library, corner of Church and Somerset streets (tel: 049-892 4248, fax: 049-892 3577 www.graaffreinet.co.za)
Open: Mon–Fri 8–5, Sat 9–12, Sun 10–12
An architectural jewel, Graaff-Reinet is the fourth-oldest town in South Africa, tucked into a horseshoe bend in the Sundays River, at the foot of the Sneeuberg. Founded in 1786 and named by the governor after himself and his wife, it remained a troubled frontier town for nearly a century. Much of its superb Cape Dutch architecture has been restored and the town is now home to 200 historic monuments (walking maps available).

Louis Thibault designed the **Drosdty Hotel** (1806), but as he lived far away in Cape Town, the local builders used their own initiative; for instance, they substituted a half-moon gable for the planned dome and bell tower. Behind the hotel, **Stretch's Court** is a complex of mid 19th-century Karoo cottages built for coloured workers and emancipated slaves. They are now used as hotel rooms. **Reinet House** (1 Parsonage Street, tel: 049-892 3801 for all museums. *Open* Mon–Fri 9–12.30, 2–5, Sat–Sun 9–12. *Admission: inexpensive*), built in 1806–1812 as the Dutch Reformed parsonage, is the local history museum, while **Urquhart House**, next door (*Open* Mon–Fri 8–12.30, 2–5, Sat 9–12. *Admission: inexpensive*), is furnished as a Victorian dwelling.

The Owl House, a strange concrete legacy of a tormented artist

The early 19th-century **Old Residency** (Parsonage Street, see Urquart House for opening times) houses the Jan Felix Laegan Memorial Collection of firearms, as well as the Middellandse Regimental Memorabilia.

The **Hester Rupert Art Museum** in the 1821 Dutch Reformed Mission church (Church Street, tel: 049-892 2121. *Open* Mon–Fri 10–12, 3–5, Sun 10–12. *Admission: inexpensive*) has an excellent collection of contemporary South African art and the **Old Library** (corner of Church and Somerset streets. *Open* Mon–Fri 8–12.30, 2–5, Sat–Sun 9–12. *Admission: inexpensive*) has Karoo fossils, San art, photography and costumes. Other fine buildings include the Dutch Reformed church, the Town Hall, the John Rupert Little Theatre (Parsonage Street), built as the church of the London Mission Society, and the Graaff-Reinet Pharmacy (24 Caledon Street), preserved as a Victorian drugstore.

To the south, the **Karoo Nature Reserve** (tel: 049-892 3476) has walks, hiking trails and a 14km (9-mile) drive up to the twisted rock formations of the **Valley of Desolation**, with superb views across the Plains of Kamdeboo.

Fifty kilometres (31 miles) north of Graaff-Reinet, in the tiny Afrikaner village of **Nieu Bethesda**, is the **Owl House▶▶** (*Open* daily 9–5. *Admission: inexpensive*), the disturbing home of artist Helen Martins (see panel).

▶ Mountain Zebra National Park   102B2

20km (12 miles) west of Cradock (tel: 048-881 2427, fax: 048-881 3943, www.sanparks.org)
Open: daily Oct–Apr, 7–7; May–Sep, 7.30–6
Admission: moderate

This 6,536ha (16,143-acre) sanctuary saved the distinctive Cape mountain zebra from extinction. There are over 200 zebras here, with more than 200 bird species, many antelope and the caracal (or lynx). There are driving routes, nature trails and day walks, while the Mountain Zebra Hiking Trail (25.6km/16 miles) offers 3 days of hiking in the rugged Karoo landscape—views are worth the effort.

HELEN MARTINS
Brought up in the strict, isolated Dutch Reformed village of Nieu Bethesda, Helen Elizabeth Martins left home abruptly in 1915, married briefly and disastrously twice, and returned to nurse her ailing parents in 1935. After their deaths, when she was about 50, she began to decorate the family home, the Owl House, covering every available surface (including chair seats) in boldly patterned ground glass, with huge sun motifs on the windows and ceilings. She also designed powerful naive concrete sculptures (actually made by coloured helpers) of owls and camels, nativity scenes and mermaids. She spent the rest of her life alone in dire poverty. In 1977, with her sight failing, she committed suicide by drinking caustic soda.

The most characteristic architecture of the Cape is the simple yet elegant style known as Cape Dutch, which evolved over the 17th to early 19th centuries. Later, the British influence made itself felt in Georgian and Victorian buildings, some of the latter epitomizing imperial pomp.

114

Top: Wrought-iron gingerbread balconies in Swellendam
Below: Elaborate 19th-century style in Grahamstown

Most early Cape Dutch buildings were farmhouses, simple rectangular structures with a wooden frame, wattle and clay infill, a steeply pitched thatched roof, central front door and symmetrically placed windows with heavy wooden shutters. The house often made up one side of a courtyard, with the barns, stables and servants' quarters on the other three. Most had whitewashed walls and dark green paintwork (the only paint available to early settlers), a decorative scheme that became traditional. Inside, the hall led to just two rooms, one for sleeping, the other for living. Floors were of polished dung or mud inset with peach pits. Furniture was basic: a solid box bed, dining table and chairs with woven gut seats. Few houses of this style survive in their original form outside museums such as those in Worcester (see page 77) and Pretoria (see page 164).

In time, as fortunes were made, the house began to sprout wings, becoming H-, T- or U-shaped, and acquired a small, raised veranda (*stoep*). The two largest rooms were in the front: the living room (*voerkammer*—front room) and the main bedroom. Behind, inter-connecting at first, but later leading off a central corridor, were a second public room (the *agterkammer*—back room), sometimes a study/office, more bedrooms, and, right at the back, the kitchen. There were no indoor bath-rooms until the mid-19th century. Before then, the lavatory was in an outhouse and the bath movable. These grander houses had ceilings and floors of highly polished yellowwood or stinkwood. The furniture became more varied and sophisticated, mirroring European fashion; the very wealthy imported everything.

It was the arrival of the gable that signalled the coming of age of Cape Dutch design. Based on the intricate gables fashionable in 17th- and 18th-century Holland, the typical Cape house had one large gable over the front door. Embellished with curved and curled edges, space for statues, the date of construction, or the arms of the family, these provided an element of chic and individuality, elevating the house from cottage to mansion. The master

architect was Louis Thibault; the master sculptor, Anton Anreith. The Cape Winelands (see pages 86–89) are littered with these beautiful houses, a number still owned by the original family and with period furnishings.

By the end of the 18th century, design was shifting away from the rectangular farm to the square, two-floor town house of Georgian England, with symmetrically positioned windows, a triangular pediment and flat roof. The façade became more intricate, with pastel shades, pilasters and plaster garlands. Inside, traditional white walls gave way to elegantly painted *trompe-l'oeil* columns and urns. Not many of these houses have survived urban progress, but there are a few outstanding examples, such as the Koopmans de Wet House (see page 56) in Cape Town. In the country towns they became the model for the tiny, square-built Karoo-style cottages, flat-roofed and with a small fanlight above the door, the interior quartered into four connecting rooms: living room, kitchen and two bedrooms. Many fine examples survive in Karoo towns such as Graaff-Reinet (see page 112) and even in the Bo-Kaap quarter of Cape Town (see page 54).

The last great shift before the modern era came in the mid- to late-19th century with the advent of neo-Gothic churches, the large-scale work of South Africa's first major architect, Sir Herbert Baker, and the prevalence of Victorian houses with steeply pitched roofs (many pitched only in front as the stunted trees did not provide sufficiently long timbers) and corrugated-iron verandas that sported elaborate gingerbread trim.

Top: Elegance in Graaff-Reinet
Above: A typical, simple rectangular house with a curved gable, in Tulbagh

OUT AND ABOUT

Numerous boat trips are on offer in Port Elizabeth, leaving from King's Beach including whale, seal, dolphin and birdwatching. For sea-going sailing trips or deep-sea fishing (tel: 041-378 2528, wwwraggycharters. netfirms.com); for scuba diving (tel: 041-368 7880, www.prodive. co.za). For adventure sports, including white-water rafting, abseiling, hiking, riding and cycling (tel: 041-378 1418). A local steam train, the Apple Express, runs from PE to Thornhill (tel: 041-583 2030), stopping at Von Stadens River Bridge, the world's highest narrow-gauge bridge. For township and cultural tours (tel: 041-581 0091 or 043-743 0472); for city orientation tours (tel: 041-585 1801).

A few early buildings have survived the redevelopment of bustling Port Elizabeth

Nelson Mandela Bay

► Port Elizabeth   *102B1*

769km (477 miles) east of Cape Town. Nelson Mandela Bay Tourism, Donkin Lighthouse, Donkin Reserve; (tel: 041-585 8884, fax: 041-585 2564, www.tourismpe.co.za/ www.nmbt.co.za)
Open Mon–Fri 8–4.30, Sat–Sun 9–3.30.

A garrison was stationed here in 1799, but the real settlement came in 1820 with a large contingent of British immigrants. The acting governor, Sir Rufane Donkin, named the port after his wife. Port Elizabeth (or PE) is now South Africa's third-largest port and fifth-largest city. There are several excellent beaches in the area, including King's (from the harbour to Humewood) and Humewood itself.

The main **Bayworld Museum** (Beach Road, Humewood, tel: 041-586 1051, www.bayworld.co.za. *Open* daily 9–5. *Admission: moderate*) has several sections. The museum itself has an interesting small collection of 18th- and 19th-century South African art, plus history, costume and marine exhibits. Far more fun, however, are the living satellites—a **Snake Park** (*Open* daily 9–1, 2–4.30; shows daily Dec–Jan, Apr 10 and 2. *Admission: expensive*), **Tropical House** (*Admission: moderate*) and **Oceanarium** (*Open* daily 9–1, 2–4.30; seal and dolphin shows daily 11 and 3. *Admission: expensive*). Here you see snakes, exotic birds, 40 species of fish, including sharks, plus African penguins, bottlenose dolphins and Cape fur seals.

Elsewhere, the **Castle Hill Historical Museum** (7 Castle Hill, tel: 041-5582 2515. *Open* Tue–Fri 10–1, 2–5, Sat 10–1, Mon 2–5. *Admission: inexpensive*) displays fine Cape furniture in PE's oldest surviving house, a former parsonage; the **Nelson Mandela Metropolitan Art Museum** (Park

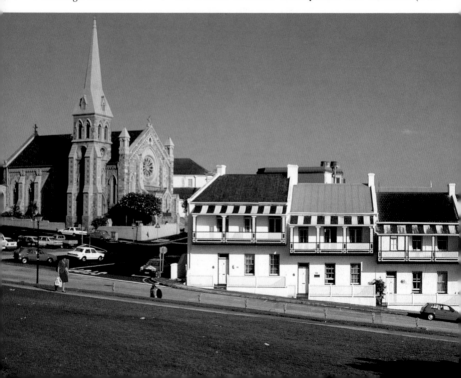

Drive, tel: 041-586 1030. *Open* Mon–Fri 9–5; closed Tue am, Sat–Sun 2–5. *Admission: free*) has 19th- and 20th-century British and South African fine art; and the The Boardwalk Casino (Marine Drive, Summerstrand, tel: 041-507 7777, www.boardwalk.co.za) is a massive new entertainment complex with Tivoli-style gardens.

▶▶ Addo Elephant National Park 102B1

72km (45 miles) north of Port Elizabeth (tel: 042-233 0556, fax: 042-233 0196, www.sanparks.org)
Open: daily 7–7
Enormous herds of elephants once roamed across the Eastern Cape. An animal without predators, the elephant met its match in man, as towns cut across the ancient paths, forests were felled, the open grassland was planted with crops, and the elephants were shot—for sport and ivory, and as a pest. By 1931, the Eastern Cape was down to its last 11 elephants. This massive reserve—which is now linked to several private reserves, more than doubling the space to create South Africa's third largest park—was created solely to protect the tiny herd and the last surviving Cape buffalo. Today, the population has risen to around 400 elephants, plus eland, kudu, red hartebeest, bushbuck and Cape buffalo, endangered Kenyan black rhino and 185 bird species. There are two walking trails, a rest camp, a restaurant and a shop.

▶ Jeffreys Bay/St. Francis Bay 102A1

About 70km (43 miles) west of Port Elizabeth
Jeffreys Bay Tourism, Da Gama Road, Shell Museum Complex (tel: 042-293 2588, fax: 042-293 2227, www.jeffreysbaytourism.com). St. Francis Tourism (tel: 042-294 0076, fax: 042-294 0675, www.stfrancisbay.co.za)
This remote corner of the coast is little known except by surfers who, like the dolphins and whales, flock here to ride such exciting waves as the 5km (3-mile) 'Supertubes'. With several low-key resorts along superb beaches, it is ideal for water sports, beachcombing (visit the **Shell Museum**, Da Gama Road, tel: 043-293 1111) and 4WD rides across the dunes.

St. Francis Bay is built around a series of pretty canals on the Kromme River estuary (boat trips available), while Port St. Francis is a chic marina and resort. Take time to visit the **Kouga Cultural Centre**, Humansdorp, off the N2 (tel: 042-295 1111), a traditional African healers' trading post and market, with ceremonies and tours of cultural sights.

The Campanile

MONUMENTAL GLORIES
A walking guide to historic PE is available from the tourist office. Look for the original Fort Frederick (Belmont Terrace), which was built in 1799 and never saw a shot fired in anger; the 51.6m/168ft (204-step) Campanile Clock Tower (harbour entrance) with a carillon of 23 bells, built as a memorial to the 1820 Settlers; the Horse Memorial (corner of Cape and Russell roads), erected in honour of all the horses that died in the Anglo-Boer wars; and Sir Rufane Donkin's stone pyramid, erected in memory of his beloved Elizabeth, next to the Donkin Lighthouse.

Shamwari has been completely restocked with game

RHINO HORN
The name rhinoceros comes from the Greek words *rhis* (nose) and *keras* (horn). The horns have no bony core but are made of heavily compacted fibres. They grow continuously but are restricted by wear and tear to about 60cm/2ft (front horn) and 25cm/1ft (rear horn). They contain no magical aphrodisiac properties, and are, in fact, made of exactly the same substance as human fingernails. This is a mild analgesic—which may be why we chew our nails in times of stress.

▶ **Shamwari and Kwandwe Game Reserve** *102B1*

Shamwari, 72km (45 miles) east of Port Elizabeth, off the N2 (tel: 042-203 1111, www.shamwari.com). Kwandwe, 160km (100 miles) from Port Wlizabeth, on the banks of the Great Fish River, via the N2. Grahamstown and Ecca Pass (tel: 046-603 3400, reservations 011-809 430, www.ccafri.com).
Shamwari (the name means 'friend') and Kwandwe ('Place of the Blue Crane' in Xhosa) are both private luxury Big Five game parks, each covering some 20,000ha (49,400 acres), a mix of former farmland and hunting preserve. Run by separate companies, both have been leaders in the conservationists' efforts to restore game to an area largely denuded of wildlife, leaving only small animals such as mongoose in the region. Many different species, from black and white rhino, elephant, lion, cheetah and wild dog to the humble dung beetle and oxpecker have been shipped in to help in the careful rebuilding of an indigenous ecology.

▶ **Tsitsikamma Forest National Park** see page 101

▶ **Uitenhage** *102B1*

38km (24 miles) north of Port Elizabeth
Tourist Information, Municipality, Market Street (tel: 041-994 1111, fax: 041-994 1210)
Uitenhage began as a wool town but now has several car factories. Among some fine historic buildings, the **Old Drostdy Museum** (tel: 041-992 2063) includes a Volkswagen motor museum alongside local history and Africana collections, while the **Old Station** (tel: 041-922 8210. *Open* Tue–Thu 10–1, 2–4.30) is a perfectly preserved Victorian setting for a small railway museum. **Cuyler Manor Cultural Museum** (5km/3 miles out of town on the Port Elizabeth road, tel: 041-922 0372. *Open* Mon–Fri 10–1, 2–4.30, Sun 2–5) has demonstrations of traditional farming, plus a mohair farm. The **Van Stadens Wild Flower Reserve** (tel: 041-561 000) is a 373ha (921-acre) reserve and bird sanctuary on the eastern rim of the Van Stadens River gorge.

The Wild Coast

Tourist Information, PO Box 52791, Umtata 5100 (tel: 047-531 5290, fax: 047-531 5291, email: ectbwc@icon.co.za)
Central Reservations for Wild Coast hotels (tel: 043-743 6181)
The great Kei River once marked the border of the Xhosa kingdom and later of the supposedly independent Transkei homeland. The region is markedly different from its neighbours; a few miles from the river's banks the ribbon of holiday homes comes to an abrupt halt, and the few towns are quite obviously poorer. From the 1970s, tourism here took the form of getaways on the Wild Coast and gambling weekends in the local casinos. But even this began to trail off, in the mid-1990s, as a strong anti-white stance regularly threatened violence.

These days, with Transkei reintegrated into South Africa, the area has opened up again. With the exception of pretty little **Port St. Johns** (Tourist Information, tel: 047-564 1187, www.ruraltourism.org.za), an increasingly popular back-packers' hangout, there are few reasons for tourists to visit the towns, although as the home of Nelson Mandela, there is a growing 'pilgrimage' trail. The Nelson Mandela Museum in Umtata covers his life and the history of the struggle against apartheid. Instead, glory in the virgin hardwood forests, the flower-strewn meadows and, above all, the sea.

The Transkei's very poverty and isolation have protected the local ecology from development. Here is a totally pristine stretch of magnificent coast, with gentle grasslands rolling down to wave-pounded cliffs, huge dunes and glistening, snake-like river estuaries. Dolphins play in the surf around the hulks of long-wrecked ships and kingfishers dart through the mangrove swamps. Occasional roads lead down to small, remote resort hotels, where you can catch your own dinner, or enjoy mounds of fresh oysters, lobster, crab, periwinkle, yellowtail and kingfish.

A hiking trail runs the full length of the Wild Coast. It takes about 14 days to walk the whole route, but you can do a shorter segment (for information and permits, contact Wild Coast Holiday Reservations, tel: 043-743 6181, fax: 043-743 6188, email: meross@iafrica.com).

PROPHECY OF DOOM
In 1856, a young Xhosa medium named Nongqawuse had a prophetic vision while staring into a pool at the Qolora River mouth. In the vision the ancestors promised that if the Xhosa would destroy all their cattle and crops they would drive away the white men and provide the Xhosa with new and better animals and grain. The elders gathered, believed her, and the order went out. The cattle were driven into the sea and the granaries and fields set alight. The gleeful British forcibly shut the missionaries' aid stations, and some 25,000 people are thought to have died in the ensuing famine.

119

The Wild Coast car ferry across Kei River mouth

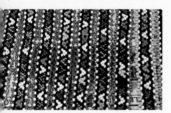

The Xhosa, Zulu and Ndebele—the latter are actually a breakaway Zulu clan—are all Nguni, a closely related cultural group whose languages are sufficiently similar for people to understand each other. They are spread across the Eastern Cape, KwaZulu-Natal, the borders of Limpopo Province and Mpumalanga.

The three cultures have a great deal in common. By tradition, all are pastoralist, the older boys herding cattle (which count as wealth), the younger boys looking after the goats, and the women growing maize, vegetables and some fruit on small farms. In their youth, the men were warriors; as elders they formed the local council. These days, however, the old structure has all but vanished. Most men work away in the mines or factories, while the women rear the children, either separately in the villages or—increasingly—in the townships.

People The Xhosa come from the hills and coast of the Eastern Cape, around the area separated off under apartheid as the Transkei and Ciskei (see page 104). The many clans of the Zulu nation, unified under Shaka in the early 19th century (see page 30), live mainly in KwaZulu-Natal. The Ndebele, who fled north away from Shaka, live on the borders of the Limpopo Province and Mpumalanga, although a large number went further still, crossing the Limpopo River into what is now Zimbabwe.

Religion The traditional religion is monotheistic: One all-important god looks after the big things in life, leaving smaller tasks to an army of ancestors. Because of this, people revere and pray to their ancestors in much the way Catholics pray to the saints. Few Nguni see any real conflict with Christianity and many happily

A young Zulu dancer dressed for a performance

Three Ndebele women

practise both religions simultaneously. They still consult the *sangomas* (diviners), who act as mediums, interpreting the wishes of the ancestors, and the *nyangas* (traditional herbal doctors)—although they may try the better-safe-than-sorry approach by visiting a Western hospital, too. There is still a belief in the evil influence of witchcraft. The only real difference made by the church has been in cutting down to some extent the number of wives each man takes in a polygamous culture.

Traditional life The life cycle is carefully marked as people progress from childhood to youth, marriage and so on. Traditionally, female dress changes at each stage, while teenage boys are circumcised before they start training for adulthood. A boy must pay *lobolo* to the family of the girl he wishes to marry; this used to be in cattle, but today is more usually cash. Her parents must provide a dowry of useful household objects and clothes. For weddings, on the eve of battle or just for a night out with the boys, every opportunity is taken to dance—energetically and competitively, with harmonizing song and rhythmic drums.

Decoration Western dress is becoming the norm, so that almost the only time you see the often magnificent traditional costume is during rituals and tourist pageants. Most people are very fond of personal adornment and bright colour. All the Nguni used animal skins and beads of ostrich shell, seashells and seeds until multicoloured glass beads were introduced by the early 19th-century missionaries. These have now become an integral part of the culture, used not only for decoration, but as a clearly understood language. Illiterate Zulu girls write love letters to their boyfriends in beads, and a woman's exact status, clan and home village can be told from the patterning of her headband and necklaces. The Ndebele took the love of adornment one stage further, the women creating jazzy geometric patterns on both inner and outer walls of their houses, at first in natural earth tones, but later, after they were introduced to acrylics, in a dazzling array of blues greens, pinks and purples. Sadly, these adornments are increasingly rare, although Ndebele designs are very popular on plant pots and souvenirs.

BEER
Beer, which is brewed by the women, has ritual and social connotations. Maize and sorghum are wrapped in wet sacks until they sprout, dried in the sun, ground into flour, boiled to a thin porridge, then strained through a woven grass tube and left to ferment, a process that takes up to 10 days. The sediment is given to the ancestors. Traditionally the beer is drunk from a communal clay or woven pot. A bowl placed face-down as a lid shows there is beer available; if it is face-up, visitors know that drinks are off.

Xhosa people still sometimes whiten their faces in the traditional way

Blesbok silhouetted against the desert sunset

▶▶▶ **REGION HIGHLIGHTS**

Augrabies Falls
page 134

**Golden Gate Highlands
National Park** page 129

**Kgalagadi Transfrontier
Park** pages 134–135

Kimberley
pages 137–139

Namakwa page 136

**Pilanesberg National
Park** pages 144–145

Sun City page 145

SEA OF SAND In the heart of South Africa, on the high plains of the Free State, mile upon mile of maize and wheat coat the endless prairies, punctuated by nothing but an occasional windmill or isolated farmhouse. To the north and west is an enormous expanse of almost empty semidesert, stretching from the Karoo through the rust-red dunes of the Kalahari to merge with the even more terrible Namib Desert, one of the thirstiest places on earth. Together, they make up a truly massive area of wind-blown sand extending from the Northern Cape to southern Zaire—the largest continuous stretch of sand in the world. Like the Sahara, the desert is expanding.

It is a harsh, bleak, wonderful environment of strange, wind-carved rock, red-gold sand and weird succulents and stone plants. Thousands of shallow round or oval pans trap tiny amounts of rain and dew in their hard, grey clay. These lifesaving water holes support a variety of life, from small reptiles to dramatically beautiful, drought-

hardened antelope such as gemsbok and springbok. Where rivers or underground water feed the grass, there are some of Africa's largest remaining wildlife sanctuaries, including the remote Kgalagadi Transfrontier Park. Even people manage to survive here, from the last few desert-wise San (see page 132) to hardy Afrikaner farmers who bleed water drop by drop from deep boreholes to support scattered herds of cattle and game.

Game-farming is increasingly popular in such difficult terrain. Live game is shown off to tourists and sold at auction; the surplus is hunted. Staggering numbers of people in all three provinces are eager to help hunters shoot the animal of their choice; many private reserves are stocked specifically for hunting, and quite a few small towns are proud of the local taxidermist. As a result, the animals are far too wary of humans to get close, limiting your chances of decent photographs. The good news is that hunting is expensive, controlled and carried out

TOURIST INFORMATION

Free State Tourism, PO Box 4041, Welkom 9460 (tel: 086-110 2185, fax: 051-430 8206. www. freestatetourism.gov.za). Northern Cape Tourism Authority, 187 Du Toitspan Road, Private Bag X5017, Kimberley 8300 (tel: 053-832 2657, fax: 052-831 2937, www.northerncape.org.za). North-West Parks and Tourism Board, 30–31 Nelson Mandela Drive, Cookes Lake, Heritage House, Mafikeng, PO Box 4488, Mmabatho 2735 (tel: 018-397 1500, fax: 018-397 1660, email: tidcmf@yebo.co.za, www.tourismnorthwest. co.za).

THE GRIQUA

The Griqua (the name is a simplification of "Kurikwa") originated in the Piketberg area— Khoikhoi people who were enslaved and became a subcaste of mixed-blood people. In the early 19th century, some of them sought freedom, wandering north as herders and cattle raiders and calling themselves Bastaards. A freed slave, Adam Kok, former cook to the governors of the Cape, was their leader. They settled around Klaarwater, where they drew in other displaced people of all races, from fragmented Tswana clans to army deserters. The surrounding area (now Griqualand West in the Northern Cape) succeeded in remaining independent until the 1860s, when diamonds were discovered in the area.

Right: The flowers of Crassula marnierana *bloom in the desert*

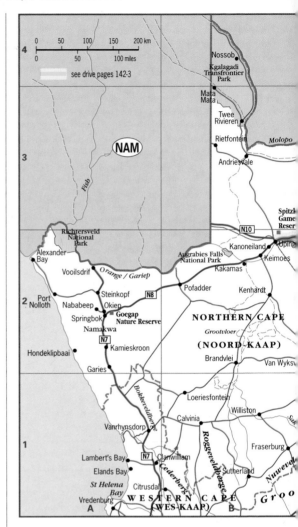

under strict supervision. Licences for big-game hunting are handed out only when culling is strictly necessary.

The thread that binds—and feeds—the region is South Africa's largest river, the Orange (Gariep) River. It rises at Maluti in the Lesotho Drakensberg, flowing northwest for 2,250km (1,395 miles) to meet the Atlantic at Alexander Bay. Its basin covers 606,700sq km/234,186sq-miles (47 per cent of South Africa) and drains 22 per cent of all water in South Africa. The country's second-largest river, the Vaal, is a tributary. The Orange River Development Project, founded in 1963 to provide hydroelectric power and irrigation, includes long tunnels and canals and two massive dams, the Gariep (Hendrik Verwoerd) and the Vanderkloof (P. K. Le Roux). From the central prairies, the river flows through the desert in a narrow strip of emerald green. The Orange River valley is one of the major wine areas of South Africa, and also produces table grapes, raisins and other fruit.

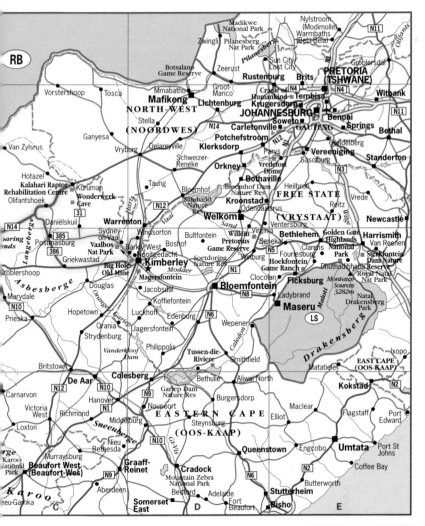

The real money, however, comes from underground. Diamonds were discovered here in 1869, and vast fortunes were made in the Kimberley area. There are still many working diamond mines in the region as well as increasing undersea harvesting of old river gravel. In April 1938, a borehole sunk on St. Helena Farm, near Welkom, drove through the lava walls of a vast underground treasure trove. Gold was found in quantities that staggered the world. By 1946, following the discovery of fabulous deposits on a farm named Geduld, at Odendaalsrus, it seemed that the Free State was the new El Dorado.

The Free State goldfields currently produce more than a third of the country's output; the names of its mines daily echo around international stock exchanges, and its goldfields rival those of the Witwatersrand as the richest in the world.

Local resources also include many other valuable minerals, from manganese and copper to uranium.

BY APPOINTMENT
Several of the most
magnificent buildings in
the President Brand
Conservation Area may be
visited by appointment
only. They include the
City Hall (tel: 051-405
8911), designed in 1934
by Sir Gordon Leith; the
twin-spired 1880
Tweetoringkerk (Charles
Street, tel: 051-430
4274); the Supreme Court
(corner of President Brand
and Fontein streets, tel:
051-447 8837); the 1929
Appeal Court (corner of
President Brand and
Charles streets, tel: 051-
447 2631); and the
Fourth Raadsaal (corner of
President Brand and
Charles streets, tel: 051-
447 8898), built in 1893,
with a magnificent Greek
Revival council chamber.

*The First Raadsaal
museum has done
duty as a council
chamber, school and
community hall*

Free State

▶ Bloemfontein 125D2

398km (247 miles) south of Johannesburg
City Tourist Information, 60 Park Road, Willow (tel: 051-405
8489/90, fax: 051-447 3859, www.bloemfontein.co.za)
Open: Mon–Fri 8–4.15, Sat 8–12

Some say Bloemfontein (Fountain of Flowers) was named
after a local Griqua (see page 124) leader, Jan Bloem,
others that it came from the flower garden planted
around the perennial spring by the first settler, Johannes
Brits. The city itself was founded by Major H. D. Warden,
British resident of the area between the Orange and
Vaal rivers. In 1854, it became capital of the new
Boer Republic, the Orange Free State. Following the
Union in 1910, Bloemfontein became—and remains—
the judicial capital of South Africa, an oddly provincial
town with imposing public buildings and museums.

Conservation Area museums Many of the most
impressive buildings, clustered around President Brand
Street (walking tour maps available), now house
museums. The thatched-roofed, dung-floored **First
Raadsaal** (95 St. George Street, tel: 051-447 9610. *Open*
Mon–Fri 10.15–3, Sat–Sun 2–5. *Admission: inexpensive*) was
built in 1848 as the first council chamber and school. It
contains a small museum of the Republic, with a collection of carriages and wagons. Highlights of the **National
Museum** (corner of Charles and Aliwal streets, tel: 051-447
9609. *Open* Mon–Sat 8–5, Sun 12–6. *Admission: inexpensive*)
are a re-created 19th-century street and an extensive
archaeological and fossil collection, including the
Florisbad skull, South Africa's earliest example of *Homo
sapiens*. The Old Government Building (1908) is now
home to the **National Afrikaans Literary (Letterkundige)
Museum** (corner of President Brand and Maitland streets,
tel: 051-405 4711. *Open* Mon–Fri 7.30–4, Sat 9–12. *Admission: free*). The opulent, Scottish baronial **Old Presidency**
(corner of President Brand and St. George streets, tel: 051-
448 0949. *Open* Tue–Fri 10–12, 1–4. Sat–Sun pre-booked
groups only. *Admission: free*) was built in 1885 on the site
of the original Bloem Fonteyn farm as official residence of
the presidents of the Free State Republic.

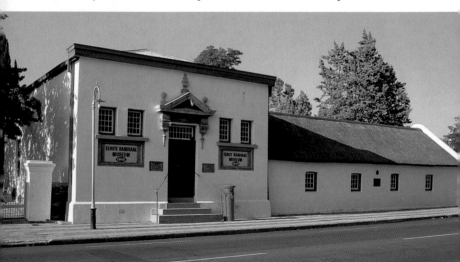

EMILY HOBHOUSE
A staunch supporter of Afrikaner independence, Emily Hobhouse spent much of her life trying to mediate between the British and Boers. In 1900, she began to raise money to alleviate the suffering in Boer concentration camps, eventually whipping up enough support to help improve conditions and force a settlement. Notably, she never visited any black camps. After the war, she established a series of 26 spinning and weaving schools for Boer girls. Regarded as a local heroine, she is buried at the foot of the National Women's Memorial.

127

Left: Painted tiles depict the Battle of Colenso Below: Memorial to Boer victims of the concentration camps. Both are in the War Museum, Bloemfontein

Other museums Colonial **Freshford House** (31 Kellner Street, tel: 051-447 9609. *Open* Mon–Fri 10–1, Sat–Sun 2–5. *Admission: inexpensive*) is full of brass, stained glass and Victoriana. The **Oliewenhuis Art Gallery** (Harry Smith Street, tel: 051-447 9609. *Open* Mon–Fri 8–5, Sat 10–5, Sun 1–5. *Admission: free*) was a neo-Cape Dutch homestead. **Queen's Fort** (Church Street, tel: 051-447 5478. *Open* Mon–Fri 10–4. Sat–Sun pre-booked groups only. *Admission: free*), built in 1848, depicts the Free State conflicts of between 1820 and 1990.

The excellent **National Women's Memorial and War Museum▶▶** (Monument Road, tel: 051-447 3447. *Open* Mon–Fri 8–4.30, Sat 10–5, Sun 2–5. Guided tours by appointment. *Admission: inexpensive*) gives a compelling (if one-sided) account of the Anglo-Boer War, with horrific details of prisoner-of-war and concentration camps (see page 39). In the grounds is a memorial to the 26,370 Afrikaner women and children who died in them.

Gardens The finest of Bloemfontein's gardens are the lush **National Botanical Garden▶** (Rayton Road, tel: 051-431 3530. *Open* daily 8–6. *Admission: inexpensive*) and rose-filled **King's Park**. The **Zoo** (King's Way, tel: 051-405 8483. *Open* daily 8–6 in summer, 8–5 in winter. *Admission: moderate*) is famous for its now dead 'liger' (a lion-tiger cross) and primates. Naval Hill includes the **Franklin Game Reserve** (Union Avenue, tel: 051-405 8124. *Open* daily 8–5. *Admission: free*). Nearby, in Hamilton Park, is the **Orchid House▶** (Union Avenue, tel: 051-405 8124. *Open* Mon–Fri 10–4, Sat–Sun 10–5. *Admission: free*).

SIR HARRY SMITH

A renowned and charismatic hothead, Harry Smith began his career as an aide to the Duke of Wellington during the Spanish Peninsular Wars. During this time he married a young Spanish noblewoman, Juana Maria de los Dolores de Leon. Smith served for a time in America and fought at Waterloo. In later life, he became governor of the Cape Colony, where he managed to stir up trouble along most of the borders, fighting bloody wars against the Xhosa and Sotho. Harrismith is named after him, while both Ladysmith in KwaZulu-Natal and Ladismith in the Western Cape are named after his wife.

Eastern Highlands
(Thabo Mofutsanyana)

Tourist Information, corner Mampoi and Mota streets, Phuthaditjhaba, Private Bag X810, Witieshoek 9870.; tel: 058-713 0012, email:victoria@statetourism.co.za

The Eastern Highlands are an area of great natural beauty and drama, where cold winters frequently blanket the higher reaches of the Maloti Mountains and the Drakensberg in snow. Traces remain of the various peoples who have lived here—in the San rock paintings, the scattered Sotho, Bakwena and Balokwa villages, and the tidy sandstone towns and churches of the Boers and British.

For tourists this area is all about the great outdoors, with a whirl of activities from birdwatching and game viewing to horseback-riding, mountain bicycling, hiking and climbing, water sports and golf. The Sandstone Steam Rail Company runs excursion trains between Bloemfontein and Bethlehem (tel: 011-799 7405). Several charming small towns with fine Victorian buildings of local sandstone make up the Maloti Route. Prosperous **Harrismith** (Tourist Information, Pretorius Street, tel: 058-622 3525, www.drakensberg-tourism.com) was founded in 1849.

Nearby are the 1,000ha (2,471-acre) **Mount Everest Game Reserve** (tel/fax: 058-623 0235, email: everest@ interest.co.za) and the 18,000ha (44,600-acre) **Sterkfontein Dam Nature Reserve** (tel: 058-622 3520, fax: 058-622 1772. *Open* daily 6–10. *Admission: inexpensive*) surrounding a lake. Stunningly situated beneath the Titanic, a huge ship-shaped wedge of rock, **Clarens** (Tourist Information, Market Street, tel: 058-256 1542, email: clarens@bhm. dorea.co.za) is a delightful village, founded in 1912 and named after the Swiss town where President Kruger died.

Bethlehem has a local history museum, a particularly fine collection of Victorian buildings and several lakes nearby. **Fouriesburg** (Tourist Information, tel: 058-223 0552, fax: 058-223 0166) was founded in 1892. Surrounded by flat-topped sandstone hillocks, many of them pierced by caves, it was a Boer stronghold during the Anglo-Boer War. An Asparagus Festival takes place here in September.

Ficksburg on the Caledon River border with Lesotho, was founded in 1867 as a bulwark between disputed Boer and Sotho territory, its history is laid out in the **General J. J. Fick Museum** (Town Square).

San rock art adorns the caves of the Imperani Mountains nearby, and the **Hoekfontein Oxwagon Camp** (13km/8 miles from town, off the R26 to Fouriesburg, tel: 051-933 3915) offers oxwagon rides.

The district surrounding the town is known for producing cherries. It celebrates this with a Cherry Festival each November.

Sotho women chatting in Ficksburg

▶ Gariep Dam

125D1

About 160km (100 miles) south of Bloemfontein
(tel: 082-407 0944, www.xhariep.co.za)

The biggest stretch of inland water in South Africa lies behind this vast dam on the Orange and Caledon rivers. The reservoir covers 374sq km (144sq miles) when full and provides water for irrigation and hydroelectric power. The dam wall (1972) is 914m (2,998ft) long and 90.5m (297ft) high. Around the shores are huge expanses of grassland and Karoo vegetation dotted with rocky outcrops and massive boulders, most of it protected by the **Gariep Nature Reserve** (tel: 052-172 ASK26) and the **Tussen-die-Riviere** (tel: 051-763 1114), which is a normal sanctuary in winter and hunting preserve in summer. **Aasvoelkop**, near the eastern boundary, preserves some San rock paintings. Both reserves offer accommodation, sailing, fishing and swimming.

The **Pellissier House Museum** (tel: 051-763 0103) in nearby **Bethulie** (Tourist Information, tel/fax: 051-763 0002) is thought to be the oldest settler structure north of the Orange River.

▶▶ Golden Gate Highlands National Park 125E2

Approximately 360km (223 miles) south of Johannesburg and 300km (186 miles) northeast of Bloemfontein
(tel: 058-255 0012, fax: 058-255 0022, www.sanparks.org)

In the upper valley of the Little Caledon River and the foothills of the Maloti Mountains of Lesotho, this reserve preserves a strange landscape of brilliant yellow, orange and red sandstone cliffs, and high outcrops and caves, pummelled into bizarre shapes by water. Early hunters were driven out of this area by the Sotho, who settled on the secure heights of the sandstone outcrop 'fortresses'. The wildlife includes black wildebeest and blue cranes and there is hiking, trout fishing and riding.

Highly coloured sandstone cliffs in the Golden Gate Highlands National Park

THE BERG MARATHON
During the Anglo-Boer War, a British major, John Belcher, insulted the citizens of Harrismith by referring to 'their' mountain, Platberg (2,395m/7,856ft), as 'that little hill of yours'. They bet that he would not be able to reach the summit in 60 minutes. He took them on, won easily, and then donated a trophy for an annual race. The course consists of a 5km (3 mile) run, climbing 605m (1,984) to the top, followed by a run along the summit and down an old bridle path back to the town.

METEOR
A newly gazetted World Heritage Site, about 100km (60 miles) southwest of Johannesburg near Vredefort and Parys, the Vredefort Dome is thought to be the world's largest meteor crater. It is certainly the oldest and most clearly visible. The damage was caused around two billion years ago when a massive meteorite 10km (6 miles) in diameter—larger than Table Mountain—struck the earth, creating an impact crater 380km (236 miles) across, with an inner circle measuring 180km (112 miles). It may even have been the 'Eden' rock, increasing oxygen levels to the point where multicellular life was possible. Plans are now underway to develop an interpretation centre and tourism facilities in the area.

▶ Jagersfontein 125D2

110km (68 miles) southwest of Bloemfontein
Tourist Information, Municipality, Market Square
(tel: 051-724 0003, fax: 051-724 0447)
A Victorian mining town, Jagersfontein has a number of attractive buildings, including four designed by Herbert Baker. The main reason to come here is the **Mining Village** (*Open* Mon–Fri 8–1, 2–5. *Admission: inexpensive*), an open-air museum on the rim of the local 'Big Hole', nearly 500m (1,640ft) both in diameter and in depth. The 971-carat Excelsior diamond was discovered here in 1883.

▶ Philippolis 125D2

Tourist Information, Transgariep Museum, 25 Kok Street
(tel: 051-773 0209, fax: 051-773 0157)
Philippolis is an oasis of white stucco and deep-green trees in the immense, dry plain. Dating from 1823, it is the oldest town in the Free State, founded as a mission station for the Griqua people (see page 124). It has some interesting Karoo architecture, including a splendid Dutch Reformed church, Adam Kok's home on Voortrekker Street and Sir Laurens van der Post's childhood home, and Memorial Garden. Emily Hobhouse (see page 127) established her first spinning and weaving schools here. The **Transgariep Museum** (tel: 051-773 0216. *Open* Mon–Fri 10–12. *Admission: free*) covers all the town's fascinating history, and each April brings out its distilling kettle for a *witblitz* (moonshine) festival.

▶ Phuthaditjhaba 125E2

Previously known as Witsieshoek, **Phuthaditjhaba** (Tourist Information see page 128), was the capital of Qwa Qwa, the former homeland of the Bakwena and Balokwa tribes. The **Balokwa Museum** covers local tribal history.
Within **Qwa Qwa National Park** (tel: 058-721 0300), a vast area of 22,000ha (54,340 acres) crossed by rich green valleys and sparkling streams interspersed with gnarled sandstone cliffs, is the **Basotho Cultural Village** (tel: 058-721 0300. *Open* Mon–Fri 9–4.30, Sat–Sun 9–5. *Admission: expensive*). Though a little like a theme park, the village is fascinating, with a display of Sotho huts, from beehive-style thatch to bright, geometric clay. You can see demonstrations of southern Sotho ways of life, too.

▶ Sandveld Nature Reserve 125D3

200km (124 miles) northwest of Bloemfontein; 10km (6 miles) from Bloemhof on the R34 (tel: 053-433 1701/2)
Stretching down to the horseshoe-shaped Bloemhof Dam, this is a wonderland of Kalahari thornveld. It has a 238km (148 miles) shoreline, softened by sandy beaches and shaded by giant camelthorn trees. White-backed vultures build huge, unruly nests in the high branches; below scuttle small mammals such as aardwolf and antbears, porcupines and springhare. Gemsbok, wildebeest, white rhino, giraffe and kudu also thrive here.

▶ Welkom 125D3

Tourist Information, Stateway Road (tel: 057-352 9244, fax: 057-352 9501)
Planned as a garden city, this industrial giant is a minescape of machinery, dumps, reduction works and

belching factories. There is a museum (Tulbagh Street), but it is worth coming here only if you want an underground tour of a gold mine (ask at the tourist office) or to visit Phakisa Freeway, South Africa's top racing circuit.

▶ Willem Pretorius Game Reserve   *125D2*

150km (93 miles) northeast of Bloemfontein off the N1; the turn-off is between Winburg and Ventersdorp (tel: 057-651 4003/4168).

Open: daily 7am–10.30pm. Admission: inexpensive

The Sand River and Allemanskraal Dam divide this 12,000ha (29,640-acre) park into a densely covered, hilly northern section, which provides a perfect habitat for baboons, bushbuck, kudu and duiker, and open grasslands to the south, teeming with springbok, wildebeest, blesbok, eland, impala and zebra. White rhino and buffalo roam freely. On the summit of Beckersberg are a restored prehistoric settlement of dry stone-walled huts and *kraals* belonging to the now-vanished Leghoya people, and a small site museum. At nearby **Senekal** (Tourist Information, tel: 058-481 2142) are the remains of a 250,000-year-old petrified forest. **Winburg** (Tourist Information, tel/fax: 051-881 0003) is a Voortrekker town with a local history museum.

Zebra, springbok and wildebeest drinking

131

The San were dubbed 'Bushmen' by the Dutch because of their knowledge of and affinity with nature. Nomadic hunter-gatherers, they are thought to be the earliest aboriginal inhabitants of southern Africa. Their lifestyle has changed relatively little over some 40,000 years.

132

The San roamed the animal-rich central plains and left archaeological evidence of their passing—paintings and engravings—in lush, mountainous areas with plentiful water, such as the Drakensberg. Some of the most recent paintings depict soldiers on horseback wearing red-and-blue tunics, proving that the last of the San did not leave the Drakensberg area until after the arrival of the Europeans in the mid-19th century.

End of an era Most were long gone by then, however, pushed into the harsher fringes of the continent by the Nguni, who began to arrive around AD500. When the Voortrekkers began to compete—often violently—for the same water sources, many of the remaining San were killed, while some were taken prisoner and turned into servants and farm labourers. Yet others died of epidemic European diseases such as smallpox and even flu, to which they had no immunity. Most mingled with the Khoikhoi, Malays and incoming Nguni, and have slowly been absorbed into the general 'coloured' population. By the early 19th century, their independent lifestyle and tribal identity had all but disappeared. Today, the last few surviving groups skilfully scratch out a meagre existence from the Kalahari sands. There are claimed to be some 60,000 San left across South Africa, Namibia and Botswana, but relatively few are pure blood and living a traditional life.

Top: San paintings are a powerful affirmation of the natural world Below: A dwindling number of San still hunt for their food

Traditional life San huts consist of a domed framework of branches, covered in grass and reeds; in the dry season, when shade is more important than a waterproof covering, partly open shelters are made from reed mats bent over a frame. Always on the move, the San have few material possessions. Both men and women traditionally wear only a small 'skirt' with front and back aprons of animal skin, hung from a beaded belt; these days it is as likely to be a loincloth or a pair of swimming trunks, while the women

San villagers at Kagga Kamma, near Ceres

133

often feel more comfortable in Western dress when strangers are around. Both sexes wear elaborate, beaded headdresses, necklaces, bracelets and anklets. Until the arrival of beads, these decorations would have been made of ostrich eggshell and seeds.

Tortoise shells are used as dishes; with one end filled in and the other corked, they also serve as containers and snuffboxes. Ostrich eggshells and dried springbok pouches are used as water containers, both for rations when on the move and for storage in the long dry season. The San have perfected a technique of skinning the animal without splitting the skin, then simply tying knots in the legs and head hole to make a watertight container.

The men hunt in groups, with bows and poison-tipped arrows, wooden clubs and spears. They also set snares, and track bee eaters in search of their most popular luxury—honey. The gathering, which accounts for most daily food, is done by the women, who search the veld for roots, tubers, berries and fruit. In the dry season, fruit such as melons are a vital source of liquid. Cooking was traditionally done in clay pots, but today the pan may well be an old tin can.

San art Above all, the San are known for their art, which adorns many caves, rocky overhangs, or even particularly smooth slabs of stone, depicting local animals, the thrill of the hunt, or a dance. The painters used natural dyes such as carbon, iron oxide or yellow ochre mixed with blood or animal fat; other pictures are engraved into the surface of the stone. The shapes are alive with movement and obviously executed with love.

*The Augrabies Falls are a
spectacular torrent of
water splitting the
barren desert rock*

Northern Cape

▶▶ Augrabies Falls 124B2

*120km (74 miles) west of Upington (tel: 054-452 9200,
fax: 054-451 5003, www.sanparks.org).*
Open: Apr–Sep 6.30am–10pm; Oct–Mar 6am–10pm
The Khoikhoi called it *Aukoerebis* ('Place of Great Noise')
after the thunder of the Orange River as it crashes down
five flights of granite falls (totalling 60m/192ft) into a
magnificent 18km (11 miles) canyon. They are the fifth-
largest falls in the world, made all the more dramatic-
looking by the massive surrounding boulders and
parched desert landscape. The 3-day Klipspringer Hiking
Trail runs along the canyon through the **Augrabies Falls
National Park**. This is full of weird rock formations and
desert vegetation such as the quiver trees, whose
branches were hollowed by the San to hold their arrows.
There are spectacular views along the rim and activities
such as whitewater rafting (contact Kalahari Adventure
Centre, tel/fax: 054-451 0177,
www.kalahari-adventures.
co.za). The park is a malaria
area, so take precautions.

▶ Colesberg 125D1

*Tourist Information, Murray
Street (tel/fax: 051-753 0678)*
This classic Karoo town
halfway between Cape
Town and Johannesburg
grew up around a water hole
at the foot of the conical
Coleskop, a landmark for
many early visitors. Its first
settlement, a mission, was
forced to close when local
farmers decided its San and
Griqua followers were a
security threat. A white
town (named after Sir Lowry
Cole, Cape governor in
1828–1833), Colesberg was
founded in 1830. Whole
streets of small Karoo block
houses survive, as well as
grander Victorian buildings.
Kemper Museum (Murray
Street. *Open* Mon–Fri 8–1,
2–4.30) is one of the best
small-town collections.

▶▶ Kgalagadi Transfrontier Park 124B4

*358km (222 miles) north of
Upington (tel: 054-561 2000,
www.sanparks.org)*
*Open: daily 6am–6.30pm, but
times vary with season*
This is a vast park up in the
northwest on the borders of

Namibia and Botswana, in the harsh Kalahari Desert. The whole area, more than 3.6 million hectares (8.9 million acres), is one of the world's largest unspoiled ecosystems, set up during the 1930s to protect the magnificent gemsbok from poachers. Much of the park is in Botswana but about a quarter is in South Africa. Access and facilities, including accommodation and fuel, are easily available only from the South African side.

There are just three roads in the whole area, two of them following the river-beds, where the animals tend to cluster around the small amounts of water. The game includes wildebeest, harte-beest and springbok, more than 280 bird species and a superb range of flora, from the creeping desert melons on the Kalahari dunes to fertile woodland and savan-nah, where there is only water enough to sustain life.

There are few or no service stations or shops on the road north from Upington, so remember to bring supplies.

The Eye of God in Kuruman is a real desert oasis

►►► Kimberley see pages 137–139

► Kuruman 125C3

238km (148 miles) northwest of Kimberley
Kalahari Tourism, Main Road, PO Box 1480, Kuruman 8460
(tel: 053-712 1001, www.roaring kalahari.co.za)

Known locally as **Gasegonyana** ('Place of the Little Calabash'), Kuruman is a lush oasis in the dusty Kalahari, built around the Eye of God, a huge spring. Twenty million litres (4.4 million gallons) of water a day gush from the dolomitic rock, never weakening even during the most severe drought. In 1821, Robert Moffat of the London Missionary Society set up a base here, and the little settle-ment was tagged the Fountain of Christianity. Moffat 's daughter married David Livingstone, who used Kuruman as a base from which to explore the hinterland and spread the gospel. Meanwhile, Moffat translated the Bible into Tswana, printing it on his own press. The mission is now a museum, and the church (1838) is still in use.

The **Kalahari Raptor Rehabilitation Centre** (Tsineng Road, tel: 053-712 3576. By appointment only) is a good place to see some of Africa's fiercest birds, and there is a **bird sanctuary** on Hotazel Road. The **Wonderwerk Cave** (40km/25 miles from Kuruman, on the Daniëlskuil Road) was inhabited from 800,000BC to 1914, and contains some fascinating rock art.

TOO HOT FOR COMFORT
Hotazel (61km/38 miles northwest of Kuruman) was named by two young prospectors who stopped here on their travels in 1917. They proclaimed the farm was 'hot as hell' and were so busy recuper-ating that they failed to notice that the land under-neath was almost solid manganese. It turned out to be the richest deposit in the world.

BIGGEST AND BEST

Upington collects statistics. It has the world's longest avenue of date palms (1,041m/0.75 miles), needed in the intense desert heat, and the longest runway in the southern hemisphere (5km/3 miles), used for land speed trials and as a possible emergency landing strip for the space shuttle. The winery is the second largest in the southern hemisphere.

In spring, the whole of Namakwa bursts into bloom

►►► Namakwa 124A2

Springbok is 559km (347 miles) north of Cape Town
Tourist Information, Voortrekker Street, PO Box 56,
Springbok (tel: 027-718 2985/6, fax: 027-712 1421,
www.northerncape.org.za)

The Northwest Cape is semidesert—harsh and dry for most of the year. With an economy based almost entirely on a few scattered copper and diamond mines, it is sparsely populated. The only reasonably sized town is the region's capital, **Springbok**. In spring (mid-Aug to mid-Sep) the area is transformed by millions of colourful daisies, aloes and lilies. The **Goegap Nature Reserve** (15km/9 miles southeast of Springbok, tel: 027-712 1880, fax: 027-718 1286. *Open* daily 8–4) has 581 plant species, 45 species of mammal and 94 bird species. The **Richtersveld Transfrontier Park** (93km/58 miles east of Alexander Bay, tel: 027-831 1506) is fascinating for botanists—half the plants here are rarities. The park is now joined to Namibia's Ai-Ais National Park and border crossings are due to open soon—4WD vehicles are needed for access.

► Upington 124B2

800km (496 miles) west of Kimberley
Tourist Information, Kantor Street (tel/fax: 054-332 6064)
Open: Mon–Fri 8–30, Sat 9–12
Green Kalahari Tourism, Siyanda Municipality Building (tel: 054-337 2804/2855, fax: 054-337 3984, www.greenkalahari. co.za). Open: Mon–Fri 7.30–4.30, Sat 9–11

By local standards Upington is a metropolis, with two interesting monuments. One, at the police station, is to the early Camel Corps; the other, commemorating the donkeys used to open up the area, is by the **Kalahari Orange Museum** (Schröder Street. *Open* Mon–Fri 8–12.30, 1.30–5). Tour the **Orange River Wine Cellars** (tel: 054-337 8800. Tastings: Mon–Fri 8–12, 2–5) or visit the vineyards on **Kanoneiland** (Cannon Island) in the Orange River. Many Koranna (mixed-race Griqua and Tswana) retained their land and still farm in **Keimoes** (Tourist Information, Main Road, tel: 054-461 6400). **Kakamas** (Tourist Information, Municipality, 11th Avenue, tel: 054-431 6300) has a network of waterwheels, canals and irrigation tunnels (1898–1901).

Kimberley

The famous diamond town lies 979km (607 miles) north-east of Cape Town and 485km (301 miles) southwest of Johannesburg. In 1871, the first diamond was discovered at Colesberg Kopje. Prospectors rushed to the area and a tented town sprang up. Originally called New Rush, the village was renamed Kimberley in 1873, after the British secretary of state for the colonies. During the Anglo-Boer War, the town was besieged by the Boers for 124 days. Over 3,000 women and children took shelter in the mine tunnels, while the mine workshops were converted to make ammunition and a huge gun, Long Cecil. The **Honoured Dead Memorial** (Memorial Road), commissioned by Rhodes, has an inscription by Rudyard Kipling and commemorates those who died during the siege. At the base stands Long Cecil. Kimberley is now a city of around 250,000 people, but diamonds are the biggest draw. The mines still produce about 568,000 carats a year.

Kimberley's wealth paid for some beautiful buildings, such as the rococo **City Hall** (1899, Market Square), the **Newton Dutch Reformed church** (1885, Hertzog Square) and the **Kimberley Club** (1882, Du Toitspan Road). Equally imposing are the mansions built by the diamond magnates, such as **Dunluce** (1897, 10 Lodge Road), the **Rudd House** (5–7 Loch Road) and the **Oppenheimer House** (7 Lodge Road). The **Diggers' Fountain** by Herman Wald, in the Oppenheimer Memorial Gardens, shows five miners holding a diamond sieve.

After John Weston made a non-stop flight of 8 minutes, 30 seconds in 1911, the country's first flight school opened in Kimberley. The **Memorial to the Pioneers of Aviation** (General Ken van der Spuy Road, 3.5km/2 miles from the airport; tel: 053-839 2700. *Open* Mon–Sat 9–4.30, Sun 2–5.30. *Admission: inexpensive*) consists of a monument, a reconstruction hangar and a replica Compton Paterson biplane.

An extraordinarily dainty town hall graces the heart of rough, tough Kimberley

BASICS

Tourist Information: Diamantveld Visitor Centre, 121 Bultfontein Road, PO Box 1976, Kimberley (tel: 053-832 7298, fax: 053-832 7211, email: francois.basson@fbdm.co. za, www.kimberley.co.za). *Open* Mon–Fri 8–5, Sat 8.30–11.30. For guided half- or full-day tours featuring Cecil John Rhodes, historical Kimberley, diamonds, SA Battlefields, townships and local ghosts, contact Steve's Tours, PO Box 3017, Kimberley 8300 (tel/fax: 083-732 3189, email: stevestours@ kimberley.co.za).

CECIL JOHN RHODES

Rhodes (1853–1902) came to South Africa in 1870 for his health. In 1871, he headed for the Kimberley diamond fields. By 1888, he had formed the De Beers Mining Company and controlled 90 per cent of the world's diamond production. He made a second fortune from the Transvaal gold-fields and, in 1889, founded the British South Africa Company (BSAC). In 1890, he became prime minister of Cape Colony, while the BSAC colonized Rhodesia (now Zimbabwe and Zambia). He died in Muizenberg, near Cape Town, but is buried in the Matobo Hills, Zimbabwe. Part of his fortune still funds the Rhodes Scholarships to Oxford University.

▶▶▶ The Big Hole and Kimberley Mine Museum   125C2

Tucker Street (tel: 053-833 1557)
Open: daily 8–6. Admission: moderate

The hole really is big, the largest man-made excavation in the world, with a circumference of 1.6km (1 mile) and a surface area of 13.38ha (33 acres). It is now part of an open-air museum that vividly re-creates old Kimberley, with over 40 carefully restored buildings, from homes and dealers' offices to stores, a church and Barnato's Boxing Gym. All are furnished in period style, with photos and plentiful explanation. A diamond exhibition hall has replicas of some of the world's most famous diamonds, plus about 2,000 gleaming carats of the real thing, including the cut and polished Eureka diamond (see page 140).

A trolley runs from the City Hall to the museum, the last vestiges of a route that began as a mule-drawn service in 1887. Near the main entrance, the **Jewel Box** has demonstrations of diamond polishing and goldsmithing, while the 19th-century-themed **Star of the West** pub is one of the busiest drinking spots in the city.

▶▶ Bultfontein Mine   125D2

Molyneux Road, Kimberley (tel: 053-842 1321)
Surface tours: Mon–Fri, 9 and 11 (no children under 8 years); underground tours: Mon–Fri by appointment, minimum age 16. Advance bookings essential. Admission: moderate

The first diamonds discovered here in 1869 were actually in the mud walls of the Bultfontein farmhouse, which was destroyed in the attempt to find more. Today there is a large hole where the house once stood. Bultfontein Mine, owned by De Beers, is still operational. To see high-tech diamond mining, take the daily surface and underground tours.

▶ The Duggan-Cronin Gallery   125D2

Egerton Road, Kimberley (tel: 053-839 2700)
Open: Mon–Fri 9–5, Sat 9–1, 2–5, Sun 2–5
Admission: donation

A. M. Duggan-Cronin was an avid photographer and recorder of 'native' life in South Africa at the turn of the 20th century, and the collection includes many photos that are fascinating, if rather dubious—it is rumoured that he carried a leopard skin on his journeys for people to wear when posing.

▶ The McGregor Museum   125D2

Atlas and Chapel streets, Kimberley (tel: 053-839 2700)
Open: Mon–Sat 9–5, Sun 2–5, public holidays 10–5
Admission: donation

Built as a sanatorium, this became a luxury hotel, and Cecil Rhodes lived and worked here during the Boer siege. Today it is a museum of Kimberley history and the ecology of the Northern Cape, with a fine collection of 19th-century furniture. The **Alexander McGregor Memorial Museum** (Chapel Street, tel: 053-842 0099. *Open* Mon–Fri 9–5. *Admission: donation*), a satellite of the main McGregor Museum, contains displays about geology worldwide and the history of the Northern Cape, as well as a small costume collection.

The Star of the West is one of the oldest pubs in South Africa

▶ Magersfontein Battlefield 125D2

32km (20 miles) from Kimberley, on the Modder River road
(tel: 053-833 7115)
Open: daily 8–3 by appointment only with guide from the
McGregor Museum. Admission: moderate
On 11 December 1899, in an effort to break the siege of
Kimberley, 12,500 British soldiers led by Lord Methuen
attacked a well-entrenched Boer force of 8,200 under
General Cronje. The battle lasted 10 days, leaving 239
Britons and 87 Boers dead. It was one of the worst British
defeats in the Anglo-Boer War. A small museum at the
site contains uniforms, weapons, documents and photos.

▶ The William Humphreys Art Gallery 125D2

Jan Smuts Boulevard (tel: 053-831 1724/5)
Open: Mon–Fri 8–4.45, Sat 10–4.45, Sun 2–2.45
Admission: inexpensive
Founded around a personal collection of 16th- and
17th-century Dutch and Flemish masters and British
and French paintings belonging to former Member of
Parliament William Benbow Humphreys (1889–1965),
this gallery is one of the best in South Africa. In addition
to the international collection, it has an innovative selection of South African art by both black and white artists.

THE BIG HOLE
Diamonds produced:
14,504,566 carats
(2,722kg/5,988lb).
Ground excavated:
25,000 tonnes.
Depth of hole: 215m
(705ft).
Depth from surface to
water: 174m (571ft).
Depth of water: 41m
(135ft).
Original depth of open
cast working: 240m
(787ft).
Original depth of
underground working:
1,097m (3,598ft).

*The aptly named Big
Hole in Kimberley was
one of the world's richest
sources of diamonds*

139

The story goes that in 1866 young Erasmus Jacobs was playing on his father's farm, near Hopetown, when he picked up a pretty pebble. A neighbour, Schalk van Niekerk, offered to buy the stone; thinking it worthless, the family gave it to him. Erasmus' plaything turned out to be the 21.25-carat 'Eureka' diamond, the trigger for the Kimberley diamond rush.

'Of course I thought when once on the field,
Every load of stone would yield,
But, I owned, after many a weary day,
That gravel is gravel, and clay is clay.'
Longlands, 1908

140

Early days In 1869, Schalk van Niekerk bartered with a Griqua shepherd for a second, larger stone, later named the 'Star of South Africa'. weighing 83.5 carats. Diamonds were also found on two other farms, Bultfontein and Dorstfontein (now known as Du Toitspan), about 40km (25 miles) south of the Vaal River. By 1871, diggings had also been opened up on the De Beers farm, Vooruitzicht and Colesberg Kopje. It was this small, rocky hill that was eventually to turn into the Kimberley Big Hole. Some 50,000 people streamed into the area from across the globe, living in tents and flimsy houses of wood and galvanized iron. There were not even the most basic facilities such as drains. Disease was rife in the hot summer months, and the diggers had to pay up to 2.5 cents for one bucket of muddy water or 10 cents for a loaf of bread. By the mid-1880s, the hills were flattened and the diggings began to hollow out the land. At 15–18m (50–60ft) down, the last of the yellow oxidized earth began to run out. Disappointed diggers were preparing to move out when, to their aston-ished delight, someone discovered that the harder blue rock beneath (now named kimberlite) was even richer in gems. They had tapped into the volcanic pipe in which the diamonds had been born, in the middle of the earth.

Above top: Production line in the De Beers diamond-sorting sheds (1900)
Above: Aerial ropeways at Kimberley

Seeking a fortune The biggest problem was the owner-ship of the diamond fields. The whole area was known as Griqualand West and claimed by the Khoikhoi Griqua people, who had lived there for 70 years. It was also on the frontier, and the governments of the Orange Free State, the South African Republic and the Cape Colony all claimed so rich a prize. In 1880, the British simply annexed it and dared the others to complain.

There was also the problem of individual claims. Each new rumour led to a frantic rush to stake claims and obtain licences. Early maps are a patchwork of tiny squares of land—eventually there were some 1,600 individual properties, each only 10m by 10m (about 30ft by 30ft), in the Big Hole alone. As they dug farther into the earth, the dividing walls collapsed. There were often brutal fights over who owned the resulting heap of earth—and it became ever harder for prospectors to reach their workings or get the gravel out of the pits. Enterprising businessmen set up pulley systems that covered the diggings like a cobweb. They used the fortunes they made to buy up small claims. Kimberley came to be dominated by a handful of key players such as Cecil Rhodes, Charles Rudd and Barney Barnato, who worked together in an increasingly powerful cartel, eventually merging to become De Beers Consolidated Mines. Today, under the Oppenheimers, De Beers still controls much of the world's diamond market, although South Africa's ranking has slipped to fifth.

❏ **Sparklers** There are six common shapes for cut and polished diamonds. The round brilliant, oval marquise, emerald cut and pear-shaped each have 58 facets; the oblong baguette has 25; and the square cut 30. The normal colour range is from white to dark yellow, but defects in the crystal lattice can produce unusual colours. Known as 'fancies', these are more expensive still. ❏

THE BIG ONE
The largest uncut diamond in the world is the 616, found at Kimberley in 1974 at Du Toitspan Mine by Abel Maratela. It was named after its carat weight, which happened to coincide with the De Beers' box number.

Below: the Cullinan diamond—530.2 carats

Left: Rough diamonds in many shapes and colours
Below: De Beers' newest major mine—Venetia, Transvaal

Diamond drive
(see map pages 124–125)

Kimberley is the heart of South Africa's diamond trade, but many other places in the neighbourhood have commercial mines, and diggers elsewhere still scratch at the river-banks under a blazing sun amid ochre sands and camelthorn trees. Allow 1 to 2 days for this tour.

Leave Kimberley on the R31 toward Barkly West. After 24km (15 miles),

There are many small diamond-digging operations, such as these near Barkly West, northwest of Kimberley

turn right to Nooitgedacht and follow the dirt road for 8km (5 miles). Here pavements of 2,500-million-year-old Ventersdorp lava were polished by glaciers 250 million years ago, then covered in engravings by the San.

Return to the main road and continue for 8km (5 miles) to **Barkly West** (Tourist Information, tel: 053-531 0673). Once known as Klipdrift, this is the site of the Northern Cape's first diamond rush to Canteen Kopje in 1869. A cairn marks the spot. In 1870, the Klipdrift diggers declared independence from the Transvaal, only to be annexed by Britain in 1871. Two years later the name was changed in honour of the governor, Sir Henry Barkly. There are mementoes of the Diamond Rush in St. Mary's church (1871). Numerous small diggings line the Vaal River in nearby Windsorton (take the R374 north for 33km/20 miles). Return to Barkly

West and continue west along the R31 through the old diamond diggings at Sydney-on-Vaal (27km/17 miles farther on). Nearby is the **Vaalbos National Park** (tel: 053-561 0088, www.sanparks.co.za. *Open* daily dawn–dusk. *Admission: moderate*), with buffalo and both black and white rhino. From here, keep going along the R31 for 96km (60 miles) to **Daniëlskuil**—literally 'Daniel's Den' (Tourist Information, Barker Street, tel: 053-384 0326). Mining began here in 1960, when a group of hopefuls found 26 diamonds in the first two hours.

Take the R31 south for 10km (6 miles), then turn west on the R385 for 49km (30 miles) to **Postmasburg** (Tourist Information, tel: 053-313 0343). Founded in 1892 as a trading base, Postmasburg discovered wealth in a meerkat burrow in 1918. The huge kimberlite pipe turned into a Big Hole (surface area of 1.4sq km/1sq-mile and depth of about 45m/148ft) that was worked until 1935. It is now filled with water and stocked with fish. You can still visit the West End Diamond Mine and ancient mine workings in the Gatkoppies (by appointment only). Around AD700, the Khoikhoi were mining a glittering black iron oxide called specularite here, which they used for personal adornment.

Head north to **Olifantshoek** (Tourist Information, tel: 053-331 0002) on the R385 (54km/33 miles) or via the N14 and the R386 (71km/44 miles, but a better road). The little town is named after the elephant whose tusks paid for the ground on which it stands. This is the gateway to the **Roaring Sands**. When disturbed air rushes through these 100m (328ft) high sand dunes, it produces curiously human moans. Below the surface is pure, sweet water.

From Olifantshoek, you can take the N14 west for 167km (104 miles) to Upington (see page 136), set amid near desert or east for 100km (62 miles) to Kuruman (see page 135), where you can stay at the marvellous

Tswalu Private Desert Reserve (see page 261). Alternatively, return to Postmasburg and head south to **Griquatown** on the R386 (96km/60 miles; Tourist Information, 6 Moffat Street, tel: 053-343 0019). Once 'capital' of Griqualand (see page 124), this small settlement under the Asbesberge (Asbestos Mountains) was a mission station, founded by the London Missionary Society. The old mission house, birthplace of David Livingstone's wife, Mary Moffat, is now the **Mary Moffat Museum** (Voortrekker Street, tel: 053-343 0180. *Open* Mon–Fri 8–1, 2–5), where curator Hetta Hager knows all there is to know, and will happily tell. Griquatown is also famous for gemstones, including jasper and tiger's eye, a semiprecious stone so common here that the British Stone

Mary Moffat, missionary and wife of David Livingstone

Fort on Prieska Koppie (80km/50 miles south) is built of it. For more, visit the **Earth Treasures** (6 Moffat Street, tel: 053-343 0121. *Open* Mon–Fri 8–4). Take the R64 back for 158km (98 miles) to return to Kimberley.

North-West Province

▶▶ Madikwe Game Reserve 125D4

90km (56 miles) north of Zeerust, off the R47 to Gaborone).
PO Box 4488, Mmabatho 2735 (tel: 083-629 8282,
www.parksnorthwest.co.za).
Admission: moderate; closed to day visitors
Created in 1991 with the translocation of over 8,000 animals, Madikwe is South Africa's fourth-largest reserve, covering about 64,000ha (158,080 acres) along the Botswana border. It offers wonderful 'big five' game-viewing, 350 species of birds, and rarities such as black and white rhino, cheetah, brown hyena and wild dog. The park is not open to self-drive visitors, but game drives in open vehicles and guided walks are available through its five classy lodges.

▶ Mafikeng and Mmabatho 125D3

Tourist Information, Lichtenburg Road
(www.mafikeng.co.za, also
www.tourismnorthwest.co.za).
Open: Mon–Fri 8–6, Sat 8.30–12
The small town now called Mafikeng ('Place of Stones') was known as Mafeking under the British Protectorate in Victorian times.
Much lauded as an example of British courage at its best, Mafeking was besieged by the Boers in 1899, a few days after the outbreak of the Anglo-Boer War. British commander, Colonel Robert Baden-Powell (founder of the Boy Scout movement), held out for 271 days before relief arrived, an event rapturously celebrated in London. The fort on Cannon Koppie has been restored, and the **Mafikeng Museum** (Old Town Hall, tel: 018-381 6102. *Open* Mon–Fri 8–4, Sat 10–12.30. *Admission: free*) outlines the history of the area and all its people, and arranges tours to nearby historic sites.

In 1977, Mmabatho, which was built on the outskirts of Mafikeng, became capital of the Tswana homeland of Bophuthatswana, a fragmented 'state' with 17 different parcels of land scattered through white South Africa. Mafikeng was incorporated into its former satellite in 1980. The **Botsalano Game Reserve** (30km/19 miles north of Mmabatho, tel: 018-386 2433. *Open* daily 6–6) has a variety of game, with a successful white rhino-breeding project.

▶▶ Pilanesberg National Park 125D4

23km (14 miles) from Sun City (tel: 014-555 5354-7, fax: 014-555 5525, www.parksnorthwest.co.za). Open: daily 6–6; times vary with season. Admission: expensive
Pilanesberg sprawls around an extinct volcanic crater next to Sun City. The terrain is dry bushveld and Kalahari thornveld, with wooded ravines and grassy plains. Several farms were taken over in the 1970s. The translocation project Operation Genesis then restocked the park with over 7,000 animals, including the 'big five'. There are also 354 bird species, walk-in aviaries, self-guided

Baden-Powell refusing to surrender Mafeking

RELIEF
The over-embellished stories of the siege of Mafeking tapped a vein of heroic imperialism but had little to do with reality. Baden-Powell loved every minute, exaggerating the number of Boers from 5,000 in 1899, to 12,000 in 1937. Throughout the siege he made a marked distinction, in all matters, between white and black: Healthy rations for the 2,000 whites were denied to the 5,000 Africans. Baden-Powell advised that 'the toe of the boot' be applied to disapproving 'grousers'.

walking trails around the Education Centre and Manyane Camp (and information centre), hides near several dams, over 200km (125 miles) of gravel roads for game viewing, and hot-air balloon flights over the park.

▶▶▶ Sun City 125D4

About 187km (116 miles) northwest of Johannesburg, 41km (25 miles) from Rustenburg (tel: Sun City, 011-780 7800; Welcome Centre, 014-557 1544, www.suninternational.com). Open: daily 24 hours, day permits at the gate. Admission: expensive

This is a place to spend money—you could easily lose your shirt in the 24-hour casino. To do it in style, stay at the superbly kitsch Palace of the Lost City, the nearest thing in South Africa to Las Vegas. Re-creating Rider Haggard's 1885 novel *King Solomon's Mines*, Sun City is like a film set; attractions include the Valley of the Waves; the 'volcanic' Bridge of Time, which erupts every hour; and an extravaganza of showgirls. Family features include Kamp Kwena for 4- to 12-year-olds, a petting zoo and National Birds of Prey Centre. The Adventure Centre offers quad-biking, clay pigeon and target shooting and archery. There's also a host of sports, including two of the best golf courses in Africa (with live crocodiles in the water hazard at the 13th). It could be ghastly, but it isn't—the Palace is splendid, the other hotels comfortable, the food good and the weather (usually) sunny. Sun International answers critics' condemnation of this extravagance amid desperate poverty by financing local schools, clinics and housing.

Inland seas and brand new ancient ruins are just some of Sun City's attractions

BUILDING TO EXCESS
The Palace of the Lost City complex cost R800 million and took 5,000 workers 19 months to build. Experts handcrafted the finishing touches, including the massive painted dome. The mosaic in the Crystal Court is made from 30 different semiprecious stones, such as jasper, malachite and amethyst.

Gauteng

Johannesburg from the Carlton Panorama

TOURIST INFORMATION
Gauteng Tourism Centre, Shop 401, Upper Level, The Rosebank Mall, Baker Street, Rosebank 2196, PO Box 2200, Saxonwold 2132 (tel: 011-327 2000/ 9000, fax: 011-327 7000, www.gauteng.net/ www.joburg.org.za). *Open* Mon–Fri 8.30–6, Sat 9–1, Sun 10–3.
Pretoria (Tshwane) Tourism, Old Nederlandsche Bank Building, Church Square West (tel: 012-358 1430, fax: 012-358 1485, www.tshwane.gov.za). *Open* Mon–Fri 8–4, Sat 9–1.

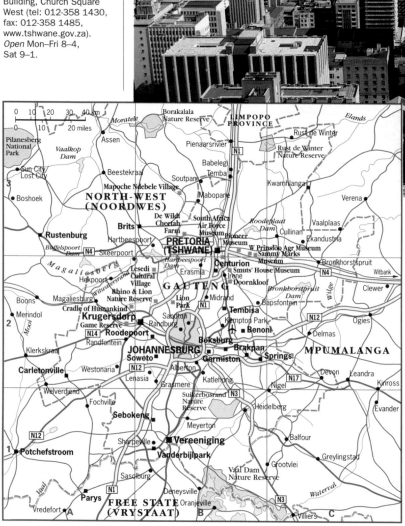

BUILT ON GOLD Gauteng means 'place of gold' in Sotho, and so does Egoli, the Zulu name for Johannesburg. A theme begins to emerge—for this is a region built, quite literally, on gold. Gauteng is a small region in central South Africa, once known as the PWV (Pretoria Witwatersrand Vereeniging). Pretoria, now renamed Tshwane, is the administrative capital of South Africa, populated almost entirely by civil servants. Vereeniging and the surrounding area, which includes the notorious township of Sharpeville (see page 43) is predominantly industrial. Between these areas is the Witwatersrand (Ridge of White Water), one of the country's main watersheds, under which lie unimaginably large reserves of gold, carbon, uranium, green diamonds, iron pyrites (fool's gold), chromite, silver and platinum.

Above these reserves tower the skyscrapers of Johannesburg, the social and economic powerhouse of the whole African continent. And beside that is Soweto, the political heart of black South Africa and now one of the largest cities in the country. The province, geographically the smallest in South Africa, has 20 per cent of South Africa's population; generates 35 per cent of the country's gross domestic product; accounts for 60 per cent of its fiscal revenue; contains about 30 per cent of the world's known gold reserves; and accounts for a staggering 28 per cent of the GDP of sub-Saharan Africa.

▶▶▶ REGION HIGHLIGHTS

Apartheid Museum
page 148

Diamond Cutting
page 151

Gold Reef City *page 152*

Johannesburg Art Gallery
pages 152–153

MuseuMAfrica
pages 154

Soweto *pages 158–159*

Union Buildings
pages 166–167

Voortrekker Monument and Museum *page 167*

Walk: Central Pretoria
pages 168–169

Willem Prinsloo Agricultural Museum
page 171

Johannesburg

In 1886, an Australian prospector named George Harrison found the first gold on the Witwatersrand at Langlaagte Farm; Johannes Joubert was sent north to investigate. Hot on his heels came the surveyor-general, Johannes Rissik, who had the responsibility of choosing a site for the new mining village that would inevitably appear. The fledgling town of Johannesburg, now known irreverently to locals as 'the Big Naartjie' (tangerine), derived its name from these two men.

Gold has always been the pulse of this boomtown. From the air, the headgear of working mines and the tell-tale yellow mounds are clearly visible. In fact, with modern techniques to help, original dumps are being remined to extract the many trace minerals left behind by the early prospectors. The city centre, built over exhausted tunnels, is steadily expanding upwards and outwards. In little over a century, it has grown into a massive conurbation covering 508sq km (200sq miles), with more than 600 parks and 260,000 trees lining its streets. There are now fewer than 40km (25 miles) between northern Johannesburg and southern Pretoria (Tshwane) and with several smaller settlements in between, it seems likely that Gauteng is destined to become one giant city.

Rosebank Mall shopping centre in Johannesburg

Johannesburg, (aka 'Joburg' or 'Jozi', is exciting, and energetic, with bubbling street life and plenty of excellent restaurants, theatres and other entertainment. To date, this is one of only a few cities in South Africa where the black Africans have moved into the central area; the whites have moved out en masse to wealthy northern suburbs such as Sandton. Crime has begun to drop and the city is certainly safer than it was, but you must still be extremely careful, take local advice and do not walk around on your own, particularly at night.

▶▶▶ Apartheid Museum · · · · · · · · · · · · 149B1

Opposite Gold Reef City, corner Norther Parkway and Gold Reef Road, Ormonde (tel: 011-309 4700, www.apartheidmuseum.org)
Open: Tue–Sun 10–5. Admission: moderate

This sombre museum is not an easy place to visit, however it should be an essential stop on all tours of South Africa. Using text, reminiscences, photos and archive film including interviews with both the architects of apartheid and its downfall, it tells the story of apartheid from its earliest beginnings in the 19th century goldfields to its official creation in 1948 and the final victory of equality in 1994. It is a welcome sign of real hope to come out of the museum and see a multiracial bunch of schoolchildren camped out in the forecourt, laughing together as they eat their sandwiches.

Greater Johannesburg is expanding rapidly as the rich move into closely guarded northern suburbs

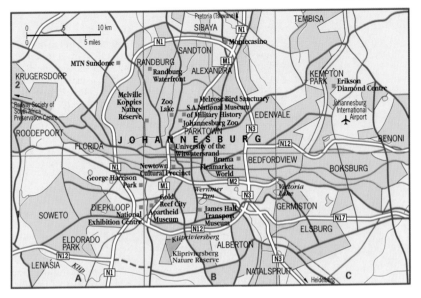

▶ Bruma Fleamarket World

149B1

Ernest Oppenheimer Drive, off Marcia and Allum roads,
near Eastgate Shopping Centre (tel: 011-622 9648)
Open: Tue–Fri 9.30–5, Sat 8.30–5, Sun 9.30–5
Admission: inexpensive

Billed as the world's only flea-market theme park, Bruma is the single largest tourist attraction in Gauteng, with 2.5 million visitors a year. It has over 300 stalls during the week, more than 600 at weekends and 15 restaurants. There are plenty of excellent souvenirs and around-the-clock entertainment, from South African tribal dancers to Tanzanian acrobats.

Sandton shopping mall has some of the most exclusive and expensive stores in Africa

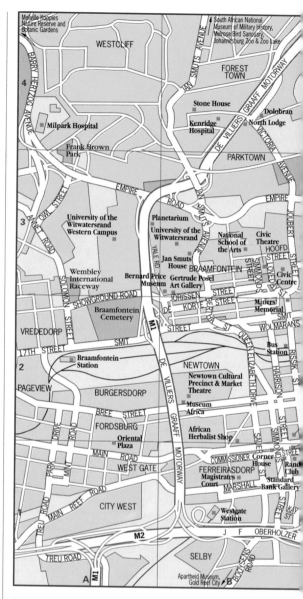

TOURING GAUTENG
These days most local tour operators offer a range of services such as city tours of Johnnesburg and Pretoria; tours of the surrounding area, including Soweto (scheduled and personalized); and airport transfers. Among the best options are **Kwathlano Tours** (tel: 012-343 2200, www.kwathlano.co.za), **Jimmy's Face to Face Tours** (tel: 011-331 6109, www.face2face.co.za), and **Gold Reef Guiding Services** (tel:011-496 1400, www.goldreef guides.co.za) who can offer tours in all major languages, locally and throughout South Africa. To tour a working gold mine (tel: 011-498 7100); advance reservations are essential.

▶▶ Constitution Hill   *151C3*

Corner Kotze Street and Hospital Street, Braamfontein
(tel: 011-274 5300, www.constitutionhill.org.za))
Open: daily 9–7. Admission: moderate; free entry Tue
South Africa's new Constitutional Court, the highest in the land and guardian of basic human rights and freedoms has risen from the blood-stained bricks of the old Johannesburg prison, set in the gounds of an early fort. Many of the leaders of the struggle against apartheid were imprisoned here, from Steve Biko to Nelson and Winnie Mandela. The fort and some elements have been left as a museum. Allow up to two hours for the full tour.

The map shows streets and landmarks of Johannesburg including:

HOUGHTON ESTATE

The Wilds

Johannesburg Hospital

Adler Museum of the History of Medicine

Johannesburg College of Education

HOUGHTON DRIVE

ST ANDREW ROAD

LOUIS

BOTHA AVENUE

Mitchell Park

RALEIGH ROAD

HARROW ROAD

HUNTER ST

ROCKEY ST

Yeoville Square

BEREA

YEOVILLE

CAVENDISH

BEZUIDENHOUT STREET

Pieter Roos Park

BRUCE ST

CLAREDON PLACE

TWIST STREET

BANKET STREET

CLAIM STREET

ABEL ROAD

HARLEY STREET

HIGHLANDS

HILLBROW

PRETORIA STREET

OTZE

Hillbrow Hospital

Mervyn King Ridge Trail

Pullingerkop

BEREA ROAD

GORDON RD

CHARLTON TERRACE

Constitution Hill

Andre Huguenot Theatre

Windybrow Theatre

SARATOGA AVENUE

Witwatersrand Technikon

Alhambra Theatre

Fuller Park

BERTRAMS ROAD

DOORNFONTEIN

Jo'burg Central Station

King George

Joubert Park

Johannesburg Art Gallery

Doornfontein Station

NEW DOORNFONTEIN

Bruma Fleamarket World

Ellis Park

SIEMERT ROAD

VAN WRIGHT AVENUE

St Mary's Cathedral

Union Grounds

CLAIM

TWIST ST

Ellis Park Station

Ellis Park Sports Stadium

VON WIELLIG

PRITCHARD ST

BEZUIDENHOUT

BREE STREET

JEPPE STREET

City Hall

Supreme Court

MARKET STREET

CITY AND SUBURBAN

COMMISSIONER STREET

Jeppe Station

JOHN PAGE DRIVE

GPO

First National Bank Museum

Carlton Centre and Panorama

Mynhardts

MARSHALL STREET

PARK STREET

ANDERSON STREET

ELOFF STREET

ROSETTENVILLE ROAD

MARSHALLTOWN

MOTORWAY M2

ELOFF EXTENSION

WEMMER

James Hall Transport Museum & Wemmer Pan

HEIDELBERG ROAD

0 400 800 m

0 400 800 yards

'An extended brickfield is the first impression: a prosperous powder-factory is the last...'
—John Buchan on Johannesburg, *The African Colony* (1903)

151

A mini Manhattan—Johannesburg at night

▶ Diamond cutting   151D1

Erikson's Diamond Centre, 20 Monument Road, Kempton Park (tel: 011-970 1355, www.eriksons.co.za). Open: Mon–Fri 8–5, Sat 8–1

Although the diamond mines themselves are elsewhere, Johannesburg is South Africa's major market and polishing centre. On a tour of a diamond cutting and polishing workshop you can learn how to turn a dull pebble into a real gem—how to pick out the quality, decide on the cut, polish, and even set the stones. There is also, inevitably, a shop. The centre also contains a moving tribute to Nelson Mandela, in exhibits at the **Madiba Freedom Museum**.

EARLY JOHANNESBURG

A few key historic buildings have survived the rush to build shiny modern skyscrapers. The 1907 Standard Bank (5 Simmonds Street) is part stone, part brick, steel-framed with a Renaissance exterior. There are visits to the old store and art gallery. The Corner House (corner of Commissioner and Simmonds streets), South Africa's original skyscraper (1903), is a curious blend of Classical and art nouveau styles. Other notable buildings include the General Post Office; City Hall (corner of Market, Rissik, President and Harrison streets), which is now the Gauteng provincial parliament; the 1930s Johannesburg Public Library (Market Square); and the 1904 Rand Club (corner of Loveday, Commissioner and Fox streets; visits by arrangement).

The Gold Reef City dancers are a top attraction

▶▶▶ Gold Reef City 149B1

Off Xavier Road (off M1), 8km (5 miles) south of the city (tel: 011-248 6800, www.goldreefcity.co.za).
Open: Daily 9.30–5. Dance shows Mon–Fri 11.30, 3, Sat–Sun 11, 2.30, 3.30. Admission: expensive

A combination of open-air museum and theme park with a mix of ersatz and real entertainments, Gold Reef City is built around a famous gold mine (No. 14 Shaft of the Crown Mines), and reconstructs the pioneering days of Johannesburg during the gold-rush era. You can watch demonstrations of pouring liquid gold into bullion, or take the elevator 220m (722ft) down the shaft into what was once the richest gold mine in the world (with a pub at the bottom). Thirty thousand men toiled in unbearable conditions below the earth's surface to produce about 1,400 tonnes of gold during its working life.

Above ground are several reconstructed Victorian streets with pubs, a hotel, restaurants, old-fashioned apothecary's shop, Chinese laundry, tailor, newspaper office, bank, brewery and early stock exchange. There are many live demonstrations, a number of fairly tame fairground rides and a Victorian amusement park, souvenir shops and plenty of places to eat and drink; you can also ride a miniature railway around the edge of the park.

Can-can dancers and the Gold Reef City International Dancers perform both traditional and gumboot dances (developed because of the miners' heavy protective footwear). Additional attractions include white-knuckle rides and a massive casino and entertainment complex.

▶▶ Johannesburg Art Gallery 151C2

Klein Street, Joubert Park (tel: 011-725 3130)
Open: Tue–Sun 10–5. Admission: free

In 1904, Lady Phillips, wife of Randlord Sir Lionel Phillips, went to London and sold a 21.5 carat diamond ring, returning home with three paintings by Wilson Steer. She spent the next five years wringing money out of wealthy friends such as Max Michaelis, Otto Beit, Abe Bailey, Julius Wernher and Frederick Eckstein to found an art gallery. Sir Edwin Lutyens (1869–1944) was commissioned to design the imposing Classical gallery, opened in 1915. Further sections were added in 1940 and 1984.

The gallery has three distinct collections. The first is European, with works by masters such as El Greco, Picasso and Rodin alongside the inevitable minor Flemish portraits. The second includes works by many of South Africa's finest artists, such as Jackson Hlungwane, J. H. Pierneef, Irma Stern and William Kentridge. Finally, the gallery now houses the somewhat eccentric Brenthurst Collection of African Art, which comprises curios originally taken back to Europe by 19th-century missionaries, explorers and scientists; most exhibits are of Nguni, Sotho or East African origin. The complex has excellent gift and coffee shops.

▶ Johannesburg Zoo and Zoo Lake 151C2

Hermann Eckstein Park, Jan Smuts Avenue, Parktown (tel: 011-646 2000, www.jhbzoo.org.za)
Open: daily 8.30–5.30, last entry 4. Admission: moderate
Zoo Lake (tel: 011-646 8807); open access (restaurant and café closed Mon). Admission: free

It may be nothing like seeing animals in the wild, but Johannesburg Zoo is a good second-best. Surrounded by impeccable gardens, the 55ha (136-acre) zoo is home to around 300 animal species, most of which are in danger of extinction. It is also a base for conservation, scientific research and education and has a good road train and fairground rides. Across the street, Zoo Lake is a popular spot for picnics.

Below: Johannesburg Zoo provides protection for endangered animals

Minor museums

The **Standard Bank Gallery** (5 Simmonds Street, tel: 011-636 4231. *Open* Mon–Fri 8–4.30, Sat 9–1) has changing exhibitions featuring the modern South African art and photography. Home of the world's largest corporate art collection, the **Absa Gallery**, (160 Main Street, Ground Floor, Absa Towers North, tel: 011-350 5130. *Open* Mon–Fri 9.30–3.30) holds changing exhibitions of up-and-coming artists. The **James Hall Transport Museum** (Rosettenville Road, La Rochelle, tel: 011-435 9485. *Open* Tue–Sun 9–5. *Admission: donations*) displays the history of land transport in South Africa. The **African Herbalist Shop** (14 Diagonal Street, Newtown. *Open* Mon–Sat 7.30–5) is a working shop, dispensing traditional African remedies, but it also runs guided tours.

The Art Gallery is a key facet of city life

GREEN SPACES

Johannesburg is one of the greenest cities in the world, with huge, shady trees lining every suburban street. It also has some magnificent parks.

Among the finest are the **Johannesburg Botanical Garden**, Thomas Bowler Street, Roosevelt Park (tel: 011-782 0517), which has the largest rose garden in the world; and the **Walter Sisulu National Botanical Gardens**, Malcolm Street, Poortview, Roodepoort (tel: 011-958 1750). *Open* daily 8–5. Guided tours can be arranged for groups. In the **George Harrison Park**, 5km (3 miles) west of the city on Main Reef Road, you can see the exterior of crumbling scaffolding of an old mine, a rock showing fool's gold and an old stamp mill. The site became a national monument in 1947.

MuseuMAfrica is a magnificent celebration of Johannesburg, past and present

► Montecasino   149B2

Fourways Junction, William Nicol Drive and Witkoppen Road (tel: 011-510 7000/7777). Hourly shuttle bus service from selected Sandton hotels (tel: 011-327 3030)

This entertainment complex, built as an imitation Tuscan village, has everything you need under one roof. Shops and restaurants line its cobbled streets, and there are trees, a pond with ducks and even washing hanging out. One area is under a night sky with stars, while others are under a blue or sunset sky. The complex also includes a casino, cinemas, theatre, health and beauty spa and luxury hotel. In addition, **The Bird Gardens** (tel: 011-511 1864. *Open* Tue–Sunday 8–6.; bird shows Mon–Fri 11 and 3, Sat–Sun 11, 1 and 3. *Admission: expensive*) house more than 12,000 birds and around 1,500 animals from around the world. There are three other huge casino and entertainment complexes in the Johannesburg area: **Gold Reef City** (see page 152); **Caesar's Gauteng**, (64 Jones Road, Kempton Park, tel: 011-928 1000, www.caesers.co.za; and **Carnival City** (corner Century and Elsburg roads, Brakpan, tel: 011-898 7000, www.suninternational.com).

►► MuseuMAfrica   150B2

121 Breë Street (tel: 011-833 5624)
Open: Tue–Sun 9–5. Admission: moderate

Several older, smaller museums scattered across the city have been closed, and their collections gathered under one roof to create one of the finest and most imaginative museums in South Africa. MuseuMAfrica is housed in an old market warehouse in the recently revived Newtown Cultural Precinct. The aim is to tell the true, multicultural story of South Africa, from Big Bang to the present.

The **Museum of South African Rock Art** contains not only a magnificent collection of original San paintings, but some of the clearest explanations on record of how these powerful works were created. The **Johannesburg Transformations** section concentrates on a few key aspects of the city's history, from local prehistoric settlements onwards. There is a special exhibition on gold, but more powerful are three interlinked sections describing township music, the growth of the townships and squatter camps, and South African politics over the last 40 to 50 years.

Beyond these are two traditional displays. The original **Africana Museum** collection, founded in 1934, includes a huge array of paintings, documents, photos, traditional African art and costumes, from the Cape to the Zambezi. The **Bensusan Museum of Photography** contains hundreds of cameras spanning the period from the magic lantern to digital imaging and CD-ROM. Photographs include everything from pioneering classics by Englishman William Henry Fox Talbot to a powerful local exhibition of South African life. Finally, the **Geological Museum** has fabulous crystals and rocks There are also changing exhibitions, workshops and activities from music and dance to storytelling.

▶▶ Newtown Cultural Precinct 150B2

Breë Street (tel: 011-832 1641).

The old fruit and spice market buildings of Newtown have been given a new lease of life, as the city's bohemian quarter, centred on the MuseuMAfrica complex and the **Market Theatre** (tel: 011-832 1641), itself once a market hall, built in 1911 with an impressive Beaux Arts façade. The theatre became renowned internationally for its courageous stand during the apartheid era; many of its powerful dramas, black and white, were openly critical of the government. The surrounding precinct has a total of four theatres, an art gallery, numerous fascinating shops including the shiny new Metro mall and the **National Design and Crafrt Centre** (in the historic Bus Factory. *Open* Tue–Fri 9–5, Sat–Sun 10–2), places to eat and drink, and a buzzing Saturday market. There are performance spaces in the Newtown Music Centre, the Dance Factory and open-air **Mary Fitzgerald Square**. It is connected to Braamfontein by the spectacular **Nelson Mandela Bridge**.

The **SAB World of Beer** (corner of President and Becker streets, tel: 011-836 4900. *Open* Tue–Sat 10–6. Tours last 90 minutes, last tour 4. *Admission:* moderate) explores the history of brewing from ancient Egypt to modern South Africa via Europe and Mesopotamia. There is a reconstructed 1960s shebeen (unlicensed bar) and several opportunities to sample the product. Nearby is a Workers' Museum (*Open* Thu–Sat 9–4) with a photographic record of industrial South Africa. The **Sci-Bono Discovery Centre** (corner of President and Miriam Makeba streets, tel: 011-832 3363. *Open* Mon–Fri 9–5, Sat–Sun 9.30–4. *Admission:* expensive) offers a broad range of interactive exhibits, great for children.

REBIRTH

Newtown was once a multicultural district of slum housing, known as Farm Bloemfontein (1853), Brookfields (1887) and Burgersdorp (1896). In 1904, the inhabitants were evacuated and the area burned, supposedly in response to an outbreak of plague. Afterwards, it was renamed Newtown. During the 1970s, in line with the Group Areas Act, much of neighbouring Fordsburg was demolished, and its Indian community moved out to Lenasia township. Now it has been reclaimed as a thriving multicultural focus for the arts and entertainment.

155

The Market Theatre, once a market hall

Sir Herbert Baker's Stone House

SHOPPING MALLS
Shopping in Jo'burg is great, with much of it in a series of malls, each with a distinct identity. Among the best and most entertaining are the classy **Sandton Mall** (tel: 011-883 2011/216 6000,) centred on chic **Nelson Mandela Square** (tel: 011-217 6045/6); **Brightwater Commons** (corner Republic and Hans Strydom roads, Randburg; tel: 011-789 5052), a family-friendly gated mall with shops, eateries, entertainment, a permanent flea market and a musical fountain; **The Mall of Rosebank** (corner Cradock and Baker roads, Rosebank; tel: 011-788 5530) with a wonderful African craft market and Sunday Rooftop flea market; **Oriental Plaza** (corner Breë and High streets, Fordsburg; tel: 011-836 6752), a taste of old India, with textiles, spices, clothes and more—haggling is the norm here; and **Mai-Mai** (corner Anderson and Berea streets, the city's oldest market, specializing in *muti* (traditional medicine)—its stalls bedecked with remedies.

► **Parktown**   150B3
For guided walks, contact the Parktown and Westcliff Heritage Trust (tel: 011-482 3349, www.parktownheritage.co.za)
Open: Mon–Fri 9–1. Admission: expensive
Johannesburg took three years to become the largest city in southern Africa; originally a typical miners' town, it was rife with crime, alcohol and prostitution. Parktown was one of the first 'respectable' leafy suburbs created by the mining magnates as a suitable environment for their wives and daughters. There are still some fine mansions, including Sir Herbert Baker's home, Stone House and Lord Alfred Milner's 'kindergarten', Moot Cottage.

► **Roodeport Museum**   150B3
Civic Centre, Christiaan de Wet Road, Florida Park (tel: 011-761 0225). Open: Tue–Thu 9.30–4.30, Fri 9.30–4, 1st Sun of the month Sun 2–5. Admission: inexpensive
The museum deals with the discovery of gold in the Witwatersrand area and the development of Roodepoort from a mining camp to the town it is today. The several rooms have late 19th- to early 20th-century furnishings.

► **South African National Museum of**   149B2
  Military History
Hermann Eckstein Park, Erlswold Way, Saxonwold (tel: 011-646 5513). Open: daily 9–4.30. Admission: moderate
This is one of Johannesburg's most popular museums. It has fighter aircraft from both world wars, tanks and artillery, uniforms and medals, displays on the Namibian and Angolan wars and a German one-man submarine.

► **University of the Witwatersrand**   150B3
  museums
Founded in 1896 as a training institute for the diamond industry, 'Wits' is now one of the largest and most highly regarded universities in South Africa, with numerous small museums. The **Bernard Price Institute for Palaeontological Research** (Jorrison Street, Braamfontein, tel: 011-716 2727. *Open Mon–Fri 8.30–4*) contains a mass of

tools and bones, such as those of *Australopithecus africanus* and *Homo erectus*, found at various sites in South Africa including the Sterkfontein Caves (see below).

The **Planetarium** (Yale Road, Milner Park, tel: 011-717 1392. Shows: Thu 2.30, Fri 8, Sat 3. *Admission: expensive*, booking essential) has a wonderful way to identify the Southern Cross and explore the unfamiliar southern skies, where the crescent moon hangs upside down. Then you can head into the bush and see the real thing. With no artificial light to dim the eyes, the sky seems to have twice as many stars. The **Bleoch Geological Museum** (Geosciences Building, East Campus, tel: 011-717 6665. *Open* Mon–Fri 8–4.30) offers a feast of beautiful rocks and minerals. **The CE Moss Herbarium** (School of Animal, Plant and Environmental Studies, tel: 011-717 6467. *Open* Mon–Fri 8–4.30) houses a large botanical collection.

Exhibits at the **Adler Museum of Medicine** (Wits Medical School, 7 York Road, Parktown, Wits, tel: 011-717 2081. *Open* Mon–Fri 9.30–4. *Admission: free*) includes a dental museum, coach house and reconstructions of a 19th-century surgery and African herbalist's shop. The **Zoology Museum** (Old Education Building, East Campus, tel: 011-717 6464. *Open* Mon–Fri 8.30–4.30) has butterflies, moths and shells.

Johannesburg environs

▶▶▶ Cradle of Humankind   150B2

Take the R563 Hekpoort Kromdraai Road, Krugersdorp North. Tel: 011-355 1208, fax: 011-337 2292, www.cradleofhumankind.co.za. Open Tue–Sun 9–4; guided tours on the half-hour. Admission: expensive. Magaliesburg Tourism Information: 014-577 1733, www.magaliesinfo.co.za.

Set into the beautiful Magaliesburg range, the Cradle of Humankind is possibly one of the most historically important World Heritage Sites ever created, a fossil bed as rich and valuable as Tanzania's Olduvai Gorge in providing crucial fossil links to the history of mankind. Covering 47,000 ha (116,090 acres) along the border of Gauteng and North West Province, it includes at least 200 dolomite cave systems, only 13 of which have been explored. At the heart of the site are the **Sterkfontein Caves**, discovered in 1896 by an Italian gold prospector on Sterkfontein farm, near Krugersdorp. Here, in 1936, Dr. Robert Broom discovered the first known adult cranium of the 2.5-million-year-old *Australopithecus africanus* ape-man, (a relative of the Taung baby, an infant skull found 12 years earlier). Known to locals as 'Mrs Ples' (although she's possibly now had a sex-change), she has become a crucial pointer to man's origins.

LIPIZZANERS
Made famous by the Spanish Riding School in Vienna, the fancy footwork of the gleaming white stallions has become a popular attraction across the world. South Africa has the world's only other troupe of the highly trained horses approved by the Spanish Riding School, descendants of horses rescued from Austria in 1944 and brought to South Africa for safety. The audience are invited round to the stable to meet and feed the horses after the performance.
(1 Dahlia Road, Kyalami, north of Johannesburg, tel: 011-702 2103, www.lipizzaners.co.za. Performances Sun 10.30am. *Admission expensive*).

Sterkfontein Caves

TOWNSHIP MUSIC
Marabi began in the shebeens, or illegal drinking dens, of the 1920s. Fast and furious, it was played on any available instrument, from an organ to a can of stones, with anyone and everyone joining in the jam sessions. Never written or recorded, it ended when the slums were bulldozed in the late 1930s. In multicultural Sophiatown, however, it fathered other forms of music, including township jazz (heavily influenced by American big bands and swing), *kwela* and *mbaqanga* (the earliest protest songs). From the mid-1970s, anti-conscription white musicians also began to use music as a form of protest.

BUILDING A CITY
From 1923, the Native Urban Areas Act tried to stop any more black people migrating to the cities and set up segregated 'locations', away from the city centres. In the 1930s, the Johannesburg council bought Klipspruit farm and built the first black township for 80,000 people, inconveniently distant from facilities such as shops and transport. Since then, Soweto (which stands for South Western Townships) has grown to incorporate 50 districts— it is now the largest city in sub-Saharan Africa. Although Soweto's official population is around 2 million, there is a huge floating population of 'unofficial inhabitants from illegal immigrants (around 4 million in the country as a whole) to families shacked up in a hut at the bottom of someone's garden and black market workers. It is estimated that this could over double the population.

In 1998, an almost complete 3.3-million-year-old skeleton, Little Foot, was also discovered, having lain unrecognized in a box since excavated here in 1998. Early tools and the fossils of other creatures from the short-necked giraffe to the giant hyena have also been found.

The caves, one of only two in the area open to the public, contain six cathedral-like chambers. As well as the cave tours, an interactive exhibition hall explains the evolution of man while wooden walkways allow visitors to see the archaeological excavations and the science laboratory. Eight kilometres (5 miles) south, at Mohale's Gate, a steel and glass burial mound marks the entrance to a four-floor interpretation facility, its lowest level a deep underground lake, which can be explored by boats which take a set path along a timeline. It here that you can see the original skeletons, including Mrs Ples.

Nearby the 2.2-billion-year-old **Wonder Cave** (tel: 011-857 0106. *Open* daily 8–5. Guided tour on the hour. *Admission:* expensive) has a huge chamber with magnificent 15m (52ft) stalactites. There is a lift, so the caves are accessible to all, but you can also abseil down if you book in advance.

Nature reserves   *146B2 and 149B2*
Several game and nature reserves lie in the Gauteng area surrounding Johannesburg, including the **Johannesburg Lion Park** (30km/19 miles north of the city, tel: 011-460 1814. *Open* daily 8.30–5. *Admission: expensive*), where 70 lions are fed on Sundays and public holidays at 12. There are also impala, wildebeest and ostrich, an Ndebele village and a small-animals area for children. The **Rhino and Lion Nature Reserve** (Kromdraai Conservancy Area, 40km/24 miles northwest of the city, tel/fax: 011-957 0109. *Open* Mon–Fri 8–5. *Admission: expensive*. Booking essential for game drives and accommodation) also has a variety of big and small game at close quarters. At the **Krugersdorp Game Reserve** (on the R24, 7km/4 miles outside Krugersdorp, tel: 011-950 9900. *Open* daily 8–6. *Admission: expensive for car and up to six people*) it's easy to see rhino, giraffe, buffalo and species of antelope, and there's also a lion enclosure. Accommodation available.

▶▶▶ Soweto   *146B2*
About 20km (12 miles) southwest of Johannesburg
For tours see page 150.
Most people have an image of Soweto, based on decades of horrific news footage, as a place of terrible deprivation dogged by unspeakable violence. Both are present, but the overwhelming impression these days is not of the horrors, but the enormous strides that have been made into creating a thriving city of over 2 million people.

There are areas of shanty settlement and many houses are just two rooms with an outside toilet and standpipe, but the streets are orderly and there is electricity, mains plumbing and rubbish collection. The city has shopping malls, cinemas, a bowling alley, a golf course, schools, a university and the biggest hospital in Africa. Many of the new black middle-class are choosing to stay rather than migrate to the former white suburbs.

Sowetans are proud of their city and actively welcome tourists to their markets, shebeens (now legal) and historic sights, offering them hospitality in a small but flourishing trade in bed-and-breakfast stays. Increasing numbers of white people are also venturing into the area after dark in search of some of Africa's finest music.

Soweto was at the forefront of the Struggle and sightseeing here focuses heavily on the dying years of

apartheid. On the spot where the first Soweto uprisings took place, the painfully moving **Hector Pieterson Monument and Museum** (corner Khumalo and Pela Sts, Orlando East, tel: 011-536 2253/0611. *Open* Mon–Sun 10–5. *Admission*: moderate). The museum has photos and TV footage of the student demonstrations. The **Mandela Museum** (8115 Ngakane Str, Orlando West, tel: 011-936 7754. *Open*: daily 9.30–5) is set in the simple four-roomed home shared by Nelson and Winnie before his arrest. The home of Archbishop Tutu is also on the Struggle tour route. The 1955 Freedom Charter was adopted in the dusty open area in Kliptown; the area has now been declared a national heritage site, the open ground renamed the **Walter Sisulu Square of Dedication**. The whole area is undergoing major redevelopment. The **Regina Mundi Church** (1149 Khumalo Street, Moroka, tel: 011-986 2546), Soweto's largest Catholic church, was once home of the unofficial black parliament.

While it is now safe to visit Soweto on your own (although you should still be careful), it is worth taking a tour as you would otherwise miss many of the sights.

Soweto is now a thriving city, and one that welcomes visitors

SOCCER CITY
This stadium (Nasrec Road, Nasrec, tel: 011-494 3640) is already the continent's largest sporting stadium (currently taking 80,000, but expanding to 100,000) and the focus of intensive development as South Africa gears up to host the 2010 Football World Cup.

Gold has been admired for its beauty since about 9000BC, but its use as currency is more recent. Even when 16th-century Spaniards were plundering Aztec hoards, gold coins were rare. In 1821, when gold became the yardstick for all currencies in the British Empire, nations had to build up bullion reserves.

160

'I tell you today that every ounce of gold taken from the bowels of our soil will yet have to be weighed up with rivers of tears...'
—Paul Kruger, ZAR president (quoted in *The Randlords*, by Geoffrey Wheatcroft)

For hundreds of years, people had known that there was gold in southern Africa—Arab traders were dealing with the inland tribes even in the 7th century. In 1853, prospectors found the first significant reserves in South Africa at Pilgrim's Rest, Mpumalanga (see page 183). It proved to be a thin seam, but it did generate a minor gold rush. By the time George Harrison struck it lucky in 1886 and discovered the Main Reef on the Witwatersrand, there were a lot of people to hand with a great deal of optimism, ready to start digging. Farms along the line of the reef were declared public property, ready for licensed claims, and a new city (Johannesburg) was laid out nearby. The God-fearing Boers, who had trekked north to get away from the crowds, were bemused by the onslaught of the rough-and-ready miners and the wave of sin. The British, led by Cecil Rhodes, started eyeing the area for a takeover—which they eventually achieved in 1902 at the end of the Anglo-Boer War.

The Transvaal Gold Rush lasted for 30 years until the discovery of far richer seams on the Witwatersrand in 1886

Pockets of wealth As in the diamond fields, the real wealth soon ended up in the hands of a privileged few, such as Cecil Rhodes and Barney Barnato, J. B. Robinson, Hermann Eckstein and Lionel Phillips. But the prospect of riches attracted countless others, including black workers, who still travel literally thousands of miles from home to work underground. South Africa's mines employ just over 400,000 men from 10 southern African countries at any given time (almost 200,000 of them in the gold mines). They come from a multitude of tribes, so a common 'pidgin', *Fanakalo*, was developed for communication. It is still used, but is no longer considered politically correct.

Lower yields Today, the mines stretch in a 500km (310-mile) arc from Evander in Mpumalanga, through the Witwatersrand and Johannesburg to Klerksdorp and south to Welkom in the Free State. Johannesburg is still the focus of the industry, but the Free State currently produces more than one third of the country's output.

In 2000 (the last year for which there were full statistics), South Africa's mines accounted for 10 per cent of the GDP and 35 per cent of export earnings. Of this,

about a third came from gold. Yet things haven't all been rosy. In 1985, the country produced 671 tonnes of gold (43 per cent of global production) and was the world's cheapest producer; by 2000, production was down to 428 tonnes (17 per cent). Only favourable exchange rates and a drastic reorganization of the industry, which has led to the closure of many marginal mines and the loss of around 260,000 jobs, has helped shore up profits. There are numerous reasons for the fall. One is economics. After years of exploitation, workers have demanded—and got—better wages, housing, conditions and safety. It is also technical. South Africa has the deepest mines in the world, with tunnels descending more than 900m (3,500ft), making costs high. The sale of massive gold reserves by various Western governments has depressed international prices. Nevertheless, South Africa still owns 39 per cent of the world's known gold deposits (30 per cent of them in Gauteng). It will be a long time before the country needs to look for an alternative source of income.

PURE GOLD
Gold is pure, malleable, does not tarnish or corrode, is almost indestructible, and can be finely moulded and remoulded without alteration. It is heavy, dense and an excellent conductor of heat and electricity. The simplest version of placer mining is panning, which uses a large sieve to collect easily separated deposits from river gravel; sluicing, hydraulic mining and dredging are similar processes on a larger scale. In underground lode-mining of quartz seams, an average 100,000oz (28.35 million grams) of ore is required to produce 1oz (28.3g) of gold. Gold is also recovered as a by-product of copper.

Liquid gold pouring into an ingot at Gold Reef City

Pretoria (Tshwane)

Born in a leisurely fashion in 1855 as a farming settlement on the Apies (Little Monkeys) River, Pretoria was roughly in the middle of the newly colonized Transvaal region, so was chosen as the capital of the South African Republic. The president, Marthinus Pretorius, named it after his father, Andries Pretorius, leader of the Boer forces at the Battle of Blood River and a great Afrikaner hero. At the Union in 1910, the city became the administrative capital of the republic. In 2001 it was incorporated into a larger metropolitan area named Tshwane, the traditional name of the Apies River. It means 'we are one because we live together'. The city takes its role seriously, with many fine statues, museums and four universities, including Pretoria University (the largest in the country) and the University of South Africa (UNISA), the world's largest correspondence university.

Jacaranda in bloom carpets the city streets in purple

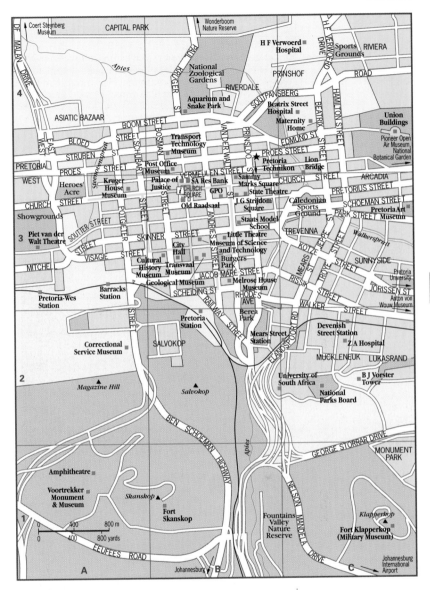

Almost totally white-collar, Pretoria was, until very recently, the only major city in South Africa where the majority of the population (estimated at 2 million) was white. Because of this fact it escaped most of the violence during the years of unrest, and is at present one of the few major cities without a significant crime problem. As a city, it is totally unlike its neighbour Johannesburg, and is mostly quiet, dignified and conservative. It could be dull, but as befits anywhere with a large diplomatic contingent, it has some of the best nightlife around, from theatres to clubs and restaurants. Until Johannesburg has sorted out its problems, you may find this a far more pleasant place to stay.

THE JACARANDA CITY
The first two jacarandas were planted in Pretoria in 1888. Today, some 80,000 mature trees line the streets of the city, providing much-needed shade and greenery. Every October, they burst into flower, coating the city in purple blossom. Pretoria celebrates with a jacaranda festival.

PRETORIA'S FORTS

In 1896, following the abortive Jameson Raid (see page 37), the Transvaal government built four forts to defend Pretoria. Beautifully constructed of stone with meticulously executed brickwork, they were guarded by stout armour-plated doors, fitted with bomb-resistant case-ments, and armed with heavy artillery. Revolving artillery pieces could be mounted on the ramparts when required, but they were never needed, and the forts were used only to accommodate Lord Roberts' troops after the British occupation in 1900. Fort Klapperkop and Fort Skanskop are still intact (both are off Nelson Mandela Road, just south of the city); Forts Wonderboom and Daspoort are in ruins. Fort Klapperkop (tel: 012-460 3235) houses a small military museum and offers fine city views.

164

FLOWER POWER

The National Botanical Garden (2 Cussonia Avenue, Brummeria, tel: 012-843 5194, www.sanbi.org. Open daily 8–6, last admission 5. Admission: moderate) is a wonderland of luxurious planting, its 76ha (188 acres) containing some 5,000 species of native and exotic plants, divided into two distinct sections by a 50m (164ft) rock outcrop. About a third of the area has been left wild, offering a home to around 198 species of bird as well as small reptiles and mammals. It has walk-ing trails, a restaurant and gift shop. Occasional events include picnic concerts between May and September.

Art museums

The **Pretoria Art Museum▶** (corner of Schoeman and Wessel streets, Arcadia Park, tel: 012-344 1807, www. pretoriaartmuseum.co.za. Open Tue–Sun 10–5, Wed 10–8. Admission: inexpensive) has works by a number of Dutch and Flemish painters, including Frans Hals and Van Dyck, as well as one of the most important collections of works by South African artists, such as Irma Stern, and local residents Anton van Wouw and J. H. Pierneef.

The Anton von Wouw Museum (299 Clark Street, Brooklyn, tel: 012-460 7422. Open Tue–Fri 10–4, Sat 10–12. Admission: free) occupies the artist's former home and studio.

▶▶ **Church Square** see Walk, page 168

▶▶ **Cultural History Museum**   163B3

Visagie Street, between Bosman and Schubart streets (tel: 012-324 6082, www.museumpark.co.za)
Open: daily 8–4. Admission: inexpensive
With some 4 million potential exhibits to choose from, and a fine custom-built home to put them in, this showcase of South African culture should be spectacular. However, the money ran out before the exhibits were complete and while the few galleries that are open use an interesting thematic approach, such as a display of hats, from the headdress of a traditional healer to a Boer bonnet, the overall impression is of underused space. There are some interesting temporary exhibitions and events.

▶ **Kruger House Museum**   163A3

Church Street West (tel: 012-326 9172, www.nfi.org.za)
Open: Mon–Fri 8.30–4, Sat–Sun 9–4
Admission: moderate
Paul Kruger, president of the Transvaal (1883–99), is to the Boers what George Washington is to Americans. He was a stubborn but deeply pious man who really believed that the Voortrekkers were the elect of God and had been led out of bondage to the Transvaal. He lived in this simple home, with its tin roof and broad veranda, from 1883 until 1900, and would sit on the doorstep and chat to passers-by. When Pretoria surrendered to the British in 1900, he went into exile and died in Switzerland, in 1904. His home is now a shrine to one of the country's most remarkable figures. The carved lions beside the entrance were given to Kruger by Barney Barnato.

Inside you can see the state coach, presidential train, the knife Kruger used to cut off his thumb following a gunshot wound, and many gifts and tributes. He worshipped and preached in the Dutch Reformed church opposite the house.

▶ **Melrose House**   163B3

275 Jacob Mare Street, entrance in Scheiding Street (tel: 012-322 2805, www.melrosehouse.co.za)
Open: Tue–Sun 10–5. Admission: inexpensive
George Heys made a fortune out of operating stage-coaches and other vehicles in the Transvaal and, like all good capitalists, aspired to the life of a gentleman. The result was Melrose House, built in 1886, a delicate confection of gables and turrets, curlicues, wrought iron,

marshmallow-pink walls and white stucco, set amid perfectly manicured gardens. Heys' new home lacked nothing, and many of its original furnishings are still *in situ*, including a fine collection of English-influenced 19th-century furniture.

In 1902, the house was requisitioned by the British and occupied by Lord Roberts, and later by Lord Kitchener. The Treaty of Vereeniging, which ended the Anglo-Boer War, was signed on the dining-room table on 31 May, 1902.

Minor museums

The **Correctional Service Museum** (Central Prison, Potgieter Street, tel: 012-314 1766. *Open* Mon–Fri 9–3. *Admission: free*) describes the development of South Africa's penal system with fascinating displays of home-made weapons, forged keys and home-made tattoo machines.

The **Science and Technology Museum** (Didacta Building, 211 Skinner Street, tel: 012-391 9300) is a hands-on museum with plenty of screens and things to play with for youg and old alike.

The **South African Air Force Museum** (Swartkops Air Force Base, Centurion, off the M1, tel: 012-351 2153. *Open* Mon–Fri 9–3.30, Sat–Sun 10–4. *Admission: free*) has exhibits on aircraft and missiles, uniforms, medals and paintings. Flights in historic aircraft are available.

The Kruger House Museum is furnished much as it was when the president lived here

165

Sir Herbert Baker's Union Buildings are among the greatest highlights of British imperial architecture

SIR HERBERT BAKER
Born in Kent, England, Sir Herbert Baker (1862–1946) was one of the most influential of the colonial architects, scattering buildings from suburban England and small neo-Gothic churches across the world. He flourished when faced with the glory of the Empire, and undoubtedly his two greatest works are the Union Buildings, Pretoria (Tshwane) and the Rashtrapati Bhavan (Secretariat Buildings) in New Delhi (over which he had a feud with the other great colonial architect of the period, Sir Edwin Lutyens). Other particularly fine buildings by Herbert Baker include Rhodes' house in Cape Town, and South Africa House in London.

▶▶ National Zoological Garden 163B4

Corner of Boom and Paul Kruger streets (tel: 012-328 3265, fax: 012-323 4540, email: zoologic@cis.co.za)
Open: daily 8–5.30 (6 in summer). Seals are fed at 11 and 3, vultures on Wed and Sun at 2. Night tours Wed, Fri, Sat 6pm; advance booking essential. Admission: expensive
Pretoria Zoo is wonderful. It has over 3,500 animals of 118 species, both indigenous and foreign, some of which, like the pygmy hippo, are extremely rare; more than 190 bird species; an aquarium with 300 species of freshwater and saltwater fish; and a reptile park. The pens are semi-natural, the surrounding gardens green and shady, and a cable car gives a bird's-eye view.

▶ Transvaal Museum 163B3

Paul Kruger Street (tel: 012-322 7632, www.museumpark. co.za). Open: Daily 8–4. Admission: inexpensive
Founded in 1893, this museum is dedicated to natural history and ethnography. The Austin Roberts Bird Hall contains the most comprehensive collection of birds south of the equator—each of them stuffed and in glass cases, with a recording of their song (there is a small Austin Roberts bird sanctuary, with the live version, in the suburbs of Pretoria/Tshwane). Roberts compiled the standard work, *Birds of South Africa*. The museum also has a large collection of mammals, reptiles and shells, and a skeleton of the extinct dodo, while the **Geoscience Museum** (Paul Kruger Street, tel: 012-322 7632. *Open Mon–Sat 9–5, Sun 11–5. Admission: inexpensive*) covers dinosaurs, fossils and the geology and mineralogy of the world (with special emphasis on South Africa) and has fascinating displays of precious and semiprecious stones.

▶▶ Union Buildings 163C4

Eastern end of Church Street (tel: 012-300 5200)
No tours; visit the exterior and gardens only
In 1910, following the Act of Union, Sir Herbert Baker (see panel) was commissioned by Jan Smuts to build a fitting administration office. Never one to stint on imperial

grandeur, he created a superb sandstone eagle of a building, swooping with outstretched wings over the city.

The site, Meintjieskop, once belonged to President Pretorius and reminded Baker of the acropolises of Greece. Two great office buildings with domed towers, representing the British and Afrikaner peoples, are linked in reconciliation by the curved colonnade of the amphitheatre. Columned loggias were intended to lure ministers out to 'lift up their eyes to the high veld'. No room was made for South Africa's black population, save a planned 'small partly open Council Place for Native Indabas (meetings), where, without coming into the Building, Natives may feel the majesty of Government'. It was never built. Since 1913, this has been the headquarters of the national government and the president's office. In 1994 Nelson Mandela was sworn in here as the country's first black president.

▶ Voortrekker Monument and Museum 163A1

Monument Hill, 6km (4 miles) from the middle of town (tel: 012-326 6770). Open: Sep–end Apr 8–6; May–end Aug daily 8–5. Admission: expensive

Completed in 1949, this 40m (130ft) high granite block is intended to be uniquely African, symbolizing the indomitable spirit of the Voortrekkers, and harmonizing with the vastness, solitude and mystery of the African landscape. Designed by Gerhard Moerdyk and apparently inspired by Great Zimbabwe, it looks more like a nuclear power plant. Outside, a symbolic *laager* (ring of wagons) protects the monument, while *assegais* (spears) at the gate represent the power of Zulu King Dingane. A statue of the mother and child represents the spread of civilization, surrounded by the figures of Piet Retief, Andries Pretorius, Hendrik Potgieter and an Unknown Voortrekker. This is hallowed ground for the Afrikaners, and the marble relief frieze of Voortrekker history surrounding the lower hall is poignant—if you can ignore the many references to 'barbaric' blacks and the 'shining light' of Afrikaner civilization. At noon on 16 December, the Day of the Covenant (see panel), a shaft of sunlight falls on the central inscription 'Ons vir jou, Suid Afrika' ('We for thee, South Africa').

The Voortrekker Museum has maps of the trek, a tapestry version of the frieze, Voortrekker weapons, clothing and other memorabilia.

THE COVENANT

On 9 December, 1838, following the massacre of Piet Retief and his companions (see page 33), a group of Voortrekkers led by Andries Pretorius took a solemn vow at Danskraal: that if God would deliver their enemies and allow them victory and vengeance, they would mark the anniversary as a holiday of thanksgiving every year forever more. On 16 December, they fought the Battle of Blood River (see page 204), and won without a single fatality; the date remains a holiday in the new South Africa, a memorial perhaps to the 4,000 Zulus who lost their lives.

167

Below: A laager of bas relief wagons
Bottom: Tapestry depiction of a Voortrekker camp in the Voortrekker Museum

Melrose House, one of Pretoria's few surviving Victorian mansions

Central Pretoria (Tshwane)

This gentle walk covers many of the finest buildings in the heart of the city. Start from Sammy Marks Square. Allow three hours. This route is best done on foot in daylight hours during the week. On weekends go by car, except for the Church Street pedestrian section. *See map on page 163.*

Take the first right onto Church Street, between **Sammy Marks Square**, named after the Randlord (see page 171), and **J. G. Strijdom Square**, dominated by a vast memorial to the former prime minister by sculptors Coert Steynberg and Danie de Jager. To one side is the **State Theatre**

(tel: 012-322 1665), one of the finest theatres in South Africa, with an opera house and five auditoriums, and a broad range of quality entertainment here, including plays by Athol Fugard, concerts from black jazz musician Hugh Masakela, and visiting overseas artists. **Church Street** runs right across Pretoria from east to west, a distance of 26km (16 miles), and is one of the longest streets in the world. This city centre section is now a busy pedestrianized mall, lined with fun craft stalls.

Continue west along Church Street for three blocks to **Church Square►►**. In 1857, the Transvaal Republic's Vierkleur flag was hoisted here for the first time—and taken down for the last time in 1902. The square housed the market and the city's first shops, with parking for ox wagons. Today, the wagons have been replaced by a central garden and Anton van Wouw's statue of Paul Kruger (paid for by Sammy Marks but set up only in 1954).

Many magnificent, early 20th-century sandstone buildings line the edge of the square. The facades, at least, have survived the developers. They include the **Tudor Buildings**, built by George Heys (who also built Melrose House); both the old and the new headquarters of the **South African Reserve Bank**; the **Old Mint**; the **Palace of Justice**, which was used as a military hospital during the Anglo-Boer War and later became the Transvaal division of the Supreme Court; and the Italian-Renaissance style **Old Raadsaal**, seat of President Kruger's republican government. The last two buildings both have lavishly decorated interiors, with cut stone, brass, stained glass and elaborate tiles. Church Square is also now the home of the Pretoria Tourist Office.

Continue west along Church Street. Three blocks on is the **Kruger House Museum** (see page 164), and two blocks beyond that is **Heroes' Acre**, the pantheon of Afrikaner greats. Those who lie buried in this cemetery include presidents Kruger and Verwoerd, Andries Pretorius, and, movingly, 'Breaker' Morant—the Australian soldier and poet who was executed by the British in 1902 for supposedly murdering a Boer prisoner and a British missionary.

Retrace your steps along Church Street for three blocks, then turn right onto Schubart Street. After three blocks, turn left onto Visagie Street to visit the **Cultural History Museum** (see page 164). Continue along Visagie Street and you will see the **City Hall** on your right, with a frieze by Coert Steynberg and statues of Andries and Marthinus Pretorius. Turn left onto Paul Kruger Street, then right after one block for the hands-on **Museum of Science and Technology** (see page 165). Retrace your steps to the City Hall. On the opposite side of the road is the **Transvaal Museum** (see page 166). Straight ahead is Herbert Baker's magnificently over-done and impractical **Railway Station** (1910), designed like an Italian Renaissance palace. It is the home of the luxurious Blue Train. Opposite is

the 19th-century colonial **Victoria Hotel**, now sadly run down. The surrounding area is the central focus of the minibus taxis, and offers a fascinating glimpse of township life. Do not walk around this area at night.

From the station, turn right along Scheiding Street and left onto Jacob Mare Street for **Melrose House** (see page 164). Behind the museum, the road leads into **Burgers Park** (*Open* daily 8–6), a charming Victorian formal garden with several monuments and a Biodome for exotic plants. Turn right to leave the park and left onto Van Der Walt Street, which leads north past the **Staats Model School**. Preserved as a typical Boer school, it is famous for being the place where Winston Churchill was imprisoned during the Anglo-Boer War. Continue down the street and back to the Tourist Office.

169

Opulent Church Square was the focus of historic Pretoria

Pretoria environs

THE CULLINAN
Found in 1905 and named after Sir Thomas Cullinan, the Cullinan was the world's largest rough diamond, weighing 3,106 carats. It is thought to have been part of an even larger diamond broken up by weathering. The Transvaal government presented it to King Edward VII, who had it cut into nine major jewels. The 530-carat Great Star of Africa (the largest cut diamond in the world) is set in the Royal Sceptre; the 317-carat Lesser Star of Africa is in the Imperial State Crown. The other seven are the property of the British royal family.

170

▶ Cullinan 146C3

Premier Diamond Tours, 99 Oak Avenue, Cullinan, 40km (25 miles) east of Pretoria (tel: 012-734 0081)
Open: Tours daily 10.30, Mon–Fri 2 (2 hours), by arrangement for guided surface tours; booking essential. 4th Fri each month an underground tour 8–12.30; max of 15 people so book early. No children under 10. Admission: expensive
The Premier Mine is one of the richest in the world. It is yielding an average of 1.5 million carats a year since 1902, including some of the world's most famous diamonds—the Cullinan (see page 141, and panel), the Centenary Diamond and the Premier Rose. Tours include the Big Hole (40ha/99 acres and 500m/1,640ft deep), the 800m (2,624ft) deep mine shaft, displays of uncut diamonds, and replicas of the most famous sparklers.

▶ De Wildt Cheetah Farm 146B3

Brits, 48km (30 miles) west of Pretoria on the R513 (tel/fax: 012-504 1921, www.dewildt.org.za)
Open: Tours (3 hours) Tue, Thu, Sat, Sun 8.30, 1.30
Reservations essential. No children under 6
Admission: expensive
Wild dog, brown hyena and cheetah, including the rare king cheetah, are bred and researched here.

▶ Hartbeespoort Dam 146B3

About 35km (22 miles) west of Pretoria
The 120km (75-mile) long, low ridge of the Magaliesberg is an attractive area, but its history is one of conflict. Early white hunters were followed by Voortrekker pastoralists, leading to savage encounters with the Ndebele in the late 1830s. Hunting for gold began here long before the Witwatersrand deposits were discovered—and you can still see old diggings, stamp mills and machinery. Anglo-Boer War forts dot the hills. In the foothills, Hartbeespoort Dam has boating, angling, swimming and birdwatching.

Zwartkoppies Hall, the former home of Sammy Marks and his family

A cableway takes visitors to a viewing site over the dam wall, built in a narrow gorge on the Crocodile River in 1923. The Elephant Sanctuary (2km/1 mile) from the Dam Doryn 4 Way Stop on the Rutensberg Road, tel: 012-258. *Admission: expensive*), is home to five tame elephants. Visit for the day or stay and play with them. Nearby, **Lesedi Cultural Village** (on the R512; tel: 012-205 1394. Shows daily at 11.30 and 4.30; booking essential) runs imaginative cultural events depicting the traditional life of the Pedi, Sotho, Xhorsa and Zulu peoples.

▶ Jan Smuts' House   *146B2*

Jan Smuts Avenue, Centurion. Take the M1 south to Irene (tel: 012-667 1176). Open: Mon–Fri 9.30–1, 1.30–4.30, Sat–Sun 9.30–1. 1.30–5. Admission: inexpensive
Jan Christian Smuts (1870–1950) was one of the great Afrikaner heroes and statesmen, commander-in-chief of the British forces during World War I, and later prime minister of the Union. Doornkloof, a modest, prefabricated farmhouse was his home until his death, and still contains original furnishings, cars and other memorabilia.

▶ Pioneer Museum   *146B3*

Take exit 3 off the N4 to Witbank (tel: 012-803 6086)
Open: daily 9–4. Admission: inexpensive
This delightfully imaginative museum, based around a restored Voortrekker cottage (built 1848), with several other early buildings and a carefully reconstructed farmyard, has plenty of hands-on demonstrations including candle-making, baking and cracking a bullwhip.

▶ Sammy Marks Museum   *146B3*

18km (11 miles) from the city centre off the R104, Old Bronkhorstspruit Road (tel: 012-802 1150)
Open: Tue–Fri 9–4, Sat–Sun 10–4. Admission: moderate
Randlord Sammy Marks (see panel) designed his own house, Zwartkoppies Hall (completed in 1886). The somewhat eccentric and richly decorated mansion contains most of its original furnishings. Tea room in the rose garden.

▶ Tswaing Meterorite Centre   *146B3*

40km (25 miles) northwest of Pretoria off the M35 (tel: 012-790 2302). Open: daily 7.30–5. Admission: moderate
A 200,000-year-old meteor crater (1.4km/1 mile across and 500m/1,640ft deep), surrounding a soda lake, is the site of South Africa's first environmental museum, with walking trails, 240 species of birds and archaeological sites (the area has been inhabited for 120,000 years). Nearby is the traditional **Mapoch Ndebele Village** (tel: 072-300 7474. *Open* daily 10–4. *Admission: moderate.* Booking essential).

▶▶ Willem Prinsloo Agricultural Museum   *146B3*

13km (8 miles) from the city centre; take exit 27 off the N4 to Witbank, or follow the R104 (tel: 012-736 2035)
Open: daily 8–4. Admission: inexpensive
People in costume deomonstrate a wide range of farm activities, from plucking geese to working in a blacksmith's shop. The museum also features an Ndebele house, a fully furnished farmhouse and the largest collection of agricultural implements in the country.

Traditional Ndebele home in the Willem Prinsloo Museum

South Africa has a long tradition of white, mainly Afrikaner, art. There have been magnificent sculptors, from Anton Anreith to Coert Steynberg, and some fine painters, from the watercolourist Thomas Baines to the expressionist Irma Stern. They have taken as their themes the landscape and people of South Africa, but their works are rooted in Europe.

Top: Jazzy masks have become a popular tourist souvenir

The 20th century also produced some fine black art, such as the sleek, tactile forms of Sydney Kumalo, Bonnie Ntshalintshali's magnificently complex confections of pure imagination and many of the weavings and etchings issuing from the Rorke's Drift school. On the whole though, most of the black art that achieved public viewing was derivative, somewhat staid, and generally unsuccessful in its attempts to emulate European media and styles.

Ethnic arts Exciting things were happening elsewhere, however. Since the first San artist picked up a flint and scratched the outline of an eland on a rock, Africa has had its own superb artistic traditions. From glass-beaded Zulu bridal veils and carved tribal fighting sticks, to burnished clay cooking

Above: Rorke's Drift weavers
Below: Awakening, *by Coert Steynberg*

pots and intricately patterned Sotho baskets, South Africa was filled with art. But it wasn't something to collect and hang on a wall. Art imbued every aspect of traditional culture, but because it was black and 'tribal', even the most creative works were dismissed as handicrafts and their artists condemned to oblivion and penury.

All that is now changing. Like the art of the Australian aborigines or Native Americans, the ethnic arts of Africa are finally trickling into view in galleries and shops across the globe. Finally, people are being invited to take a serious look at these creations of amazing beauty, and to gain some knowledge and understanding of their creators' identity.

Township images The townships spawned a different and very vibrant art, as vivid as jazz, its feet planted in a sense of black rather than tribal identity. Some of it is born of necessity. Penniless youngsters, too poor to afford toys, patiently squat on the street corners, constructing ingenious bicycles, cars and aeroplanes (complete with moving parts) from tangles of old wire.

172

Bored security guards while away the long night hours by weaving *imbenge* (shallow baskets) from psychedelic telephone cable wires. Others have been more ambitious, creating innovative and exciting fine art that uses exclusively urban themes, progressing with the struggle from the day-to-day street scenes of 'township art' to the brutal battering of 'protest art', howling with the pain of oppression. More exciting is Durban's jazzy, multi-artist Peace Wall, painted to commemorate the history of the struggle. The movement has become known as 'transitional art', and there, for the moment, it stays, searching out a new identity in these days of multicultural harmony.

Repression repressed South Africa is fertile ground for creativity, for cultural sanctions cut it off from the mainstream and its talents were tempered by repression. The galleries of the world are now expecting great things. There are still two separate traditions of art-making in the country: the European, in love with the land, and the African, searching for spirituality. Both still hark back to colonialism and apartheid, and it will be a long time before their scars fade and are forgotten. Meanwhile, like everything else South African, art is in great demand across the world, and artists with real talent are likely to be successful.

Among those who have arrived are Robert Hodgins, a painter and graphic artist of figures and urban life; Jackson Hlungwani, a self-taught sculptor in wood of both religious works and symbolic animals; the Ndou brothers (Goldwin and Owen); sculptor Noria Mabasa; and painter and sculptor Malcolm Payne. Also be on the lookout for works by Willie Bester, David Koloane (co-founder of the first black art gallery in South Africa), Penny Siopis and William Kentridge.

Olive Pickers, *by Irma Stern*

WHERE TO BUY
Cape Town Johans Borman Fine Art Gallery, Upper Buitengracht Street (tel: 021-423 6075); Michael Stevenson Contemporary, Hill House, de Smidt Street, Green Point (tel: 021-421 2575); Association of Visual Arts, 35 Church Street (tel: 021-424 7436).
Johannesburg Gallery on the Square, Nelson Mandela Square, Sandton (tel: 011-784 28478); Goodman Gallery, 163 Jan Smuts Avenue, Rosebank (tel: 011-788 1113); Everard Read Gallery, 6 Jellicoe Avenue, Rosebank (tel: 011-788 4805); Zuva Gallery, 14 The High Street, Melrose (tel: 011-684 1214).
Durban African Art Centre, 1st Floor, Tourist Junction, 160 Pine Street (tel: 031-301 2717).

173

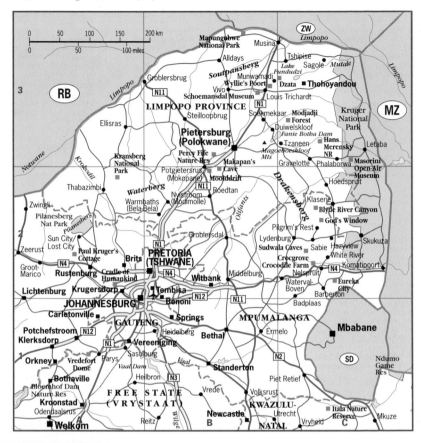

*Giant baobabs dwarf
the scrublands of the
northern lowveld*

FORESTED MOUNTAINS Much of Mpumalanga ('the place of the rising sun') lies in the northernmost section of the Drakensberg, which run from the Swaziland border and taper off as they near the Limpopo River. Considerably lower than the KwaZulu-Natal section (see pages 208–209), the peaks nevertheless rear up to form a 2,300m (7,544ft) rim around the central plateau before the land plunges down over the edge of the escarpment to the true lowveld. The Limpopo, Olifants and Crocodile rivers, together with a host of smaller streams, flow eastwards to water the rocky plains beneath.

The area is spectacularly beautiful, with several hiking trails (for information, tel: 013-764 1058). Agriculturally, it supports everything from tea to bananas, tobacco and nuts, lemons and lettuces. Above all, however, it grows trees—mainly pine and eucalyptus—and is home to the world's largest man-made forest, covering 250,000ha (617,500 acres).

When the early underground mines were first opened, the local indigenous forests were decimated for building materials, mine props and firewood. By 1876, a farsighted local timber merchant, Joseph Brook Shires, was replanting with fast-growing trees; about half of this timber is now used for pulp and paper, one-fifth for the mines, and the rest for (continued on page 176)

Mpumalanga & Limpopo Province

▶▶▶ REGION HIGHLIGHTS

Blyde River Canyon
page 182

Drive: Rim of the escarpment
pages 184–185

Kruger National Park
pages 186–187

Pilgrim's Rest *page 183*

THE BAOBAB

The baobab, *Adansonia digitata*, is one of the largest trees in the world, not because of its height, which rarely exceeds 20m (65.5ft), but because of its enormous and slightly fleshy trunk. The tree prefers a hot, dry climate and can live for at least 1,000 years. It has large white, waxy flowers in October to November and furry, gourd-shaped fruit in April to May. Numerous local legends abound—one says that the baobab once offended God, was uprooted and replanted upside down; another that the flowers are inhabited by spirits and that anyone picking them will be eaten by lions.

176

LIMPOPO PROVINCE TOURIST INFORMATION

PO Box 2814, Pietersburg (Polokwane) 0700 (tel: 015-290 7300, fax: 015-291 4140, www. limpopotourism.co.za)

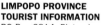

Huge, hardy, horned cattle in the Venda bush

telegraph poles and furniture. The eucalyptus has proved very damaging; each tree soaks up an enormous quantity of water, which drains the watershed and leads to severe drought on the plains below. Efforts are being made to change to more eco-friendly species, such as hardy Californian pine and mahogany.

The hot, arid area to the north and west feels like a different country. It used to be one. This was once the Boer Zuid Afrikanische Republiek (ZAR), known since the Union as the Transvaal. Most of it was not colonized until the mid- to late 19th century, so the hunters and farmers failed to kill off all the wildlife before it came under legal protection.

The black tribes in the region are a mix of refugees from the Zulu Mfecane (such as the Ndebele and Shangaan) and people like the Venda, who are most closely related to the Zimbabwean Karanga-Rozwi group. Even the white 'Vaalies' are considered a breed apart by the rest of South Africa. The descendants of the hardiest of pioneers, they are large, tough, rugby-playing, beer-drinking, hard-line conservatives, with a broad sentimental streak.

The region's population is scattered widely, with few towns of any great size and huge farms roamed by wild horned cattle. The Limpopo Province survives almost entirely on farming, but has been hit severely by protracted drought at various times. In common with many other parts of the world, it sees tourism as its salvation.

Both the Limpopo Province and Mpumalanga have a number of thermal spring and spa resorts. The most popular are **Badplaas** in the highveld, where the hot sulphur spring emerges from the ground at a rate of 30,000L (6,600gal) per hour, **Warmbaths (now known as Bela-Bela),** in the bushveld, **Tshipise** (beneficial for diabetes), and **Sagole**, in Venda territory bordering the Limpopo River.

Badplaas, once known as *Emanzana* ('the healing waters') and Warmbaths, known in Tswana as *Biela bela*

Kruger National Park

('the water that boils on its own') are the most highly developed, and both have accommodation. Bela-Bela has a variety of treatment facilities. Its springs have been in use since the Iron Age—and were long popular with wild animals who, like the settlers of the 19th century, liked to wallow in the warm, mineralized mud.

However, the main focus of the entire region is **Kruger National Park** (see pages 186–187), a vast stretch of protected land, quite literally the size of a country, stretching north along the Mozambique border. Around it cluster countless smaller reserves, infinite numbers of hotels, and tour companies offering every permutation, from training as a game ranger to whitewater rafting.

Currently, most of the activity is concentrated at the southern end of the park in Mpumalanga, but everyone has a vested interest in spreading the honey farther north. The Limpopo Province needs its share of tourist dollars and the park needs to control the number of tourists in any one area if it is to avoid overstressing the animals and refute the accusation that it is a large zoo.

As Nelspruit built its airport, tiny Pietersburg (Polokwane) was converting its old airforce base into an international airport; the road north was being dramatically improved, and even little Hoedspruit has converted the local airforce base into what it hopes will be an international airport. Two hours drive north of Johannesburg, the Waterberg area is now a flourishing patchwork of game ranches.

The Gaza-Kruger-Gonarezhou Transfrontier Park was launched in 2002, when South Africa, Mozambique and Zimbabwe pulled down fences to create a massive reserve covering more than 36,000sq km (13, 896sq miles), opening elephant migration routes.

GEOLOGICAL SAUCER
Millions of years ago, the whole Transvaal area was completely flat. As the volcanoes settled down it became an inland sea, and a layer of mud and sand solidified and was turned into shale and quartz. A later eruption poured lava across the middle, pushing it down and forcing up the sides to create a vast saucer. Since then, much of the soft shale has weathered away, leaving the hard granite outcrops exposed. The gold-bearing reefs discovered in the cliffs of Mpumalanga are the same geological strata as those found deep underground in Gauteng.

The rain queen's village is surrounded by wooden staves carved with faces and figures. The first rain queen was Modjadji, a Karanga princess from Zimbabwe, who fled south in the 16th century, taking with her the rainmaking secrets of the ruling family. For a long time she was considered to be immortal and omnipotent, and her secrets have been passed down through the centuries. When old, the queen hands over to the next generation and commits suicide. Modjadji is said to have been Rider Haggard's inspiration for the immortal queen in the novel *She*.

178

Limpopo Province

▶▶▶ **Kruger National Park** see pages 186–187

▶ **Letaba District** *174C3*

Tourist Information, Tzaneen (tel: 015-307 1294, fax: 015-307 1271, www.tzaneen.co.za)

Tzaneen (from *dzana*, a Karanga word meaning 'to dance') is an attractive settlement on the Letaba River (Tourist Information, 25 Danie Street, tel: 015-307 1294). Nearby, the spectacular **Magoeboeskloof Mountains** climb 610m (2,000ft) up the escarpment, through primeval forest and banana and tea plantations. Tours are available around the **Sapekoe tea plantations** (tel: 083-627 1494. *Open* daily 10–5. Tours Tue–Sat 11, booking advised). Visit the **Debengeni Falls**, on the Ramadipa River, a popular picnic site. Both the **Fanie Botha Dam** and **Ebenezer Dam** have nature reserves, birdwatching, water sports and angling. In the **Hans Merensky Nature Reserve** (tel: 015-386 8633. *Open* daily 8–4) the **Tsonga Kraal Museum** (tel: 015-386 8727. *Open* for tours Mon–Fri 7.30–4) is dedicated to the Tsonga and Shangaan peoples. **Moria** is the headquarters of the Zion Christian church

The **Modjadji Forest** (28km/17 miles northeast of Duiwelskloof) has the world's largest concentration of cycads, the 50-million-year-old 'Modjaji palm'. This is also the home of the rain queens (see panel), who have protected the forest for many generations. A huge baobab in the forest has a bar inside (tel: 015-309 9039).

In Modjadji, the rain queen guards cycads as old as dinosaurs

▶ **Phalaborwa** *174C3*

114km (70 miles) east of Tzaneen. Tourist Information, tel: 015-781 1767). Open: Mon–Fri 8–4.30, Sat 9–12

Phalaborwa's name derives from the Tsonga term *pala borwa*, which means 'to smooth the bow', after the sandpaper-like leaves of the *Ficus capreifolia*, which grows commonly in the area. Millions of years ago, massive geological explosions forced millions of tonnes of magma up from the depths of the earth, bestowing the area with rich deposits of phosphate, copper and iron ore. The **Masorini Open-Air Museum** (in the Kruger National Park) is a reconstruction of an Iron Age village; archaeological findings reveal that the area was first mined in about AD800. Tours are available around the **Phalaborwa Copper Mine** (tel: 015-780 2911), one of the world's five largest open-cast mines. The **Foskor Museum** (Tambotie Street, tel: 015-789 2024. *Open* Mon–Thu 10–4) charts the area's archaeological, mining and ethnographic history.

At nearby **Hoedspruit** you can see wildlife close up in the **Moholoholo Wildlife Rehabilitation Centre** (tel: 015-795 5236. Tours Mon–Sat 9.30 and 3; reservations essential), with sick and orphaned animals; the **Cheetah Project▶** (tel: 015-793 1633. *Open* daily 8–4. Tours on the hour—3

ROVING AUTHOR
John Buchan (1875–1940), author of *The Thirty-Nine Steps*, lived and travelled in the Tzaneen area between 1901 and 1903. He set the novel *Prester John* in the region, and later expressed a desire to return and be buried here. There is a small memorial to him on the Georges Valley Road (R538) overlooking the Ebenezer Dam.

hours. *Admission: expensive*), a breeding and research operation for cheetah, king cheetah and Cape wild dog; and the **Swadini Reptile Park** (tel: 015-795 5203. *Open daily 8–5. Admission: moderate*).

▶ Pietersburg (Polokwane)   *174B3*

Tourist Information, Civic Centre, corner of Landros Maré and Bodenstein streets (tel: 015-290 2010, also for all city museums). Open: Mon–Fri 8.30–4

Capital of the Limpopo Province, Pietersburg (now Polokwane) is a rather dull town. There are four museums: the Victorian **Irish House Museum** (corner of Mark and Vorster streets); the **Hugh Exton Photographic Museum** (on Civic Square); the **Art Museum** (Library Gardens, Jorissen Street); and the **Bakone Malapa Ethnic Museum** (9km/5.5 miles south on the R37 Chuniespoort road), dedicated to the Northern Sotho people.

▶ Potgietersrus (Mokopane)   *174B2*

Tourist Information, 97 Voortrekker Street (tel: 015-491 8458). Open: Mon–Fri 7.30–4.30

This attractive town was established in 1852 and eventually named after Piet Potgieter, who was shot in 1854 during the 30-day Makapansgat Siege, a retaliatory strike for the massacre of 28 Voortrekkers at **Mooiddrift** (marked by a monument). The new name, Mokopane, commemorates an Ndebele chief. Nearly 2,000 Tlou tribesmen died of thirst and starvation in the huge **Makapans Caves**, where archaeological digs have unearthed plant fossils and remains of *Australopithecus africanus*. (Visits must be arranged in advance.) The **Arend Dieperink Museum** (Voortrekker Street, tel: 015-491 9735. *Open Mon–Fri 7.30–4. Admission: inexpensive*) follows local culture from prehistory to the pioneers. The **Game Breeding Centre** of the National Zoological Gardens of Pretoria (tel: 015-491 4314) specializes in rare African species such as *tsessebe* (antelope) and black rhino.

MAPUNGUBWE NATIONAL PARK

Located in the far north, near Musina and the Zimbabwe border (tel: 015-534 2014, www.sanparks.org. *Open*: daily 6–6) this park covers 28,000 (69,160 acres). Mapungubwe or 'place of the stone of wisdom' is the newest national park and a World Heritage Site. It is part of a project to create a transfrontier conservation area (with Zimbabwe and Botswana). The landscape is a dramatic rubble of vast granite boulders and kopjes interpersed by giant baobabs with lush riverine forest near the water. The game viewing is excellent, with the Big Five and over 400 species of bird. It is also important for the archaeological evidence of South Africa's first major kingdom, dating back to the 13th century. A museum and information facility is under construction.

One of the shining velvet tea plantations that carpet the Magoeboeskloof Mountains

179

Many Venda homes still use traditional thatch

▶ Venda   174B3/C3

In the southern foothills of the **Zoutpansberg** mountains. The area has excellent hiking and 4 x 4 trails, mountain climbing plus the Medike and Lajuma rock art sites. The **Ivory Route** (tel: 015-295 3025) was set up to follow trails used by early ivory hunters, gold and slave traders. Here, too, is the small town of **Makhado** (formerly Louis Trichardt. Tourist Information, on the N1, at northern edge of town, tel: 015-516 0040. *Open* Mon–Fri 8–5, Sat 8–1). **Schoemansdal Museum** (16km/10 miles west of the town, tel: 015-516 3254. *Open* daily 8–4.30) is a vivid open-air reconstruction of early pioneer life.

  Wyllies Poort, a narrow gorge of cliffs, leads to an intensely hot area of wide plains and high plateaux, pitted by deep valleys. In 1979, it was designated the Venda tribal homeland, with its capital at **Thohoyandou**.

  It is a land of ancient indigenous forests and lakes, magic and legend. Near **Lake Fundudzi** (see panel), on the Mutali River, is the sacred **Thathe Vondo Forest**, burial ground of the chiefs of the Thathe clan and forbidden to visitors. At **Dzata** is a ruined stone city similar to those of Zimbabwean culture. There are **museums** of Venda history at Dzata and Thohoyandou. The many magnificent forests, waterfalls and hot springs at **Munwamadi** and **Sagole** are well worth visiting; the sandstone caves at Sagole feature San paintings and the largest known baobab tree in southern Africa.

▶▶ Waterberg   174B2

Approx 200km (124 miles) north of Johannesburg, off the NI. Tourist Information, Bela-Bela Waterfront, tel: 014-736 3694.
Hills rather than true mountains, the Waterberg form part of the shore of the vast superlake that once covered so much of Limpopo Province (see margin, page 177). Never the country's most productive farmland, the past 10 years have seen the area transformed into an excellent game viewing area and adventure playground, only a couple of hours drive from Johannesburg. The area has also

received UNESCO Biosphere status. There are a couple of relatively small national reserves, such as the Lapalala Wilderness Reserve, but much of the land is a series of privately owned game reserves such as Jembisa, to the Welgevenden Reserve, with over a dozen lodges, some commercial, some private, or Entabeni with five lodges. Accommodation ranges from inexpensive self-catering and B&Bs to luxury lodges to rival those of the Kruger. Most are relatively child-friendly. Many properties have Big Five game viewing and good birding; other activities include horse-and-elephant back rides, nature walks, quad biking, helicopter rides and bush barbecues. Best of all, the area is malaria free.

The main town in the area is Bela-Bela (meaning Boiling-Boiling and formerly known as Warmbaths), source of hot mineral water springs and there are hot water pools, but no luxury hotels with all the trimmings nearby.

TOURISM INFORMATION
Mpumalanga Tourism Authority, Hall's Gateway, Parksboard Building, Block F, Mataffin, Nelspruit, Mpumalanga (tel: 013-752 7001, fax: 013-759 5441, email: mtanlpsa@cis.co.za, www.mpumalanga.com. *Open* Mon–Fri 8-4.30).

Statue of Jock of the Bushveld

The De Wildt-Shingwedzi Cheetah and Wildlife Ranch (32 km/19 miles) from Bela-Bela, tel: 014-734 1735. Tours Tue-Sat 10 & 4 by appointment, plus accommodation) is a satellite of the main centre (see page 170) where adult cheetah and wild dogs are released to live in safety in the wild.

Mpumalanga

▶ **Barberton**   *174C2*
43km (27 miles) south of Nelspruit. Tourist Information, Crown Street (tel: 013-712 2121). Open: Mon–Fri 8–1, 2–4.30, Sat 8.30–12
On 21 June 1884, Graham, Fred and Henry Barber discovered a rich gold reef in Rimer's Creek. A few days later, the mining commissioner, David Wilson, visited their camp to verify the find, naming the area Barberton. Over 1,400 fortune-hunters rushed into the area and Barberton turned into a town of music halls, gambling dens, tin shanties, shops and canteens. When news of the Witwatersrand reach Barberton, however, the town was deserted. **Pilgrim Streeet** has fine old buildings, and you can visit several others, including the 1886 **Stopforth House** (Bowness Street), the 1904 **Belhaven House** and 1890s **Fernlea House** (both on Lee Road), while the **museum** (in the Library) covers gold-rush history and local geology.

Today, the town is most noted for the Barberton daisy, first exported to Kew Gardens in London in 1884, and now a staple of many gardens across the world.

The **Fortuna Mine Trail** is a 2km (1 mile) walk through Barberton's indigenous tree park and the 600m (1,968ft) tunnel of an old gold mine. Take a torch.

JOCK OF THE BUSHVELD
Percy FitzPatrick arrived from England at the age of 22, and became a transport rider, accompanied always by his faithful dog, Jock. In 1907, he published the story of their adventures together and the book became an instant best-seller and local classic. It has never been out of print. A statue to the canine hero stands in front of the Town Hall in Barberton.

One of Africa's most dramatic views, the Three Rondavels in the Blyde River Canyon

RIVER OF HAPPINESS
In 1844, a party of Voortrekker men went ahead to look for a route to the coast, leaving their women and children camped on the top of the escarpment. After one month, they had not returned, and the grief-stricken women assumed that they were dead. The women turned back, naming the river beside their campsite the Treur (River of Sorrow). A couple of days later, as they reached another small river, the overdue men returned. Amid the celebrations, the new river was named the Blyde (River of Happiness).

▶▶▶ **Blyde River Canyon** 174C2

About 60km (37 miles) north of Graskop on the R532. Tourist Information, Bourke's Luck Potholes (tel: 013-769 6019)
Protected by a nature reserve, this spectacular canyon—26km (16 miles) long and 350–800m (1,148–2,624ft) deep—was gouged from the earth's crust by the humble Blyde River over 60 million years. There are superb views, the finest of them overlooking the **Three Rondavels**, conical mini-mountains that look like traditional thatched huts. The canyon floor is a true wilderness, accessible only by a 2-day, 38.5km (24 mile) hike along the river. Early Stone Age human remains have been discovered here, and San cave art is abundant. Highlights nearby include **Marieskop**, the highest peak in the district (1,946m/6,383ft), a 200m (656ft) waterfall and **Bourke's Luck Potholes** (see page 184).

▶ **Echo Caves** see page 184

▶ **Hazyview** 182C2

421km (262 miles) east of Johannesburg
Panorama Information and Central Reservations, Simunya Centre (tel: 013-737 7414, fax: 013-737 7415)
This is one of the most convenient places to stay in Mpumalanga, with every hilltop crowned by a delightful hotel. The town itself has little to offer, aside from lively roadside market stalls. A 1-hour tour of **Bombyx Mori Silk Farm** (85km/53 miles north of Hazyview, tel: 015-795 5813. *Open: Mon–Sat 9–4; tours at 9, 10.30, 12, 1.30 and 3. Admission: expensive*) takes in the production and weaving facilities and a wonderful shop. About 9km (5.5 miles) north of Hazyview on the R535, the **Shangana Cultural Village** (tel: 013-737 7000, www.shangana.co.za. Tours: 9, 10, 11, 3, 4 and 6, with dinner. *Admission: expensive*) is an entertaining cultural village with dancing, a traditional sangoma and mopane worms to eat.

▶▶▶**Kruger National Park** see pages 186–187

▶ **Nelspruit** *174C2*

330km (205 miles) east of Johannesburg
Lowveld Tourism, 1 Nelstreet, Civic Centre
(tel: 013-755 1988, fax: 013-755 1350, www.lowveldinfo.com)
Open: Mon–Fri 8–4.30
Capital of Mpumalanga, Nelspruit is an attractive small town garlanded with bougainvillea and surrounded by citrus groves. Named after the Nel brothers, who used the area as winter grazing for their cattle in the 1870s, the town developed around the railway but is now a trading base for local farmers. Nearby is **Lowveld Botanical Gardens** (on the R40/R37 junction, 6km (4 miles) from town, tel: 013-752 5531. *Open* Oct–end Apr daily 8–6; May–end Sep daily 8–5.15. *Admission: inexpensive*) and **Crocgrove Crocodile Farm** (about 25km/15 miles west on the R539, tel: 013-752 5511. *Admission: expensive*).

▶▶ **Pilgrim's Rest** *174C2*

Tourist Information, opposite Royal Hotel,
Main Street (tel: 013-768 1060). Open: daily 9–12.45, 1.45–4
After Alec Patterson found the first commercial gold at Pilgrim's Creek in 1873, Pilgrim's Rest grew up as the adjacent miners' village. It is said to have been named by the first group of diggers, who called themselves 'The Pilgrims' because they were always in search of spirits (reputedly they arrived complete with a wagonload of whisky). There were rich pickings; the largest nugget found here weighed 11kg (24lb). The miners did not stay for long, but the little town, with its houses of galvanized iron, has survived almost intact. A walking map leads visitors around the cemetery, shops and old houses, many of which are vacation cottages. There are several small museums, including the **Diggings Site**, the **Drezden Shop and House** and the typical wood and corrugated-iron **House Museum**. (A single ticket, valid for all the museums, is available from the tourist office.)

▶ **Sabie** see page 185

▶ **Sudwala Caves** *174C2*

About 35km (22 miles) northwest of Nelspruit, off the R539
(tel: 013-733 4152). Open: daily 8.30–4.30. Tours last 1 hour.
Admission: expensive
The Sudwala Caves snake for over 30km (19 miles) through the dolomitic Mankelekele in the northern Drakensberg. Tourists normally go no farther than 600m (1,968ft) underground, yet even this section is spectacular, with giant chambers and twisted rocks. Strange fossil algae such as stromatolites—the earliest identifiable forms of life—date the rocks to 2,000 million years, nearly half the age of Earth. Below the entrance is the **P. R. Owen Dinosaur Park**, with life-size replicas of prehistoric beasts.

▶ **White River** *174C2*

Lowveld Information (tel: 013-750 1073)
This small farming town grew up as a resettlement area for British soldiers after the Anglo-Boer War. Just outside town, **Rottcher Wineries** (Nutcracker Valley, tel: 013-751 3884) specializes in orange and ginger wines.

REFUGE
In the 19th century, Somquba, son of the Swazi king Sobhuza I, stole a number of royal cattle, then fled. He and his followers hid in the Sudwala Caves while his brother, Mswati, laid siege outside. On several occasions, Mswati tried to smoke out the fugitives, but the caves have a natural ventilation system and they survived. Somquba was eventually killed by Mswati's troops but survivors stayed on, led by Sudwala (Somquba's officer), for whom the caves are named.

183

The beautiful Sudwala Caves, one-time refuge for a royal thief

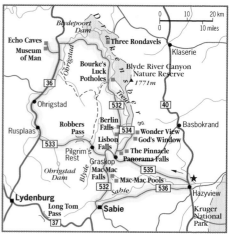

Drive

Rim of the escarpment

The scenery is stunning and the air cool and crisp, with the scent of a million wildflowers. Allow at least one long day. Start at Hazyview, take the R40 north, then turn left on the R535 to the market town of **Graskop** (Panorama Information, tel: 013-767 1377).

Leave Graskop on the R532 heading north, then turn right onto the R534, a 15km (9 miles) panoramic loop with tumbling views off the escarpment and across the lowveld to the Mozambique coast. There are four main viewing points, at **Panorama Falls**, **The Pinnacle**, **God's Window**►► and **Wonder View**. God's Window has the most breathtaking views, and featured as the edge of the world in the film *The Gods Must Be Crazy*. As the road rejoins the R532, paths lead to two fine waterfalls, the 92m (302ft) **Lisbon Falls** and 150m (492ft) **Berlin Falls**.

The R532 continues north for about 50km (31 miles) to **Bourke's Luck Potholes**► (tel: 013-769 6019. *Open daily 7–5. Visitor centre 8–5. Admission: inexpensive*), which mark one end of the **Blyde River Canyon** (see page 182). This is the confluence of the Treur and Blyde rivers, a dramatic landscape of strange pools and cauldrons of rock, carved over the millennia by tempestuous water. The 30m (98ft) potholes are named after a 19th-century surveyor, Thomas Bourke, who found a great deal of gold here. Unfortunately, he worked for a big mining conglomerate and so never reaped the rewards. The visitor centre has a museum, and walking trails for visitors with visual or physical disabilities. A little farther along the road you reach the first and most dramatic of several panoramas, with a magnificent view of the **Three Rondavels** (see page 182) and **Blydepoort Dam**.

The road wriggles along the rim of the canyon before looping south to join the R36. After about 10km (6 miles), a turn-off to the right leads to **Echo Caves**►, a huge dolomitic complex of tunnels and caverns (the largest is 100m/328ft long and 45m/148ft wide) in the Molapong Valley. Tap the stalactites and they echo. The eastern end is open to the public, while the western end is home to millions of bats. A neighbouring San rock shelter now houses the small **Museum of Man**, displaying archaeological finds from the caves. Return to the R36 and continue south for 36km (22 miles). A turn-off to the left, onto the R533, leads over Robbers Pass to **Pilgrim's Rest** (see page 183).

Continue along the R533 towards Graskop for 17km (10 miles), then turn right onto the R532 in the direction of Sabie. After about 12km (7 miles), you come to the **Mac-Mac Falls** and, 2km (1 mile) farther on, the **Mac-Mac Pools** on the Sabie River. Site of an alluvial gold strike in 1872, these delightful pools and falls were named by President Burgers, who looked at the 1,000-odd miners scratching for gold and was astonished to find that most of them were Scots. The water originally fell in a single stream, but was split by a dynamite blast in an attempt to reach the gold-bearing quartz on the bank.

Thirteen kilometres (8 miles) on, the town of **Sabie▶** (Tourist Information, Market Square, tel: 013-764 1125, fax: 013-764 1134. *Open* Mon–Fri 9–5, Sat–Sun 9–1) was founded in

Left: the Mac-Mac Falls
Below: Bourke's Luck Potholes

1871, when someone fired a stray bullet during a shooting party, chipped off a piece of rock, and revealed a rich gold reef. Today, wood provides the lifeblood of the town and local forests supply half of all South Africa's needs. The **Forest Museum** (7th Street, tel: 013-764 1058. *Open* Mon–Fri 8–4.30. *Admission: inexpensive*) has a varied display on the timber industry, from chain saws to a model church made of matches. Little, grey-stone **St. Peter's church** was designed by Herbert Baker in 1913. The surrounding area has many waterfalls, while **Long Tom Pass**, on the R37 to Lydenburg, is one of the most spectacular mountain roads in South Africa. A disabled Long Tom field gun stands at the top as an Anglo-Boer War memorial. Take the R536 along the Sabie River valley for 45km (28 miles), back to Hazyview.

185

THE SABIE RIVER

There are several opinions on how this river got its name. One option derives from the Shangaan name Ulusaba ('River of Fear'). Some say it is haunted by black soldiers killed during tribal wars, whose bodies were thrown into the river without being ripped open to release the spirits. Others, more prosaically, suggest a healthy respect for the river's strong currents and large crocodile population. A more credible option comes from the Karanga word *save*, meaning 'sand': this is the name of one of the major tributaries and of the main river farther downstream in Mozambique.

Termite hills feature among the scrubland of Kruger National Park

▶▶▶ Kruger National Park   174C2/C3

Descend the precipitous heights of the ruggedly beautiful escarpment, and the transition from the highveld to the subtropical lowveld, with its well-watered acacia and mopane woodland, is complete. The rolling plain seldom rises above 350m (1,148ft) as it stretches eastwards towards the Mozambique coast. It is a habitat perfectly designed for antelope and lion, elephant, giraffe and hippo. Intensely hot and dry in summer, and a natural home to diseases such as malaria and sleeping sickness, the plain is less accessible for man. Ironically, the fever allowed a small corner of wild country to survive South Africa's farmers. Today, a substantial part of this area is the home of Kruger National Park. Founded in 1903, the park is 350km (217 miles) long, up to 60km (37 miles) wide, and covers an area the size of Wales or Israel. Kruger has five major rivers, 300 species of tree, 114 species of reptile, 507 species of bird and 147 species of mammal. At any given moment, there are thought to be around 8,000 elephants, 1,500 lions, 1,900 white rhinos, 220 black rhinos, 15,000 buffalos and up to 900 leopards in the park.

In 1993 the fences between the park and the surrounding private reserves were taken down. Traditional elephant migration routes were reopened in 2002 when South Africa, Zimbabwe and Mozambique pulled down their fences to create the vast Gaza-Kruger-Gonarezhou Transfrontier Park (see page 177).

In general, the farther north you go, the drier and hotter the climate, the more desolate the vegetation, the fewer the tarred roads, and the more rudimentary the camps. Most visitors huddle in the southern half of the park, within a day's drive of Skukuza, the main camp and park administration base, which has room for 3,000 visitors on any one night. Keep away from here if you want solitude.

Practicalities From north to south, the gates are: Pafuri, Punda Maria, Phalaborwa and Orpen in the Limpopo Province; Paul Kruger, Numbi, Crocodile Bridge and Malelane in Mpumalanga. The busiest is Paul Kruger, which is the nearest entry point for Skukuza Camp (500km/310 miles from Johannesburg; reception tel: 013-735 4152. *Open* Nov–end Feb 5.30am–6.30pm; Mar and Oct 5.30m–6pm; April, Aug–end Sept 6–6, May–end July 6–5.30. *Admission: expensive*). Scheduled air services operate to Kruger Mpumalanga Airport near Nelspruit and Phalaborwa/Hoedspruit. There are about 22 camps (tel: 012-428 9111, fax: 012-343 0905, www.sanparks.org), ranging from small remote camping areas to the main camps, which all have a shop, restaurant and cafeteria, picnic facilities, toilets, fuel and diesel, telephones, first aid and accommodation.

The Kruger is a malarial area, so take precautions. Do not leave your vehicle, drive off the road or feed the animals. Speed limits are 50kph (30mph) on tarred roads, 40kph (25mph) on dirt roads. Park authorities also run three-day wilderness hikes, camping rough.

Private game parks Along the western edge of the park are several private game reserves, built up by rich, ardent conservationists to contain luxury lodges and hunting grounds. The five major blocks, from south to north, are

Sabie Sands, **Manyeleti**, **Timbavati**, **Klaserie** and **Umbabat**, of which Sabie Sands is by far the most important for tourism and home to a dozen different luxury game lodges such as Sabi Sabi, Exeter and Inyati (see page 262). Here you can stay in quiet luxury, with game coming to you at the waterhole or river below the terrace. Most lodges are unfenced, and you could find a buffalo or herd of kudu peering through your bedroom window; and while your ranger may not be allowed to track an elephant onto someone else's land, the animals roam freely across all boundaries. You are more likely to see the 'Big Five' at the lodges than in the main park, as you will be in an open Land Rover with qualified rangers and trackers, who are able to leave the road and take you on night drives or on foot, activities usually curtailed.

Massive, graceful, and spellbinding, elephants and giraffes are highlights of any visit to Kruger

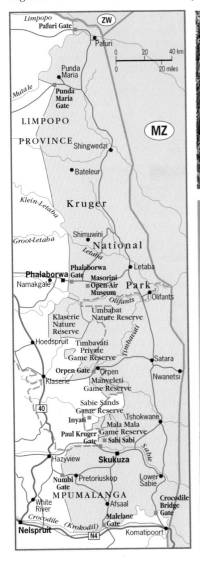

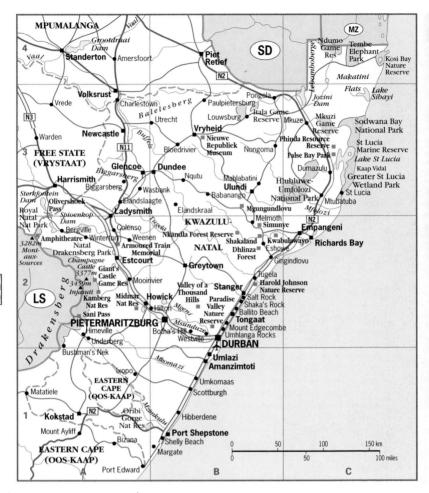

BITTER BEGINNINGS On Christmas Eve, 1497, the Portuguese navigator Vasco da Gama dropped anchor off a lush, green, subtropical coast. In tribute to the day, he named the land Natalia. Oblivious to this fact, its inhabitants continued to raise and rustle cattle, the numerous small tribes squabbling constantly and violently. Nothing disturbed this existence until about 1809, when a formidable Mthethwa ruler, Dingiswayo, began to conquer and absorb many small groups and clans. His successor, the great Shaka, continued the task from 1815 onwards. The Mfecane (see pages 30–31) marked the true birth of the Zulu nation.

At much the same time as this, the early Voortrekkers were beginning to look covetously at the fertile valleys, while the British were keeping a beady eye on any territory that the Boers might open up. In 1838, the inevitable happened. The Zulus massacred a party of Boer settlers (see page 33) and the territorial disputes dissolved into bitter bloodshed. The Boers then annexed much of the Zulu territory and broke away from the Cape Colony, creating the Republic of Natalia.

▶▶▶ **REGION HIGHLIGHTS**

The Drakensberg
pages 208–209

Dundee *page 202*

Eshowe and environs
pages 212–213

Golden Mile
pages 194–195

Hluhluwe-Umfolozi
National Park *page 213*

St. Lucia *page 214*

uShaka Marineworld
page 197

Tour: The Disputed
Territory
pages 204–207

Pietermaritzburg
pages 210–211

INDIAN DURBAN
With a huge Indian population, parts of Durban seem a continent apart. Start at the Victoria Street Market (corner of Queen and Victoria streets, tel: 031-306 4021. *Open* Mon–Sat 6–6, Sun 10–4) and surrounding Grey Street trading area, a district clouded with spices and billowing gilt-embroidered silk. Other stops should include the beautiful Muslim Juma Mosque (155 Queen Street, tel: 031-306 0026), the Hindu Ganesha Temple (Mount Edgecombe), the Shree Ambalvanar Alayam Second River Temple (Bellair Road) and the Hari Krishna Temple of Understanding (Florence Nightingale Drive, Chatsworth, tel: 031-403 3328. *Open* daily 4–9).

Durban's Golden Mile, the perfect place for a suntan

The British took it all back in 1843, naming the new colony Natal. In 1877, they tried and failed to annex the Boer territory in northern Natal, and then focused on the Zulu heartland, deposing King Cetshwayo and absorbing his kingdom into the Empire. By 1902, with the final defeat of the Boers, the British had conquered the whole area.

INDIAN IMMIGRANTS Natal was immensely fertile, with sugarcane and cotton in abundance, but there was a severe shortage of labour to work the fields. Slavery had been abolished in 1834 and the Zulus showed no interest in working for the white farmers. On 16 November, 1860, a paddle-steamer from Madras, the SS *Truro*, docked in Durban. On board were 342 indentured Indian workers (including 75 women and 83 children under the age of 14): the first of many shipments. Thousands of poverty-stricken Indians were persuaded to sign five-year contracts that forced them to work under appalling conditions. They included Hindus, Muslims and a few Christians, and came from all areas of the Indian subcontinent, although most were from the south and west. Other wealthier, free Indians also arrived to set up as traders. In 1913, the Natal government, alarmed by the competition from these hard-working merchants, banned general Indian immigration, and in 1920 the system of indentured labour was finally ended, under pressure from Mahatma Gandhi. Today, South Africa has an Indian population of about 1.25 million, 928,000 of them living in and around Durban. The community is renowned for its success in business, while a number of Indians hold high office in government. About 70 per cent are Hindu, 20 per cent Muslim and the remainder Christian. There are several fine temples and mosques across the province, fascinating Indian markets and some of the best curries in the world. The remains of Gandhi's first *ashram* still stand at Durban's Phoenix Settlement.

A MODERN KINGDOM Modern KwaZulu-Natal covers 91,481sqkm (35,311sq miles) on South Africa's eastern seaboard. It is administered jointly from the old white capital Pietermaritzburg and Ulundi, the traditional royal seat of the Zulu kings. The monarchy was restored in 1951, although it has no actual power. Nevertheless, the current king, Goodwill Zwelithini, is revered by his people and is a significant force in national affairs.

Of all nine provinces in South Africa, KwaZulu-Natal is the only one that did not submit happily and peaceably to the new constitution. However, things have now quietened down with the Inkatha Freedom Party—led by the prime minister of KwaZulu, Mangosotho Buthelezi (himself the grandson of King Dinizulu)—preferring to agitate for further autonomy from the floor of the Houses of Parliament. There is still some friction, but the violence that marred the mid-1990s and hopes of a peaceful transition is for now all in the past.

KwaZulu-Natal is the most populous (about 9.6 million) state in South Africa, with rich resources, including plentiful water, coal, minerals and agricultural land (Natal produces 75 per cent of South Africa's sugar, along with timber, beef, dairy products, maize, poultry and fruit). Durban is the largest port in Africa (and ninth-largest in the world), while the bulk export harbour at Richards Bay is one of the world's largest coal export terminals. The province also has the most comprehensive tourist infrastructure in the country (with around 3.2 million visitors every year), even though only about 26 per cent of foreign visitors come here. The rest of them are missing a treat.

The province has truly magnificent scenery, from the soaring peaks of the Drakensberg to the forest-covered dunes and lagoons of St. Lucia. Superb Indian Ocean beaches and remote, dramatic game parks equal or surpass even the Kruger, but with a fraction of the number of visitors. And it has history. It is a land for storytellers, with tales of confrontation and conflict, bloody treachery, and glorious heroism. It is indeed a land fit for kings.

The Hindu Shree Ambalvanar Temple in Bellair Road, Durban

NATAL PARKS
Most reserves in KwaZulu-Natal come under the jurisdiction of KZN Wildlife, Head Office, PO Box 13069, Cascades, Pietermaritzburg 3202 (tel: 033-845 1002 (information), 033-845 1000 (parks bookings, 033-845 1067 (wilderness trails bookings), fax: 033-845 1001, www.kznwildlife.com), the successor to the old Natal Parks Board. *Open* Oct–Mar 5am–7pm; Apr–Sep 6–6. *Admission: expensive.* A Golden Rhino Passport offers free entry to all Board properties, but you need a special permit to take vehicles onto the beaches. Most Zululand reserves are malarial. Accommodation ranges from A-frame chalets to three-bedroom cottages, and fully serviced lodges with restaurants.

TOURIST INFORMATION

Tourist Junction, Station Building, 160 Pine Street, Durban (tel:031-366 7500, fax: 031-305 6693, www.zulu.org.za. *Open* Mon–Fri 8–5, Sat–Sun 9–2) is a one-stop shop for tourist information about KwaZulu-Natal. This excellent office also has desks for Durban Africa (tel: 031-304 6196, fax: 031-304 3868, email: funinsun@iafrica.com, www.durban.gov.za) for information on the Greater Durban area and to organize walking tours of the city; several local tour operators, car rental, travel and accommodation agencies; and KZN Wildlife. There are also tourism information offices at Durban Airport and the uShaka Marine Park.

Durban

This thriving metropolis is known as Durban to the British, eThegwini to the Zulus, Banana City to the irreverent and the 'city where the fun never sets' to its marketing department. Its population is approaching 3 million and it is growing faster than any other city in the world except Mexico City. It also has a multiple personality, with the normal sprawl of poverty-stricken townships around the edge, tight enclaves of white suburbia and a decidedly Asian feel in the middle. Indians make up nearly one-third of the city's population, and many, particularly the more confident and better educated,

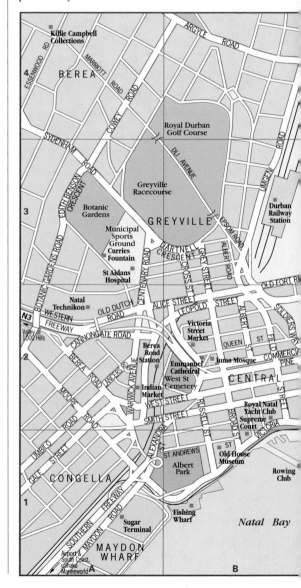

have moved out of the shadows of apartheid and into the city centre. The city is famous for its curries and for the fascinating spice market that perfumes the air.

Durban is really about water. It has a port so busy that ships sometimes have to line up for days before berthing, and a long fringe of sand so perfect that it could have been custom-crafted for the thousands of sun-worshippers who flock to the sun-parched waterfront. Although it can be very humid in summer, when the tip of the southwest monsoon brushes the coast, the normally pleasant subtropical climate provides 320 days of sunshine a year, and promotes a laid-back outdoor lifestyle with swimming and water sports all year round.

Today, towering office buildings dwarf the Victorian City Hall

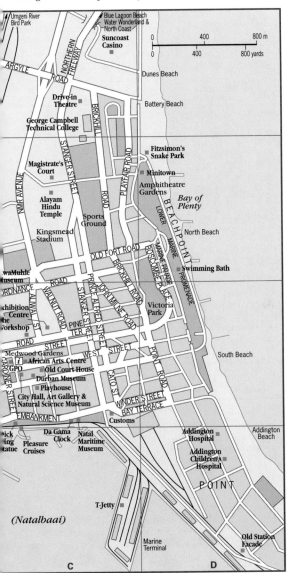

(Natalbaai)

Dick King, one of Durban's local heroes

DICK KING
SAVED NATAL MAY 1842

HEROES PARADE
Victoria Embankment is a gallery of memorials to local heroes. The Da Gama Clock (corner of Aliwal Street), donated by the Portuguese community in 1897, commemorates Vasco da Gama's first visit on Christmas Eve, 1497; the statue of Dick King (corner of Gardiner Street) honours a man and his horse, Somerset, who journeyed 960km (596 miles) to Grahamstown in 10 days to raise the alarm and bring relief to besieged British troops in Durban's Old Fort; and 14-year-old John Ross, who made an epic journey to the coast on foot to obtain medical supplies for the Durban settlers.

▶ **African Arts Centre** 193C2
1st floor, Tourist Junction, 160 Pine Street, Durban (tel: 031-304 7915). Open: Mon–Fri 8.30–5, Sat 9–1
This non-profit gallery is one of South Africa's finest platforms for traditional African art. Browse among the best of the best, from imaginative township crafts to traditional Hlabisa baskets, Rorke's Drift weaving, wood carvings from Empangeni and Tugela River beadwork. You should even find plenty of affordable souvenirs.

▶ **City Hall and museums** 193C2
City Hall, Smith Street
Francis Farewell Square has been the site of the local market since Durban's first European settlers, Henry Fynn and Francis Farewell, set up a trading post here in 1824. It is now dwarfed by Durban's overblown City Hall (1910), a replica of the city hall in Belfast, Northern Ireland.

Inside, the **Natural Science Museum** (tel: 031–311 2256; *Open* Mon–Sat 8.30–4, Sun 11–4. *Admission: free*) has hundreds of stuffed animals, birds, reptiles and fish, a life-size model dinosaur, a virtually complete dodo skeleton and South Africa's only Egyptian mummy. The Insect Arcade can make the flesh creep.

On the second floor, the **Durban Art Gallery** (tel: 031–311 2264. *Open* Mon, Tue, Thu–Sat 9.30–5; Wed 9.30–2, Sun 2.30–5. *Admission: free*) has fine collections of Victorian paintings, Chinese ceramics and French Lalique glass, as well as a powerful range of contemporary South African art, including magnificent Hlabisa basketware.

▶▶ **Golden Mile** 193D3
Durban's Golden Mile now stretches for 6km (4 miles) from Addington Beach along snazzy, fun-filled Marine Parade to Blue Lagoon Beach. Its sand gleams silver and gold, the water is clearest sapphire and the foam-topped waves were designed for surfers. It is also so jam-packed with hot, happy bodies that you can hardly pick your way between their legs. For the more adventurous, there are surfboards, bikes and paragliders (Addington Beach), and opportunities to sail, fish, snorkel and scuba dive. Lifeguards are on duty daily 7am–10pm. Be sure to leave valuables at home; pickpockets do good business here.

The buzzing promenade is filled with souvenir and ice-cream sellers. **Fitzsimon's Snake Park** (240A Snell Parade, tel: 031-337 6456. *Open* Daily 9–4.30. *Admission: moderate*) wriggles with snakes, crocodiles and iguanas. **Funworld** (Marine Parade, tel: 031-332 9776. *Admission: moderate*) has roller coasters, swings and bumper cars.

The **Amphitheatre** park has a busy Sunday flea market. Nearby is the **rickshaw** stand. Since 1893, public transport in Durban has included two-wheeled rickshaws. By 1904 there were over 2,000 clattering through the streets, laden with people and packages. The last commercial venture folded in the 1970s, but around 15 now offer rides for tourists. The runners wear colourful costumes and, when posing for photographs, add towering headdresses. There are also a few auto-rickshaws (tuk-tuks), familiar to anyone who has been to India or the Far East. **Minitown** (114 Snell Parade, North Beach, tel: 031-337 7892. *Open Daily 9.30–4. Admission: moderate*) displays scale replicas of Durban's best-known buildings. Across the road, the seafront hotels host a wide array of bars and restaurants.

At **North Beach**, you can also visit **Waterworld** (Snell Parade, tel: 031-337 6336. *Open Mon–Fri 9–5, Sat–Sun 8.15–5. Admission: expensive*) for pulsating and looping water-propelled slides, and the **Umgeni River Bird Park** (490 Riverside Road, off the N2 , tel: 031-579 4600. *Open daily 9–5; flight displays at 11 and 2. Admission: expensive*), where 30m (98ft) cliffs with tumbling waterfalls and lush gardens of palms and cycads are home to over 3,000 birds of 400 species.

WHEEL OF FORTUNE
The Suncoast Casino (Suncoast Boulevard, Battery Beach, tel: 031-328 3000, www.suncoast casino.co.za) is a pastel art deco confection with a casino, multiplex cinema, shopping and food arcades and entertainment venues. Its beach is regularly patrolled and is secure, with regular open-air events from jazz to sports. There is another huge casino complex farther along the coast, Sibaya (1 Sibaya Drive, Umhlanga, tel: 031-580 5555, www.suninternational.co.za) offers the Zulu Fire Cultural Expeience.

The rickshaw runners are one of the city's most colourful sights

195

The Killie Campbell Collection houses a fascinating account of traditional ethnic dress in South Africa

TOURS

There are several different ways to see Durban. The Ricksha Bus (tel: 031- 466 2282) runs sightseeing tours of the city on an open-topped bus, as well as shuttle services between the city centre and beaches. For guided city walking tours, tel: 082-672 1191. Umkumbane Tours (tel: 031-309 5021) run fascinating tours of multi-ethnic Durban. For helicopter tours contact INC Helicopters (tel: 031-563 9513).There are plenty of opportunities for spending a day out in a boat, from harbour tours to deep-sea fishing charters. Coral Sea Charters (tel: 031-467 0585) and Isle of Capri Pleasure Cruise (tel: 031-305 3099) do harbour cruises, whale- and dolphin- spotting, wreck diving and deep-sea fishing. For other options, contact the Durban Charter Boat Association (tel: 031-301 1115).

SHOPPING

Durban may well be the country's finest source of souvenirs. There are several market areas, including the predominantly Indian Grey Street area; the Victoria Street Market, with an enticing mix of Asian and African goods, from traditional potions to spices; the Zulu Dalton Road Market; the huge Sunday flea market in the Amphitheatre; and the Church Street Arts and Crafts Market.

Good malls include the Village Walk at uShaka Marineworld, the Wheel and the Workshop and the central Bat Centre, the Suncoast Casino, the Heritage Market on the road up to the Valley of a Thousand Hills and the north coast Gateway Casino.

▶▶ Killie Campbell Collection   *192A4*

*Corner of Marriott and Essenwood roads, Berea
(tel: 031-207 3711). Open: Mon–Fri 8.30–4.30, Sat 9–12
Guided tours by appointment*

Sugar baron Sir Marshall Campbell built himself a magnificent neo-Cape Dutch mansion, Muckleneuk, overlooking Durban. Now swallowed up by the suburbs, it is replete with suitably imposing furnishings collected by his son, William Campbell. His daughter, Dr. Margaret Roach Campbell—a keen anthropologist—created one of South Africa's finest private libraries of Africana. She also collected superb African cultural items, including musical instruments, pottery and costumes. A set of 250 superb paintings of tribal dress by local artist Barbara Tyrell complete the **Mashu Museum of Ethnology**.

▶ KwaMuhle Museum   *193C3*

*130 Ordnance Road (tel: 031-311 2223)
Open: Mon–Sat 8.30–4, Sun 11–4. Admission: free*

KwaMuhle means the 'place of the good one'. This thought-provoking museum, housed in the 1930s offices of the Bantu Administration Board, honours J. S. Marwick, a civil servant during the Anglo-Boer War, who—with his *iduna* Prince Pika Zulu—helped 7,000 migrant workers to escape from the Transvaal to Natal and Zululand. The museum covers the 20th-century history of Durban and South Africa as seen through the non-white communities.

▶ Natal Maritime Museum 193C2
*Bayside end of Aliwal Street, use Victoria Embankment
entrance (tel: 031-311 2231)*
Open: Mon–Sat 8.30–4, Sun 11–4. Admission: inexpensive
Durban is all about boats, as proved by this harbourfront
museum. Sea View Cottage is a re-created early settler's
home. There are excellent views of the docks from the
deck of the **Harbour Terminal** (Stanger Street).

▶ Old Court House 193C2
Corner of Aliwal and Smith streets (tel: 031-311 2233)
Open: Mon–Sat 8.30–4, Sun 11–4. Admission: free
Built in 1863, Durban's first public building now houses a
fascinating museum of local history. The exhibits
comprise an eclectic mix of architecture, fashion, sugar,
shipping, stamps, maps, documents and fine art relating
to the city's history.

▶ Old House Museum 192B1
31 St. Andrews Street (tel: 031-311 2261)
Open: Mon–Sat 8.30–4, Sun 11–4. Admission: donation
This is an exact replica of a settler homestead, built by
John Goodricke in 1894. It remains fully furnished and
equipped with domestic items dating from 1850 to 1900.

▶▶▶ uShaka Marineworld *Off map 192A1*
*Bell Street, Point, tel: 031-328 8000. Open: Sea World daily
9–5 (winter), 9-6 (summer), Sun-Tue 6-9pm, Snorkel Lagoon,
OceanWalker and Xpanda Shark Dive closed Mon; Wet'n'Wild
Wed–Sun 9–5 (winter), 9-6 (summer). Admission: expensive
(Village Walk free).*
The showpiece of the Point Waterfront Development
which is transforming huge areas of the old Durban
docks, uShaka Marineworld is a vast tourism project,
with the Village Walk, a glitzy mall full of shops and
restaurants, wrapped around a stunning
marine park. One of the world's largest
aquariums, Sea World includes a 1,200
seater dolphinarium with regular shows, a
seal pool, penguin rookery, dive tank
(including shark diving), a snorkel reef
and touch pool. The centrepiece shipwreck contains a couple of excellent
restaurants, while Wet'n'Wild theme park
has water slides and rides for young and
old, its water heated in winter.

Parks
Botanic Gardens▶ (70 St. Thomas Road,
Berea, tel: 031-201 1303. *Open* daily
Apr–Sep, 7.30–5.15; Oct–Mar, 7.30–5.45.
Admission: free) These botanic gardens are
the oldest and most beautiful in Durban,
with delightful woodlands, ancient
cycads, a sunken garden, a scented garden
for the blind and a superb **Orchid House**
(*Open* daily 9.30–12.30, 2–5) with over
3,000 specimens. There are also enchanting **Japanese Gardens▶** for those in search
of peace (Tinsley Road, Durban North, tel:
031-563 1333. *Open* daily 7.30–4).

OTHER MUSEUMS
Museums in the Durban vicinity include the Bergtheil Museum (16 Queens Avenue, Westville, tel: 031-203 7107) a 19th-century farmhouse full of memorabilia of the 1848 German settlers; the Cato Manor Heritage Centre (Intuthuko Junction, 750 Francois Road, Cato Manor, tel: 031-261 6640) with its apartheid history; the Private Garden And Bead Museum (Meriwinkle Estate, Kloof, tel: 031-767 0361), with beautiful gardens and collection of African beadwork and traditional objects; the Phansi Museum (Cedar Road, tel: 031-206 1591), more tribal objects in a Victorian mansion; and Coedmore Castle (Coedmore Ave, Yellowwood, tel: 031-462 3005), a grandiose old family home built in 1885.

197

*Hand-feeding the sharks
in Durban's uShake
Marineworld*

If South Africa has one obsession, it is sports. Top rugby and cricket players rank with film stars, and everyone watches compulsively, both indigenous competitions and foreign fixtures such as the English soccer league. During the 1980s sanctions, the loss of international sporting links caused real heartache.

Since 1994, South Africa has leaped back into the international arena with impressive prowess. In 1995, Nelson Mandela wore a rugby jersey to watch the Springboks win the Rugby World Cup on home ground. Subsequently, South Africa has taken on the cricketing fraternity, and hosted—and won—soccer's 1996 African Nations Cup. The country already has some of the finest golf courses in the world. Andwork has already started on preparation for the 2010 Football (Soccer) World Cup.

Sports, except for soccer, still represent primarily a white-man's world. The 1995 winning rugby team had only one black player, and few black townships or schools have the money for more than a dusty square of open ground where children can kick a ball around. For those with the money, anything you care to mention is on offer, from a full range of competitive sports to riding, hiking, climbing, water sports, ballooning and hang-gliding, canoeing, fishing, tennis and golf. Facilities are always excellent.

Triumph for South Africa in the 1995 Rugby World Cup

Spectator sports Cricket, rugby and soccer are the three top spectator sports, with keenly contested local and national leagues as well as the revitalized, headline-grabbing international competitions. For information contact **United Cricket Board of South Africa** (tel: 011-880 2810, www.cricinfo.com); **South African Rugby Football Union** (tel: 021-685 3038, www.sarugby.net); **South African Football Association** (tel: 011-494 3522, www.safa.net); **Premier Soccer League** (tel: 011-402 2424).

Golf Golf is immensely popular in South Africa, with multiple courses in major cities and tourist areas such as the Garden Route, Mpumalanga and Sun City (home of the Million Dollar Golf Challenge, the biggest cash prize on the

international circuit).
Up in the Northern Cape, there is an all-sand desert course close to Upington. Visitors are welcome at most clubs during the week by prior arrangement (South African Golf Association, tel: 011-442 3723, www.saga.co.za). Equipment is available to rent at hotels with their own courses. Costs (inclusive of green fees, caddy fees and tips) vary, but are not too high.

Fishing There are excellent opportunities for deep-sea and coastal fishing, spear fishing and freshwater trout and coarse fishing. The deep-sea fishing season is November to April (marlin and sailfish) in the north, and September to April (long-fin and yellowfin tuna) in the south. Boat charters include the cost of equipment, bait and rods. Permission is not needed to fish in public freshwater, but you may need a licence. This is compulsory for fishing in proclaimed trout angling waters. Anglers Corner (tel: 011-793 3321) is a Johannesburg fishing emporium that can supply gear and answer all questions.

Casting from the beach, East London

Water sports Surfing conditions are excellent, with the Eastern Cape coast, around Jeffrey's Bay and Cape St. Francis, drawing top surfers from around the world. The Gunston 500 International Surfing Championship is held each July. Sunscene (www.sunscene.co.za) runs surfing tours from Cape Town. Waterskiing can be arranged on both inland lakes and offshore (South African Waterski Federation; tel: 011-634 0430, www.sawaterski.co.za). There is windsurfing year round on inland lakes and seaside lagoons, but most offshore locations are too rough. Boats available for rent range from rowing boats and dinghies to power boats and racing yachts (South African Charter Boats Association, tel: 031-301 1115).

MORE INFO
www.southafrica.co.za/sports is an excellent travel website that provides links to hundreds of sporting websites in or about South Africa, covering every possible option from archery to surfboarding. Adventure Safaris and Sports, PO Box 32176, Camps Bay 8040, Cape Town (tel: 021-438 5201) is a specialist sports tour operator offering everything from golf to shark diving.

Durban environs

▶ North Coast   188B2

Sugar Coast Tourist Information, Umhlanga Rocks (tel: 031-561 4257); Dolphin Coast Publicity, Ballito (tel/fax: 032-946 1997, www.dolphincoast.co.za)

This is an attractive, but increasingly built-up area, with an abundance of places of historical or natural interest.

The **Sharks Board** 1a Herrwood Drive, Umhlanga, 18km (11 miles) north of Durban (tel: 031-566 0400, www.shark. co.za. *Open* Mon–Fri 8–4; shows and dissections Tue–Thu 9 and 2, Sun 2. *Admission: expensive*) has shows that are not for the faint-hearted. For early boat tours, tel: 082-403 9206. From **Ballito Beach**, the area is tagged the 'Dolphin Coast' after the local bottlenose dolphins.

At **Shaka's Rock**, Zulu warriors proved their manhood by leaping into the sea, and the women collected salt from tidal pools at **Salt Rock**. **Tongaat** is the oldest Indian community in South Africa, and features the **Vishwaroop Temple** and the **Juggernnath Puri Temple** (1901).

In Stanger, next to the King Shaka Memorial—site of his death and grave—the **Dukuza Interpretive Centre** (23 King Shaka Road, tel: 032-552 7210. *Open* daily 8–4. *Admission: free*) has displays about the Zulu royal dynasty. Across the road, at the **Dukuza Museum** (tel: 032-551 3091 ext. 116. *Open* Mon–Fri 9–3.30. *Admission: donation*) there's a sugar mill, Zulu art and weapons and the history of Indian life on the sugar plantations. At the Tugela River mouth, the **Harold Johnson Nature Reserve** surrounds **Fort Pearson** (1878) and the **Ultimatum Tree**, where, in 1878, the British demanded that Cetshwayo yield his sovereignty and army to imperial rule.

▶ South Coast   188B1

www.hibiscuscoast.kzn.org.za

The 'Hibiscus Coast', as it is known, should be a paradise of golden sand, limpid waters and tangled coastal forests. Unfortunately, its popularity has engendered a continuous strip of small resorts that have spoiled the look although there are five pristine Blue Flag beaches. There are also great surfing waves and whale and dolphin watching tours.

The **South African Sugar Terminal** (51 Maydon Wharf, corner of Maydon and Leuchars roads, Durban, tel: 031-365 8153. Tours Mon–Fri 8.30, 10, 11.30, 2 except Fri. *Admission: inexpensive*) tells you about sugar production and has tours of the silos.

Even crocodiles have charm in the baby stage

Amanzimtoti (Tourist Information, Beach Road, tel: 031-903 7498), known as 'Toti', is a booming family resort with great beaches and entertainment. The **Amanzimtoti Bird Sanctuary** (Umdoni Road, tel: 031-903 7498. *Open* daily 6–6. *Admission: free*) has a self-guided, 30-minute walking trail and hides. **Scottburgh** (tel: 039-976 1364) has a miniature railway and **Croc World** (Old South Coast Road, tel: 039-976 1103. *Open* daily 8.30–4.30. Feeding times Tue–Sun 11, 3), with 10,000 crocodiles, an aquarium and Zulu dancing. **Port Shepstone** (tel: 039-682 2455) is home to the narrow-gauge **Banana Express** railway (see page 235), and has a small **Maritime Museum** (near the beach, tel: 039-682 2455. *Open* Wed, Thu 12–4). Nearby is the spectacular **Oribi Gorge**, carved out by the Umzimkulwana River. Offshore, a 3km (2 mile) fossilized sand dune, the **Aliwal Shoal**, and the nearby **Protea Banks** offer some of Africa's best dive sites (see panel, page 214).

Margate is popular with the young, with freshwater and tidal pools, amusement park and an **Art Museum** (Viking Street, tel: 039-312 2525. *Open* Tue–Fri 9–5, Sat 10–3).

▶ **Valley of a Thousand Hills**   *188B2*
Tourist Information, Old Man Road, Botha's Hill
(tel: 031-777 1874, www.1000hills.kzn.org.za)
Open: Mon–Fri 8–4, Sat–Sun 10.30–1.30
The uplands surrounding the huge Umgeni River valley have quintessentially English villages, cool breezes and dramatic views. The **Paradise Valley Nature Reserve** (tel: 031-702 3443. *Open* daily 7.30–5. *Admission: inexpensive*) has coastal bush with waterfalls and walking trails. **Phezulu** (Botha's Hill, Durban, tel: 031-777 1000. *Open* daily 8.30–4.30. *Admission: expensive*) is a Zulu village spectacular, safari park and crocodile and snake farm.

On Air Raptor Displays (north of Phezulu on the T1 road to Pietermaritzburg, tel: 031-777 1871. *Admission: expensive*) offers dazzling flight shows Tue–Fri 10.30, Sat–Sun 10.30, 3. The **1000 Hills Choo-Choo** steam train operates from Kloof Station, Inchanga twice a month (tel: 082-353 6003, booking essential).

The extravagantly named Valley of a Thousand Hills

REGAL FRATRICIDE
In 1825, Shaka built a royal *kraal* of some 2,000 beehive huts at Stanger, known as KwaDukuza ('place of the lost person') because of its labyrinthine layout. He conducted meetings under an old *mkuhla* (Natal mahogany) tree, which still survives in Roodt Street. On 22 September, 1828, he was murdered by his half-brothers, Dingane and Mhlangane, who then burned the entire town. A memorial in Stanger marks Shaka's deathsite and grave.

SARDINE RUN
In July each year, vast schools of pilchards (*Sardinops ocellata*) migrate north from the Cape coast, coming inshore to avoid the fast-flowing Mozambique current. Driven ashore by rampaging predators, they beach themselves in great flopping heaps. Locals pour down to the beach and simply pick them up.

TOURIST INFORMATION
Battlefields Route
Association (tel: 083-802
1643, www.battlefields.
kzn.org.za)

SHOPPING STOPS
Elandskraal, near Dundee,
is a country town so in
touch with its German
roots that it still has an
'oompah' band. The very
cheap and very basic local
trading store is used as a
supply base by the local
tribespeople, who wander
the aisles dressed in
traditional beads and
blankets. At Wasbank,
Tactile Carpets (tel:
034-651 1678) sells
individually designed
and created carpets
and tapestries.

DRESSING FOR WAR
During the Anglo-Zulu
Wars, the British wore
single-breasted red tunics,
blue trousers and pith
helmets. They carried
.45 Martini Henry rifles,
capable of firing 55
rounds every three
minutes, with a range of
900m (2,952ft). Zulu
warriors went into battle
wearing a loincloth and
small headdress (to distin-
guish regiments). They
carried a shield, a short
stabbing *assegai* (spear), a
knobkerrie (heavy wooden
battle hammer), and
throwing spears. By the
outbreak of war, they also
had an estimated 10,000
obsolete rifles. They
picked up 800 modern
Martini Henry rifles, with
ammunition, after the
Battle of Isandlwana.

Battlefields

▶ Colenso 188A2

Tourist Information, 36 Sir George Street (tel: 036-422 2111)
Colenso, on the Tugela River, was founded in 1855 and named after the controversial John Colenso, Bishop of Natal (1853–1883). Notable historic buildings include the **R. L. Stevenson Museum** (tel: 036-422 2111. *Open* Mon–Fri 8–6; keys available from the police station next door) in the Old Toll House (1879) next to Bulwer Bridge, which houses relics of the Anglo-Boer War's Battle of Colenso. On 15 December, 1899, Sir Redvers Buller made his first serious attempt to relieve the siege of Ladysmith (see pages 206–207). Fought along the river to the east and west of Colenso, the battle was a triumph for the Boer commander, General Louis Botha, resulting in the deaths of 1,500 British and only eight Boers. Many of the dead lie in the nearby **Ambleside Military Cemetery**, **Chieveley Military Cemetery** and **Clouston Field of Remembrance**.

Close by, the **Armoured Train Memorial** (between Frere and Chieveley on the R103) marks the spot where Winston Churchill, then war correspondent of the *Morning Post*, was captured by the Boers in 1899.

▶▶ Dundee 188B3

320km (198 miles) from Durban
Tourist Information, Victoria Street (tel: 034-212 2121,
fax: 034-218 2837, www.tourdundee.co.za)
Open: Mon–Fri 9–4.45, Sat 9–12
Founded by Peter Smith from Dundee in Scotland, this quiet town in the foothills of the Biggarsberg Mountains saw the first true battle of the Anglo-Boer War (see page 206). The **Talana Museum▶▶** (Vryheid Road, tel: 034-212 2654. *Open* Mon–Fri 8–4.30, Sat–Sun 10–4.30. *Admission: inexpensive*. The museum arranges tours of all the battle-fields) is one of the most impressive local museums in South Africa, built around Peter Smith's cottage (used as a dressing station during the battle) and many of the battle's gun emplacements and forts. Displays include the towns' development, the local Stone Age site of Nkupe Cave, Zulu history, glass, blacksmithing, carpentry and early mining. The coach house has wagons, farming and vehicle exhibits. Best of all are some stunningly graphic exhibitions on the Zulu and Anglo-Boer Wars.

The small **MOTHS Museum** (corner of Beaconsfield and Wilson streets, tel: 034-212 1250. *Open* on request, ask at the tourist office) has a fascinating collection of military memorabilia from 1879 onwards. About 32km (20 miles) from Dundee, the **Maria Ratschitz Mission** (tel: 034-212 651 1722. *Open* by arrangement) was built at the base of Hlatikulu Mountain in 1886 by Trappist monks. It is a delightful building with fine paintings and stained glass.

▶▶ Ithala Game Reserve 188B3

Louwsburg, about 70km (43 miles) east of Vryheid
(tel: 034-938 2540, www.kznwildlife.com)
For opening times see panel page 191
Most of this beautiful 29,653ha (73,243-acre) park in the Pongola River valley is made up of rocky kopjes, deep valleys and bushy thickets but about a quarter of the area is rolling golden grassland. It is well stocked with all the

major animals except lion, and includes a healthy rhino population. There are guided drives, night drives and game walks. Those who want a real experience of the bushveld should join one of the 3-day hiking trails.

▶▶ **Ladysmith** see pages 206–207

▶ **Vryheid**   *188B3*
345km (214 miles) northeast of Durban
Tourist Information, corner of Market and Landrost streets
(tel: 034-982 2133, email: information@vhd.dorea.co.za)
Open: Mon–Fri 7.30–1, 1.30–4
In 1884, the Boers in northern Natal helped Dinizulu, son of Cetshwayo, dispatch his rivals and take the throne. In return, he granted them land to establish a Boer republic. The pristine market town remains heavily Afrikaner.

There are three interesting museums (*Open* Mon–Fri 7.30–4. *Admission: inexpensive*). The 1884 Cape Dutch revival **Lukas Meijer House** (Mark Street) was the home of the president and now a museum, with period furnishings and exhibits on banking, printing, mining and Zulu crafts. The **Nieuwe Republiek Museum** (Landrost Street, tel: 034-982 2133 ext. 2287) was built in 1885 as the council chambers and offices of the Volksraad, and tells the story of the short-lived republic; the fort and prison cells added in 1887. The **Old Carnegie Library** (1906, corner of Mark and Landrost streets) houses the local history collection.

Three of the major battles of the Anglo-Zulu War were fought not far from Vryheid: one at **Ntombe Drift** (12 March 1879), closely followed by those at **Hlobane** (28 March 1879) and **Kambula** (29 March 1879).

THE PRINCE IMPERIAL
In 1879, Prince Napoleon Louis Eugène Jean Joseph, son of Napoleon III and the Empress Eugénie, begged to be allowed to head for South Africa with the British troops. Despite official misgivings, he was eventually allowed to go as an observer, and he set off on 1 June without a suitable escort. His party was attacked by Zulus and, while his retinue managed to escape, he had trouble mounting a frightened horse and was stabbed 17 times. His death marked the end of the Bonaparte pretensions to the throne of France.

203

Red wool and brass buttons—a hot and visible uniform for an African war

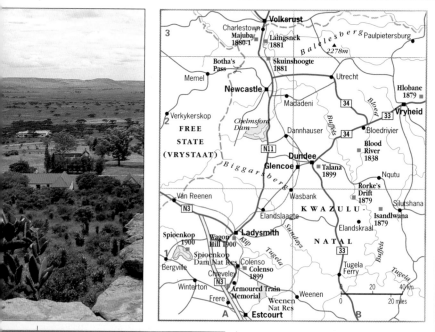

Tour

The Disputed Territory

For over 50 years, the grasslands of northern Natal saw bitter conflict as a result of the territorial ambitions of the Zulus, Boers and British. The area has South Africa's largest concentration of battlesites; most remain untouched and are intensely evocative of the action and tragedies that once drenched them in blood.

The official Battlefields Route covers 11 towns, over 50 battlefields and museums, war graves and memorials. Maps, guides, tapes and tours are available. Many sites are reached via minor roads and it is impossible to create a continuous route between them. Instead, they are arranged below chronologically (see also **South Africa Was**, pages 30–39, **Battlefields**, pages 202–203 and **Zululand**, pages 212–213).

Boer-Zulu War (1838)
Blood River (48km/30 miles east of Dundee, tel: 034-632 1695. *Open daily 8–5*). Following the massacre of Piet Retief (see page 33), a Boer unit of 464 men and 64 wagons, led by Andries Pretorius, took a solemn vow of retribution (see panel, page 167). On 15 December, they circled the wagons into a D-shaped formation at the confluence of the Ncome River and a *donga* (large ditch). Next morning, they found themselves surrounded by over 10,000 Zulus. Three times the Zulus were driven off by fierce rifle fire, then Pretorius led a mounted charge— the Zulus fled, trapping their own reserve in the river. In all, 3,000 Zulus died, with only three Boers wounded. The river was renamed after the slaughter and 16 December remains a national holiday. Today, 64 bronze wagons mark the battlefield; a small interpretation centre and a monument stand nearby. Across the river, the **Ncome Museum** (*Open daily 8–5. Admission: donation*) tells the story from the Zulu perspective.

Anglo-Zulu War (1879)
Isandlwana (80km/50 miles) south-east of Dundee, off the R68, tel: 034-271 0634. *Open daily 9–4. Admission: inexpensive*) was a tragic mistake.

Left: Rorke's Drift battlefield, from the Zulu perspective. Above: Memorial wagons at Blood River

Neither side intended to fight, but at about 11.30am on 22 January 1879, a British patrol stumbled over the Zulu army of 20,000, who were forced to attack the main British column of 1,774 men. Within 2 hours, 1,329 British and over 1,000 Zulu soldiers lay dead. Survivors fled across **Fugitive's Drift**, where most were then killed.

Rorke's Drift (42km/26 miles from Dundee, off the R68, tel: 034-642 1687. *Open* daily 8–4. Crafts centre open Mon–Fri 8–4; Sat 10–3.

Admission: inexpensive) is named after James Rorke, a British soldier who set up a trading post here in 1849. In 1878, the farm became a Swedish mission and a British military base. At 3.15am on 22 January 1879, two survivors of the battle at Isandlwana raised the alarm here. The tiny garrison of 139 soldiers, 35 of them hospital patients, began to fortify the base using everything from maize sacks to biscuit boxes. The attack, by four Zulu regiments (4,000 men) led by King Cetshwayo's brother, Dabulamanzi, began at 4.30. Twelve hours later the Zulus finally withdrew, leaving behind nearly 600 dead. Only 17 British soldiers were killed. Eleven Victoria Crosses were awarded to the defenders—more than for any other single engagement. The rebuilt hospital is now an interpretation centre.

First Anglo-Boer War (1880–1881) Majuba (on the N11 between Volksrust and Newcastle. *Admission: inexpensive*). On 12 April 1877, the British annexed the South African Republic; on 13 December 1880, guerrilla resistance blossomed into full-scale war. The governor of Natal, Sir George Colley, marched north, only to lose 150 men at Laingsnek (28 January) and a further 150 at Skhuinshoogte (8 February).

A 19th-century engraving of the battle at Rorke's Drift

On 27 February, Sir George assaulted the Boer-held Hill of Doves, Majuba, with a force of 579 men. By morning, 91 British, including Colley, were dead. It was the deciding point in the war. The British signed an armistice on 6 March, returning the ZAR to the Boers.

Second Anglo-Boer War (1899–1902)

Talana (Dundee, see also page 202). By the time war was declared on 9 October 1899, 4,000 British troops were stationed in Dundee, ready to protect the local coalfields. On 20 October, **Talana Hill** (hiking trail from the Talana Museum) became the scene of the first battle of the Anglo-Boer War when a 14,000-strong Boer army attacked the British camp. In a hard-fought struggle, the British eventually repelled their attackers, leaving 51 British and 145 Boers dead. Two days later, the British retreated. (This was the first time the British abandoned their red coats in favour of practical khaki.)

Ladysmith▶▶ (231km/143 miles from Durban. Tourist Information, Town Hall, Murrchison Street, tel: 036-637 2992, www.ladysmith.co.za. *Open* Mon–Fri 9–4, Sat 9–12) became a focal point for the Anglo-Boer war following the British rout at Nicholson's Nek on 30 October 1899. From 2 November, the little town on the Klip River was besieged by the Boers for 118 days, while 53,000

troops fought a series of bitter and bloody encounters near by. The siege was eventually lifted by Sir Redvers Buller on 28 February 1900. Like Mafeking, it captured the public imagination, and Ladysmith became a household name across the Empire. It finally proved disastrous for the

> ❏ **Life under seige**
>
> At the start of the siege, there were nearly 20,000 people crowded inside the 27km (17-mile) perimeter of Ladysmith, 12,500 of them fighting men, many others battle-weary refugees from northern Natal. There were also 4,000 cattle and a good supply of rations. Although regularly shelled by the Boers, surprisingly little damage was done to people or property. As time wore on, however, the effects of poor sanitation and inadequate fresh food meant that about 30 people were dying every day. When Sir Redvers Buller finally arrived, he found 2,800 people sick and wounded, and 3,037 soldiers and 54 civilians dead. ❏

Boers, who had pinned down too many troops in an area with no lasting strategic value.

The **Siege Museum** (Murchison Street, tel: 036-637 2231 ext. 318. *Open* Mon–Fri 8–4; Sat 9–1. *Admission: inexpensive*) has vivid displays and graphic descriptions of events, and will provide a detailed guide to local sites, best appreciated from the high ground on one of the encircling hills. The museum building, originally the local market hall, was used as a rations store during the siege. Next door, the **Town Hall** (1893) acted as a hospital, but was still shelled by the Boers, who did not believe that the Red Cross flag was genuine. In front stand two British 160mm (6.3in) Howitzer RML guns, Castor and Pollux and a replica Boer

A British Howitzer gun outside the Town Hall in Ladysmith

Spioenkop, a battle that ended in ignominious defeat for the British

Long Tom field gun. Behind it, the **Emnambithi Cultural Centre** (25 Keate Street, tel: 036-637 2231 ext. 2712. *Open* Mon–Fri 9–4. *Admission: inexpensive*) showcases Ladysmith's cultural achievements and heroes, such as Ladysmith Black Mambazo and boxer Sugarboy Malinga.

Inside **All Saints Anglican church** (1882), memorial tablets list those who died in the siege and the relief, alongside stained-glass windows and the Regimental Standard, presented to the Natal Carbineers by the Prince of Wales in 1925. In the gardens of the Hindu **Vishnu Temple** is a statue of Mahatma Gandhi, who was a stretcher bearer with the relief column. The Muslim **Sufi mosque** is considered one of the most beautiful in South Africa. The **Blockhouse Museum** (6km/4 miles from Ladysmith, off the Harrismith road, tel: 036-635 4091. *Open* by appointment) is a replica of a British blockhouse, with a collection of Zulu and Boer War objects.

Wagon Hill (Platrand, 5km/3 miles south of Ladysmith) was a key British defensive position during the Siege of Ladysmith. On 6 January 1900, Boer commandos stormed the hill, but had to retire after a fierce battle. Various fortifications are visible and there are several memorials. The modern

❑ **Long Tom** The Boers had only four of these famous field guns. Made in France, the 155mm (6in) Creusot weapons fired 43kg (95lb) shells over a distance of about 1km (0.5 miles). Each gun weighed 7 tonnes and was pulled by 16 oxen. ❑

Burgher Memorial, with its seven stylized stone hands, commemorates the 781 Natal Boers who died during the war, 310 of whom are buried here.

Spioenkop (off the R600, west of Ladysmith. *Admission: inexpensive*). On 23 January 1900, this small, rocky hill was attacked by 1,700 British troops. The 15 Boers fled, leaving it deserted. In the dark, misty conditions, the British sited their lines wrongly. The next morning 3,600 Boers attacked in earnest. Although the battle lasted all day, the *kopje* was never reinforced from the 25,000 British troops below, command was confused, and a massacre ensued. By the evening, with 243 dead and over 500 wounded, both sides believed they had lost, and withdrew. Several hours later, the astonished Boers found the hill deserted and moved in. The battlefield is now part of the **Spioenkop Dam Nature Reserve** (tel: 036-488 1578. *Open* Oct–Mar, 6am–7pm; Apr–Sep, 6–6).

TOURIST INFORMATION
DRAKENSBERG
www.drakensberg-tourism.com
Northern and Central: Drakensberg Adventure, Winterton (tel: 036-488 1988; Okhahlamba Drakensberg Tourism, Bergville, tel: 036-448 1296; Drakensberg Tourism Association, Bergville (tel: 036-448 1555).
Central: Winterton (tel: 036-488 1207); Bushmans River Tourism Association, Estcourt (tel: 036-352 6253).
Southern: Kamberg Valley Tourism, Rosetta (tel: 033-267 7028); Nottingham Road Tourism (tel: 033-394 5561; Southern Drakensberg Escape, Underberg (tel: 033-701 1471).
Mountain Rescue Service: (tel 031-307 7744 or 082-990 5877).

208

DRAKENSBERG MUSEUMS
In Estcourt, Fort Durnford (Kemps Road, tel: 036-352 3000, *Open* Mon–Fri 9–12, 1–4.30, weekends by appointment), the largest fort in Natal (1847), is now a military and social museum. Winterton Museum (Kerk Street, tel: 036-488 1885. *Open* Mon–Fri 9–3; Sat 9–12. *Admission: inexpensive*) covers local geology, flora, fauna and history. In Himeville, a loop-holed fort, is a museum of rural life (tel: 033-702 1184. *Open* Wed, Fri, Sat, Sun 10–12. *Admission: inexpensive*).

GUIDED HIKES
The Mountain Backpackers' Club (tel: 031-266 3970) runs regular guided hikes through the Drakensberg and can provide information for those wishing to set out on their own. For other information, contact KZN Wildlife (see page 191).

The Drakensberg

The high Drakensberg, which run for 200km (125 miles) along the western border of KwaZulu-Natal, are part of a much longer chain of basalt stretching from the Cape to the Limpopo. Now a World Heritage site, they were known to the Zulus as *uKhahlamba* (Barrier of Spears); the Afrikaners named them Dragon Mountains.

With jagged 3,000m (9,840ft) peaks, flowing fields of red-gold grass, meadows as rich in flowers as a medieval tapestry, San rock paintings, raptors soaring on the thermals and gushing waterfalls, man-made attractions would seem superfluous. The mountains are preserved as a recreational wilderness, with unsurpassed walking, hiking and climbing. Detailed maps are available at trailheads; permits are needed for most longer hikes. There are also numerous small resorts, cottages and campsites, with gentle strolls through the lower-lying hills. Activities include trout fishing, climbing, birdwatching, riding and hot-air ballooning. The best months to visit are probably April and May. The frosty winters are too cold, while in midsummer mist and rain may obscure the views.

►►► Central Drakensberg   188A2
This section has the highest mountains in the country, crowned by Injasuti (3,459m/11,346ft). Close behind are Champagne Castle (3,377m/11,076ft), Giant's Castle (3,314m/10,870ft) and Cathkin Peak (3,149m/10,329ft). Cathedral Peak (3,004m/9,853ft) is the easiest climb in the Natal range. Below them, the **Giant's Castle Game Reserve** has splendid herds of ˜eland, while its birds include black eagle and lammergeier. Carcasses are laid out at the **Lammergeier Hide** (May–Sep, Sat–Sun only; tel: 036-352 4617; booking essential, arrive before 8am) to attract the huge, rare, bearded vultures.

The area is also one of the world's richest stores of San art. The **Main Caves** (2km/1 mile south of Main Camp. *Open* daily 9–3; ask here for information on other caves in the area. *Admission: moderate*) have over 500 paintings in a single large shelter and a small Bushman Site Museum.

The **Kamberg Nature Reserve** has excellent trout fishing (season 1 Sep–30 Apr; permits obtainable from the office), while the 4km (2.5-mile) **Mooi River Trail** is specifically designed for travellers with disabilities. The **Ardmore Studio** (D275, off Champagne Castle road, tel: 036-468 1314, www.ardmore.co.za. *Open* daily 9–4.30) is a collective of 35 superb Zulu and Sotho artists. Off the main road from Winterton into the mountains **Kwazulu Weavers** (tel: 036-488 1098) produces handwoven wool and mohair rugs. There is a candle factory and shop next door.

►►► Northern Drakensberg   188A2
The north is dominated by the **Amphitheatre**, an 8km (5-mile) crescent flanked by two peaks—the Sentinel (3,165m/10,381ft) and the Eastern Buttress (3,047m/9,994ft). Between them, the skinny **Tugela Falls** skip over several cascades before plummeting 614m (2,014ft). With a combined drop of 948m (3,110ft), these are the second-highest falls in the world (the highest are Angel Falls, Venezuela). Drive to the base of Sentinel Peak, and walk to the waterfall along the rim of the Amphitheatre on

reasonably flat ground, or climb the summit of the Sentinel via a hiking trail and chain ladders. The Tugela River is only one of five major rivers, which include the Orange, born on **Mont-aux-Sources** (3,282m/10,765ft). Much of this area lies within the **Royal Natal National Park**, which is home to over 200 bird species and has several sites with San rock paintings. The road from **Bergville** to Harrismith leads over the breathtaking 2,095m (6,872ft) **Olivershoek Pass**.

▶▶▶ Southern Drakensberg   *188A2*

Although close to the coast and major cities, this is the most rugged of the three areas, with several small nature reserves and some heavy-duty hiking for those who want a challenge. The **Giant's Cup Trail** (60km/37 miles, 5 days) runs south from Sani Pass to Bushman's Nek, and is part of the National Hiking Way.

The remote, tortuous, rugged and spectacularly beautiful **Sani Pass** is the highest in South Africa, climbing from 1,200m to 2,874m (3,936–9,427ft) as it crests the jagged dragon's back. It follows the upper valley of the Mkomazana River and was always the traditional crossing between the Drakensberg and Lesotho. Much of the road runs through protected wilderness areas (a four-wheel-drive vehicle and passport are required).

THE SOUND OF MUSIC
The Drakensberg Boys Choir is magnificent. The school near Winterton educates boys from 9 to 15 years old. The choir has toured in the United States, Europe, Israel and the Far East. When at home, it holds regular concerts on Wednesdays at 3pm in term time in the school auditorium (tel: 036-468 1012, www.dbchoir.co.za).

The Amphitheatre is the most dramatic and instantly recognizable rock formation in the Natal Drakensberg

The Colonial Buildings in Pietermaritzburg

MARATHON
In May each year, South Africa's athletes have their day with the running of the Comrades Marathon. It covers a staggering 82km (51 miles) between Durban and Pietermaritzburg, uphill and downhill in alternate years.

Pietermaritzburg and the Natal Midlands

▶▶▶ Pietermaritzburg   188A2

Pietermaritzburg Publicity Association,
177 Commercial Road (tel: 033-345 1348, fax: 033-394 3535,
www.pmbtourism.co.za)
Open: Mon–Fri 8–5, Sat 8–3

Founded by the Voortrekkers in 1838, and set in the fertile Msunduze valley, Pietermaritzburg was named after two Boer trek leaders killed by the Zulus, Piet Retief and Gerrit Maritz. Since 1845 it has been capital of KwaZulu-Natal (currently sharing the role with Ulundi).

The streets around **Church Street** reveal a feast of magnificent Victorian and Edwardian architecture, in particular the towering red-brick **City Hall** (1900). Also noteworthy are the 1889 **Old Natal Parliament** (tel: 033-355 7708/26. *Open* Mon–Fri 8–5); **Old Government House** (home of the governors until 1910); and Philip Dudgeon's fine **Standard Bank** (1882). A statue of Mahatma Gandhi by Phil Kolbe stands in front of the old **Colonial Buildings**. Bishop John William Colenso, who established the Church of England in Natal, is buried in the **Cathedral of St. Peter** (1872). **St. George's Garrison Church** (1898) is part of **Fort Napier** (1843). There is also a fine Hindu temple, the **Sri Siva Soobramoniar and Marriamen Temple** (Lower Longmarket Street. *Open* Mon–Sat 7–6, Sun 8–6).

Museums

The **Natal Museum** (237 Loop Street, tel: 033-345 1404. *Open* Mon–Fri 9–4.30, Sat 10–4, Sun 11–3. *Admission: inexpensive*) covers dinosaurs, marine life, pan-African art, from San rock paintings to Asante wooden pillows, Portuguese shipwrecks, and settler history. **Macrorie House Museum** (11 Loop Street, tel: 033-394 2161. *Open* Mon 11–4, Tue 9–1. *Admission: inexpensive*), the atmospheric Victorian home of Bishop Macrorie, is now restored and contains beautiful antiques and costumes.

The **Tatham Art Gallery** (corner of Church Street and Commercial Road, tel: 033-342 1804. *Open* Tue–Sun 10–6. *Admission: free*) is housed in the **Old Supreme Court** (1871) and displays late 19th- and early 20th-century paintings, porcelain and glass, and an exciting collection of contemporary South African art. The annexe shows ethnic arts being made. The **Voortrekker Museum** (Longmarket, tel: 033-394 6834. *Open* Mon–Fri 9–4, Sat 9–1. *Admission free*) is in the old Longmarket Girls' School and gabled **Church of the Vow**, built in 1841 in repayment of the Covenant (see page 167). Next door, **Welverdient House** was the home of Andries Pretorius (see page 162).

The **Comrades Marathon House** (Connaught Road, Scottsville, tel: 033-394 3511. *Open* Mon–Fri afternoon, Sat–Sun by arrangement. *Admission: free*) is dedicated to the gruelling, annual race (see panel opposite).

Parks and gardens

The **Garden of Remembrance** has a memorial to 13,000 South Africans who died at the Battle of Dellville Wood in World War I, with a Weeping Cross that supposedly oozes sap on its anniversary. The beautiful **KZN National Botanic Gardens** (2 Zwartkop Road, Prestbury, tel: 033-344 3585. *Open* Oct–end Apr daily 6–6; May–end Sep daily 8–5. *Admission: free*) contain plants indigenous to Natal.

▶ The Midlands   *188A2/B2*

Between the Drakensberg and the coastal belt, the **Midlands Meander** leads through rolling, green hills and delightful country towns, visiting artists' studios, tea gardens and antiques shops. In **Howick** (Information, tel: 033-330 5305), go to the 95m (312ft) **Howick Falls** on the Mgeni River, walk down into the gorge, and visit **Howick Museum** (Fallsview, tel: 033-330 6124, ask for museum. *Open* Tue–Sat 9.30–4.30. *Admission: inexpensive*) for local history and militaria. **Midmar Public Resort and Nature Reserve** (tel: 033-330 2067. *Open* daily 8.30–4.30. *Admission: moderate*) has small-game viewing and water sports.

GANDHI IN AFRICA
On 7 June 1893, at Pietermaritzburg station, a young high-caste Indian lawyer, Mohandas Karamchand Gandhi, was ejected from first class and told to sit in the luggage wagon. When he protested, he was thrown off the train. The incident was a turning point in his life. For the next 20 years, he fought for the rights of Indians, developing his theories of *satyagraha* (passive resistance) and influencing the course of South African nationalism. He returned to India in 1914, was given the honourific 'Mahatma' (Great Soul), and went on to change the course of world history and philosophy.

211

EMBLEMS
Pietermaritzburg's coat of arms, supported by wildebeest, had to be altered in 1908 as the original version showed the animals running in the wrong direction—a symbol of cowardice. The elephant is a Zulu symbol for a great ruler's place, Umgungundhlovu.

The elephant marks Pietermaritzburg's status as a capital

THE BLOODSTAINED KING

In 1828, Dingane (c1795–1843) assassinated his half-brother Shaka and became the Zulu king. In 1838, he met with Piet Retief and a party of 101 Boers to negotiate a treaty. He supposedly signed a land deal, but then killed the Boer party and attacked Boer camps at Bloukrans River and Boesmans River. Afrikaner retribution (see page 204) led to his eventual downfall. In 1840 his half-brother Mpande overthrew him, and he fled to Swaziland.

KWABULAWAYO

Shaka built a *kraal* overlooking the Nkwalini Valley (about 25km/16 miles from Eshowe on the P230). Here he executed all those who had tormented his mother during their struggle, naming it KwaBulawayo ('the place of killing'). Warriors who returned without their spears were punished at Coward's Bush.

Men build the frame of the house, but women do the thatching in Zulu communities

Zululand

▶ Eshowe and environs   188B2

Tourist Information, Osborne Road (tel: 035-474 1141, fax: 035-474 4733, email: eshowe@uthungulu.co.za) Open: Mon–Fri 7.30–4, Sat 9–12.

Eshowe ('the sound of wind in the trees') is a lovely hill town near the last remnants of the indigenous **Dhlinza Forest** ('a gravelike place of meditation') with a boardwalk through the forest canopy (tel: 035-474 4029, email: boardwalk@zbr.co.za. *Open daily Sep–Apr 6–6, May–Aug 8–5. Admission: inexpensive).* Massive **Fort Nongqai** (1883) garrisoned the Natal Native Police. It now houses the **Zululand Historical Museum** (Nongqai Road, tel: 035-474 1141. *Open Sun–Fri 9–4, Sat on request. Admission: donation*), with fine furniture, royal *ingxothas*, Zulu household items, and a silver beer mug given to King Cetshwayo by Queen Victoria in 1882. Next door, the **Vukani Museum** (tel: 035-474 5274. *Open daily 9–4. Admission: inexpensive*) has wonderful Zulu basketry and pottery. Just out of town, the hilltop **Martyr's Cross** (KwaMondi Road) celebrates Eshowe's first Christian martyr (1877).

Cetshwayo's first *kraal* (1860) at **Gingindlovu** ('swallower of the elephant') commemorated Cetshwayo's victory over his brother, Mbulazi, for the Zulu throne. The king died in 1884 and is buried in unspoiled indigenous **Nkandla Forest** ('place of exhaustion').

Between Eshowe and little colonial Melmoth are several excellent Zulu cultural villages, all with dance troupes, a living village and a *sangoma* (healer). **Shakaland** (14km/ 9 miles from Eshowe on the R68, tel: 035-460 0912, www. shakaland.com. *Open* daily, tours at 11, 12, or stay overnight) was created for the TV series *Shaka Zulu* in 1985, as the *kraal* of Shaka's father, Zenzangakhona. It

puts on a good show. **Simunye** (about 45km/28 miles from Eshowe, off the D256, tel: 035-450 3111, www.shakaland.com) combines Zulu heritage with the Voortrekker experience, including ox-wagon rides, in an excellent hideaway camp (overnight guests only).

Nearby, **KwaBhekithunga** (Stewart's Farm, off the R34 between Empangeni and Melmoth, tel: 035-460 0644, email: kwabheki@netactive.co.za. *Open* for tours by appointment. *Admission: expensive*) has a fine craft centre.

▶▶ Hluhluwe-Umfolozi National Park   *188C3*

Established in 1897, this is a complex of two parks linked by a corridor of land 8km (5 miles) wide, with a range of habitats. It shares with St. Lucia the distinction of being the oldest wildlife sanctuary in Africa. In the 1960s, it was the home of Operation Rhino, a project to ensure global survival of the white rhino, and still has the world's largest concentration of black and white rhino. It also has all the other major species, a wide range of birds, and a small conservation centre with an excellent craft shop, café and the chance to see animals awaiting translocation.

Dumazulu (about 9km/6 miles south of Hluhluwe Village, tel: 035-562 0144. *Open* 8.15, 11, 3.15 for tours and dance displays; and at 6pm including dinner—minimum 20 people. *Admission: expensive*) is a good Zulu cultural centre, snake and crocodile park. Nearby, **Ilala Weavers** (tel: 035-562 0630) is a magnificent shop stocked with art from 1,200 Zulu craftspeople; **Emdoneni Lodge** (tel: 035-562 2256, email: sunseeker@iafrica.com. *Open* daily. *Admission: expensive*) has some cheetahs and servals in pens.

The private **Phinda Resource Reserve** (run by CCAfrica; 29km/18 miles north of Hluhluwe village, tel: 011-775 1000) includes sand forest, mountain, wetlands and river valleys. The whole area has been restocked with a wide range of game, including the 'big five'. and has several luxury lodges that offer their excellent game watching, bushwalks, canoe safaris and river cruises.

▶ Mgungundlovu   *188B3*

In 1828, Dingane moved the Zulu capital to Mgungundlovu ('the place of the great elephant') in the Mfolosi Valley. It was here, in 1838, that he murdered Piet Retief and his followers. The city was torched when Dingane abandoned it in 1839, but its core has been accurately rebuilt. There is an obelisk **memorial** to Piet Retief and his followers. Most of the ancestors of the Zulu royal lineage, including Senzangakhona (father of three kings: Shaka, Dingane and Mpande) and Dinizulu (1884–1913), are buried nearby at **eMakhosini** ('the place of kings').

Impala at a water hole in Hluhluwe-Umfolozi National Park

213

DUNES
St. Lucia has the highest
forested sand dunes in
the world, towering moun-
tains of golden sand
knitted together by
ancient root systems.
Unfortunately, the sand
contains huge deposits of
valuable titanium and
zirconium, which is
already being mined on
unprotected dunes in the
uMhlathuze (Richards Bay)
area. Environmentalists
have finally won a bitter
battle with the mining
consortiums, who wanted
to tap the deposits within
the national park. For
visits to the Richards Bay
Minerals dune-mining
operations and the
Mananga Heritage Centre,
which exhibits archaeological finds from the dunes,
tel: 035-901 3444.

Northern KwaZulu

Traditional homeland of the Tonga and Mabudu peoples,
this remote Maputaland region of KwaZulu-Natal, near
the Mozambique border, covers 9,000sq km (3,475sq
miles) of hot, flat, sandy, tree-covered terrain, crisscrossed
by rivers. It has heavy summer rains, dense populations of
hippo and crocodile, and a staggering array of birds. Much
of the area is now carved up into magnificent game parks,
rich in game and empty of people. Notable are the **Mkhuze
Game Reserve** (335km/208 miles northeast of Durban), an
area of fever trees and fossils in the foothills of the
Lebombo Mountains, and **Sodwana Bay National Park**
(about 400km/248 miles from Durban via the Lower
Mkuzi road, tel: 035-845 1000), with lakes, coastal dune
forest and tidal and coral reefs—a magnet for divers.

In the far north, the large inland **Ndumo-Tembe National
Park** comprises the **Ndumo Game Reserve**, often
described as a miniature Okavango, teeming with
wildlife, fish and over 400 bird species, and the 300sq km
(114sq-mile) **Tembe Reserve** (tel: 031-202 9090,
www.tembe.co.za), set up to provide a safe haven for
Mozambique's elephants. On the coast, **Kosi Bay Nature
Reserve** (accessible only by four-wheel-drive vehicles)
protects towering dunes, mangrove swamps and golden
sand beaches where leatherback and loggerhead turtles
waddle ashore to lay their eggs. Farther south, magnificent coastal forests surround **Lake Sibaya**, South Africa's
largest freshwater lake. Inland is another huge lake, the
Pongolapoort Dam, built artificially for irrigation.

▶▶▶ St Lucia   188C3

*Tourist Information, corner of Katonkel and McKenzie streets
(tel: 035-590 1247, email: shakabarker@futurenet.co.za)*
The unique **Greater St Lucia Wetland Park**, one of the
three most important wetlands in Africa, surrounds an
ancient 40sq km (15sq-mile) lake, with several distinct
ecosystems including coastal dune, wetland, bushveld,
coastal forest, mangrove swamp and grassland. It is a
magnificent birdwatching area, with 450 species including
large colonies of pelicans and flamingos, herons, fish
eagles and three species of kingfisher. **False Bay Park** on
the northwestern shore of Lake St Lucia comprises 2,247ha
(5,550 acres) of dry forest and coral ridges. Hundreds of
rare pink-backed pelicans congregate in the trees on the
banks of the Hluhluwe River from December to April.

The **Crocodile Centre** (*Open* daily 8–4.30; feeding time
Sat 3. *Admission: moderate*) has a small ecology museum
and live crocodiles of every species in Africa. An 80-seat
launch, the *Santa Lucia* (tel: 035-590 1340. Tours, taking 2
hours, daily at 8.30, 10.30, 2.30. Booking essential.
Admission: expensive), runs regular trips around the lake.
You can also rent private boats from Charters Creek and
Fanies Island. There is good fishing (except in the Marine
Reserve), but swimming and water sports are not a good
idea, with about 2,000 crocodiles, 800 hippos, black-fin
sharks and Zambezi River sharks. Deep-sea fishing is
available from St. Lucia town. The **Marine Reserve**
stretches along the coastline from Sodwana Bay in the
north to Cape Vidal in the south and 3km (2 miles) out to
sea. It contains the southernmost coral reefs in the world.

ANIMAL TRAFFIC
Increasing numbers of South Africa's farmers and game reserves hold regular auctions at which anything from a cheetah to a dung beetle may be sold. The inclusion of species such as rhino is part of a serious drive to save them from extinction; gentler animals, such as antelope and zebra, may be bought purely for domestic use. Many new hunting or game reserves are opening for tourists, and there is a move to farm game for the table.

Northern Natal, with its rich tropical waters, offers excellent fishing in the lagoons, lakes and open sea

► **Ulundi**   *188B3*

Tourist Information, Khulani Park, 93 Princess Mkabayi Street (tel: 035-870 0034, email: amafahq@mweb.co.za)
Every Zulu king founded his own new capital, abandoning that of his predecessor, and in 1873 Cetshwayo built Ulundi. On 4 July, 1879, British troops, led by Lord Chelmsford, defeated 20,000 Zulus at Mahlanathini Flats. The military power of the Zulus was finally broken: King Cetshwayo was soon captured and his kingdom annexed to the British Empire. Ulundi is now joint capital of KwaZulu-Natal and seat of the **Legislative Assembly**, where amazing tapestries depict the history of KwaZulu (viewing by appointment only, tel: 0358-202 101).

Ulundi was succeeded as capital by **Ondini** ('the heights'), then destroyed by Swazi invaders. Archaeologists have uncovered the foundations, and the royal *kraal* has been rebuilt, with *uhlongwa* (dome-shaped woven grass dwellings), as part of the **KwaZulu Cultural Museum** (King Cetshwayo Highway, tel: 0358-702050. *Open* Mon–Fri 8–4, Sat–Sun 9–4. *Admission: inexpensive*). There is also a kitchen garden and crafts market.

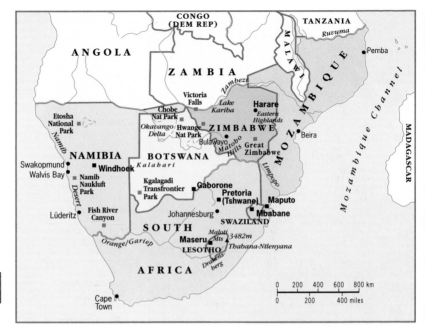

PRACTICALITIES

Check before leaving whether you need a visa to enter any of these other countries. If you need one for South Africa, make sure it is multi-entry. A quick trip across the border, or even the shortcut through Swaziland, will cancel your initial entry. Namibia, Botswana, Zimbabwe and Mozambique all have cerebral malaria and you must take prophylactics. Few car rental companies will allow you to take a vehicle over the border, so shop around or arrange for a new vehicle to meet you at the border. The tap water should be safe in all countries except Mozambique.

Right: Namibia's sand dunes are the highest in the world

South Africa has six neighbours—tiny mountainous **Lesotho**, tucked into the Drakensberg; the gentle kingdom of **Swaziland**, which tumbles off the escarpment between Kruger National Park, Mozambique and KwaZulu-Natal; poverty-stricken **Mozambique**, still emerging tentatively from the devastation of war and flood; the vast desert expanse of **Namibia**, famous for its diamonds and the shipwrecks of the Skeleton Coast; triumphant **Botswana**, which has quietly proved a stable democracy in the whirlwind of African politics; and **Zimbabwe**, home to the Victoria Falls, one of the seven natural wonders of the world, and the magnificent stone city of Great Zimbabwe, heart of a mighty kingdom from the 13th century, but tragically now devasted by a corrupt and vicious government.

South Africa is at present orderly, organized, and—by African standards—sophisticated. Its population is largely urban and increasingly distanced from its heritage and traditions. By contrast, its neighbours were colonized for far shorter periods, with foreigners not taking full possession until the late 19th century, and handing back the reins of power far sooner than in South Africa. With extraordinary luck and political cunning, Lesotho and Swaziland managed to remain independent protectorates throughout the colonial period. The result is that all have the distinct, flamboyant cultures that are hard to find in South Africa itself. There can also be a greater degree of what may seem like chaos, but is all part of the diverse, exciting experience that is Africa. Some have more severe problems, such as Zimbabwe's economic and political meltdown and the desperate poverty in troubled Mozambique, but tourism carries on regardless.

Because these countries have far smaller populations than that of South Africa, most have managed to set aside

much larger areas as national parks and reserves. You have a chance to experience nature in the raw from the many small camps dotted across the wide landscapes. Namibia and Botswana both have world-class game parks, with few of the crowds that gather at Kruger. And then there are the spectacles—the biggest waterfalls, highest sand dunes, and second-largest canyon in the world; and the great rivers—the Zambezi, Limpopo, Chobe and Okavango.

All distance is relative, and in Africa people happily travel hundreds of kilometres for a weekend. South Africa's neighbours may seem far away, but it is easy to hop on a plane and sample an exciting and different view of Africa.

Lesotho

Lesotho, made up almost entirely of rugged mountains
and totally surrounded by South Africa, calls itself the
'Kingdom in the Sky'. In the 1820s a Sotho chief, Moshoeshoe the Great, fled to the mountains from the Mfecane
wars raging across the highveld. Eventually he settled in
a natural fortress, Thaba Bosiu (the 'Mountain of the
Night'), near modern Maseru, where he and some 40,000
followers formed the BaSotho nation. For almost a
century, the tiny kingdom battled to survive, against
other refugees, Trekboers and the British. The king skilfully steered a middle course, maintaining his kingdom's
independence until his death in 1870. Basutoland eventually became a British colony in 1884 and voted to remain
one in 1910 during the Union of South Africa, thus escaping apartheid. In 1966 it became an independent
constitutional monarchy.

Above all, Lesotho is for lovers of the great outdoors. It
has only one museum, at the **Morija** mission station, while
the capital, **Maseru** ('red sandstone'), is a quiet, pleasant
but undistinguished place. However, the scenery is stunning, and there are vast
mountain vistas, including
Thaba-Ntlenyana, the highest peak in southern Africa
(3,482m/11,421ft). Walkers
can ramble on moorland, by
rocky streams, and through
woodland. Pony trekking
and fishing are specialties.
You can find fossil-laden
cliffs and faint, ancient San
paintings in caves and under
overhangs. Villages dot the
hills and a thriving crafts
industry makes fine wool
and mohair tapestries,
basketry, leather, jewellery
and pottery. And the Katse
Dam water development
project will provide Lesotho
with a base for water sports.

*The Sotho are great
horsemen*

NATIONAL HATS
The national dress of
Lesotho is a colourful
blanket and a conical
straw hat, the *mokorotlo*,
a word denoting disagree-
ment. The hat is said to
take its shape from the
mountain of Qiloane, part-
ing sight of Moshoeshoe's
son, who left court
because he disagreed
with dealings with the
British. It became a
symbol of nationalism.

Swaziland

Swaziland tumbles off the African plateau between South Africa and Mozambique, with high montane forest in the west and burning savannah lowveld in the east. Founded by King Sobhuza I during the upheavals of the Mfecane in the early 19th century, the country narrowly escaped absorption into South Africa. In the early 20th century, a fund was established to buy back land from the Boers, ensuring legal title for the Swazi people. The country was a British protectorate for 66 years, gained independence in 1968, and is an absolute monarchy under the benign rule of King Mswati III. It is a peaceful, largely agricultural country with a population of about 800,000, and survives on the sugar crop and income from immigrant workers to the South African mines. South African tourists come here for the outdoor activities, but most visitors are passing through en route to Durban or Kruger National Park.

The capital, **Mbabane**, is a pleasant, small, low-rise city. From here, a road leads southeast to Manzini through the **Ezulwini Valley**, the "heavenly place," heart of royal Swaziland. **Lobamba** has the Houses of Parliament, the National Museum, a traditional Swazi village, and several fine crafts workshops. Nearby are the **Mlilwane Wildlife Sanctuary** and **Mantenga Falls**. **Piggs Peak**, in the mountainous northwest, offers spectacular views, walking and other outdoor activities. There are three further game parks in the eastern section, **Hlane Royal National Park**, **Mbulizi Game Reserve** and **Mkhaya Game Reserve**.

The country blends ancient traditions and Western culture with traditional villages and people wearing national dress. Twice a year there are major festivals. In the male **Ncwala**, or First Fruit Ceremony (December/January), the young men bring ocean foam and *lusekwane* (acacia) branches to the king, who dances with his warriors. The female **Umhlanga** (reed) dance (August/September) is in honour of the Queen Mother (see panel).

ROYAL SUCCESSION

The new king is never the eldest son of the old king but is chosen from the royal clan, the Dlamini. The Queen Mother, who will automatically become regent, must be from a different clan. The new king is chosen when young and unsullied. In order to secure the throne against family feuds, he must be a single son, unmarried, and have no child of his own at the time of his coronation. Afterwards, he may marry many times and have many children.

PRACTICALITIES

There are good road connections and flights from South Africa. The currency is the *lilangeni* (plural *emalangeni*) linked to the SA Rand. Swazi Plaza Tourism Information Office, Swazi Plaza, Mbabane, PO Box A1030, Mbabane, tel/fax: 268-404 2531). In South Africa tel: 012-344 1917; in the UK tel: 020-7630 6611, www.welcometo swaziland.com; in the USA tel: 202/362 6683.

219

The Organ Pipe Donga, in the Mkhondvo Valley

Zimbabwe

*Zimbabwe, ruinous capi-
tal of great priest
emperors, has handed its
name on to a new country*

Due north of South Africa, across Kipling's famous 'great, grey, green, greasy Limpopo River, all set about with fever trees', is landlocked Zimbabwe, with a turbulent history as the renegade colony of Southern Rhodesia. There are only two cities of any real size: **Harare**, the capital, in the northeast and **Bulawayo** in the southwest. The Nyanga, Vumba and Chimanimani mountain ranges together form the lush, green **Eastern Highlands**, whose pine forests, coffee farms, and mountain lakes are popular with locals escaping the searing summer heat. There are plenty of activities including golf, riding, trout fishing and hill walking. In the far southwest, the outer fringes of the Kalahari Desert creep across the border to the magnificent rocky **Matobo Hills**. Most of the country is a high plateau (at around 1,000–1,500m/3,280–4,920ft), perfect for farming and wildlife.

There are two main tribes, the majority Shona and the Ndebele, an offshoot of the Zulus, whose first leader Mzilikaze fled north to escape Shaka's wrath (see pages 30–31). Shona art has become world famous since the late 1980s, and Zimbabweans are also brilliant musicians, with names like the Bundu Boys, Stella Chieweshi and Thomas Mapfumo achieving some international and a great deal of African fame. Many people are immensely hospitable and charming, with an infectious sense of humour.

THE VICTORIA FALLS One of the wonders of the natural world, known locally as Mosi Oa Tunya ('the smoke that thunders'), these waterfalls on the massive Zambezi River are the largest on earth. They are 61–105m (200–345ft) high, 1,688m (5,537ft) wide, and in full flood some 545 million litres (120 million gallons) of water cascade over the brim every minute, sending a jet of rainbow-sparkling spray 500m (1,640ft) into the air. The town has a lot to offer, from elephant and hot-air balloon rides to traditional dancing, but the most popular activities are river-based. Leisurely cruises run upstream from the Falls, while downstream, rafts tumble through 8km (5 miles) of twisting gorges tossed in some of the world's wildest white water.

LAKE KARIBA The Kariba Dam across the Zambezi is 126m (413ft) high; it contains 1,050,000cu m (1,372,350cu yd) of concrete and 11,000 tonnes of steel. Behind it is the fifth-largest man-made lake in the world, 290km (180 miles) long, up to 32km (20 miles) wide and up to 120m (394ft) deep. A booming holiday trade has grown around it, with numerous water sports, sailing, houseboats, fishing and beaches

and beer for sunseekers. Away from Kariba town, several small, remote reserves have excellent game viewing.

HWANGE NATIONAL PARK This vast game park, covering 14,650sq km (5,655sq-miles) in the northwest corner of Zimbabwe, is one of the finest in Africa. It has 107 mammal and 410 bird species, but is renowned above all for its herds of elephant and for the stately sable antelope, national emblem of Zimbabwe. There are several comfortable Parks Board camps and an increasing army of private game lodges offering luxury accommodation, guided drives by day and night, and even bush walking and riding. Only three are actually within the park (operated by Wilderness Safaris).

GREAT ZIMBABWE From the 13th to the mid-16th century, this was the capital of an empire that stretched halfway across southern Africa and traded for gold and ivory with the Arabs and Portuguese. In its latter years it was ruled by the Mwene Mutapa ('Great Plunderer'), an autocratic, semi-divine priest-king. The city, the most magnificent of a number of virtually unknown stone-built towns in the region, is thought to have had a population of some 50,000 in its heyday. Today, abandoned to the baboons, it is an atmospheric ruin, one of the largest stone structures in Africa. Although only a short detour from the main Jo'burg–Harare road near Masvingo, it is off the beaten track for most Zambezi tourists.

Victoria Falls, the largest and one of the most beautiful waterfalls in the world

PRACTICALITES
There are still flights and good roads from South Africa. Most visitors require visas and must apply well in advance of travel at their nearest embassy. Zimbabwe Tourist Authority, PO Box CY286, Causeway, Harare (tel: +263-4-752570, fax: +263-4-758 826, www.zimbabwe tourism.co.zw). UK Embassy, 429 The Strand, London WC2R 0SA (tel:020-7836 7755, fax: 020-7379 1167 (also tourist board). US Embassy, 429 1608 New Hampshire Ave NW, Washington DC 20009 (tel: 202-3327 1000, fax: 202-483 9326).
For an independent view of the country, visit www.swafricaradio.com.

PRACTICALITIES

There are good roads and train services and regular flights from South Africa to Gaborone and Maun. Nationals of most Commonwealth and EU nations and the USA may enter without a visa. The currency is the *pula*. Botswana Tourist Board, Private Bag 0047, Gaborone (tel: 267-3953 024, fax: 267-3908 675). In the UK, tel: 01344 298 982, www. botswanatourism.org.uk.

Canals and reeds in the Okavango Delta

Botswana

Once the British colony of Bechuanaland, Botswana is as large as France or Texas but with a population of only about 1.6 million, mostly of the SeTswana tribal group. With nearly three-quarters of the country covered by uninhabitable Kalahari sand, almost the entire population is clustered in the lush green hills of the southeast corner around the capital, **Gaborone**.

At independence in 1966, Botswana was one of the 10 poorest countries in the world; today, it is one of the wealthiest in Africa, thanks to the discovery of huge diamond fields and the successful development of the beef cattle industry. It is peaceful, stable and democratic.

Nearly 20 per cent of the country is national park. In the far south, the huge arid **Kgalagadi Transfrontier Park** crosses the South African border, next to the smaller **Mabuasehube Game Reserve**. The first 'peace park' in southern Africa, it covers an area far larger than the Kruger, although the scarcity of water and the scrubby vegetation do not allow the same density of wildlife to survive. There are few roads and facilities in the Botswana section.

In the middle of the country is the even larger and more remote **Central Kalahari Game Reserve**, set up originally as a home for the San people. In the far north, near the Zimbabwe border, the **Chobe National Park** is the richest in game and facilities of all Botswana's parks, offering game viewing equal to the great parks of Kenya and Tanzania, and particularly famous for its massive herds of elephant.

Pride of place, however, goes to the **Okavango River**, which heads south and west from Angola towards the sea but never makes it, fanning out instead into the magnificent, 13,000sq km (5,018sq-mile) inland **Okavango Delta**, with over 350 bird species. It is a fantastic wilderness of reeds and water lilies, much of it only negotiable by canoe. The neighbouring **Moremi Game Reserve** has excellent game viewing.

Namibia

Namibia is four times the size of Germany, with a population of a little over 1.8 million. A German colony known as South West Africa from 1890, it was handed over to South Africa at the start of World War I and remained part of that country until independence in 1990. There is a distinctly Germanic air to the architecture, especially in the little coastal towns of **Luderitz** and **Swakopmund** and in the hilly capital, **Windhoek**. German cakes, sausages, beer and oompah bands add a slightly surreal quality to local festivals, and there is still one tribe, the Herero, whose married women wear the full heavy skirts of 19th-century German missionaries, adding their own towering cloth headdresses.

Most of Namibia is desert, with the Kalahari merging into the even more forbidding **Namib Desert**. Even the coast is desolate. A huge area in the far south is forbidden territory, left to the diamond diggers, while the northern section is known as the **Skeleton Coast** after the many who died in shipwrecks on its terrifying rocks. Between them is the **Namib Naukluft Park**, an enormous reserve of red-gold sand dunes, including the 300m (1,000ft) high **Sossusvlei Dunes**, the highest in the world.

Inland is another geological marvel, the **Fish River Canyon**. This giant ravine, second in size only to the Grand Canyon, is 161km (100 miles) long, 27km (17 miles) wide and up to 550m (1,804ft) deep. A 25km (15-mile) road leads to viewing platforms and a rugged 90km (56-mile), five-day hiking trail runs along the bottom.

In the north, where the desert gives way to acacia savannah, the 22,270sq km (8,598sq-mile) **Etosha National Park** is focused around a 5,000sq-km (1,930sq-miles) pan. The name means 'place of dry water' but there is still enough water to support one of the largest concentrations of wildlife in Africa. Yet more excellent game viewing can be found in the **Caprivi Strip**, the neck of land that stretches out into the Zambezi Valley in the far north.

PRACTICALITIES
There is a good road north and regular flights to Windhoek from Johannesburg and Cape Town. Most EU and US citizens can enter without a visa. The currency is the Namib dollar, which has the same value as the SA Rand. Namibia Tourism, Ground Floor, Sanlan Centre, corner Fidel Castro and Werner List streets, Private Bag 13244, Windhoek (tel: 061-284 2111, fax: 061-284 2364, www.namibiatourism.com. na). In South Africa, tel: 021-422 3298 or 011-785 4626; in the UK, 6 Chandos Street, London W1M 0LQ (tel: 020-8487 9881, www. namibiatourism.co.uk).

22.

The wind whips the Namib Desert into towering pinnacles of red-gold sand

Spectacular view from God's Window, across the lowveld to the Mozambique coast

TOURIST INFORMATION
Fundo Nacional do Turisomo–FUTUR, Avenue 25 de Setembro 1203, PO Box 4758, Maputo (tel: +258-1-307 320/3, fax: +258-1-307 324, www.futur.org.mz.

PRACTICALITIES
All visitors must obtain a visa before arrival. The currency is the *metical*, but many places may ask for payment in US dollars or SA rand. Roads across Mozambique are gradually opening up, but it may be safer to fly and you should always get local advice before visiting. Do not stray beyond clearly marked settlements, as there are an estimated 2 million land mines still to be located and defused. Be warned, local tourism information is still in its infancy.

Mozambique

A long, skinny country running north for 1,960km (1,215 miles) up the Indian Ocean coastal plain, Mozambique began as part of the Omani Sultanate, at the southernmost tip of the Arab gold, ivory and slave trade. It is hot and humid, and the swamp fevers nearly defeated the earliest Portuguese traders, but the promised prizes inland were worth the hardships and it became a Portuguese colony. Best known as a scruffy but charming Mediterranean-style playground for white Rhodesians and South Africans, it used to be a source of good food, wine and loose women, with some of the finest beaches in Africa.

Independence changed all that. In 1975, the Portuguese withdrew abruptly and some 80 per cent of whites departed, decimating the infrastructure. Frelimo, a hard-line Marxist organization, took power and instituted extreme socialist government. Almost at once civil war broke out between Frelimo and the anarchic Renamo (Mozambique Resistance Movement), largely funded by Rhodesia and South Africa. When peace was restored after nearly 20 years, the country had become one of the poorest in the world.

Today, Mozambique has renounced its hard-line policies and is trying desperately to reconstruct some sort of life for its citizens. Roads are gradually opening, power restored, and the land cleared for agriculture so that the hundreds of thousands of refugees can return. The first glimmerings of renewed tourism are also in view. The capital, **Maputo**, has several luxury hotels, including the historic Polana, and you can again stroll the boulevards and eat *peri-peri* prawns, while several small beach resorts have sprung up within day-trip distance. The second city and largest port, **Beira**, is also making great efforts to re-create a holiday environment. However, most tourism is still concentrated on **Vilanculos** and its classy, offshore resort islands of **Santa Carolina** and **Benguela**. For now, the rest of the country is suitable only for those with a good four-wheel drive and a strong sense of adventure.

Practicalities

The luxurious swimming pool area at the Saxon Hotel, Johannesburgh

Accommodation

Middle-class South Africans have an exceptionally high standard of living, and even higher expectations, so while the tourist industry murmurs self-deprecatingly about pulling standards up to the international norm, South Africa actually provides excellent accommodation, with service often surpassing European and US levels.

Luxury Few locals can afford international five-star prices but the hoteliers have been jumping on the bandwagon as tourism and business boom. Johannesburg and Cape Town both have an excellent collection of top-end hotels, from glitzy newcomers such as the Michelangelo in Jo'burg to historic properties such as the venerable Mount Nelson in Cape Town. Outside these cities, there are fewer large five-star properties, but scattered across the entire country is a network of wonderful small luxurious hotels, such as the Cellars-Hohenort in Cape Town, Grand Roche in Paarl and Coach House in Tzaneen. Many are in historic buildings or stunning settings, with lush gardens, antiques, impeccable service and food to die for, most are marketed through organizations such as Small Exclusive Hotels of Southern Africa or the Portfolio of Country Places. In recent years, most upscale properties have sprouted spas—an essential; it would seen in city and game reserve alike.

Chains For those who cannot afford this sort of luxury there are several chains with cross-country facilities, although here you pay for comfort and convenience, not atmosphere. Holiday Inns are well represented, from the classy Crowne Plazas to the basic and very affordable Garden Courts. Protea, the largest, has a huge network, but the ratings, price and efficiency vary widely from property to property, so check before booking.

Game lodges A trip to Africa would not be complete without at least a couple of nights' game viewing. If you have the cash, head for one of the exclusive game lodges, such as Londolozi or Sabi Sabi in Mpumalanga, Phinda, or Ndumo in Natal, Shamwari or Kwandwe in the Eastern Cape. Not only are they totally delightful, but the game viewing is superb and the knowledge of the rangers encyclopaedic. You can also get off the roads, and do walks and night drives, activities still largely taboo in the national parks.

The facilities offered within the national parks are much less expensive. Most have at least one full-service lodge, they all have chalets with kitchens, *rondavels* (small,

FURTHER INFORMATION
For central booking numbers and hotel listings, see pages 258–263. Most guest-houses have only two or three rooms available, so few are listed here. SATOUR and the South African AA both publish annual guides to recommended guest-houses, farmhouses, bed-and-breakfast, and self-catering establishments, as does Portfolio. There are also numerous excellent websites offering a wide range of properties. Alternatively, ask at the local tourist office.

simple circular rooms), camping and caravanning facilities, a camp shop with basic foods and a filling station.

Lord Milner Hotel, Matjiesfontein

Self-catering If you want to travel cheaply, this is the way to do it. There is a very wide choice of accommodation with kitchens, and many establishments offer a range to satisfy all tastes and pockets. There are many timeshare properties along the KwaZulu-Natal coast, most of which can be rented by casual visitors. Cape Town has increasing numbers of apartments to let. Rural retreats offer full service or self-catering in furnished chalets, tents with fitted bathrooms, simple huts or real bush camping. In most small towns someone has a spare cottage, often attractively furnished, at a ludicrously low price. The only drawback is that you will have to take cutlery and crockery for picnics and supply yourself with the basic foodstuffs—feasible only if you have your own transport.

Guest-houses The bed-and-breakfast business is also booming throughout the country. Usually tucked away in residential suburbs, many are delightful historic houses, such as Cape Dutch farms, as well as rambling Victorian mansions with four-poster beds and patchwork quilts. Prices are reasonable and you will get a huge cooked breakfast and a warm welcome from a (probably) middle-aged Afrikaner lady who wants nothing more than to sell the delights of her country to you.

HOLIDAY HOMES
A growing potential market, right along the coast, but clustered around Cape Town and Durban, are the casual short-term rentals of various holiday homes that belong to South Africans, as well as the increasing number of foreigners investing in the property boom. Rates and facilities can be excellent, but the trick is to find what is available. There are only a few small agencies; most are managed by local real estate agents. The best place to look is on the web.

South African bed-and-breakfast is affordable and often delightful

Food and drink

South Africans like meat—lots of meat. It may be beef, lamb or pork, or a variety of more exotic options from springbok or impala to crocodile and ostrich, but it must come in large quantities. They also have a very sweet tooth. If anything is a South African staple today, it is a vast slab of steak, usually smothered in barbecue sauce.

In the small towns, there is often little choice about where to eat, but the meal you get will be filling and wholesome, and you can request half portions, sauceless steaks and salads. Along the coast, in the main cities and in the top hotels, the story is very different, with South Africa offering fine and imaginative cuisine, often based on traditional recipes and using the finest of local ingredients.

Cape Dutch food The famous Cape Dutch cuisine grew from several intertwined influences. The newly arrived Dutch brought their traditional thick soups, stews, *frikkadels* (meatballs) and breads, adapting them to available ingredients. Many had Cape Malay servants, and the spices and curries of the East Indies and South India soon crept into the diet. Later arrivals included German settlers who brought their sausage-making skills, and French Huguenots who brought *konfyt* (preserved

Menus offer a wide choice in South Africa

Tomato bredie *(left) and* bobotie *(right) are two of the classic mainstays of Cape Dutch cuisine*

fruits) and endowed the Cape Winelands with a taste for fine dining that survives to this day.

The Voortrekkers had to survive away from civilization for years on end, in intense heat, and very primitive conditions. *Biltong*, strips of meat salted, spiced and dried, was probably their best way of carrying protein. It can be eaten dry or reconstituted as part of a stew, can be made from beef or game shot en route, and can be cured easily in the sun on a drying rack. *Biltong* is still a universal food in South Africa and is now even creeping into high society, with fine shavings in soups and salads.

The *braaivleis* (literally 'roasted meat') is a ritual as central to the white South African lifestyle as the 'barbie' to Australians—and for much the same reason. It began with whatever could be shot being grilled over an open fire—tough food for tough men. Today, the central ingredient is still steak, and with it comes *boerewors* (literally 'farm sausage'), highly spiced pork, mutton and beef sausage, flavoured with coriander, ginger, mace, cloves, nutmeg, thyme, fennel, rosemary, mint and red wine or vinegar. *Sosaties* are kebabs marinated for several days in sweet and sour sauces, based on Indonesian satay. On the side are the salads, roasted mealies (corn on the cob), pot bread (baked in a cast-iron pot) or *roosterkoek* (bread cooked on the coals or ashes)—and plenty of alcohol.

HEALTHY DIET
Traditionally cooked over an open fire, the black African staple is a thick porridge (*pap*) of indigenous sorghum or maize, introduced to the continent by the 15th-century Portuguese sailors. Accompanying this come thin stews of spinach, beans, pumpkin, tomatoes and onions with added chicken, mutton or beef on special occasions. Other protein comes from sour milk, mopani worms, grasshoppers, ants and edible beetles. It is a remarkably healthy diet, with little fat, salt or excess sugar, but is being compromised by a dependency on sugary soft drinks, bottled beer and white bread.

229

Stews, known as *bredies* in the Cape and *potjiekos* in the Transvaal, are traditionally fat-tailed mutton or venison cooked very slowly in a three-legged cast-iron cooking pot (a *potjie*—pronounced 'poykey') over an open fire. Any available vegetable can be thrown in, but common additions are tomato, pumpkin, butternut squash, beans, onion, potato and *waterblommetjie* (water lily). The savoury stew is often served with something sweet, such as a compote of dried fruit, sweet potatoes glazed in orange caramel or sugary pumpkin fritters.

Biltong is still a South African staple

Pancakes make a handy snack

ALCOHOL
Maheu, a thick white beer made from sorghum, is the drink of choice for all social occasions in traditional black society. Most South Africans wash down their *braai* (barbecue) with a lager (Castle, Lion, Ohlssons or Amstel) or some Cape wine (see pages 88–89). Finish your meal with a local liqueur, such as the *naartjie* (tangerine)-based Van der Hum or Amarula Cream (made from the fruit of the wild marula tree). Beware local moonshine firewaters—*mampoer* or *witblitz*—unless you have a head like iron or a death wish.

Asian cuisine Alongside those dishes that have been adopted and adapted into the white diet, there is still a strong tradition of 'Malay' and Indian cuisine; this received a fresh injection of authenticity with the arrival of the Indian cane workers in Natal in the early 20th century. Here are the real curries and rice-based *breyanis* (similar to the Indian biriyani), served with *sambals* (chutneys) and *atjar* (pickles). Most famous of the Malay dishes is *bobotie*, a mild baked curry of minced lamb with dried fruit, topped with an egg custard, which has been designated the South African national dish.

Fish With two oceans and plentiful fresh water available inland, one of the greatest treats in the country is the extraordinary range of fish to choose from. In addition to oysters, mussels, limpets, crayfish and perlemoen (abalone), there are superb white fish such as kingclip, yellowtail, snoek and kabeljou. The finest prawns are said to be from Mozambique, served Portuguese style in a marinade of olive oil, lemon juice, garlic, bay leaves, chilli and ground cloves. Alternatively, look for Cape Malay pickled fish (Cape salmon, kingclip, yellowtail or any other firm white fish), served traditionally at funeral feasts. Inland, try the smoked salmon trout or barbel.

Desserts To finish off your typically South African meal, you should leave room for a calorie-laden dessert such as *melktart* (a cinnamon-flavoured milk tart of Dutch origin), Cape brandy pudding (a British-style steamed pudding laden with brandy) or *koeksisters* (small braided dough-nuts that have been soaked in honey or a thick syrup of concentrated fruit juices).

Shopping

Souvenirs of South Africa are plentiful—some tacky, many expensive and some exquisitely beautiful. Unfortunately, many of the best—ostrich feathers, huge stone statues, fire-baked pots, helicopters made of wire, 2m (7ft) tall wooden giraffes—are extremely difficult to transport.

Animal products Ostrich farms sell expensive shoes or handbags, and cheap feather dusters or blown ostrich eggs (plain, filled with fruit, painted—usually badly—or carved). Antelope skins are legal if you can face the social comment, but do not buy ivory—you are not allowed to bring it home.

Few of the more spectacular shells and corals you see are actually South African. Most shells for sale are collected live, an activity that is illegal in protected areas and is certainly not eco-friendly. Collect your own abandoned shells on the beach; they come free and you will not harm the environment. The rich blue perlemoen shells or jewellery made from them are fine, as the contents are harvested for food.

Baskets, bowls and beads Many traditional crafts, such as stunningly patterned baskets made by the Sotho and Zulus, and simple hardwood bowls and spoons, are still going strong. Intricate Zulu beadwork is magnificent at its best; look for traditional aprons and veils or simpler (and less expensive) pen holders.

Jewels and gemstones Gold and diamonds are both sold in abundant quantities, as are many gemstones, from emerald earrings to huge slabs of amethyst crystal. For an entertaining half-hour, head for the gemstone scratchpatches, found in all the main cities. These contain huge cans filled with tumble-polished semi-precious stones. You can select your favourites and buy by weight at unbelievably low prices.

Food, wine and flowers Look for estate-bottled wines, dried or glacé fruit, *konfyt* or jams (try more unusual flavours such as prickly pear) or fresh proteus *biltong* (vacuum-packed).

Curios Finally, there are the almost obligatory soapstone heads, wooden hippos, copper ashtrays and T-shirts, which range from the pleasant to the totally awful.

Pots and baskets in Umgababa Market, near Durban

231

Entertainment

There is surprisingly little entertainment in South Africa. Most socializing is done at home, though people are beginning to eat out more, and most towns of any size have a cinema with the latest-release international films. But outside the cities there are few lively bars and clubs. Many people get up with the sun, so dining is early and most nightlife is over by 11pm.

Traditional music and dance Tribal dance is now almost exclusively a tourist attraction. Several 'tribal villages', particularly in KwaZulu-Natal, put on dance displays. Go to at least one, as the Zulu and Shangaan dancers are spectacular and it will probably be your only chance to see something of a fast-vanishing lifestyle. The quality of the performances and explanations varies, so choose carefully. Some of the best are found in and around Durban, at Simunye, Dumazulu, Shakaland and KwaBhekithunga (see pages 201 and 212–213); and in Gauteng, at Gold Reef City, and Lesedi (see pages 152 and 171).

Township jazz Headed by such luminaries as Miriam Makeba, Ladysmith Black Mambazo and Hugh Masekela, South Africa's township musicians combined tribal rhythms with jazz and swing to create a unique, thriving heritage of music and dance. Many of its themes, such as the *toyi-toyi* (Struggle dance of the people), the *mapantsula* (township jive) and *isicatamiya* (a choir tradition from the mines and men's hostels) grew out of the Struggle. Music was one of the few relatively safe ways to protest against apartheid. For safety reasons, most township shebeens (once illegal pubs), in which the movement has its roots, should be visited only on organized tours; fortunately the musicians are beginning to move into mainstream venues.

CAPE TOWN
The Green Dolphin, V&A Waterfront (tel: 021-421 7471, www.greendolphin.co.za). Nightly jazz in the premier club. **The Jazz Café**, 41 The Drive, Camps Bay (tel: 021-438 0783). Nightly gigs in a popular venue, with three restaurants.

DURBAN
The Bat Centre, Maritime Place, off Victoria Embankment (tel: 031-332 0451). Very lively small mall, combining the best of crafts shopping with the traditional **African Zansi Restaurant and Bar**, a café, craft workshops and regular jazz nights, dance and classical theatre. There are jazz nights at the Hilton Hotel every Thursday and, when in town, **Ladysmith Black Mambazo** play regular Saturday nights at the Beatrice Street Hostel.

The costumes of the Gold Reef City dancers are carefully designed not to offend family sensibilities

JOHANNESBURG
Carfax, 39, Pimm Street, Newtown (tel: 011-834 9187). Most progressive arts café in Jozi.

PRETORIA
There are no downtown jazz clubs; for the best go to the shebeens. However, the street musicians in **Hatfield Plaza** (tel: 012-362 5842) give excellent concerts.

The classics The cultural boycott isolated South Africa from the rest of the world, but it also forced the country to rely on its own resources, resulting in flourishing local culture. The Market Theatre in Johannesburg was particularly dynamic, creating a theatre of protest that drew rave reviews in London and New York. Today, classical music and theatre are under siege, with government funds being diverted to lay drains and build houses, while the outbreak of peace has left many writers temporarily silent.

Each of the main cities has its own orchestra and theatres, although most are likely to have their funding cut unless they become more multicultural. The focus is firmly European, but artists broke the race barrier long before most, and the townships are beginning to produce some highly talented, classically trained black actors, dancers and singers.

CAPE TOWN
Artscape Theatre Centre, Foreshore (tel: 021-421 7695; box office: 021-421 7839, credit card bookings www.artscape.co.za). Concerts, theatre, opera and ballet.

DURBAN
Natal Playhouse, Smith Street (tel: 031-369 9555). Home of the Natal Philharmonic Orchestra. Four theatres—The Cellar, The Drama, The Loft and The Studio.

JOHANNESBURG
Civic Theatre, corner of Loveday and Hoof streets, Braamfontein (tel: 011-877 6800).
Market Theatre, corner of Breë and Wolhuter streets, Newtown (tel: 011-832 1641, www.markettheatre.co.za).

PRETORIA
State Theatre, Church Street (tel: 012-392 4027). Six auditoria offering ballet, opera, music and some of the most dynamic theatre in the country.

Sun City is South Africa's answer to the glitter of Las Vegas

233

ENTERTAINMENT INFO
To find out what's on, check the relevant section of local daily newspapers, the national *Weekly Mail & Guardian* (published Friday), or the regional Metro sections of the *Sunday Times*. In Cape Town, look at *Cape Review*, while Cape Town and Durban both have a monthly *What's On* available free. In Cape Town, also look for the monthly *Day & Night* or log onto www.capetownevents.co.za. In Johannesburg, buy *Blakes Guide to Johannesburg and its Environs*, or *Johannesburg Alive!*, published by *The Star*.
Buy tickets for major venues from Computicket (tel: 083-915 8000, online booking: www.computicket.com. *Open* daily 8–8).

Hobby steam services run by enthusiastic amateurs include the South African National Railway and Steam Museum's weekly (Sun) Magaliesburg Express (from Johannesburg Station, Gauteng, tel: 011-888 1154, www.mogalecity.gov.za; and Port Elizabeth's narrow-gauge railway, the Apple Express (tel: 041-583 2030, www.nmbt.co.za). In Cape Town there is a small vintage train from the city centre to Spier wine estates (tel: 021-411 5222), while Biggsy's Train (tel: 021-788 7760, www.capemetrorail.co.za) offers a comfortable commute with restaurant and winebar from Simon's Town.

234

The Outeniqua Choo-Tjoe train crosses a bridge over the sea at Knysna

Trains

South Africa has a magnificent network of railway lines—but virtually no trains. Half the tracks are derelict, many run only freight, and even major intercity routes have only one scheduled passenger service a day. Cape Town and Johannesburg have reasonably efficient suburban networks, but these suffer from major security problems.

Main-line Racism and snobbery killed off the passenger services, which were seen as low-class and dangerous. In fact, while second class is not that comfortable for long journeys, Shosholoza Meyl service is inexpensive, safe, comfortable and spacious. Trains are slow, but you can stretch out between crisp white sheets for a leisurely night's sleep, after an old-fashioned dinner. There are not enough services to make touring by train practical, but they are excellent for cross-country journeys.

The Blue Train is the successor to the original Union Limited, and replaced the venerable steam service in 1939. It is now one of the most famous—and expensive—trains in the world, running regular scheduled services between Pretoria and Cape Town, a sybaritic 24-hour journey; and from Cape Town to Port Elizabeth, with charter options from Pretoria up to Hoedspruit, for the Kruger and via Botswana to Victoria Falls. For details, contact The Blue Train (tel: 012-334 8459, fax: 012-334 8464, www.blue train.co.za).

The Pride of Africa, run by Rovos Rail, Victoria Hotel, PO Box 2837, Pretoria 0001 (tel: 012-323 6052, www.rovos.co.za), vies with The Blue Train as the 'world's most luxurious train'. From its base in Capital Park, Pretoria, the company runs to Cape Town, along the Garden Route to George, from Pretoria to Durban, and via Victoria Falls to Dar es Salaam (Tanzania). With vintage locomotives (some steam) and refurbished original cars, the train is less a mode of transport than a holiday in itself.

For historical accuracy try the **Union Limited**, (tel: 021-

International commuters between Zimbabwe and South Africa at the taxi rank beside Messina (Musina) station

449 4391, www.transnetheritgefoundation.co.za), whose locomotives and cars are all restored originals. There are 6–15 day-trips a year from Cape Town to the Winelands and nearby areas, with infrequent 9- and 15-day safaris to the Garden Route, Mpumalanga and the Zambezi. Profits go towards preservation work at the Transnet Museum.

The **Shongololo Express**, named after a shiny brown millipede, aims for a high standard of comfort at more affordable prices. There are three itineraries: the Good Hope Adventure (16 days, Johannesburg–Cape Town); Southern Cross (15 days, six countries of southern Africa); and the Dune Adventure (16 days around Namibia). They also run shorter itineraries along along the Garden Route, from Durban to Kruger, and through the Winelands and Karoo among others. Shongololo Express (tel: 011-781, www.shongololo.com).

Bushveld Train Safaris, PO Box 237, Bela-Bela (Warmbaths) 0480 (tel: 014-736 3025, www.boon.co.za) run a wide range of trips from Pretoria. Aimed at the local market and popular with school groups, they are simple and relatively inexpensive.

The **Banana Express** (tel: 039-315 7065) is based at Port Shepstone on the South Coast. There are two itineraries: a 90-minute journey through the banana and sugar plantations to Izotsha (weekly), and a 3-day trip to Paddock and the Oribi Gorge (daily in season; three days a week out of season; booking essential). In the Western Cape, the **Outeniqua Choo-Tjoe**, one of the most enjoyable and scenic services in the country, runs through the heart of the Garden Route between George (tel: 044-801 8288) and Knysna (tel: 044-382 1362, www.onlinesources.xo.za) several times a day in season.

MAINLINE RESERVATIONS
Book first- and second-class tickets at least 24 hours in advance, either at the stations or by phone. Order your bedding at the same time. Cape Town: information 021-449 2991, reservations 021-405 3871; Durban: information 031-361 3388, reservations 0860-008888; Johannesburg: information 011-773 5878, reservations 011-773 2944; Pretoria: information 012-315 2757, reservations 012-315 2401.

Practicalities

TOP TRAILS—1
Boland Trail, Hottentots-Holland Reserve, Western Cape (40km/25 miles, 2- or 3-day options, tel: 028-840 4826); Cederberg Mountains, Western Cape (1–7-day routes, tel: 027-482 2812); Drakensberg Mountains, KwaZulu-Natal (1 hour–10 days; tel: 033-845 1000); Blyderivierspoort Trail, Mpumalanga (65km/40 miles), 5 days, tel: 013-151 2307); Klipspringer Trail, Augrabies Falls National Park, Northern Cape (40km/25 miles, 3 days,tel: 012-428 9111).

Up Table Mountain, the hard way

Hiking

There is superb hill walking in the Cederberg, KwaZulu-Natal and Mpumalanga Drakensberg; coast and forest paths along the Garden Route; savannah, and even desert walking in the Northern Cape and Limpopo Province. There are over 200 designated long-distance trails and a multitude of other options, from short strolls to more arduous day-trips. Most are accessible by anyone of reasonable fitness, and a few are even laid out for wheelchair access. Brochures and sketch maps of many walks are available, and most are clearly route-marked.

Selecting your trail Take note of local terminology. What South Africans call a 'backpacking trail' is actually an area crossed by trails, usually fairly rugged, where you can make multiday hikes, choosing your own campsite as you go. A 'hiking trail' is a designated route, marked by painted footprints or stakes, and usually several days in length. There is basic accommodation in huts or chalets, but you will be expected to pack all your own supplies. 'Day walks' are precisely what you'd expect, energetic, self-guided days out. 'Guided wilderness trails' are usually relatively easy day-trips in the parks and reserves, led by a knowledgeable ranger. 'Interpretive trails' are short, well-cleared and marked paths with regular explanatory displays.

Many trails limit the number of people in any party and on the route, so reserve a place in advance. You may also need a permit. The local tourist office will be able to give you details. Alternatively, buy one of several detailed hiking guides available. Or log onto www.footprint.co.za, a useful website with detailed descriptions and booking details for many of South Africa's hiking trails. This is the website of the Footprint Hiking Club (tel: 021-462 0992) offering commerically operated guided hikes acorss the country, as well as rafting, mountain biking and more.

On the track Never underestimate the environment and do not hike on your own. Ideally, go in a group of at least three or four. Get a detailed route map and study it carefully, for gradient as well as distance. Always let someone know where and when you are going and when you expect to return, so they can raise the alarm should you fail to show. Keep a safe distance from all wildlife, big or small. For more on safety in the bush, see Surviving in the wilds, page 252.

Take the climate into consideration when deciding on the degree of difficulty you are prepared to tackle. South Africa's mountains are not particularly high and you will not have to acclimatize to the altitude, but they do produce some treacherous and very fast-moving weather. Several people are killed each year in the Drakensberg and even on Table Mountain, trying to escape from incoming fog. If the mist comes down, find shelter and sit it out. In winter the mountains can be cold, wet and slippery, while in bright sunshine the glaring heat and harsh light can damage pale skin and eyes.

The problems of heat are greatly increased in the savannah of the Limpopo Province or the Kalahari scrub of the Northern Cape, where in midsummer it can be like hiking in the Sahara. Treat the sun with extreme respect, do not try to be too energetic during the midday hours, and make sure you drink far more water than you think you need. Savage thunderstorms may whip across the country on summer afternoons. Keep well clear of trees or prominent rocks in case of lightning, and stay out of riverbeds, however dry they may seem, in case of flash floods. Never start an unprotected fire or throw away a match. The vegetation is often tinder dry and a bush fire can rampage for kilometres before it burns out or is brought under control.

The Drakensberg is relatively painless hiking territory

TOP TRAILS—2
Magoebaskloof Trail, Limpopo Province (two sections—Dokolewa, 36km/22 miles, 3 days; Grootbosch, 50km/30 miles, 3 days, tel: 012-481 3500); Otter Trail, Tsitsikamma Coastal National Park, Eastern Cape (41km/25 miles, 5 days, tel: 012-428 9111); Swartberg Trail, between the Great and Little Karoos, Western Cape (65km/40 miles, 5 days, tel: 044-279 1739).

Game walks offer a quieter and more intimate bush experience

OTHER USEFUL ADDRESSES

Association of Southern African Travel Agents (ASATA), PO Box 1234, Saxonwold 2132 (tel: 011-327 7803, general@asata.co.za).

Southern African Tourism Services Association (SATSA), PO Box 806, Cramerview 2060, Gauteng (tel: 011-463 6559).

Qualitour Tourism Classification, PO Box 7119, Centurian 0046, Gauteng (tel: 012-664 9080, fax: 664 9081, www.qualitour.co.za). A private agency classifying standards across the tourism board, from hotels to tour operators.

FAMILY HOLIDAYS

Bushbaby Travel (tel: 020-8780 0363, www.bushbabytravel.com) is a UK-based tour operator specializing in family holidays to South Africa.

Tours and safaris

GENERAL TOUR OPERATORS

Abercrombie & Kent Safaris, PO Box 782607, Sandton 2146 (tel: 011-781 0740, fax: 011-781 0733, www. abercrombiekent.com. In the UK, tel: 020-7730 9600; in the US, tel: 800/323 7308 toll-free or 630/954 2944). This is a smart, worldwide operator, running organized tours and tailor-made itineraries in South Africa and surrounding countries.

Cedarberg Travel, De Heinings, PO Box 20, Clanwilliam 8135 (tel: 027-482 2444, fax: 027-482 1420, www. cedarbergtravel.com). Imaginative tailor-made, escorted and self-drive tours at different budget levels, including specialist tours and walking safaris.

Rennies Travel, Head Office, 10th Floor, Safren House, 19 Ameshoff Street, Braamfontein, PO Box 9395, Johannesburg (tel: 011-407 2800, fax: 011-403 3698, www.rennies.travel.co.za. In the UK, tel: 01733-330111; in the US, tel: 805/855 1572). One of the largest incoming tour operators in South Africa, and the local Thomas Cook representative, with some 70 branches nationwide.

Springbok Atlas, 48 Tulbagh Road, Pomona, PO Box 14884, Bredell (tel: 011-396 1053, fax: 011-396 1069, www.springbokatlas.com). One of South Africa's largest operators, with many local offices and tours of most major cities, day-trips and safaris, as well as countrywide long-distance bus tours.

SOUTH AFRICA BY AIR

African Ramble Air Safaris, PO Box 736, Knysna 6570, Western Cape (tel: 044-533 9006, fax: 044-533 9012, email: aframble@mweb.co.za). Personalized, fly-in tours to eco-tourist and off-beat destinations in southern Africa.

Bill Harrop's 'Original' Balloon Safaris, PO Box 67, Randburg 2125 (tel: 011-705 3201/2, fax: 011-705 3203, www.balloon.co.za). Hot-air balloon rides over the Magalies River valley, Gauteng.

Civair Helicopters, PO Box 120, Newlands, Cape Town 7725 (tel: 021-419 5182, fax: 021-419 5183, info@civair.co.za). Tailor-made and charter helicopter tours of Cape Peninsula and the Winelands, plus whale-spotting.

Dragonfly Group, 18 Rivonia Road, Illovo (tel: 011-268 2000, fax: 011-268 2010, www.dragonfly.co.za). Helicopter tours of Sun City, Mpumalanga, Johannesburg, Cape Town and Durban. Safaris and day-trips across the country.

Sport Helicopters, Cape Town (tel: 021-419 5907/8, fax: 021-419 4044, www.sport-helicopters.co.za). Charters, tailor-made tours and regular sightseeing flights over Cape Pensinsula, the Winelands and the west coast.

SPECIALIST NATIONWIDE OPERATORS

Adventure Safaris & Sports Tours, PO Box 32176, Camps Bay, Cape Town 8040 (tel: 021-438 5201, fax: 021-438 4807, email: adventurepic@icon.co.za). Short breaks, mini-safaris and special interest tours including golf, bicycling, diving, hiking, fishing, hunting, river-rafting, game-viewing, whale-watching, wine-tasting and sailing.

C Africa Tours, PO Box 882, Benoni 1500 (tel: 011-845 1194, fax: 011-421 8550, www.cafrica.net). Tailor-made and small group tours following Kosher or Hallal customs.

CCAfrica/Afro Ventures, Pinmill Farm, Block F, Katherine Street, Sandown, Private Bag X27, Benmore, 2010, Gauteng (tel: 011-809 4300, fax: 011-809 4400, email: information@ccafrica. com). Two of Africa's best luxury safari companies have merged to form one of the most influential upscale providers of lodges, tailor-made, and mobile camping safaris in southern Africa.

Classic Twin Tours, PO Box 141, Koelenhof 7605 (tel: 021-865 2558, email: enquiries@classictwintours.com). Harley Davidson tours of the Western Cape, Mpumalanga and Namibia.

Dive the Big Five, PO Box 2209, White River 1240, Mpumalanga (tel: 013-750 1832, fax: 013-750 0018, email: info@divethebig5.com). Shark, reef and wreck diving coupled with a safari. Tailor-made or packaged options.

Dive South, PO Box 38890, Faerie Glen 0043 (tel: 012-991 3134, fax: 012-991 5523, email: Karin@divesouth.co.za). Dives for everyone—sharks or wrecks or swim an d relax with dolphins.

Drifters Adventours, PO Box 48434, Roosevelt Park, Johannesburg 2129 (tel: 011-888 1160, email: drifters@drifters.co.za). Small group, off-beat camping safaris throughout southern Africa.

Felix Unite, PO Box 2807, Clareinch 7740, Cape Town (tel: 021-683 6433, fax: 021-683 6486, www.felixunite.com). Premier adventure tour operator with trips on the Gariep, Tugela, Doring, Cunene and Breede rivers, along with horseback safaris, extreme sports and overland tours.

Which Way Adventures, PO Box 2600, Somerset West 7129 (tel: 021-845 7400, fax: 021-845 7401, www.nomadtours. co.za). 4WD and camping safaris, white-water rafting and abseiling on the Doring, Breede and Gariep rivers.

GOLFING HOLIDAYS

The following companies offer golf, mixed with game-viewing for nongolfers.
Golf Adventures International, PO Box 536, Randburg 2125 (tel: 011-293 2077, email: info@golfadv.co.za).
Golf & Game Safari Company, PO Box 543, Pennington 4184, KwaZulu-Natal (tel: 0323-975 3164).
South African Golf Safaris, PO Box 3051, Paarl 7620, Western Cape (tel: 021-863 8833).
South African Golf Tours, Greenways 4501, Beach Road, Strand (tel: 021-852 8909, info@sagolftour. co.za. Ascot Golf Tours, Milton's Way, 11 Bell Crescent, Westlake Business Park, Westlake, Cape Town 7945 (tel: 021-701 1201, info@ascottours.co.za.

239

Elephants keep a wary eye on passing safaris

Tours and safaris

REGIONAL SPECIALISTS
For day-trips around major cities, see the A–Z listings.

Western Cape
The Capevine, PO Box 3799, Tygerpark 7536, Cape Town (tel: 021-913 4580). Classy tailor-made tours of the Western Cape—wine, food, culture and wildlife.
Stormsriver Adventures, (tel: 042-281 1836, fax: 042-281 1609, www.stormsriver.com). Tubing, abseiling, diving, fishing, hiking and more in the Tsitsikomma region.
Vineyard Ventures, PO Box 554, Sea Point, Cape Town 8060 (tel: 021-434 8888, www.vineyardventures.co.za). Half- to 7-day tours of the Winelands, with tastings.

Guateng
Kwathlano Tours and Safaris, PO Box 75928, Lynnwood Ridge, Pretoria 0040 (tel: 012-343 2200, fax: 012-343 2198, www.kwathlano.co.za). Sightseeing tours of major cities, plus airport transfers. Also cross-country tours.

KwaZulu-Natal
180° Adventures, PO Box 1011, Umhlanga Rocks (tel: 031-556 4955, fax: 031-556 5381, www.180.co.za). Bicycling, 4WD, rafting, kayaking, climbing, hiking and diving.
Andy Cobb Eco Diving, PO Box 386, Winkelspruit 4145 (tel: 031-916 4239). Diving and game park safaris.
Strelitzia Tours, PO Box 1462, Westville 3630, Durban (tel: 031-266 9480, fax: 031-266 9404, www.strelitziatours.com). Short trips, including townships, Zulu experience and golf.

Mpumalanga
Lawson's Specialised Tours, PO Box 16849, Westacres, Nelspruit 1200 (tel: 013-741 2458, fax: 013-741 3681, www.lawsons.co.za). Bird-watching, wildlife and photo tours.
Lowveld Environmental Services, PO Box 5747, Nelspruit 1200 (tel: 013-744 7636, www.les-safaris.com). Kruger safaris.
Safarilandia, PO Box 2978, Nelspruit (tel: 082-338 9055, email: safarilandia@yebo.co.za). Open-vehicle safaris.

Hikers by the Mac-Mac pools

Limpopo Province
Equus Horse Safaris, PO Box 975, Vaalwater 530 (tel: 014-721 0062, fax: 014-721 0062, www.equus.co.za). Riding and camping in the Lapalala Wilderness Area (Waterbergs).

Northwest Province
Airtrack Adventures, PO Box 630, Muldersdrift 1747 (tel: 011-957 2322). Hot-air balloons over the Pilanesburg National Park and Crocodile River.

Travel Facts

Arriving

Arriving by air
Of the three major international airports, the biggest is **Johannesburg International**, 25km (15 miles) east of Johannesburg, tel: 011-921 6262 (inquiries).
Cape Town International is 22km (14 miles) east of Cape Town (tel: 021-937 1200); airport shuttle (tel: 021-934 4440) Magic Bus (tel: 021-934 5455).
Durban International is 20km (12 miles) southwest of Durban (tel: 031-451 6667); Super Shuttle (tel: 0860-333444).
Kruger Mpumalanga International is 22.5km (14 miles) northeast of Nelspruit (www.kmiairport.co.za) is the main gateway to the Kruger National Park.

There are scheduled flights from all over the world. Destinations of the state airline, **South African Airways (SAA)**, include New York, Miami, Hong Kong and Sydney, with regular services from London Heathrow to Johannesburg, Cape Town and Durban (www.flysaa.com). As a

Short-term parking at Cape Town International

member of the Star Alliance, partner airlines fly round the world. Business and first class offer comforable lie-flat beds. An arrival **tax** is included in the price of an international or domestic ticket. For all airports: www.airports.co.za; automated flight information (tel: 086-727 7888).

SAA offices abroad:
UK St. George's House, 61 Conduit Street, London W1S ZNE (tel: 020 7312 5000, fax: 020 7312 5009, reservations 0870 747 1111)
USA 515 E. Las Olas Boulevard, Fort Lauderdale, FL 33301 (tel: 954-769 5000, fax: 954-769 5079).

Airline offices in South Africa:
South African Airways (SAA)
SAA Call Centre: 0861-359 722 (in SA), +27-11-978 5313 (from abroad) Cape Town, 4th floor, JDN House, corner Shortmarket Street and St. Georges Mall (tel: 021-449 1122, fax: 021-449 1131. Johannesburg International Airport, Airways Park, Jones Road (tel: 011-978 1111. Durban International Airport (tel: 031-450 2277).
Air France International Departure area, Johannesburg International

Airport (tel: 0861-340 340,
www.airfrance.com).
British Airways PO Box 535,
Parklands, 195 Jan Smuts Avenue,
Rosebank (tel: 011-441 8600,
www.britishairways.com).
KLM Royal Dutch Airlines c/o Air
France, www.klm.com
Qantas 2nd Floor, Grosvenor Court,
195 Jan Smuts Avenue, Parkton North,
PBI Parklands 2121 (tel: 011-441 8550,
www.quantas.com).
Virgin Atlantic Building C, 50 Sixth
Road, Hyde Park, Johannesburg (tel:
011-340 3400, www.virgin-atlantic.com).

Arriving by land

South Africa borders Namibia,
Botswana, Zimbabwe, Mozambique,
Swaziland and Lesotho. Most cross-
ings are open at least 8am–6pm daily.
There are good roads, and bus and
train links with Namibia, Botswana,
Mozambique and Zimbabwe.

If you intend to take a shortcut
through Lesotho and Swaziland ask
for a multiple-entry visa, allowing
unlimited border crossings within a
specific period.

Arriving by sea

Several cruise companies, including
Hebridean Island Cruises, Cunard
Line, Crystal Cruises and Holland
America Line, stop in South Africa.
The RMS *St. Helena* (www.rms-st-
helena.com) runs four scheduled
services a year between the UK and
Cape Town (tel: South Africa 021-425
1165, UK 020 7575 6480) and round
trips from Cape Town to St. Helena.
Several other companies provide
passenger services on cargo freighters.

Long and straight—the Free State roads

Customs regulations

Duty-free allowance For visitors over
18 years old, the allowance is 200
cigarettes, 250g of tobacco and 50
cigars, 1 litre of spirits, 2 litres of
wine, 50ml of perfume and 250ml of
toilet water. Duty of additional
goods to the value of R12,000 will be
charged at 20 per cent.
Drugs Narcotics and habit-forming
drugs are prohibited. If you are using
prescription drugs, carry a letter
from your doctor.

Travel insurance

Make sure you have travel insurance
that covers medical treatment, air
ambulance and repatriation, loss or
theft of luggage, papers or money,
and travel delays or cancellation.

Documents

Visitors need a full passport, valid
for at least six months beyond the
intended stay and one blank page.
Visas are not required by most
Europeans, Northern Americans,
Australians and New Zealanders,
other nationatilies should check
before travelling (www.home-
affairs.pwv.gov.za) . If you arrive by
air you will need to show your return
ticket. If you arrive at a border you
may need to show a credit card or
proof of funds and a ticket out.

Your national driver's licence is
valid if it is written in English and
has your photo. If not, get an international driver's licence, valid for up
to three years (depending on the type
of permit) before leaving home.

Essential facts

Climate

As a whole, South Africa has an average annual rainfall of 464mm (18in) a year and an average of 8.5 hours of sunshine a day. Average midwinter (June–July) temperatures range from 0°C (32°F) at night to 20°C (68°F) at midday. Average midsummer (December–January) temperatures are 15°C (59°F) at night to 35°C (95°F) at midday.

This means little, however, as there are several distinct climatic zones in the country dependent on longitude, latitude, vegetation and altitude. It can be cool and grey in temperate Cape Town, hot and sticky in monsoon Durban, crisp and chilly in the high Drakensberg, and hot and dry in the Kruger, all at the same time. It can also go from cool and overcast to blasting sun in the same place in the space of a few minutes. Always check local conditions, and always add sunblock, a hat, an umbrella and a sweater or jacket when packing.

National holidays

1 January	New Year's Day
21 March	Human Rights Day
March/April	Good Friday
March/April	Easter Sunday
March/April	Easter Monday
March/April	Family Day
27 April	Freedom Day
1 May	Workers' Day
16 June	Youth Day
9 August	National Women's Day
24 September	Heritage Day
16 December	Day of Reconciliation
25 December	Christmas Day
26 December	Day of Goodwill

Time differences

South African Standard Time is 2 hours ahead of Greenwich Mean Time (Universal Standard Time), 7 hours ahead of US Eastern Standard Time, and 8 hours behind Australian Eastern Standard Time.

Opening times

Banks: Mon–Fri 9–4, Sat 9–11. Most have 24-hour ATMs outside.
Businesses: Mon–Fri 8–5, with an hour for lunch between 12 and 2. Some are open limited hours on Saturday morning.
Filling stations: Most open 7–7 daily; many are open 24 hours a day.

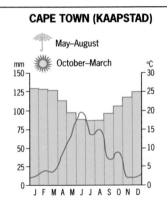

CAPE TOWN (KAAPSTAD)

May–August
October–March

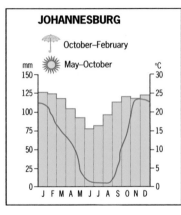

JOHANNESBURG

October–February
May–October

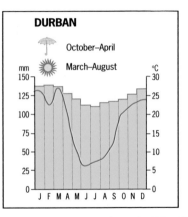

DURBAN

October–April
March–August

244

Post offices: Mon–Fri 8.30–4.30, Sat 8–11.30/12.30.
Shops: Mon–Fri 8–5, Sat–Sun 8.30–1 (cities only)—although hours are often longer in the main shopping areas and vary from province to province.

Many small towns, still controlled by the Dutch Reformed Church, close down completely on Sunday.

Money matters

Currency The South African currency is the rand (R), divided into 100 cents. Banknotes are issued in denominations of R200, R100, R50, R20 and R10.

Exchange facilities Most banks have exchange facilities for major currencies, but it is advisable to carry US dollars or UK pounds sterling. There are plenty of ATMs in larger towns and cities, and you can obtain money from most if your national cheque card or credit card bears a Maestro logo.

Thomas Cook (Rennies) and American Express operate bureaux de change in all major cities. Banks wil require ID for you to change money.

Cheques and credit cards Many hotels, shops and restaurants in tourist and urban areas accept traveller's cheques. Most businesses,

Shelves are piled high in the back street grocery stores

tour operators, airlines, hotels and restaurants accept international credit cards including Visa, MasterCard, American Express and Diners Club. To report the loss or theft of a card, call the following numbers: American Express SA (tel: 011-359 0200); Diners Club (tel: 0800-112 017); MasterCard SA (tel: 0800-990 418); Visa SA (tel: 0800-990 475). Thomas Cook MasterCard Travellers Cheque Refund Centre (24-hour service—report loss or theft within 24 hours), tel: 0800-998 175.

Prices There is a secondary economy, based on the former townships, where prices are a fraction of those in the old white habitat. For most tourists, however, the exchange rate has made South Africa affordable, if not as cheap as a few years ago. Fashionable hotel and tour prices are based on the US dollar and compare with US prices.

VAT Value Added Tax at 14 per cent is levied on most items and services, including accommodation, goods, vehicle rental and tours. Keep receipts on goods over R250 and claim back the tax when you are leaving the country. You may have to show the receipts, www.taxrefunds.co.za.

Getting around

By car

Car rental Budget, Hertz, Imperial and Avis have offices throughout the country, including all main airports; you can rent from one office and return at another (for a premium). Local firms offer a less expensive, more limited service. Everything from an economy compact to 4WD, chauffeur-driven limousine or motor home (RV) is available, all in excellent condition. Rental is not expensive, but base rates can be doubled by extras such as Collision Damage Waiver and insurance. Shop around for deals and, with huge distances to cover, always look for unlimited mileage. You should not need 4WD, even in the game parks, but check that your insurance covers you for dirt roads (some policies forbid them, which cuts out serious game viewing). Make sure you have a full set of spares and a jack before setting out.

Car Rental Central Reservation:

Avis (tel: 011-923 3660 or toll-free 0861-021111, www.avis.co.za)
Budget Rent a Car (tel: 011-392 0123 or 0860-016 622, fax: 011-392 0124, www.budget.co.za)
Europcar (tel: 011-394 8831 or toll-free 0860-011 344; fax: 011-394 8833, www.europcar.co.za)
Hertz (tel: 021-935 4800, fax: 021-935 4801, www.hertz.co.za)
Imperial Car Rental (tel: 011-574 1000 or toll-free 0861-131 0000, www.imperialcarrental.co.za).

Driving tips South Africa has excellent roads. Traffic is light, tempting drivers to go too fast, many drive drunk at night and the country has an appalling accident record. Concentrate every second—anything can appear from nowhere. There are a growing number of toll roads; keep some change handy for the tolls, which are reasonable.

Service stations are plentiful on major routes, infrequent elsewhere. Most will accept credit cards, but carry some cash, just in case. Window washing is standard. On long journeys, check the oil, water and brakes before setting out, take a can of fuel (you can buy cans at larger filling stations), together with spare tyres (and jack) and fan belt. Always carry a mobile phone, water, emergency rations and a blanket.

Regulations Driving is on the left. The speed limit is 60kph (37mph) in built-up areas, 100kph (62mph) on rural roads and 120kph (74mph) on freeways, unless otherwise indicated. There are severe fines for exceeding the designated speed limit. Give way to the right at intersections and traffic circles. Seat belts are compulsory. Always carry your driving licence, and do not drive under the influence of alcohol. Traffic laws are strictly enforced and penalties are harsh.

The **Automobile Association of South Africa** (tel: 082-16111, www.aa.co.za) has reciprocal arrangements with many other driving associations and will give advice and travel information as well as arrange emergency rescues.

By air

Several small airlines create an excellent network of domestic flights, serving surprisingly small towns and many of the main tourist sights. Fares, on the whole, are not particularly inexpensive, but there are usually discounts for advance booking and they can be less expensive if you reserve internal flights in conjunction with your international ticket.
SAA (www.flysaa.com, see page 242) and its offsrint SA Express and SA Airlink, fly to and between many destinations in South Africa, inlcuding Jo'burg, Cape Town, Durban, Sun City, Hoedspruit, Kruger Mpumalanga, East London and Port Elizabeth. **Kulula** (www.kulula.com, call centre tel: 0861-585 852 (in SA), +27-22-921 0111 (from abroad) is the country's first real low-cost airline with services to main cities. British Airways (www.britishairways.com, see page 242) also has a good network of domestic flights in the country.
By train see pages 234–235

By bus

Long-distance buses are popular, with services around the clock on all intercity routes. Reserve in advance.

Greyhound (tel: 083-915 9000 or 011-276 8500, fax: 011-276 8550, www.greyhound.co.za)
Intercape (tel: 021-380 4400, fax: 021-380 2076, www.intercape.co.za)
Translux (Central Reservations: 011-774 3333, fax: 011-774 3831, www.translux.co.za)
The Baz Bus (tel: 021-439 2323, fax: 021-439 2343, www.bazbus.com). Inexpensive hop-on-hop-off bus around main tourist attractions.

By minibus taxi

The least expensive (but most uncomfortable) way of getting around is via the growing army of taxis. They are now fanning out to provide a countrywide network of routes. There is no advance booking and no schedule; they simply wait until full (and that can mean 22 people in an eight-seater).

Standards of maintenance and driving are sometimes dodgy, with a high accident rate, and the city depots are usually in the former townships. This method of getting around is not usually recommended for tourists.

Hitchhiking

Hitchhiking is not recommended anywhere in the country.

City travel

Things are improving but there are still relatively few efficient, safe ways of getting round the cities other than by private taxi. In **Cape Town**, contact **Metro Transport Info** (tel: 0800-656 463, www.mti.co.za) for details of public transport and taxis; **Cape Metrorail** (tel: 021-449 4210, www.capemetrorail.co.za); and **Golden Arrow** buses (tel: 021-937 8000, www.gabs.co.za).
Johannesburg's services are improving but safety is a consideration. Buses are run by **Metrobus** (tel: 011-403 4300, www.mbus.co.za). Commuter rail services are more efficient and safer with plans underway for the Gautrain, a high-speed link between Pretoria and Jo'berg.

Taxis are common, metered, and expensive in major cities, almost nonexistent in smaller towns. You cannot hail them on the street and taxi stands are rare. Most shops and restaurants are happy to call one for you, even if you just walk off the street.
Cape Town Marine Taxi (tel: 021-434 0434)
Durban Mozzie Cabs Taxis (tel: 086-066 9943)

Durban is the only city in South Africa with a good local bus service

247

Johannesburg Maxi Taxis
(tel: 011-648 1212)
Pretoria Rixi Mini Cabs
(tel: 012-325 8072).

Student and youth travel
There is a growing range of good cut-price backpackers' accommodation, and student and youth discounts. Take an International Student Identity Card (ISIC).
South African Student Travel Service (SASTS), Cape Town: 11 Breë Street, CT 8001 (tel: 021-418 3794, fax: 021-418 3795); Johannesburg: 3rd Floor, South Wing, Hyde Park Shopping Centre, corner Jan Smuts Avenue and Sixth Road, Sandton 2004 (tel: 011-325 5899, fax: 011-325 5894, www.sasts. org.za, organizes working holidays.

Communications

Media
Television and radio The South African Broadcasting Corporation operates three television services in 11 languages and 22 radio services in 11 languages. e-TV is a local independent TV channel (English). A full range of satellite channels is available. M-Net is the local movie/prime-time station; most hotels offer CNN, Sky and/or World Service. One of the best radio stations is the English-language SAfm. BBC World

Service and Voice of America both broadcast here.

The press There are five daily and five Sunday national newspapers. The *Sowetan* has the highest circulation, followed by *The Star*, and the *Sunday Times*. The weekly *Mail & Guardian* has international news. International papers are available in major cities, if a day or two late.

Post
There is a good postal service. For post office hours, see page 245. General delivery facilities are available in the main post office in each town; take identification to claim mail.
Cape Town GPO, corner of Parliament and Darling streets (tel: 021-464 1700)
Durban GPO, corner of West and Gardiner streets (tel: 031-336 3333)
Johannesburg GPO, Sandton City (tel: 011-783 6312)
Pretoria Church Square Post Office (tel: 012-339 8000).

Telephones
The telephone system is good, with a reasonable number of public phones in the larger towns. Phonecards for green phone booths are sold in pubs, at newsstands and other outlets. Cash telephone kiosks operate on a minimum of 20 cents. Standard rates are Mon–Fri 7am–5pm. Prices for overseas calls are high and the markups in hotels are huge. The mobile phone network is excellent, using the GSM system (compatible with European phones; North Americans will need tri-band. **MTN** and **Vodacom** have 24-hour desks at all major international airports, offering rental of mobile phones. Sim 4 Travel (www. sim4travel.co.uk) and Go-Sim (www.gosim.co.uk) are schemes offering heavily discounted international calls in a wide range of countries.
- International dialling code for South Africa 27
- Domestic information 1023
- Domestic operator services 0020
- International information and other enquiries 0903
- International operator 0900
- International direct dial 09 + the country code

• International codes:
Australia 61; Botswana 267;
Canada 1; Lesotho 266; Namibia 264;
New Zealand 64; Swaziland 268;
UK 44; US 1; Zimbabwe 263.

Electronics
Most hotels and businesses have fax facilities. Local stationers or 'copy shops' have public fax machines. Fax numbers are listed in the local telephone directory. Business hotels can arrange email connections and there are many Internet cafés in cities and major towns. Multinational servers are present.

Language
There are 11 official languages in South Africa—English (the language of government and administration), Afrikaans, Ndebele, Northern Sotho, Southern Sotho, Swazi, Tsonga, Tswana, Venda, Xhosa and Zulu. Most people speak at least a smattering of English and Afrikaans. There is discussion at present as to whether the Samn language should be turned into a 12th official language as part of the effort to keep it alive.

Caution for all—multilingual do's and don'ts

Emergencies

Police
To contact the South African Police (SAP), see listing SA Police Service under 'Government Departments' in local telephone directories.

Emergency telephone numbers
Police, Emergency and Crisis Services (ambulance, fire, mountain rescue, etc): 10111 and ask for the relevant service
AA Breakdowns: toll free: 082-16111

Embassies and consulates
For a full list of SA embassies and foreign embassies in SA visit www.dfa.gov.za
South African embassies abroad
Australia Rhodes Place, State Circle, Yarralumla, Canberra, ACT 2600 (tel: 02-6273 2424, fax: 02-6273 4994)
Canada 15 Sussex Drive, Ottawa, Ontario K1M 1M8 (tel: 613-744 0330, fax: 613-741 1639)
United Kingdom Trafalgar Square, London WC2N 5DP (tel: 020 7451 7299, fax: 020-7451 7284)
United States 3051 Massachusetts Avenue, N.W., Washington D.C.

20008 (tel: 202/232 4400, fax: 202/265 1607).
Foreign embassies in South Africa
Australia 292 Orient Street, Arcadia, Pretoria (tel: 012-342 3740, fax: 012-342 8442)
Canada 1103 Arcadia Street, Hatfield, Pretoria (tel: 012-422 3000, fax: 012-422 3052)
Ireland 1st Floor, Southern Life Plaza, 1059 Schoeman Street, (corner Festival Street, Arcadia, Pretoria 0083 (tel: 012-342 5062, fax: 012-342 4752)
New Zealand 1110 Arcadia Street, Hatfield, Pretoria (tel: 012-342 8656, fax: 012-342 8640)
UK 'Greystoke', 255 Hill Street, Arcadia, Pretoria (tel: 012-421 7500, fax: 012-483 1302)
USA 877 Pretorius Street, Arcadia, Pretoria (tel: 012-431 4000, fax: 012-342 2244).

Health
Inoculations For your own peace of mind, it is worth taking polio, typhoid and tetanus boosters and the 10-year hepatitis A vaccination.

Medical help Medical and hospital standards are excellent. Doctors are listed in local telephone directories under 'Medical Practitioners'. Pharmacies include:
Cape Town Rustenburg Pharmacy, Fountain Shopping Centre, Main Road, Rondebosch (tel: 021-685 5998. *Open* daily 8.30am–10pm)
Durban No 24-hour pharmacies. Medicine Chest Chemist, 155 Berea Road, Berea (tel: 031-305 6151. *Open* daily 8am–midnight)
Daynite Pharmacy, 9a Nedband Circle, corner of Point Road and West Street (tel: 031-368 3666. *Open* daily 7.30am–10.30pm)
Johannesburg Daelite Pharmacy, Sandton (tel: 011-883 7520. *Open* daily until 8pm)
Pretoria Unitas Hospital, 39 Clifton Avenue, Lyttleton (tel: 012-677 8000. *Open* 24 hours).

Hazards AIDS is endemic—49 per cent of the sexually active population is estimated to be HIV positive: practise celibacy or safe sex. Condoms are freely available. Blood for medical use is carefully screened and treated.

Rabies is fatal if not caught in the early stages, so get treatment immediately if bitten by any animal. Check with a doctor if you are bitten by a snake, spider or scorpion, or if you stand on any creature in the sea. Treat even minor grazes with caution, as there are parasites and poisonous plants to which you will have no immunity. Clean, disinfect and cover any wound and see a doctor if it seems to be going septic.

Malaria is found only in the Limpopo Province, Mpumalanga, northern areas of the Northern Cape, and KwaZulu-Natal. You must take prophylactics if going into these areas or any of the surrounding countries. You will need to take the pills before you leave and after you return home. Follow the pharmacist's advice. As the disease can take up to six months to develop, you should check with your doctor if you have flu-like symptoms within this period.

Tap water is safe. In bush camps, check before drinking. Do not drink from rivers or lakes without purifying the water, and don't swim or paddle in natural water without checking. In certain areas, the water may be infected with bilharzia—and there is the possibility that crocodiles or hippos are lurking.

Wear a hat and high-factor sunblock, and stay in the shade during the intense midday heat. If you feel giddy in the sun, go indoors, drink large quantities of cool liquid, and have a cool bath. If you don't feel better, call a doctor.

If you are hiking in the mountains or in the desert, see **Surviving in the wilds** on page 252.

Survival

The urban jungle The crime rate has fallen dramatically but most South African cities still have a bad security problem. Central Cape Town and Durban require normal vigilance and precautions in daylight hours, but large segments of Johannesburg are virtual no-go areas.

The first rule is to try not to look rich. Don't walk the streets festooned in cameras or wearing jewellery. Use

Guard against pickpockets on beaches

traveller's cheques and credit cards wherever possible instead of carrying cash; take only what you need for the day, and always keep your money in several places. Never walk the streets after dark—take a taxi, however short the journey.

If you are mugged, hand over your valuables—do not resist. Wait until your assailant is out of sight before heading for the phone.

Try to make long-distance journeys in daylight and to reach your destination before dark. Keep car doors locked and wind up windows at traffic lights.

Do not pick up hitchhikers or stop to help people. If they seem to be in real trouble, telephone the nearest police station. Always park in well-lit and preferably busy places.

The former townships are still unsafe for foreigners unless you go with an informed local or escorted tour.

The **Travel Buddy** stystem (www.satravelbuddy.co.za) is a network of local people and organizations, including the tourist industry and police, throughout South Africa, linked by email and moble phones. Members will meet and greet visitors and provide information. The entire network can be mobilized within minutes to give assistance to those in distress.

Surviving in the wilds However cuddly they seem, many wild animals will happily take your hand off. Do not attempt to pet or feed animals, or even get out of the car for a better photo, without an experienced armed ranger.

When bush walking, always tell somebody where you are going and when you plan to be back. Wear desert boots with good treads and ankle support, thick socks and long trousers to protect your legs against thorns and wildlife. Take a hat, sunglasses and high-factor sunblock, a long stick for dealing with unwanted wildlife, a water

Camping is popular and facilities are excellent

bottle and emergency high-energy rations (such as trail mix). A foil space blanket, some analgesic tablets, water purifiers, anti-histamines in case of any allergic reaction (after a bite), insect repellent and sticking plasters are useful for emergencies. If you stumble on a snake, try not to provoke it. If you are bitten, stay calm, but get immediate help. Keep checking for spiders, scorpions and ticks; if you are bitten seek immediate medical advice.

When camping, take warm clothes for the evening and wet- and cold-weather gear in the mountains. Shake out your sleeping bag before you get in and hang your shoes upside down to deter creepie-crawlies. Ensure food is kept well sealed and out of reach of ants and monkeys.

Be careful about swimming on empty beaches. The African seas are treacherous with dangerous currents and riptides. Never let children swim unattended or go into the surf on rafts. If the beach is packed but nobody is swimming, there is probably a good reason. Many beaches have lifeguards but they are not on duty around the clock.

Other information

Camping

South Africa has a network of pleasant campsites, with shady pitches and good washing and cooking facilities (including your own *braai*/barbecue and a generous stack of wood). Larger sites may have self-catering cottages, a shop, filling station, swimming pool and restaurant. Visitors with caravans or campers (RVs) are unlikely to find individual hookups for electricity, water, and so forth. The South African Automobile Association publishes an annual guide available from them (tel: 011-483 3044) or local bookshops.

Camping rough is not a good idea for security reasons.

Camper rental:

Britz (Johannesburg tel: 011-396 1860, fax: 011-396 1937, www.britz.co.za). South Africa's largest campervan and 4WD rental with offices around SA.
Buffalo Camper and 4x4 Hire (tel: 011-704 1300, fax: 011-462 5266, www.buffalo.co.za)
Campers Corner (Johannesburg tel: 011-787 9105, fax: 011-789 2327, www.campers.co.za)

Children

South Africa is probably the most child-friendly country in Africa, with a fine climate, glorious beaches, entertainment, good food and hygiene and excellent health care. There are plenty of family accommodation options, including some with self-catering and camping, and for fussy eaters pizzas and hamburgers are on tap. Shops are well stocked with all the essentials from nappies to formula baby food, and finding reliable babysitters is easy.

The only drawbacks are the various stinging and biting creatures that lurk in long grass and under water; the ferocity of the midday sun; and the enormous distances covered when touring. Take plenty of snacks and entertainments and make sure your children wear sunblock,

hats and shoes when outside. Keep them in view and make sure they are properly supervised by a strong swimmer in the sea. There can be treacherous tides and waves as well as jellyfish, sea urchins and the occasional stray shark.

Only children over the age of four are permitted on game-viewing expeditions organized by private safari companies and lodges. If you have your own vehicle, they can start younger, but remember that children have a limited attention span and are not disposed to sit quietly while watching the animals. Also, peak game-viewing times are early morning and late afternoon/early evening—which may disrupt schedules for young children. Some game lodges such as Garonga (see page 262) and Ulusaba (ww.ulusaba.co.za) arrange family safaris and activities. Tour operators (see page 238–240) will put together family-based itineraires. Many smart hotels will not accept children under 12.

Parent-free breaks
The National Environmental Adventure Trust, 10 Parl Drive, Crestholeme, Durban (tel: 031-776 3334) offer parent-free adventure breaks, from one day and upwards, for older children (usually seven to nine years and up), with everything from abseiling to canoeing to ecology classes.

Visitors with disabilities

Many major sights and hotels have ramps and toilets for people who use wheelchairs, but facilities vary. Staff are usually willing to assist those with special requirements.

Eco-Access, PO Box 1377, Roosevelt Park, Johannesburg 2129 (tel: 011-477 3676, fax: 011-477 3675, www.eco-access.org) is a South African organization set up to help provide access to nature for those with disabilities.

Flamingo Adventure Tours/Disabled Ventures, PO Box 60554, Flamingo Square 7441, Western Cape (tel/fax: 021-557 4496, www.flamingotours.co.za).

Tours of the Western Cape for visitors with disabilities, with specially adapted vehicles and a registered nurse as tour guide. Also mainstream tours.

For information before you travel, contact:

UK RADAR (Royal Association for Disability and Rehabilitation), 12 City Forum, 250 City Road, London EC1V 8AF (tel: 020 7250 3222, fax:

020-7250 0212, minicom: 020 7250 4119, www.radar.org.uk).

USA SATH (Society for the Advancement of Travel for the Handicapped), 347 Fifth Avenue, Suite 610, New York NY 10016 (tel: 212/447-7284, fax: 212/725-8253, www.sath.org).

Senior citizens

There are some facilities but most are for South African nationals only. Keep proof of your age handy and you may be able to get discounts on some national parks accommodation, cinema and theatre tickets and some restaurants. **The Association for Retired Persons and Pensioners (ARP&P)** (tel: 021-531 2953).

Maps

There is a wide range of free maps of the country, regions and cities available from SA Tourism (see page 256 for contact details). Most of these are as good or better than anything on

The Jama Madjid mosque, Durban

254

sale, other than the full A–Z city plans, which are very comprehensive.

CNA booksellers are probably the best places to buy commercial maps, while hiking trail maps are available from the national parks shops.

Measurements
South Africa uses the metric system.

Places of worship
You will find Christian churches of every denomination, from Catholic, Anglican and Dutch Reformed to a variety of evangelical sects throughout the country.

With large Jewish, Indian and Malay populations, there are also synagogues, mosques and Hindu temples. Check the telephone directory for those nearby, or ask your hotel for advice.

Electricity
South Africa uses 220–240V AC, 50 Hertz, and plugs have three round pins. Power is reliable in cities, but you may experience some problems in remote areas, and bush camps may not be equipped with electricity, so take a torch (flashlight). US appliances may need a transformer.

Tipping
Tipping is common, but not obligatory. Give waiters and taxi drivers 10 per cent and porters R4–R5 per bag. Many hotels run a staff box at the front desk for one lump sum on checkout.

Otherwise, give a few rand to the room staff and doorman. Tip tour guides and game rangers at least R30 each per day.

Toilets
Most tourist venues, service stations and shopping malls have good public toilets. In nature reserves, parks and at the seaside they can be primitive but are usually spotless. There may be a small fee.

Tourist services

Tourist services in South Africa
The South African Tourist Board has only one office in South Africa:

CONVERSION CHARTS

FROM	TO	MULTIPLY BY
Inches	Centimetres	2.54
Centimetres	Inches	0.3937
Feet	Metres	0.3048
Metres	Feet	3.2810
Yards	Metres	0.9144
Metres	Yards	1.0940
Miles	Kilometres	1.6090
Kilometres	Miles	0.6214
Acres	Hectares	0.4047
Hectares	Acres	2.4710
Gallons	Litres	4.5460
Litres	Gallons	0.2200
Ounces	Grams	28.35
Grams	Ounces	0.0353
Pounds	Grams	453.6
Grams	Pounds	0.0022
Pounds	Kilograms	0.4536
Kilograms	Pounds	2.205
Tons	Tonnes	1.0160
Tonnes	Tons	0.9842

MEN'S SUITS

UK	36	38	40	42	44	46	48
Rest of Europe	46	48	50	52	54	56	58
US	36	38	40	42	44	46	48

DRESS SIZES

UK	8	10	12	14	16	18
France	36	38	40	42	44	46
Italy	38	40	42	44	46	48
Rest of Europe	34	36	38	40	42	44
US	6	8	10	12	14	16

MEN'S SHIRTS

UK	14	14.5	15	15.5	16	16.5	17
Rest of Europe	36	37	38	39/40	41	42	43
US	14	14.5	15	15.5	16	16.5	17

MEN'S SHOES

UK	7	7.5	8.5	9.5	10.5	11
Rest of Europe	41	42	43	44	45	46
US	8	8.5	9.5	10.5	11.5	12

WOMEN'S SHOES

UK	4.5	5	5.5	6	6.5	7
Rest of Europe	38	38	39	39	40	41
US	6	6.5	7	7.5	8	8.5

255

SA Tourism Head Office, Bojanala House, 90 Protean Road, Chislehurston, Sandton 2196; Private Bag X10012, Sandton 2146 (tel: 011-895 3000. Info/brochures 083-123 6789, fax: 011-895 3001, www.southafrica.net.
Provincial tourist office addresses are listed at the start of each chapter in the A–Z section of this book. Local details are given in each town listing.

SA Tourism abroad
Australia Level 1, 117 York Street, Sydney, PO Box Q120, QVB NSW 1230 (tel: 02-9261 5000. Info/brochures 1-800-238 643, fax: 02-9261 2000
Benelux: Jozef Israëlskade 48, N-1072SB Amsterdam (tel: 020-471 3181. Info/brochures 0900-202 0433, fax: 662 9761)
UK 5 Alt Grove, London SW19 4DZ (tel: 020 8971 9351. Info/brochures 0870-155 0044, fax: 020-8944 6705)
USA 500 Fifth Avenue, 20th Floor, New York, NY 10017 (tel: 212/730-2929. Info/brochures 1-800-593 1318, fax: 212/764 1980). Email for all via the website www. southafrica.net).

National Parks
Most game parks provide accommodation with basic *rondavels* (huts) and

A self-drive tour in the Kruger

camping; larger ones have a lodge with hotel-standard accommodation. All have at least one restaurant, a provisions store and fuel; some have their own post office, fax and laundry facilities. Opening hours for all parks are from dawn to dusk (roughly 6–6); reach the gate well before then to allow time to drive to the camp. The self-catering camps are very popular and it is worth booking in writing well in advance (up to a year), especially in local school and public holidays. For details of individual parks, see the A–Z section. (See also **Surviving in the wilds**, page 252.)
National Parks Board PO Box 787, Pretoria 0001 (tel: 012-426 5000, reservations 012-428 91111, www.sanparks.org). Operates 11 of the major parks, including Kruger.

Each of the provinces has a local department, while many smaller parks and reserves run by local conservation bodies offer walking, hiking and climbing. For information:
KZN Wildlife PO Box 13069, Cascades, Pietermaritzburg 3202 (tel: 033-845 1000, fax: 033-845 1001, www. kznwildlife.com). Manages all parks in KwaZulu-Natal.
Cape Nature Cape Nature House, Belmont Park, Belmont Road, Private Bag X29, Rondesbosch 7701 (tel: 021-659 3400, reservations 021-426 0723, fax: 021-423 9611, www.capenature.org.za

Hotels and Restaurants

ACCOMMODATION

Central Booking

Bed-and-Breakfast South Africa
Sandringham, Johannesburg 2131
www.bedandbreakfast.co.za
Bed-and-breakfast website with properties all over the country.

Caraville Group
PO Box 1166, Westville, Durban 3630
tel: 031-266 0030 fax: 031-266 0205, in the UK tel: 020-8943 4747 www.caraville.co.za
Marketing and sales company representing around 100 smaller hotels and resorts throughout southern Africa.

CCAfrica
Pinmill Farm, Block F, Katherine Street, Sandown, Private Bag X27, Benmore 2010
tel: 011-809 4300 fax: 011-809 4400 email: information@ccafrica.com www.ccafrica.com
Small, exclusive and very luxurious lodges on private game reserves.

Holiday Inn
PO Box 782553, 2146 Sandton
tel: 011-780 0143 fax: 011-780 0106 bookings, in the UK tel: 0870 400 9670 (toll-free); in the US (toll-free)
tel: 800-421 8905 www.basshotels.com
Large chain of hotels, including the local Holiday Inns in their many incarnations.

Hostelling International South Africa
3rd floor, St. George's House, 73 St. George's Mall (PO Box 4402), Cape Town 8000
tel: 021-424 2511 fax: 021-424 4119
www.hisa.org.za
The local youth hostel affiliate.

Jacana Country Homes and Trails
PO Box 95212, Waterkloof 0145
tel: 012-346 3550/1 fax: 012-346 2499
email: info@jacanacollection.co.za
Central marketing for a wide range of farm stays and country cottages.

Legacy Hotels and Resorts
Tel: 011-806 6888 fax: 011 806 6899
www.legacyhotels.co.za.
Rapidly growing chain of luxurious city hotels, coastal resorts and bush lodges.

National Parks South Africa
643 Leyds Street, Muckleneuk (PO Box 787), Pretoria 0001 tel: 012-428 9111
fax: 012-426 5500 www.sanparks.co.za
Accommodation in the national parks, from campsites to lodges.

Portfolio Town and Country Retreats
Shop 5E, Mutual Square, Oxford Road, Rosebank, 2196 Johannesburg
tel: 011-880 3414 fax: 011-788 4802
www.portfoliocollection.co.za
Offers a wide range of guest-houses and small hotels, from the most basic to the most luxurious.

Protea Hotels
5th Floor, Nedbank Foreshore Building, Heerengracht, Cape Town 8000
tel: 021-430 5000 fax: 021-430 5320
www.protea-hotels.co.za
The largest South African chain; most hotels are comfortable and reasonably priced, if lacking in atmosphere.

Relais Hotels
PO Box 654, Cape Town 8000
tel: 021-423 1426 or 0800-600 889 (toll-free)
fax: 021-423 1439 www.relais.co.za
Luxury small and suite hotels, most in the Cape.

Sun International
PO Box 784487, 2146 Sandton
tel: 011-780 7444 fax: 011-780 7726
In the UK tel: 01628 421 511;
in the US tel: 954/331-3252
Hotels range from very comfortable to the totally luxurious, including Sun City. Most with casinos.

The best budget accommodation is in small bed-and-breakfasts that have only a couple of rooms and have not been listed here. Ask agencies or local tourist offices for recommendations. The following recommended hotels have been divided into four price categories:

- inexpensive ($)—under 500 Rand
- moderate ($$)—500–1,500 Rand
- expensive ($$$)—1,500–3,000 Rand
- very expensive ($$$$)—above 3,000 Rand

WESTERN CAPE

Cape Town and the Cape Peninsula

Cape Grace ($$$$)
West Quay, V&A Waterfront, Cape Town
tel: 021-410 7100 fax: 021-419 7622
www.capegrace.com
Luxury country-house style hotel right on the V&A Waterfront, with seamless efficiency, comfort and excellent food.

Cellars-Hohenort ($$$)
93 Brommersvlei Road, Constantia
tel: 021-794 2137 fax: 021-794 2149
www.collectionmcgrath.com
Magnificent small Cape Dutch hotel with extensive gardens, great views of Table Mountain and two superb restaurants. Swimming pool, riding.

Commodore and Portswood Hotels ($$$)
Portswood Road, V & A Waterfront
Commodore tel: 021-415 1000 fax: 021-415 1100; Portswood tel: 021-418 3281 fax: 021-419 7570 www.legacyhotels.co.za
Sitting side by side these two hotels offer good value, comfortable accommodation in a superbly convenient location. Good views from some rooms, good restaurants and shared pool.

De Waterkant Village ($/$$)
PO Box 51105, Waterfront 8002, Cape Town
tel: 021-422 2721 fax: 021-421 5054
www.dewaterkant.com
Delightful collection of 65 carefully restored cottages with kitchens, many with fine views, splash pools or roof terraces, all in the lively Cape Malay Bo Kaap district of town.

Grandwest ($$/$$$)
1 Vanguard Drive, Goodwood
tel: 021-505 7777 fax: 021-505 7132
www.suninternational.com
Spectacular hotel and casino complex focused around the architectural heritage of the Cape. There are two hotels, the luxury Grand Hotel and

the less expensive City Lodge, several restaurants, an ice rink, multiscreen cinema, go-carts and more keep the children occupied while you spend money.

iKhaya Guest Lodge ($$)
Dunkley Square, Wandel Street, Cape Town
tel: 021-461 8880 fax: 021-461 8889
www.ikhayalodge.co.za
Small African-style lodge in the heart of the city, magnificently designed with carvings and hand-crafted furniture. Also apartments with kitchen.

Kensington Place ($$)
38 Kensington Crescent, Higgovale
tel: 021-424 4744 fax: 021-424 1810
www.kensington-place.co.za
Small, luxurious furnished guest-house (eight rooms) in a residential suburb at the foot of Table Mountain. It also has a pool.

Mount Nelson ($$$$)
76 Orange Street, Cape Town
tel: 021-483 1198 fax: 021-483 1109
www.mountnelsonhotel.orient-express.com
An elegant pink hotel in the heart of the city, the 'Nellie' is one of the world's greatest historic hotels. It also has three of Cape Town's finest restaurants. Swimming pools.

The Town House ($)
60 Corporation Street tel: 021-465 7050
fax: 021-465 3891 www.townhouse.co.za
Modern, well-designed city-centre hotel.

Travellers Inn ($)
208 Long Street, Cape Town
tel: 021-424 9272 fax: 021-424 9278
email: travellersinn@intekom.co.za
A clean, budget backpackers' B&B in a historic Victorian gingerbread mansion in the city.

Victoria Junction ($$)
Corner of Somerset and Ebenezer roads,
Gallows Hill, Cape Town tel: 021-418 1234
fax: 021-418 5678 email: vicjunct@icon.co.za
A Protea hotel in the middle of the city, heavy on the chrome, glass-brick and spotlights.

The Vineyard ($$)
Colinton Road, off Protea Road, Newlands
tel: 021-657 4500 fax: 021-657 4501
www.vineyard.co.za
Large Georgian country-house hotel, built originally for a local socialite, Lady Anne Barnard. It was carefully restored and is now furnished with antiques. Set in beautiful gardens on the Liesbeeck River, with superb mountain views, a swimming pool and an excellent French restaurant.

The Winelands, Breede Valley and West Coast

L'Auberge du Quartier Français ($$/$$$)
Huguenot Street, Franschhoek
tel: 021-876 2151 fax: 021-876 3105
www.lequartier.co.za
Elegant country-house hotel, with two superb restaurants: Le Quartier, serving formal French cuisine, and the outdoor Café Français, with Cape Provincial cuisine. Booking advised.

Bushman's Kloof ($$$)
PO Box 53405, Kenilworth 7645, Cape Town,
33km (21 miles) from Clanwilliam, off the
R364 tel: 021-797 0990 fax: 021-761 5551
www.bushmanskloof.co.za
Luxury manor set in a vast private reserve with 34

species of mammal, over 140 species of bird and a magnificent collection of San art in some 125 sites. Pool, game drives, art walks, birdwatching and many other activities.

Clanwillian Hotel ($/$$)
Clanwilliam tel: 027-482 1101
fax: 027-482 2678
Relaxing, historic hotel. Good restaurant and tea room. Swimming pool.

De Ouwe Werf ($$)
30 Church Street, Stellenbosch
tel: 021-887 4608 fax: 021-887 4626
email: ouwewerf@iafrica.com
www.ouwewerf.com
B&B in a centrally located house built in 1803. Light lunches, traditional Cape and continental fare and tasty cakes. Swimming pool.

The Farmhouse ($$)
Langebaan tel: 022-772 2060
fax: 022-772 1980
www.thefarmhouselangebaan.co.za
Country house with a swimming pool overlooking the Langebaan lagoon, serving classic Mediterranean cuisine.

Grande Roche ($$$)
5 Plantasie Road, Paarl tel: 021-863 2727
fax: 021-863 2220 www.granderoche.com
A sumptuous hotel in the heart of the famous Paarl vineyards. Long wine list. Swimming pool.

Kagga Kamma ($$$)
100km (62 miles) north of Ceres
tel: 021-872 4343 fax: 021-872 4524
www.kaggakamma.co.za
'The Place of the Bushmen' is a private game reserve, with resident San population, in the Cederberg. Accommodation consists of a camp with chalets and the Bushmen Lodge. The price includes all meals and excursions.

Lanzerac Hotel ($$$)
Jonkershoek Road, Stellenbosch
tel: 021-887 1132 fax: 021-887 2310
email: info@lanzerac.co.za
Hotel based around a 150-year-old Cape Dutch homestead in one of South Africa's most famous vineyards on the outskirts of Stellenbosch. The restaurant serves traditional Malay fare.

Mooikelder Manor House ($$)
Agter–Paarl Road, North Paarl
tel: 021-8698787 fax: 021-863 8361
email: mooikel@mweb.co.za
Close to Paarl, this lovely Cape Dutch homestead (1835) includes Cecil John Rhodes among its past owners. Friendly, enthusiastic hospitality and antique furnishings. Normally bed-and-breakfast; other meals on request. Pool.

The South Coast, Garden Route, and Karoo

Arniston Hotel ($$)
Arniston tel: 028-445 9000
fax: 028-445 9633 www.arnistonhotel.co.za
A comfortable hotel in a 200-year-old fishing village. Good seafood restaurant. Pool and water sports. Alternatively, book a cottage ($) from Arniston Seaside Cottages (tel: 028-475 9772).

Belvidere Manor ($$)
Duthie Drive, Knysna tel: 044-387 1055
fax: 044-387 1059 www.belvidere.co.za

259

Historic house with Victorian-style cottages, each with a fireplace, next to Knysna lagoon. Excellent restaurant. Swimming pool, boating.

Eight Bells Mountain Inn ($$)
35km (22 miles) from Mossel Bay on the Oudtshoorn road tel: 044-631 0000 fax: 044-631 0004   www.eightbells.co.za
Superbly situated for the coast and the Karoo, this is a luxurious little resort with *rondavels* (huts), Swiss-style chalets and excellent restaurant.

Fancourt Hotel and Country Club ($$)
Montague Street, George tel: 044-804 0000 fax: 044-804 0700 www.fancourt.com
Exclusive and luxurious health, golf and leisure complex. Also has a play outlet for children.

Hunter's Country House ($$)
10km (6 miles) from Plettenberg Bay on the N2 to Knysna tel: 044-532 7818 fax: 044-532 7878 www.hunterhotels.com
Exclusive country hotel, with intimate thatched cottages scattered across manicured gardens on the edge of the last remaining indigenous forests. Superb dinner. Swimming pool, riding.

Klippe Rivier Homestead ($$)
10km (6 miles) west of Swellendam, PO Box 483, Swellendam tel: 028-514 3341 fax: 028-514 3337 www.klipperiver.com
A delightful Cape Dutch homestead with antique furnishings, close to historic Swellendam.

Lord Milner Hotel ($/$$)
Logan Road Matjiesfontein 6901 tel: 023-551 3011 fax: 023-551 3020 email: milner@mweb.co.za www.matjiesfontein.com
The tiny village of Matjiesfontein is a national monument, and this is basically all part of the resort, with options ranging from luxury rooms in the 'big house' to family apartments. There is a variety of restaurants (some requiring jacket and tie) as well as a Victorian country pub.

Old Post Office Tree Manor ($$)
Market Street, Mossel Bay tel: 044-691 3738 fax: 044-691 3104 www.oldposttree.co.za
Comfortable central guest-house with antique furnishings, in the third-oldest building in town.

The Plettenberg ($$$)
Plettenberg Bay tel: 044-533 2030 fax: 044-533 2074 email: plettenberg@pixie.co.za www.plettenberg.com
Highly comfortable, modern hotel on a rocky headland, with magnificent views and a fine restaurant. Swimming pool.

Rosenhof Country Lodge ($$)
264 Baron van Rheede Street, Oudtshoorn tel: 044-272 2232 fax: 044-222 3021
Delightful small Victorian hotel with antique furnishings and a fine country restaurant.

EASTERN CAPE

The Cock House ($)
10 Market Street, Grahamstown 6140 tel/fax: 046-636 1295 email: cockhouse@imaginet.co.za
A delightful small guest-house, built in 1830 and now a National Monument. The food is highly recommended.

Die Tuishuise ($)
36 Market Street, Cradock tel: 048-881 1322 fax: 048-881 1295 email: tuishuise@caraville.co.za
A wonderful hotel with 11 lovingly restored houses, all filled with antiques and each distinctively different. The price of a room gets you a whole house.

Drostdy Hotel ($$)
30 Church Street, Graaff-Reinet tel: 049-892 2161 fax: 049-892 4582
Designed in 1806 by the noted Cape Dutch architect Louis Thibault, and carefully restored. The rooms are in 1855 slave cabins. Pool.

Hacklewood Hill Country House ($$)
152 Prospect Road, Walmer, Port Elizabeth tel: 041-581 1300 fax: 041-581 4155 www.pehotels.co.za
This delightful, sophisticated Victorian house has been restored and furnished with magnificent antiques. The atmosphere is calm and elegant, the welcome friendly and the food delicious.

The Halyards Resort Hotel ($$)
Port Alfred 6170 tel: 046-624 2410 fax: 046-624 2466 www.halyards.com
Resort hotel at the mouth of the Kowie River. Rooms have private balconies overlooking the marina. Water sports, riding.

Settlers Inn ($$)
N2 Highway, below the 1820s Settlers Memorial, Grahamstown tel: 046-622 7313 fax: 046-622 4951 www.settlersinn.co.za
A pleasant modern hotel with good food, a pool and views.

Shamwari Game Reserves ($$$$)
72km (45 miles) from Port Elizabeth on the banks of the Bushmans River tel: 042-203 1111 fax: 042-235 1224 www.shamwari.com
Luxury private game reserve, with accommodation in a restored manor house and settler homes. Swimming pools. Game viewing. Expensive, but includes all meals and game drives.

Tsitsikamma Lodge ($)
on the N2, about 14km (9 miles) from the entrance to Tsitsikamma National Park tel: 042-2880 3802 fax: 042-280 3702 www.tsitsikamma.com
Comfortable log cabins, pretty gardens, a pool, forest walks and fishing at this early-to-bed resort.

Umngazi River Bungalows ($$)
about 18km (11 miles) west of Port St. Johns, Wild Coast tel: 047-564 1115-9 email:umngazi@iafrica.com, www.umngazi.co.za
A coastal hideaway with whitewashed thatched cottages and grassy slopes down to the river, dunes and coastal forest. Fishing, hiking, water sports. Other less expensive Wild Coast hotels include **Trennery's** (tel: 047-498 0004) and the **Kob Inn** (tel/fax: 047-499 0011).

THE FREE STATE, NORTHERN CAPE, AND NORTH-WEST PROVINCE

The Free State
Cranberry Cottage ($)
37 Beeton Street, Ladybrand tel: 051-924 2290 fax: 051-924 1168 www.cranberrycottage.co.za email: crancott@xsinet.co.za

A prettily decorated old sandstone house filled with antiques and fine art in the heart of the Eastern Highlands, with terraces, mature gardens and real log fires.

De Oude Kraal Country Estate ($$)
35km (22 miles) south of Bloemfontein
tel: 051-564 0636 fax: 051-564 0635
www.oudekraal.co.za
Historic country house with pleasant rooms and excellent traditional restaurant.

Franshoek Mountain Lodge ($)
3km (2 miles) east of S384/S385 junction,
Ficksburg, Eastern Highlands
tel/fax: 051-933 3938
Small, intimate sandstone and thatch lodge in a valley at the foot of the Witteberg. Good country cooking. Swimming pool, hiking, fishing, climbing, polo.

Northern Cape
Chateau Guesthouse ($)
9 Coetzee Street, Upington
tel/fax: 054-332 6504
Comfortable, art deco-style central B&B.

Edgerton House ($)
5 Edgerton Road, Belgravia, Kimberley
tel: 053-831 1150 fax: 053-831 1785
email: edgerton@kimberley.co.za
A superbly restored and beautifully decorated historic home run by a diamond history enthusiast. Swimming pool and tea garden; lunch and dinner on request.

Tswalu ($$)
PO Box 420, Kathu 8446, near the Kgalagadi
Transfrontier Park tel: 053-781 9234
fax: 053-781 9238 www.tswalu.com
The largest private game reserve in South Africa, exclusive Tswalu is made up of a stone and thatch lodge with nine cottages, set in 900sq km (347sq miles) of desertscape, from scrub bush to rolling red-gold sand dunes. There are around 40 species of mammal and 250 species of bird. Activities include game drives, walks and horseback rides.

North-West Province
Lindbergh Lodge ($$)
PO Box 412331, Craighall 2024, on the main
Johannesburg/Kimberley/Cape Town road
tel: 011-884 8923/4 fax: 011-884 8925
www.lindberghlodge.co.za
Luxury lodge in 5,000ha (25,000-acre) game reserve, close to a water hole with hide. Cottages, swimming pool, tennis, golf. Game-viewing, walks, mountain bikes, horses.

Madikwe River Lodge ($$)
Derdepoort tel: 014-778 0891
fax: 014-778 0893
email: lodge@madikwe.threecities.co.za
'Big five' game viewing at this exclusive game lodge close to the Botswana border, with luxury chalet overlooking the Marico River. Price includes everything. Swimming pool.

Sun City ($/$$/$$$)
75km (46 miles) from Rustenburg; bookings
through Sun International tel: 014-557 8100;
welcome centre tel: 014-557 1544
South Africa's first and largest casino and entertainment complex. Accommodation to suit all pockets: simple family units with kitchen at the Cabanas, the comfortable but ordinary Sun City itself, the plusher Cascades and the ultra-luxurious Palace at the Lost City. Magnificent swimming pools, golf course, water slides and other sporting activities. See also page 145.

GAUTENG

Johannesburg
McKenna Cottages ($)
30 Gill Street, Observatory
tel: 011-487 2829 fax: 011-487 2404
email: mckenna@iafrica.com
Stylish stone and thatch cottages in large grounds with pool, English gardens and a hiking trail; dinner on request. Less than 20 minutes from the airport.

The Michelangelo ($$$$)
Nelson Mandela Square, Sandton,
Johannesburg tel: 011-282 7000 fax: 011-
282 7171, www.legacyhotels.com
fax: 011-678 7913
A Leading Hotel of the World, The Michelangelo may not be architecturally stunny but it a large sumptuous city hotel with every comfort, superb restaurant and friendly and efficient staff plus a very convenient location in the heart of Sandton.

Thandidille Mountain Lodge ($$)
5 Linda Place, corner of Cliffside Cresent,
Northcliff tel: 011-476 1887 ext. 12
fax: 011-678 7913
Ten luxurious, individually designed rooms with private patios overlook lush gardens and fine views. Lunch and dinner on request.

The Westcliff ($$$)
67 Jan Smuts Avenue Westcliff 2193
tel: 011-646 2400 fax: 011-646 3500
www.orient-expresshotels.com
The Orient Express run the Westcliff, a magnificent salmon-pink place set on a hillside with superb city views. The food is excellent, the service impeccable and a shuttle bus runs up the steep hill between the rooms and reception.

261

Pretoria
Court Classique ($$)
Corner Schoeman and Beckett streets,
Arcadia, Pretoria tel: 012-344 4420 fax: 012-
344 4419 www.courtclassique.co.za
This low-rise all-suite hotel has a comfortable homey feel while provide all modern conveniences. Eat in the restaurant or cook for yourself. The garden has an attractive small pool.

The Farm Inn ($$)
The Willows, on main road east of Pretoria
tel: 012-809 0266 fax: 012-809 0146
www.farminn.co.za
Thatched cottages spread across a working farm with domestic animals, game and swimming pool. Children welcome.

Oxnead ($$)
Morreleta Park, Pretoria
tel: 012-993 4515 fax: 012-998 9168
www.oxnead.co.za
This pretty Cape Georgian-style guest-house serves superb food and vintage wines in a luxury setting. Swimming pool.

Elsewhere in Gauteng
Lesedi Cultural Village ($$)
*Honeydew, 41km (26 miles) from
Johannesburg on the R512 tel: 012-205 1394
fax: 012-205 1433 www.lesedi.com*
An imaginative development that is based on
Pedi, Sotho, Xhosa and Zulu traditional culture,
with accommodation in traditionally built village
houses.
Mount Grace Hotel ($$$)
*Old Rustenburg Road, Magaliesburg
tel: 014-577 1350 fax: 014-577 1202
www.grace.co.za*
Rustic chic is the keynote at this country house
hotel with its thatched cottages and traditional
English gardens. The food is excellent and there
are monthly classical concerts. Lovely spa.

LIMPOPO PROVINCE

The Coach House ($$/$$$)
*Agatha, 15km (9 miles) from Tzaneen, in the
Magoebaskloof Mountains
tel: 015-307 3641 fax: 015-306 8008
email: coachhouse@mweb.co.za*
This 19th-century coaching inn has delightfully com-
fortable rooms, panoramic views, a swimming pool,
spa, and some of the finest food in South Africa.
Entabeni ($$$)
*Waterberg tel: 014-743 6000/012-346 2229
(reservations), fax: 012-346 2243
www.entabeni.co.za*
Stunning beautiful 'big five' reserve with five lodges,
each of a different character and price. The most
luxurious, with excellent spa, overlooks the river.
Garonga ($$$)
*Near Hoedspruit tel: 0082-4403522/011-537
4620 (reservations) fax: 011-447 0993
UK: 01403 243619 www.garonga.com*
Enchanting small luxury lodge with tented rooms
overlooking a dry riverbed. The 'big five' game are
present but not always guaranteed. Family-run, laid
back and relaxing—and you can have a massage.
Jaci's Safari Lodge and Tree Lodge ($$$)
*57km (35 miles) from Molatedi Gate, inside
the Madikwe Game Reserve tel: 014-778
9900 fax: 014-778 9901 www.madikwe.com*
This luxury camp has eight thatched tents and
eight tree houses, all with private balcony. The tree
houses also have private pools. Although expen-
sive, the price includes all game drives and meals.
Excellent game viewing and 340 species of bird.
Gates close at 8pm.
Jembisa ($$/$$$)
*Waterberg tel: 014-755 4415 fax: 014-755
4444 UK: Cedarberg Travel, see page 238
www.jembisa.com*
Rent a whole family home (sleeping 10) in your
personal game reserve, fully staffed with game
guides for drives, rides (horse and elephant) and
walks. Good game but not 'big five'. Pool.
Mhondoro ($$$)
*Waterberg tel: 011-678 0401 fax: 011-678
2431 www.mhondoro.co.za*
African-style thatch-and-wood lodge with great
views over the plain and waterhole. Small pool and
comfortable accommodation in the Big Five
Welgevonden Reserve. Some 350 species of bird.

Thornybush Game Reserve ($$$$)
*Northlands, Hoedspruit
tel: 011-883 7918 fax: 011-883 8201
email: res@thornybush.co.za
www.thornybush.co.za*
Four separate camps range from a bush lodge to
a tented camp in this luxury private reserve on the
Kruger fringes.

MPUMALANGA

Luxury lodges at Kruger
Most of the lodges scattered through Sabi Sands
and Timbavati (see pages 186–187) are similar in
style, with a large private game park and small
camps. The complex is usually open to the bush
with animals roaming through. All meals are outdoors in good weather. Dinner is taken around the
bonfire in a *boma* (fenced enclosure). All those
listed provide the highest quality service, accommodation, food, atmosphere and game viewing. All
have swimming pools. Prices are high, but are usually inclusive (check before booking). You pay not
only for luxury accommodation, but for the upkeep
of an expensive private game reserve.
Inyati ($$$)
*Sabi Sands tel: 011-880 5909/07
fax: 011-788 2406 and 013-735 5032
www.inyati.co.za*
Small, friendly lodge, with luxurious thatched
chalets, on the Sand River.
Londolozi ($$$$)
*Sabie Sands tel: 011-809 4300 fax: 011-809
4400 email: information@ccafrica.com*
Five luxurious camps along the Sand River. The
Conservation Corporation also operates nearby
Ngala Lodge, the only private lodge within the
boundaries of the park itself.
Sabi Sabi ($$$$)
*Sabi Sands tel: 011-483 3939 UK: tel: 014-
0321 3619 www.sabisabi.com*
Four deluxe lodges of very differing styles, superb
game viewing, expert, personalized service, luxuri-
ous accommodation and a superb spa.
Singita ($$$$)
*Sabi Sands tel: 021-683 3424 (reservations)
fax: 01421-683 3502 UK: tel: 0131-661 6000
US: tel: 858-350 1354 www.singita.co.za*
A group of five award-winning lodges in an 18,500-
ha (45,714-acre) private concession. Excellent 'big
five' game viewing, luxurious accommodation and
a fine spa.

Hotels outside Kruger Park
Casa do Sol ($$/$$$)
*near Hazyview, on R536 to Sabie
tel: 013-737 8111 fax: 013-737 8166
www.casadosol.co.za*
A Spanish village in little Ilanga Nature Reserve,
with African waiters in berets and smocks—it is
great fun, very comfortable and the food is excel-
lent. Riding, walking, tennis, golf, fishing.
Cybele Forest Lodge ($$$)
*22km (14 miles) from Hazyview, off the R40 to
White River tel: 013-764 1823 fax: 013-764
1810 www.cybele.co.za*
Exclusive, mountain retreat, with beautiful grounds,
spa and superb meals. Easy access to Kruger Park.

Hippo Hollow Country Estate ($)
off the R535 near the R40 junction, Hazyview
tel: 013-737 7752 fax: 013-737 7673
www.hippohollow.co.za
Complex of thatched, family-oriented chalets
with kitchen surrounding an excellent full-service
restaurant. They also have private verandas with
river views.

The Royal Hotel ($$)
Main Street, Pilgrim's Rest
tel: 013-768 1100 fax: 013-768 1188
email: royal@mweb.co.za
Beautifully restored and atmospheric Victorian
hotel at the heart of this little mining town.

KWAZULU-NATAL

Durban and environs
Beverley Hlls Hotel ($$$)
Lighthouse Road, Umhlanga Rocks
tel: 031-561 2211 fax: 031-561 3711
www.southernsun.com
Glitzy 5-star hotel with all the trimmings, catering
for tourists and business visitors, on a private
beach. The rooms all have balconies and sea
views. Spa, pool and an excellent restaurant, café
and bar.

The Country Lodge ($$)
Southbroom, South Coast
tel: 039-316 8380 fax: 039-316 8557
www.the countrylodge.co.za
email: destafr@venturenet.co.za
Lovely, friendly lodge tucked into a cycad forest
near the beach. Excellent restaurant.

The Royal Hotel ($$$)
267 Smith Street, Durban
tel: 031-304 0331 fax: 031-304 5055
email: theroyal@ifrica.com www.theroyal.co.za
The Royal has been collecting awards as the
city's best hotel and best restaurant for years.
It has a central position in town, making it ideal
for exploring and shopping. Other benefits include
a swimming pool.

Selborne Country Lodge and Golf Resort ($$)
Pennington, South Coast tel: 039-975 1133
fax: 039-975 1811 www.selborne.com
Elegant country lodge, golf club and spa on a
superb 80ha (198-acre) estate on Natal's south
coast, 40 minutes' drive from Durban. Swimming
pool.

Shortens Country House ($$)
Opposite the Umhlali Country Club,
North Coast tel: 032-947 1140
www.shortenshotel.com
Elegant historic homestead set in magnificent
gardens, surrounded by 14 individually
decorated chalets. Excellent restaurant.

Battlefields and Zululand
Fugitive's Drift ($$)
15km (9 miles) from Rorke's Drift, near
Dundee tel/fax: 034-271 8053
www.fugitivesdrift.com
Comfortable family-run lodge on a natural heritage
site beside the Buffalo River, overlooking
Isandlwana. Extensive library of Africana; the
owner is a registered battlefield tour guide and one
of the best raconteurs in the region.

Hilltop Camp ($$)
Hluhluwe-Umfolozi National Park
Booking through KZN Wildlife, see page 191
This large building has luxury chalets and more
basic units. Superb views across the plain, and
wildlife wanders through from time to time. There
are also three smaller luxury lodges, Mtwazi,
Muntulue and Munywaneni, in the park.

Isandlwana Lodge ($$$)
Near Rorke's Drift, outside Dundee
tel: 034-271 8301 fax: 034-271 8306
www.isandlwana.co.za
Sit on the veranda and follow the whole pattern of
the events of Isandlwana battlefield at this friend-
ly, classy stone and thatch lodge. Good for explor-
ing the battlefields and local game reserves.

Phinda Resource Reserve ($$$)
*about 30km (18 miles) north of Hluhluwe vil-
lage (reservations: CCAfrica, see page 258)*
Pristine, private, 'big five' game reserve with six
lodges in different styles, including the stunning
Japanese-influenced glass cabins of Forest Lodge.

Rocktail Bay Lodge ($$$)
Maputaland Coastal Forest Reserve, south
of Kosi Bay. Book through travel agents
www.wilderness-safaris.co.za
Small, remote lodge with wood-and-thatch chalets
on stilts, next to a deserted turtle beach. Private
dive site and outdoor activities.

Simunye Zulu Lodge ($$)
off R68 about 49km (31 miles) north of
Eshowe tel: 035-450 3111 fax: 035 -450
2534 www.protea-hotels.co.za
The best of several Zulu cultural villages in the
Eshowe area, with comfortable accommodation in
a cliff-face rock lodge or beehive huts, and transport is in an ox wagon, on horseback or in a 4WD.
The Simunye has good food, and runs an excellent
cultural scheme.

Drakensberg and Midlands
Cathedral Peak ($$)
31km (19 miles) from Winterton tel: 036-488
1888 fax: 036-488 1889
www.cathedralpeak.co.za
Comfortable, popular, well-run mountain hotel
with great scenery, pools and outdoor activities.

Didima Camp ($)
Cathedral Park tel: 036-488 8000(reservations
through KNZ Wildlife see page 191)
A comfortable camp with 66 thatched chalets that
can be used as 2-bedrooms or 4-bed family accom-
modation. Great walks and views. Self-catering and
restaurant available. Fireplaces in winter.

Old Halliwell Country Inn ($$)
Howick tel: 033-330 2602
fax: 033-330 3430 www.protea-hotels.co.za
A welcoming inn dating from the 1830s, near the
historic hamlet of Curry's Post.

Rawdons ($$)
Nottingham Road tel: 033-263 6044
fax: 033-263 6048 www.rawdons.co.za
Elegant, thatched country house hotel.

Sandford Park Lodge ($$)
Bergville tel: 036-448 1001
www.sandford.co.za
Delightful former coaching inn. Good food, lush
gardens and a roaring log fire in winter.

263

RESTAURANTS

South Africa now has several chains of eateries selling excellent food at affordable prices. Look out for the **Cattle Barons** if you like steak, **Ocean Baskets** for fish, and the **Mug and Bean** for wonderful coffee, cakes, breakfasts and light meals (as ever in this country, the portions are vast).

In many instances, particularly outside the major cities, the finest restaurants are attached to good hotels. To save space they are not listed here twice, so try consulting the hotel list when choosing where to eat.

Food is very reasonably priced. The following recommended restaurants have been divided into three price categories:

- inexpensive ($)—under 80 Rand
- moderate ($$)—80–160 Rand
- expensive ($$$)—over 160 Rand

Prices are per person, based on a three-course meal, including taxes but not drinks or tips.

WESTERN CAPE

264

Cape Town and environs
The Africa Café ($/$$)
Heritage Square, corner of Buitengracht and Shortmarket streets tel: 021-422 0221
A wonderful introduction to African food in a friendly, cheerful environment. Historic building with a roof terrace. Dinner only.
Aubergine ($$$)
39 Barnet Street, Gardens tel: 021-465 4909
Elegant town-house restaurant with a terrace, chic furnishings and some of Cape Town's most innovative food, fusing the best of European and Eastern influences. Booking advised.
Blues ($$$)
The Promenade, Victoria Road, Camps Bay tel: 021-438 2040
Highly popular seaside restaurant serving California-style salads, seafood and Asian fusion food. Booking advised.
Buitenwerwachting ($$$)
Klein Constantia Rd, Constantia tel: 021-794 3522
Superb French and Italian food in the glorious surroundings of one of Constantia's finest wineries. Closed Sun–Mon and 1 Jul–14 Aug.
Constantia Uitsig Restaurant ($$$)
Spaanschematriver Road, Constantia tel: 021-794 4480
One of South Africa's top restaurants, set in a top vineyard, offering a mainly Provençal menu. Booking essential.
Kloof Street ($/$$)
Rapidly becoming the food capital of a food-obsessed city, Kloof Street is lined with excellent eateries of all sorts, from **Melissa's Deli** to the ultra-trendy **Café Camissa**, via pancakes, salads, coffee, cakes and full-blown feasts.
Leinster Hall ($$$)
7 Weltevreden Street tel: 021-424 1836
South African cuisine from Knysna oysters to Karoo lamb, in a 19th-century Cape house. One of the finest restaurants in South Africa.

Madame Zingara ($$)
192 Loop Street tel: 021-426 2458
Haute boho in a fortune-teller's tent is how you might describe this venue. Expect contemporary Italian food.

The Winelands, Breede Valley, and West Coast
Evita se Perron ($$)
Old Darling Railway Station, Darling tel: 022-492 2831
A huge draw for the entertainment as much as the excellent, if wildly named food, this is the hangout of Pieter Dirk Uys, South Africa's most famous satirist. Breakfast and lunch daily. Booking essential.
Mayo at Spier ($/$$$)
on the R130 between Cape Town and Stellenbosch tel: 021-809 1100
African food as theatre. Al fresco dining to the sound of drums. Pan-African buffet; Egypt to Ghana, Morocco to South Africa.
Paddagang ($$$)
23 Church Street, Tulbagh tel: 023-230 0242
Traditional Cape specials, including smoked snoek (barracouta) pâté, *waterblommetjie bredie* (water-lily stew) and *bobotie* (mild curry), on a delightful terrace in central Tulbagh. Open daily, breakfast, tea, lunch and wine tastings. Booking advised.
La Petite Ferme ($$)
Pass Road, Franschhoek tel: 021-876 3016
Simple, delicious, fresh food, especially rainbow trout. Wonderful views across the Franschhoek valley. Lunch and tea daily. Booking essential.
Rhebokskloof ($$$)
Agter–Paarl Road, Paarl tel: 021-863 8606
Haute cuisine and Cape Dutch food at a welcoming winery. Try the seven-course, seven-wine *dégustation* menu.
Die Strandloper ($$$)
On the beach, Langebaan tel: 022-772 2490
Outdoor, literally on the beach, with paper napkins and fingerbowls—ideal for delicious seafood in a totally relaxed atmosphere. Booking essential.

The South Coast, Garden Route, and Karoo
Copper Pot ($$$)
12 Montague Street, George tel: 044-870 7378
Elegant dining with an emphasis on seafood and impeccable silver service in one of the best restaurants on the Garden Route.
De Fijne Keuken ($$)
114 Baron van Rheede Street, Oudtshoorn tel: 044-272 6403
Old home with wood-panelled walls and a broad veranda that's now a welcoming restaurant serving everything from salads to crocodile and, of course, ostrich.
The Islander ($$)
8km (5 miles) from Plettenberg Bay on the N2 to Knysna tel: 044-532 7776
Casual, buffet-style seafood restaurant. Always very busy.
CC's ($$)
Wilderness Centre tel: 044-877 0731
Great seafood in laidback surroundings.

Cornuti Restaurant and Bar ($$)
1 Perestrella Street, Plettenberg Bay
tel: 044-533 1277
Best pizza on the coast. Laidback beach style with busy ambience and great views.
Cruise Café ($$)
Remembrance Avenue, Waterfront, Knysna
tel: 044-382 1693
Right on the lagoon, come for prego rolls at lunch and oyster fresh from the bay.

EASTERN CAPE

Andries Stockenström House ($$$)
100 Cradock Street, Graaff-Reinet
tel: 082-783 2360
Friendly service at this oasis of fine dining, known for its local lamb dishes, prepared by a famous French-trained chef, Beatrice Bernard.

Michaela's of Cintsa ($$)
Main Road, Cintsa East, East London
tel: 043-738 5139
Take the funicular to the top of the dune to watch whales and dolphins from the veranda of this cheerful, family restaurant. Closed Tue.

THE FREE STATE, NORTHERN CAPE, AND NORTH-WEST PROVINCE

Le Must ($$)
12 Murray Avenue, Upington
tel: 054-332 3971
Popular, pretty restaurant with tasty local dishes.
The Butcher Brothers ($$)
Shop 5/7, Lock Laogan Waterfront, Bloemfontein *tel: 051-430 1253*
Expect well-matured steak here in very generous portions, and pastas and salads.
Catch 22 ($$)
Shop 30a, Upper Level, Mimosa Mall, Bloemfontein *tel: 051-444 6877*
Meat, seafood pasta, salad—take your pick—at one of the city's best restaurants.

GAUTENG

Johannesburg
Bukhara ($$$)
Shop U114, First Floor, Nelson Mandela Square, Sandton, Johannesburg
tel: 011-883 5555
The best-ever northern Indian food you'll get in South Africa. Portions are huge so choose carefully.
Carnivore ($$)
Muldersdrift Estate, off D. F. Malan Drive
tel: 011-950 6000
Little brother to the famous Nairobi venue, this large, cheerful restaurant cooks all sorts of meat, including game, over an open fire. Also soups, salads and vegetarian options.
Circle Restaurant and Champagne Bar ($$)
141 Greenway, Greenside, Johannesburg
tel: 011-646 3744
Busy, happening and chic; you can expect trendy dining and fusion style at one of the city's snappier new venues.

Gramadoelas at the Market ($/$$)
Market Theatre Precinct, corner of Breë and Wolhuter streets *tel: 011-838 6960*
A must for all visitors, this is one of the great exponents of African food, from Cape Malay dishes to ostrich omelettes and mopani worms. Closed Sun.
Icon ($$$)
5 Greenfield Road, Greenside, Johannesburg
tel: 011-646 4162
Part of a new wave of funky, young and very stylish Jo'burg restaurants, this time selling Greek food. Go for the meze.
Linger Longer ($$$)
Wierda Road East (off Johan), Wierda Valley, Sandton *tel: 011-884 0465*
Renowned and elegant restaurant with innovative French cuisine. Closed Sun.
Mastrantonio Ristorante ($$)
3 Rivonia Road, Illovo Square, Johannesburg
tel: 011-268 6754
If you want north Italian food the South African way, this is where it's at. Steak, pasta, calamari—it's all good.

Pretoria
All Turka ($$)
Serene Street, Garsfontein, Pretoria
tel: 012-993 0286
Turkish staples popular with the resident foreign diplomats.

Grillhouse ($$$)
The Sheraton, corner Wessels and Church streets, Arcadia *tel: 012-429 9999*
In a region of meat-eaters, this is a must. Best of local tastes at home in the city's smartest hotel.
La Madeleine ($$$)
123 Priory Road, Lenwood Ridge, Pretoria
tel: 012-361 3667
This Belgian-run restaurant, serving classic French cuisine, is one of the finest in South Africa. Closed Sun–Mon.

KWAZULU-NATAL

Durban and environs
Harveys ($$$)
77 Goble Road, Morningside
tel: 031-312 9064
Suburban home turned into a chic temple to haute cuisine.
Jaipur Palace ($$/$$$)
3 Riverside Hotel Complex, 10 Northway, Durban North *tel: 031-563 0287*
Curry is almost obligatory in Natal, but this is several cuts above the average, with a wonderfully oriental atmosphere and sea views to match some of Durban's finest food.
Roma Revolving ($$$)
John Ross House, Victoria Embankment, Durban *tel: 031-337 6707*
Delicious Italian seafood and pasta in a revolving 31st-floor restaurant. Due to the spectacular views, booking is strongly advised. Closed Sun.
Royal Grill ($$)
Royal Hotel, 267 Smith Street, Durban
tel: 031-304 0331
Still the city's best hotel, this is old-fashioned dining—anything from seafood to curry.

265

Safari Guide

TEEMING WITH LIFE

South Africa has over 130 bird and game sanctuaries, covering over 8 million hectares (20 million acres). It hosts a staggering 870 bird species; about 160 species of mammal; 115 species of snake, approximately a quarter of which are poisonous; some 5,000 spider and scorpion species; and a vast multitude of other reptiles and insects.

UP BEFORE DAWN

To see the best of the game, go out between dawn and 10am, and from 4pm to dusk. Most animals simply melt into the shade to sit out the heat of day. Wear neutral shades and ideally use a vehicle that gets you above the line of the bushes. In the game parks, animals are used to vehicles and will not be startled as long as there are no loud noises or strange shapes. Talk quietly, don't stand up or wave your arms out of the window, and above all stay in your vehicle.

WATCH THE BIRDIE!

South Africa has six broad bird habitats: *fynbos* (heathland) in the Cape; desert and semidesert in the northwest; thornveld and broad-leaved woodland in the northeast; grasslands in the centre; tropical forest along the Natal coast; and the coastal strip itself. Probably the single most satisfying area for birdwatching is northern KwaZulu-Natal, where Hluhluwe, Ndumo, and St. Lucia together provide almost the whole range of options.

Bird Life

Out of southern Africa's 870 species of bird, about 500 are either local in distribution, retiring or classed as vagrants. Consequently, only about 300 can be seen regularly and identified by the non-specialist, and of these, some—including many of the females—are small, drab 'LBJs' (little brown jobs). Keen birdwatchers need a good guide, binoculars and a great deal of time. Heretical as it may seem to say so, most ordinary tourists simply want to identify those birds which are large or flashy—ideally both.

Savannah dwellers The largest of all, and instantly identifiable, is the huge, flightless **ostrich** (8) which, in the wild, wanders the *vlei* (open savannah grasslands) in company with zebra, antelope and wildebeest. In practice, you get a far better view of them on farms, in and around Oudtshoorn (see page 80). There are plenty of other options in the grasslands, however. Pride of place goes to the gawky **secretary bird** (7), whose grey wings, black legs and crest resemble a clerk's jacket, trousers and quill pen. The **kori bustard** (13), the heaviest bird in the world still capable of sustained flight, strides the veld on long legs, with a tawny back, white underparts, black-spotted upper wings, black-and-white feathering on the neck and a black crest.

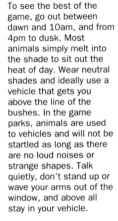

The pure white **cattle egret** (11) follows the herds, whether cattle or rhino, picking up the insects dislodged by their feet, while the little brown **red-billed oxpecker** actually catches a ride on their backs, feeding off their ticks and fleas.

Ungainly **hornbills** are unbalanced by their huge, heavy beaks. The **ground hornbill** (10) is as big as a turkey, black all over except for bald red eyes and throat, and flies clumsily only when pushed; the smaller and more agile **yellow-billed hornbill** has a black-and-white patterned back, white front and yellow beak. Less commonly seen are **trumpeter, grey** and **red-billed** (9) species.

The **red-eyed dove** (15), **ring-necked Cape turtle dove**, black-faced **Namaqua dove** and gentle little **laughing dove** (16) in its pastel coat of pinks and blues coo in the dawn from the acacia trees. Game birds scuttle underfoot: the white-spotted **helmeted guinea fowl** (20) with its blue and red head, and the round, sandy **crested francolin** (19). Seen frequently in similar habitats is the pout-chested, pointy-tailed **Namaqua sandgrouse** (17).

Storks are sociable birds, building large, scruffy nests in tenement trees and often forsaking the bush for the rich pickings of the agricultural lands. The **white stork** has a white upper body, black wing tips and tail and a red bill and legs. **Abdim's stork** (18) is shorter, squatter and largely black with white underwings. Also found in the region are **saddle-billed, African open-billed** (29) and **yellow-billed storks**. With them you will often find the very noisy, curious and gregarious **Hadada ibis** (12), greyish-brown with a wickedly curved beak.

As dusk draws in, the **nightjars** flutter down to take dust baths and the eyes of the owls blink open. There are numerous species of owl, big and small—**African Scops, white-faced Scops** (14), **barn, spotted eagle, pearl-spotted eagle** and **Verreaux's eagle owls**.

Raptors The great raptors wheel over the veld on the morning thermals. Largest of all is the majestic **lammergeier** (21). The **bateleur** (25) has a dark body with a reddish back patch, pale wings and scarlet beak and claws, and there are two species of **fork-tailed kites**—the dusty brown black and the black-shouldered, whose markings are similar to those of a gull. The large black-breasted **snake eagle** has a dark brown back and head, white belly and white underwings, banded with black, while the **long-crested eagle** (24) is smaller, dark brown with a distinctive crest, white-feathered legs and white patches on the wings. Other hunters roaming the skies include several species of **buzzard**, **falcon**, **kestrel** and **goshawk**, of which the most interesting are probably the

jackal buzzard, with dark brown upper body and back and bright chestnut breast, and the pale grey and white **chanting goshawk** (22).

Freshwater fishers Inland waterways and estuaries are bursting with bird life of every shape, size and shade. King of them all, the black-and-white **African fish eagle** (23), plummets from a high dead branch, its raucous shout of triumph still filling the sky as it spears a glistening fish. On lower branches, dark **great** and **reed cormorants** (28) hang their wings out to dry and a **darter** weaves its snakelike neck around in search of food. The elegant **little egret**, white with a black beak and yellow toes, is sometimes mistaken for a heron. The **herons** themselves, **grey**, **black-headed** and **goliath** (26), stand stock-still, frozen as sculptures in the dappled light. The black-headed **sacred ibis** (30) waits ankle-deep, while an **African spoonbill** (31) sweeps its head from side to side, filtering food with its curiously flattened, grey and red bill. A softly grey **blue crane** walks along the shore, proud as a model on a catwalk, trailing its darker tail feathers like a dirty train. In the grass nearby stalks a magnificent **crowned crane** (27), with a charcoal-grey body, gold wingtips, black-and-white face, red chin and proud crown of golden bristles.

32

33

34

35

36

Tawny **hamerkops**, **blacksmith** and **crowned plovers**, and **black-winged stilts** wade the shallows in search of frogs and insects, **spur-winged** and **Egyptian geese** gather in noisy crowds, stately parties of **white-faced** and **yellow-billed ducks**, **Cape** (32) and **red-billed teals** float gently by, the **moorhens** scrabbling furiously through the water in an effort to keep up. There is a flash of colour in the reeds from a lurking **purple gallinule**, and another from the overhanging branches as a shining turquoise and orange **malachite kingfisher** streaks past, far outstripping even its own pretty cousins, the **woodland**, **brown-hooded** (38), **giant**, **pied** and **striped kingfishers**.

By the sea To the north, in the Natal dunes, salmon-pink **greater** (3) and **lesser flamingos** stroll the shallow lagoons as heavy flights of **white** and **pink-backed pelicans** (36) zoom overhead. Down on the far south of the Cape coast, colonies of **African penguins** (33) strut the rocks with self-importance. From the skies above, **Cape cormorants** dive-bomb a shoal of sardines. The inshore waters are patrolled by raucous flocks of **terns**, **grey-headed gulls** and **Cape gannets** (35), with yellowy heads and black-tipped wings. Far out to sea, swooping over the ocean are the massive **black-browed albatross** (34) and smaller **yellow-billed albatross**, the geometrically painted black-and-white **pintado petrel**, the **white-chinned petrel** and the **sooty shearwater**, the birds of legend and storm.

Great little showoffs What they lack in size, many of South Africa's smaller birds make up for in vivid colour. The chestnut head, black-and-white back and distinctive crest of the **hoopoe** and the orange breast and punk-like crest of the **purple-crested lourie** positively pale beside the chestnut back, turquoise, lilac and black of the **lilac-breasted roller** (40) or the green, yellow, black and chestnut of various **bee-eaters**. Some starlings are drab, but the incandescent **glossy** and **plum-coloured starlings** (43) with their petroleum sheen more than make up for it. Bright yellow **weaver birds** drip-hang neat, round nests from the trees and fluffy little **yellow, blue** (37) and **violet** (41) **waxbills** descend in flocks on new-mown lawns. **Red bishops** (39) parade in black and orange robes; even the **long-tailed widow** makes up for its funereal garb by a dramatically trailing tail. The brightest of them all must be the tiny **sunbirds** that dart through the flower beds like fiery jewels: the all-green **malachite**, the **orange-breasted** with its iridescent blue-green head, the **marico** with green head and back, black belly and purple and turquoise stripes across the chin, and the lesser **double-collared** (42) with green head, blue back and scarlet chinstrap.

Scavengers Often treated with contempt, the carrion-eaters perform a valuable service, keeping the bush clean. To track a kill, look for the **Cape** (44), the **lappet-faced** and **white-backed vultures** (45) circling overhead. Often found at the same sites, or on a rubbish dump, the huge **marabou stork** is one of the ugliest birds around, with a heavy hunched body, white front and black back, bald pink head and neck, pink fleshy pouch and huge yellowish bill.

Antelope

Blesbok *Damaliscus dorcas phillipsi*; **Bontebok** *Damaliscus dorcas dorcas*; **Tsessebe** (49) *Damaliscus lunatus* Three closely related antelope: The blesbok (95cm/37in), found only in the north and east, has a rich brown coat with off-white underparts and blaze. The southwestern bontebok (90cm/35in) from the Cape has a purple-brown coat, white underbelly, rump, socks and blaze. The tsessebe (120cm/47in) has a dark red-brown coat, tan underbelly and a hump. The long, ridged horns splay out and back.

Bushbuck (46) *Tragelaphus scriptus* These nocturnal browsers live alone in well-watered woodland. The rump is higher than the shoulder (80cm/31in), giving them a hunched appearance. Males have thick, slightly twisted horns, up to 30cm (12in) long. There are over 40 sub-species, varying from grey-brown to chestnut, but always with white neck patches and white spots on the flanks.

Duiker The duiker ('diver' in Afrikaans) is one of the smallest of the African antelope. Nervous, nocturnal browsers living alone or in pairs, they are widely distributed from rocky hills to grassland. There are three species in South Africa: the common grey duiker,

Sylvicapra grimmia (50cm/20in), the smaller, rarer red duiker, *Cephalophus natalensis* (43cm/17in) and the blue duiker, *Cephalophus monticola* (30cm/12in; actually greyish-brown). All have rounded backs and black marks on the face and top of the tail.

Eland (50) *Taurotragus oryx* The massive eland (2m/7ft tall; 1 tonne in weight) has a light sandy body, faint white stripes across the back, and strips of black hair along the spine and belly. Both sexes have long, backward-lying horns with a tight spiral at the base. Timid diurnal browsers, they live in herds in scrubland and semidesert.

Gemsbok (51) *Oryx gazella* The beautiful gemsbok (1.2m/4ft) inhabit the semidesert scrub of the Kalahari, where they eat grass, leaves and tubers and need no additional water. They have a heavy body, a sandy coat with a black tail, black stripe along the flanks and upper thighs, white legs and black knee patches. The face has black-and-white patches and they have very long, thin, straight horns.

Grysbok These small, nocturnal creatures (50cm/20in) have a hunched back and chestnut coat sprinkled with white hair. The Cape grysbok, *Raphicerus melanotis*, a grazer, lives only in the far south. Sharpe's grysbok (48), *Raphicerus sharpei*, is a browser and grazer found in the far north. It has a redder coat, a dark band along the muzzle and whitish belly and inside legs.

Impala (47) *Aepyceros melampus* Largest of the gazelles (1m/3ft), impala are charmingly pretty and easily seen, living in herds in open grassland. They have a russet back and nose, a white belly, white rings around the eyes and black stripes on the tail and rump. Males have long, lyre-shaped horns. Both browsers and grazers, they can jump up to 3m (10ft) high and reach speeds of 96kph (60mph).

Klipspringer, *Oreotragus oreotragus* Little klipspringers (55cm/21in) browse and graze in small groups on rocky hillsides, bouncing on tiptoe from boulder to boulder on hooves the consistency of hard rubber. Their long, bristly, speckled coat varies from yellow-brown to charcoal grey. Males have short, straight horns.

HARD WORK
Most herd antelope split into male and female groups. The young males are driven out when nearing maturity to join a bachelor herd. The dominant male must remain tireless as he carves out and defends a territory, and guards and services a harem of anything up to 30 females and calves. To establish his own herd, a young male must either defeat him or cut out and kidnap a significant number of females.

RARE SIGHTINGS
Other antelope seen infrequently in South Africa include the huge, magnificent black-and-white sable, *Hippotragus niger*; the heavy strawberry-grey roan, *Hippotragus equinus*, similar to the gemsbok with its black-and-white face; the small beige-and-white oribi, *Ourebia ourebi*; and the tiny red-gold suni, *Neotragus moschatus*.

27

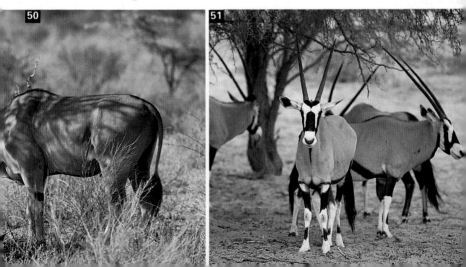

50

51

POT BUCK
You are just as likely to find an antelope on your plate as in the bush these days, with many farmers turning their attention to animals that are low maintenance, perfectly adapted to the environment, resistant to many local diseases, and that produce delicious low-cholesterol red meat for the health-conscious. Popular species include eland, kudu, impala, springbok and gemsbok. Ostrich and crocodile are also widely farmed, while warthog and zebra are sometimes shot for the table, too.

Kudu (56) *Tragelaphus strepsiceros* Found in the north and east, the powerful greater kudu (1.5m/5ft) has a sloping back, light greyish-brown coat with faint white stripes, a white crest along the spine, black beard and white band between the eyes. Males have magnificent horns that curl backward in an open corkscrew. They are browsers, living in small groups in scrubby woodland.

Nyala (55) *Tragelaphus angasii* Similar to the kudu, nyala (1.3m/4ft) are found in northern KwaZulu-Natal. They have a dark brown coat with faint white stripes across the back, white-spotted flanks, black mane and beard, white crest along the spine and a white patch on the nose. Males have long, twisting, back-facing horns. Diurnal browsers, they live in small groups in dense thickets near water.

Red hartebeest (53) *Alcelaphus buselaphus caama* The hartebeest is large (1.6m/5ft) with a steeply sloping back, a rich red-tan coat with dark patches along the spine and thighs and a long, gloomy face. Both sexes have thick, ridged, backward-twisting horns, shaped like a candelabrum. Diurnal grazers, they live in large herds in open grassland.

Reedbuck The Southern Reedbuck (54) *Redunca arundinum* (90cm/3ft) inhabits marshland near water. Usually found in pairs, they are grazers with a dirty yellow to greyish-brown coat with a white throat patch. Smaller Mountain Reedbuck, *Redunca fulvorufula* (73cm/28in) live in small groups in rocky hills or steep river beds. They have a shaggy greyish coat with white underparts and a reddish-brown head and neck. Both males have short, forward-curving horns.

Grey rhebok *Pelea capreolus* Small, grey, furry antelope (75cm/29in) with powerful back legs and a hunched back, rhebok are browsers and grazers who live on rocky hills and slopes in groups of 2–20. They have large ears, white rings around the eyes and a white rim to the tail. Males have thin, straight horns.

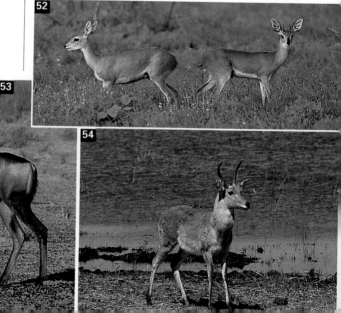

Steenbok (52) *Raphicerus campestris* Similar to the grysbok, the little steenbok (50cm/20in) often lurks in long grass or a disused burrow for safety. They have a chestnut coat and a white belly. The male has short, straight, very sharp horns. They browse and graze in open land, usually during the day, although they become nocturnal if under threat.

Waterbuck *Kobus ellipsiprymnus* Heavyset waterbuck (1.7m/5.5ft) graze in small groups in reedbeds and river valleys. Their shaggy grey-brown coat is covered in a musky secretion that not only acts as waterproofing but smells and taints the flesh, guarding against most predators. They have a distinctive white circle on the rump. The males have long, ridged horns that curve out and forward.

Wildebeest Technically an antelope, the wildebeest or gnu (1.5m/5ft) is said to have been made up of the pieces left over at the end of creation—'the forequarters of an ox, the hindquarters of an antelope and the tail of a horse'. It also has the long face of a hartebeest, a thick black mane and buffalo horns. They are gregarious, grazing open grassland in large herds. There are two species in South Africa, the common blue or brindled *Connochaetes taurinus* (57), with a greyish-brown coat and faint black striping, and the rarer black *Connochaetes gnou*, with a darker coat and white muzzle and tail.

NATIONAL SYMBOL

The springbok (6), *Antidorcas marsupialis*, has become South Africa's symbol and has given its name to the country's national sports teams. Little could be more different from a rugby player than this dainty little gazelle. The only true gazelle south of the Zambezi, springbok (75cm/30in) are gregarious browsers and grazers who thrive in large herds in the dry open scrublands on the Kalahari fringe. They have a rich tan back, white underparts, rump and face, and black stripes along the flanks and tail and beneath the eyes. Males and females have ridged, lyre-shaped horns that curve out and back before hooking in at the top.

277

58

PRESENT PERFECT
In the 13th century, the
king of Malindi (Kenya)
sent the emperor of China
a present of a giraffe, an
oryx and a zebra. The
court was so impressed
with the giraffe that the
animal became the
Chinese emblem of
Perfect Virtue, Perfect
Government and Perfect
Harmony in the Empire
and in the Universe.

FAMILY LIKENESS?
The African elephant
differs from the Asian in
several key points. It is
noticeably larger with
bigger ears, has a flat
forehead, ringed trunk,
concave back and carries
its head higher. In spite of
many tall tales, it is no
more ferocious and just
as capable of domestica-
tion as its Asian cousin.
Extraordinarily, the
elephant's closest
relatives are the rock
hyrax or dassie (like an
overgrown brown guinea
pig, about the size of a
rabbit) and the marine
dugong (said by early
sailors to be mermaids).

Plains animals

Buffalo (58) *Syncerus caffer* Deceptively cowlike but irritable and dangerous when roused, buffalo are huge (1.6–2m/5–7ft), with powerful bodies, dark-brown coats and short, massively heavy horns that clamp the brow like a Viking helmet. They browse and graze in grassland and forest, live in herds and wallow in mud for heat regulation.

Elephant (1) *Loxodonta africana* The largest land mammal— 3m (10ft), 6,000kg (13,200lb), with tusks up to 3.4m (11ft)— is a magnificent and surprisingly gentle giant, although swift to anger if alarmed. Sociable and intelligent, they live in matriarchal groups with a complex social structure. Infants stay with their mother until the age of five, sexual maturity is at 15 and life expectancy is 60–70 years. African elephants adapt to a range of habitats, from desert to montane forest, but are happiest in savannah woodland.

Giraffe (62) *Giraffa camelopardalis* Extraordinarily graceful and gentle, the giraffe (5–6m/16–19ft tall) has a hide resem- bling tan and chestnut crazy paving, a heavy, sloping body, camel-like face and small, fleshy horns topped with rounded knobs. There are only seven vertebrae in the immensely long neck and special valves regulate the blood flow to the brain when they bend. Giraffes live in large herds in open woodland and browse on the high leaves of acacia trees. Their only real defence is a powerful kick.

Hippopotamus (61) *Hippopotamus amphibius* Hippos (1.5m/5ft tall; 1,500kg/3,300lb) have massive barrel bodies, short legs, tight, shiny grey skin and a long, flat- tened face. They live in colonies of up to 15 and enjoy wallowing in shallow pools, surfacing to breath every 5 minutes, or lying with nostrils poking out of the water. At night, they walk up to 30km (18 miles) in search of good grazing. Totally vegetarian and placid when undisturbed, they kill more humans than almost all other wild animals combined, by biting people, and even canoes, in half.

Rhinoceros The white rhinoceros, *Ceratotherium simum* (1.8m/6ft; 2,300kg/5,000lb), is named not for its colour but from the Afrikaans word *weit*, meaning wide-mouthed. These grazers inhabit grasslands and open scrub. The mouth is square and the front horn much longer than the back. The black rhinoceros (2), *Diceros bicornis* (1.6m/5ft; 850kg/1,900lb), is a browser, living in thick bush. A darker charcoal-grey than the white, it has a pointy hooklip, the horns are more even in length and it is smaller and more aggressive. Both species nearly died out through poaching, but successful breeding and relocation projects have increased the number of whites. The black is still very rare.

Warthog (60) *Phacochoerus aethopicus* Large, brown, hairy pigs (70cm/27in), with dark mane, small wide-set eyes, knobbly face and short, sideways curving tusks, these prodigious diggers live in burrows and eat tubers and grass. Usually seen as a family of male, female and two to three infants, they run in a line, tails straight up in the air. Their nocturnal relative, the bushpig, *Potamochoerus porcus* (65cm/25in), has a smoother face and squarer muzzle, has larger litters and keeps its tail down when running.

Zebra These sociable grazers live in large herds on open grassland. The irregular stripes act as camouflage and a system of identification as unique as fingerprints. The common Burchell's zebra (59), *Equus burchelli* (1.3m/ 4.25ft), has brown shadow stripes on the white sections. The rare Cape mountain zebra, *Equus zebra zebra* (1.25m/ 4ft), is slightly smaller, with longer pointed ears, narrower stripes with no shadow and a plain white belly.

THE BIG FIVE
To see the 'big five' is considered the goal of any successful safari. The definition of the five—lion, elephant, rhino, buffalo and leopard—came not from their rarity value or even their beauty, but from the early hunters. These were considered to be the most difficult and dangerous animals to shoot, and therefore the finest trophies. Lion, elephant and buffalo are relatively easy to find, while there are more rhinos in South Africa than anywhere else on the continent. Leopard are widespread but virtually impossible to see.

Predators

Cheetah (63) *Acinonyx jubatus* Long (2m/65ft), lithe and built for speed, cheetahs have gold coats with black spots and neat triangular heads. A few genetically aberrant so-called king cheetahs, with larger black splotches, are found in the far north. The fastest animals on earth, clocking up speeds of 112kph (70mph) over short distances, they live in family groups and hunt in the early morning and evening.

Foxes The bat-eared fox, *Otocyon megalotis* (80cm/31in long), has a speckled grey-brown coat, darker bushy tail, small triangular face,and huge round ears. It lives in semi-arid grass and scrub, in burrows. The unrelated Cape fox (64), *Vulpes chama* (90cm/35in), has a shiny golden-grey coat and a dark tail and lives in semidesert scrub and mountain *fynbos*. Often shot as pests, both are harmless and even beneficial, eating mice, reptiles and insects.

Hyena The common spotted hyena (67), *Crocuta crocuta* (85cm/33in), roams the open savannah and woodland in the north and east, while the smaller, rarer brown hyena (66), *Hyaena brunnea* (79cm/30in), inhabits the Kalahari region. Both have powerful shoulders, weak back legs and a sloping back. The spotted has a gold coat with black spots, a small, neat head and rounded ears; the brown has a dark brown coat, stripy legs and pointed ears. They are mainly nocturnal scavengers, but also prey on young, old and sick animals. They live alone or in pairs, gathering in groups during the mating season. The spotted has an eerie cry, ranging from a yap to a manic laughter.

Jackal Regarded as scavengers, jackals (length 1.15m/3.75ft) resemble a European fox and behave in a similar fashion. They do hang around kills, farmyards and dustbins, but they are also efficient hunters of small animals, and even eat fruit and vegetables. There are two species common in

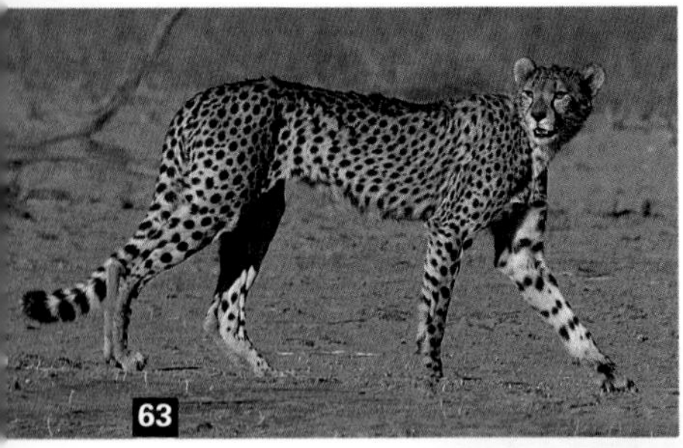
63

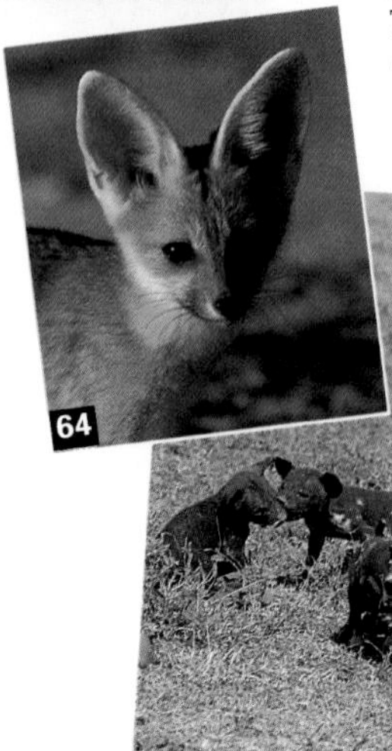
64

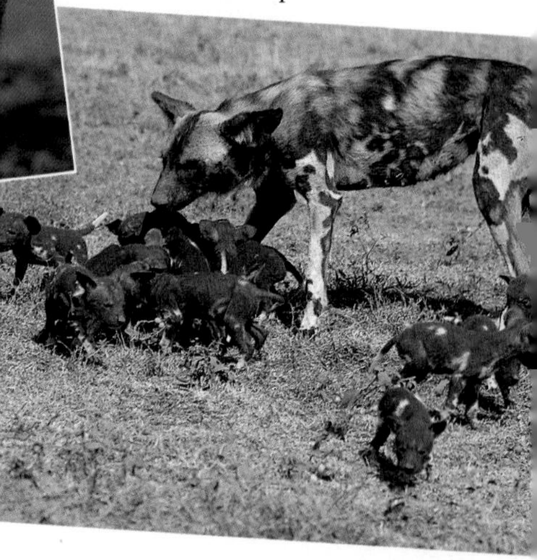
65

the region, the aggressive, diurnal black-backed (68) *Canis mesomelas* and the timid, nocturnal *Canis adustus*, with a white flank stripe.

Leopard (5) *Panthera pardus* Leopards (2m/6.5ft long) prefer wooded hills, but accept a wide range of terrain. They are solitary, nocturnal and very difficult to see. Their low-slung bodies have a red-gold coat with clusters of black spots. They hunt anything from mice to antelope, hauling carcasses into trees away from scavengers.

Lion *Panthera leo* The lion (90cm/35in tall; 2.6m/8.5ft long) is the largest cat in the world. The young (69) have spots, but adults are a uniform gold; males have a mane that can range from light coloured to almost black. They live in prides of up to 20 or 30 beasts. The smaller females do almost all the hunting, usually at night or dawn. Not particularly speedy, they rely on stealth, breaking the victim's neck with a blow from a paw or clamping the throat and suffocating it.

Wild dog (65) *Lycaon pictus* Wild, or Cape, hunting dogs have been feared and hunted by man and are now one of the rarest animals in Africa. About 68cm (26in) tall, they have long, skinny legs, powerful jaws and huge ears. Their coat is brindled black, dark brown, yellow and white, the patterning on each dog unique. Strictly diurnal, they once lived and hunted in packs of up to 40 members.

RUN RABBIT RUN
There are several species of rabbit in South Africa, but those you see are most likely to be escaped European domestic rabbits. There are two common species of hare, the Cape hare, *Lepus capensis* and the scrub hare, *Lepus saxatilis*. The spring hare, *Pedetes capensis*, is not a hare, but a marsupial, with powerful back legs and tiny forelegs, rather like a small kangaroo.

282

70

71

Primates

Bushbaby Small, tree-dwelling primates with huge eyes, bushy tails and a piercing cry uncannily like the wail of a hungry baby, bushbabies are closely related to lemurs. They live in colonies, feeding at night on small birds, reptiles and insects, eggs, fruit and leaves. There are two species in South Africa, the thick-tailed, *Otolemur crassicaudatus* (50–60cm/19–23in long) and lesser, *Galago moholi* (35cm/14in long).

Chacma baboon (71) *Papio ursinus* Chacma baboons are large (1.2m/4ft long), with thick yellowy-grey coats, a long black muzzle and kinked tail. Highly organized socially, they live in troops of up to 50 in rocky, wooded hills. Omnivorous team players, they work together smoothly to hunt or defend, using formidable teeth as weapons. Their call is a sharp coughlike bark.

Monkeys South Africa's two species of monkey are both diurnal and gregarious, living in troops of up to 30, led by a dominant male. The vervet (70) *Cercopithecus pygerythrus* (1.1m/3.5ft long) has a grey-brown back, pale stomach and black face ringed by a white ruff. The male has a bright blue scrotum. They prefer open savannah woodland, but range widely, are fearless and are highly curious. The elusive samango, *Cercopithecus albogularis* (1.35m/4.5ft), is larger and darker with tufty side whiskers and a dark brown face. They live in the upper reaches of dense montane forest.

Small mammals

Anteaters Africa's vast army of termites supports several species of anteater, all solitary, nocturnal and rarely seen. The pangolin, *Manis temminckii* (80cm/31in long), has a heavy scaled, rounded body, flat tail, tiny legs, small triangular snout, formidable claws and a long, sticky tongue. It has heavy, scaled armour and when threatened it curls up and exudes a foul smell. The aardvark or antbear, *Orycteropus afer* (60cm/23in), is low-slung, with a heavy body, short legs and pointy face. It has pale gold fur, a thin almost bald tail, long sharp ears and piglike snout. They create vast networks of tunnels. The aardwolf, *Proteles cristatus* (90cm/35in), resembles a hyena, with rounded back, long streaked black-and-tan fur, black muzzle and pointed ears.

Cats There are four local species of small cat, all nocturnal and rarely seen, hunting small creatures, birds and reptiles. The caracal, *Felis caracal* (1.1m/3.5ft long), has a red-gold coat, small head and large, pointed ears, tufted with black fur. The serval, *Felis serval* (1.1m/3.5ft long), has a tan body and black spots and stripes on the neck and tail. The African wild cat, *Felis lybica* (90cm/35in long), looks like a domestic tabby, but with a sharper face and longer ears. Even more like a tabby, the small spotted cat, *Felis nigripes* (50–60cm/19–23in long), has a tan coat, black spots and stripes and a rounded face.

Honey badger *Mellivora capensis* Also known as a ratel, the honey badger (95cm/37in) has a light grey back, a white stripe along the flank and deep brown head and underparts. They are nocturnal, largely carnivorous and regarded as pests because of their fondness for chickens and eggs. Although small, they are aggressive.

Mongoose There are 11 species of mongoose in South Africa, of which six are common: the yellow, *Cynictis penicillata;* slender, *Galerella sanguinea;* white-tailed, *Ichneumia albicauda;* water (marsh), *Atilax paludinosus;* banded, *Mungos mungo;* and dwarf, *Helogale parvula*. All eat a varied diet of insects, small animals and eggs, and between the species they cover the full range of habitats. Closely related is the scrawny suricate or meerkat (72), *Suricata suricatta*, a highly gregarious desert dweller.

Porcupine (74) *Hystrix africaeaustralis* Solitary, nocturnal and vegetarian, this extraordinary rodent (75cm/29in long) has a dark face, white bristly mane and coat of hard, pointed black-and-white banded quills, which puff up to double their size and rattle when the animal is alarmed or angry.

FALSE CATS
Often described as cats because of their appearance, genets and civets are actually related to the mongoose family. With stretched bodies, short legs and black-and-tan stripes and spots, they are nocturnal omnivores, the genets nesting in trees or underground burrows while the largest of them, the civet, *Civettictis civetta* (1.3m/4ft long), is strictly terrestrial. The small-spotted genet, *Genetta genetta* (95cm/37in long), has a white-tipped tail; the large-spotted (73), *Genetta tigrina* (1m/3ft), a black tip.

75

76

SNAKE DRILL

South African pharmacies sell snakebite serum kits—make sure you know how to use them before venturing into the bush. Don't clamber over rocks without checking where you put your hands; snakes will usually clear out of your way if you make enough noise. Should someone in your party be bitten, wrap the limb tightly with a crepe bandage, use a splint to immobilize it and treat the patient for shock. Try to suck out the poison (do not swallow) but do not cut the wound. Only use a tourniquet if you are several hours from medical assistance. Never assume that the snake was harmless, get medical help as fast as possible, and give the doctor an accurate description of the snake.

Reptiles

Of all South Africa's reptiles, the Nile crocodile (75), *Crocodylus niloticus* (up to 5m/16ft long), is king. Smaller, but still dramatically big, is the largest of the lizards, the water leguaan or monitor, *Varanus niloticus* (up to 1.6m/5ft long). Many other lizards, skinks and 10 species of agama thrive in hot sand and rocky crevices. Some, such as the blue-headed southern rock agama, *Agama atra*, or the red, green and blue common flat lizard, *Platysaurus intermedius*, are as bright as a rainbow. Pale pinky-brown geckos lurk on bedroom ceilings and there are at least 20 species of slow-moving, rainbow-changing chameleon (4). Other reptiles include tortoises, terrapins and turtles; green, loggerhead (76), leatherback and hawksbill turtles all breed on the beaches of northern KwaZulu-Natal.

Snakes have poor eyesight, but a keen sense of smell and excellent hearing; they prefer to stay out of the way. The great exception is the short, fat, black-and-tan patterned puff adder, *Bitis arietans*, which likes sunbathing on open ground, relies on camouflage, and is all too easily trodden on. Other poisonous snakes to watch out for are the bright-green, tree-dwelling boomslang, *Dispholidus typus* (77); the Cape cobra, *Naja nivea;* the rinkhals or spitting cobra (78), *Hemachatus haemachatus;* the black mamba, *Dendroaspis polylepis;* and green mamba, *Dendroaspis angusticeps*. The largest snake in South Africa is the common African python, *Python sebae* (3–5m/10–16ft long). It is not poisonous, killing by squeezing or constriction. Pythons are a protected species.

77

78

Principal references are given in **bold**

A

Aasvoelkop 129
Absa Gallery 153
accommodation **226–227**, **258–263**
Addo Elephant National Park 117
Adler Museum of the History of Medicine 157
African Arts Centre 194
African National Congress (ANC) 22, 41, **42**, 43
Afrikaans 87
Afrikaans Language Museum 87
Agulhas Lighthouse 95
AIDS 250
airports and air services 238, **242–243**, 246
Albany Museum 109
Albertinia 96
Alexander McGregor Memorial Museum 138
Alice 107
Amanzimtoti 201
Amathole Museum 107
The Amphitheatre 208
Anne Bryant Art Gallery 106
Anreith, Anton **54**, 55, 57, 69, 115
Anton von Wouw Museum 164
apartheid 10, 14, 21, **40–41**
Apple Express 116, **234**
Ardmore Studio 208
Arend Dieperink Museum 179
Armoured Train Memorial 202
Arniston 95
Ashton 77
Augrabies Falls National Park 134

B

Barberton 181
Backsberg 92
Baden-Powell, Robert 144
Badplaas 176
Baker, Sir Herbert 59, 67, 71, 115, 156, **166**, 185
Bakone Malapa Ethnic Museum 179
Bakoven 73
Ballito Beach 200
Balokwa Museum 130
Banana Express 201, **235**
banks 244–245
baobabs **176**
Barkly West 142
Bartolomeu Dias Museum Complex 97
Basotho Cultural Village 130
Bathurst 110
battlefield sites **202–207**
Beaufort West 78
Beck House 77
Beira 224
Bela-Bela (Warmbaths) 176–177
Benguela 224
Bergville 209
Bernard Price Institute 156–157
Bertram House 54
Bethlehem 128

Bethulie 129
Betty's Bay 82
Bible Monument 108–109
Big Hole **138**, 139
Biko, Steve **43**, 104
bird life 268–273
Bisho 105, **107**
Blockhouse Museum 207
Bloemfontein 12, **126–127**
Blood River 204
Blue Train 234
Blyde River Canyon **182**, 184
Bo-Kaap **54**, 64, 65, 115
Boers **32–33**, 34–35
Bombyx Mori Silk Farm 182
Bonnievale 77
Bontebok National Park 83
Boschendal 92
Botanic Gardens and Orchid House 197
Botsalano Game Reserve 144
Botswana 216, 217, **222**
Boulders Beach 70
Bourke's Luck Potholes 184
Bredasdorp 94
Breede River Valley 76–77
Bruma Fleamarket World 149
Buchan, John 178
Buffalo Hills Game Farm 101
Bulawayo 220
Bultfontein Mine 138
bungee jumping 96
Burgher Memorial 207

C

C. P. Nel Museum 81
Calgary Transport Museum 106
camping 252–253
Camps Bay 73
Cango Angora Rabbit Farm 79
Cango Caves 79
Cango Ostrich Farm 81
Cango Wildlife Ranch 79
Cannon Island 136
Cape Agulhas 72, **94–95**
Cape architecture 114–115
Cape Flats 68
Cape of Good Hope 26–27, 28, 46, **71–73**
Cape Malays 16, 54, **64–65**
Cape Muslims 64–65
Cape Town 12, 46, **50–67**, 232, 233
Caprivi Strip 223
carnival 65
car rental 246
Castle of Good Hope 54–55
Castle Hill Historical Museum 116
Cathedral of St. Mark 98
Cederberg 84
Central Kalahari Game Reserve 222
Ceres 76
Cetshwayo 212, 213, 215
Chamonix 92
Chapman's Peak Drive 72–73
Cheetah Project 178–179
children 253

Chobe National Park 222
Churchill, Winston 169, 202
Ciskei 104
Citrusdal 84
Clanwilliam **84**, 85
Clarens 128
Clifton 73
climate 244
coelacanth **106**, 109
Colenso 202
Colesberg 134
coloureds 16, **64**
Company's Garden 50, 55, **66–67**
Comrades Marathon House 211
Constitution Hill 150
conversion charts 255
Correctional Service Museum 165
Cradle of Humankind 157–158
Cradock 112
credit cards 245
cricket 198
crime 19, 148, **251**
crocodile farms 79, 87, 98, 183, 200, 201, 214
Crossroads 68
cruise ships 243
Cullinan 170
Cultural History Museum 164
currency 243, 245
customs regulations 243
Cuyler Manor Cultural Museum 118

D

Dana Bay Nature Reserve 97
Daniëlskuil 143
Darling 85
De Beer Centenary Art Gallery 107
De Hoop Nature Reserve 95
de Klerk, F. W. 22, 41, 44
De Tuynhuys 67
De Wildt Cheetah Farm 170
Debengeni Falls 178
Dhlinza Forest 212
diamond cutting 151
diamonds 125, 138, 139, **140–141**, 170
Die Braak 90
Die Tuishuise Hotel 260
Die Vonds Snake Park 87
Dingane **212**, 213
District Six 55
Dorp Street 91
Double Drift Game Reserve 111
Drakensberg 208–209
drinking water 251
driving 243, **246**
Drostdy Museum (George) 98
Drostdy Museum (Swellendam) 83
Drostdy Hotel 113
drugs 243
Duggan-Cronin Gallery 138
Duiker Island 73
Dukuza Interpretive Centre 200
Dumazulu 213
Dundee 202
Dunn, John 213
Durban 190, 191, **192–197**, 232, 233

Durban Art Gallery 194
Dzata 180

E

East London **106**
Eastern Cape 102–121
Eastern Highlands 128–131
Eastern Highlands (Zimbabwe) 220
Ebenezer Dam 178
Ecca Nature Reserve 111
Echo Caves 184
Elands Bay 85
Elandskraal 202
electricity 255
Elim 94
embassies and consulates 250
emergencies 250–252
entertainment 232–233
Erikson Diamond Centre 151
Eshowe 212
Etosha National Park 223
Ezulwini Valley 219

F

Fairview 92
False Bay Park 214
Fanie Botha Dam 178
Fernkloof Nature Reserve 83
Ficksburg 128
First Raadsaal 126
Fish Hoek 71
fishing 199
Fish River Canyon 223
flora 74–75
food and drink 228–230
Forest Museum 185
Fort Beaufort 111
Fort Durnford 208
Fort Hare University 104, **107**
Fortuna Mine Trail 181
Foskor Museum 178
Fouriesburg 128
Franklin Game Reserve 127
Franschhoek 86
Free State, Northern Cape, and North-West Province 122–145
Freshford House 127
Funworld 195
fynbos 74–75

G

Gaborone 222
game lodges 226
Gamkaskloof 78
Gandhi, Mahatma 42, 190, **211**
Gansbaai 82
Garden Route 47–48, **96–101**, 105
Gariep Dam 129
Gariep Nature Reserve 129
Gately House Museum 106
Gauteng 146–171
Gaza-Kruger-Gonarezhou Transfrontier Park 177, 186
Genadendal 82
General J. J. Fick Museum 128
geography 12–13
George 98
Geoscience Museum 166
Giant's Castle Game Reserve 208
Giant's Cup Trail 209

285

Index

Gingindlovu 212
God's Window 184
Goegap Nature
    Reserve 136
gold 35, 37, 125,
    160–161
Gold of Africa Museum 58
Gold Reef City 152
Golden Gate Highlands
    National Park 129
Golden Mile 194–195
golf 198–199
Goudini 77
Government of National
    Unity 22
Graaff-Reinet **112–113**,
    115
Grahamstown **108–109**
Graskop 184
Great Fish River
    Museum 112
Great Karoo 78
the Great Trek **32–33**, 103
Great Zimbabwe 221
Greater St. Lucia Wetland
    Park 214
Greenmarket Square 55
Griqua 124
Griquatown 143
Groot Constantia 68–69
Groot Karoo 78
Groote Kerk 55

H

Hans Merensky Nature
    Reserve 178
Harare 220
Harold Johnson Nature
    Reserve 200
Harold Porter National
    Botanical Garden 82
Harrismith **128**, 129
Hartbeespoort Dam
    170–171
Hartenbos 98
Hazyview 182
health 250–251
Hector Pierson Monument
    and Museum 159
Heidelberg, Western
    Cape 96
Helshoogte Pass 87
Hermanus 82–83
Heroes' Acre 169
Herolds Bay 98
Hester Rupert Art
    Museum 113
Heuningberg Nature
    Reserve 94
Highgate 81
hiking 208, **236–237**
history 23–44
    Anglo-Boer Wars **34**,
        38–39, 205,
        206–207
    Anglo-Zulu Wars 202,
        204–205
    apartheid 10, 21,
        40–41
    Boer-Zulu War 204
    British rule 34–35
    colonialism 28–29
    European trade 26–27
    the Great Trek 32–33
    Jameson Raid 35, 37,
        38
    Karoo 47, 78, **112–123**
    political emancipation 44
    prehistory 24–25
    proto-humans 24–25
    Randlords 36–37
    the Struggle 42–43
    Union of South Africa 35
    Zulu empire-building
        30–31

hitchhiking 247
Hlane Royal National
    Park 219
Hluhluwe-Umfolozi National
    Park 213
Hobhouse, Emily 39,
    127, 130
Hoedspruit 178
Hoekfontein Oxwagon
    Camp 128
Hogsback 107
Holocaust Centre 56
Honoured Dead
    Memorial 137
Horse Memorial 117
Hotazel 135
hotels 226
Houses of Parliament 56
Hout Bay 73
Howick 211
Hugh Exton Photographic
    Museum 179
Hugo Naudé House 77
Huguenot Memorial 86
Huguenot Museum 86
Huguenots 86
Hwange National Park
    221

I

Inkatha Freedom Party 22,
    191
inoculations 250
International Library of
    African Music 109
Irish House Museum 179
Irma Stern Museum 56
Isandlwana 204–205
Itala Game Reserve
    202–203

J

jacarandas 163
Jagersfontein 130
James Hall Transport
    Museum 153
Japanese Gardens 197
Jeffreys Bay 117
Jewish Museum,
    Cape Town 56
Jock of the Bushveld 181
Johannesburg 147,
    148–159, 160, 233
Johannesburg Art Gallery
    152
Johannesburg Botanical
    Garden 154
Johannesburg Lion Park
    158
Johannesburg Zoo and Zoo
    Lake 152–153
Julius Gordon Africana
    Museum 96

K

Kagga Kamma 76
Kakamas 136
Kalahari Raptor
    Rehabilitation Centre
    135
Kalk Bay 71
Kamberg Nature Reserve
    208
Kanoneiland 136
Kariega Game Park 111
Karoo 47, 78, **112–123**
Karoo National Botanical
    Garden 77
Karoo National Park 78
Karoo Nature Reserve
    113
Keimoes 136
Kemper Museum 134
Kenton on Sea 111

Kgalagadi Transfrontier
    Park 123, **134–135**,
    222
Khayelitsha 68
Khoikhoi 16, **28**, 83, 103,
    124, 143
Killie Campbell Collection
    196
Kimberley **137–139**, 141
King William's Town **107**
King's Park 127
Kirstenbosch National
    Botanical Gardens **69**,
    75
Klein Karoo 78, **79–81**
Kleinmond 82
Kleinplasie Museum 77
Kleinplasie Reptile
    World 77
Klondyke Cherry Farm 76
Knysna 99
Knysna Elephant Park 101
Knysna Forest 100–101
Knysna Museum 100
Knysna Oyster
    Company 100
Kommetjie 72
Koopmans de Wet House
    56–57, 115
Kosi Bay Nature Reserve
    214
Kouga Cultural Centre 117
Kowie Museum 110–111
Kraal Kraft 183
Kruger House Museum
    164
Kruger National Park 177,
    186–187
Kruger, Paul 34, 38, 160,
    164
Krugersdorp Game
    Reserve 158
Kuruman 135
KwaBhekithunga 213
KwaMuhle Museum 196
Kwandwe Game Reserve
    118
KwaZulu Cultural
    Museum 215
KwaZulu–Natal 22,
    188–215
KWV Brandy Cellars 77
KWV Wine Cellars 87, 93
KZN National Botanic
    Gardens 211

L

Ladysmith 38, **206–207**
L'Agulhas 94, 95
Lake Fundudzi 180
Lake Kariba 220–221
Lake Sibaya 214
Langa 68
Langebaan 85
language **16–17**, 249
Lesedi Cultural
    Village 171
Lesotho 216, **218**
Letaba District 178
Limpopo Province
    174–180
Little Karoo 78, **79–81**
Livingstone, David 135,
    143
Lobamba 219
Logan, James 79
Long Beach 72
Long Street 57
Long Tom Pass 185
L'Ormarins 93
Louis Trichardt 180
Lovedale College 111
Lowveld Botanical
    Gardens 183

Luderitz 223
Lukas Meijer House 203
Lutheran Church 57

M

Mabuasehube Game
    Reserve 222
Mac-Mac Falls and Pools
    185
Macrorie House Museum
    211
Madiba Freedom Museum
    151
Madikwe Game Reserve
    144
Mafikeng (Mafeking) 144
Magersfontein Battlefield
    139
Magoebeeskloof
    Mountains 178
Main Caves 208
Majuba 205
Makapaan's Caves 179
malaria 251
Malgas Pont 95
Man, Museum of 184
Mandela Museum 159
Mandela, Nelson **22**, 41,
    44, 66, 70, 104, 107,
    111, 167
Mantenga Falls 219
Mapoch Ndebele Village
    171
Maputaland 214
Maputo 224
Margate 201
Maria Ratschitz
    Mission 202
Marieskop 182
Marine Reserve 214
Market Theatre 155
Marloth Nature Reserve 83
Martins, Helen 113
Mary Moffat Museum
    143
Maseru 218
Mashu Museum of
    Ethnology 196
Masorini Open-Air Museum
    178
Matabo Hills 220
Matjiesfontein 79
Mbabane 219
McGregor 79
McGregor Museum 138
medical treatment
    250–251
Melrose House 164–165
Memorial to Pioneers of
    Aviation 137
Mgungundlovu 213
The Midlands 211
Midlands Meander 211
Midmar Public Resort and
    Nature Reserve 211
Military History Museum
    111
Millwood 101
mineral deposits 14, 37,
    125. See also
    diamonds; gold
Mining Village 130
Minitown 195
Missionary Museum 107
Mkhaya Game Reserve
    219
Mkhuze Game Reserve
    214
Mlilwane Wiildlife
    Sanctuary 219
Mmabatho 144
Model Shipyard (Mossel
    Bay) 97
Modjadji Forest 178

Moholoholo Wildlife Rehabilitation Centre 178
money 245
Monkeyland 101
Montagu 77
Montecasino 154
Monbijou Stately House 77
Mooi River Trail 208
Mooiddrift 179
Moremi Game Reserve 222
Moria 178
Morija 218
Mossel Bay 96–97
MOTHS Museum 202
Mount Everest Game Reserve 128
Mountain Zebra National Park 113
Mozambique 216, **224**
Mpumalanga and Limpopo Province 174–187
Muizenberg 71
Munwamadi 180
MuseuMAfrica 154
music and dance, traditional 232

N

Namakwa 136
Namib Desert 223
Namib Naukluft Park 223
Namibia 216, 217, **223**
Natal Maritime Museum 197
Natal Museum 211
Natale Labia Museum 71
National Afrikaans Literary Museum 126
National Assembly 22
National Botanical Garden 127
national holidays 244
National Museum 126
national parks 256
National Women's Memorial and War Museum 127
National Zoological Gardens 166
Natural Science Museum 194
Ndebele 17, **120–121**
Ndumo Game Reserve 214
Ndumu-Tembe National Park 214
Nelson Mandela Bay 116
Nelson Mandela Metropolitan Art Museum 116
Nelspruit 177, **183**
New South Africa 10–11
newspapers 248
Newtown Cultural Precinct 155
Nguni 17, **120–121**
Nieu Bethesda 113
Nieuwe Republiek Museum 203
Nkandla Forest 212
Noordhoek 72
North Coast 200
North-West Province 144–145
Northern Cape 134–143

O

Observatory Museum 109
Oceanarium 116
Okavango River 222
Old Carnegie Library 203

Old Court House 197
Old Drostdy Museum 118
Old Harbour Museum 82–83
Old House Museum 197
Old Library 113
Old Natal Parliament 211
Old Presidency 126
Old Residency 113
Old Station 118
Old Town House 58
Oliewnhuis Art Gallery 127
Olifantshoek 143
Olivershoek Pass 209
Ondini 215
Oom Samie se Winkel 91
opening times 244–245
Orange River (Gariep) 13, **124**
Orange River Valley 124–125
Orange River Winery 136
Orchid House 127, 197
Oribi Gorge 201
ostriches 80–81
Oude Drostdy 77
Oude Kerk Volksmuseum 76
Oudtshoorn 80–81
Outeniqua Choo-Tjoe 98, 235
Overberg 82–83
Owl House 113

P

P.R. Owen Dinosaur Park 183
Paarl 87
Pan African Congress (PAC) 41, 43
Panorama Falls 184
Paradise Valley Nature Reserve 201
Parktown 156
passports 243
Peddie 104–105, **111**
Peers Cave 71
Pellissier House 129
Phalaborwa 178–179
pharmacies 250
Phezulu 201
Philippolis 130
Phinda Resource Reserve 213
Phuthaditjhaba 130
Pietersburg (Polokwane) **179**
Pietermaritzburg 210–211
Piggs Peak 219
Pilanesberg National Park 144
Pilgrim's Rest 183
The Pinnacle 184
Pioneer Museum 171
Pioneers of Aviation Memorial 137
places of worship 255
Planetarium 157
Plettenberg Bay 101
police 250
politics and government 22
population 10–11, **16**
Port Alfred 110
Port Elizabeth 116–118
Port St. Johns 119
Port Shepstone 201
post offices 245
postal service 248
Postmasburg 143
Potgietersrus (Mokopane) 179
Premier Mine 170
Pretoria (Tshwane) 12,

147, **162–171**, 233
Pretoria Art Museum 164
Pride of Africa 234–235
public transportation **234–235, 246–247**

Q

Queen's Fort 127
Qwa Qwa National Park 130

R

rabies 251
railways 234–235
rain queens 178
Ratanga Junction 63
Rawsonville 77
Reconstruction and Development Programme (RDP) 14–15, 19
Reinet House 113
religions 17, 120–121
Rembrandt Van Rijn Art Museum 91
restaurants 264–265
Rhino and Lion Nature Reserve 158
rhino horn 118
Rhodes, Cecil 35, 36, 37, 58, 69, 71, **138**, 160
Rhodes Memorial 58
Richtersveld Transfrontier Park 136
rickshaws 195
Riversdale 96
Roaring Sands 143
Robben Island 43, 61, **70**
Robberg Nature Reserve 101
Robertson 77
Roodeport Museum 157
rooibos 85
Rorke's Drift 205
Le Roux Townhouse 81
Royal Natal National Park 209
rugby 198
Rust en Vreugd 58–59

S

Sabie 185
Sabie River 185, **186**
safari guide 266–284
Safari Ostrich Farm 81
safety **236–237, 251–252**
Sagole 176, **180**
St. Francis Bay 117
St. George's Cathedral 59
St. Helena Bay 85
St. Lucia 214
Saldanha Bay 85
Sammy Marks Museum 171
San 79, 103, **132–133**
San art **133**, 208
sanctions 14
Sandveld Nature Reserve 130
Sandy Bay 73
Sani Pass 209
Santa Carolina 224
Sapekoe tea plantation 178
Sasol Art Museum 91
Schoemansdal Museum 180
Schreiner, Olive 112
Schreiner House 112
Sci-Bono Centre 155
Science and Technology, Museum of 165
Scottburgh 201
scuba diving 214
Sea Point 73

Sendinggestig Museum 59
Senekal 131
senior citizens 254
Shaka **30–31**, 201, 212
Shakaland 212
Shamwari and Kwandwe Game Reserve 118
Shangana Cultural Village 182
sharks 200
Sharpeville **43**, 147
Shell Museum (Jeffreys Bay) 117
Shipwreck Museum 94
shopping 156, **231**, 245
Siege Museum 206
Signal Hill 60
Simon's Town 70, 72
Simunye 213
Skeleton Coast 223
Slave Lodge 60
Slave Tree 98
Smith, Sir Harry **128**
Smuts' House, Jan 171
snake parks 116, 179, 194, 201
Soccer City 159
Sodwana Bay National Park 214
Sophiatown 158
Sossusvlei Dunes 223
SA Airforce Museum 165
SAB World of Beer 155
SA Fisheries Museum 73
SA Library 60
SA Maritime Museum 60
SA Museum and Planetarium 61
SA National Gallery 61
SA National Museum of Military History 156–157
SA Naval Museum 70
SA Police Museum 71
SA Rock Art, Museum of 154
SA Sugar Terminal 200
South Coast 82–83, 200–201
Soweto 18, 19, 43, 148, **158–159**
spa resorts 176–177
Spier 93
Spioenkop 207
sports 198–199
Springbok 136
Staats Model School 169
Standard Bank Gallery 153
Stanger 201
State Theatre 168
Stellenbosch 90–91
Sterkfontein Caves 24, 25, **157**
Sterkfontein Dam Nature Reserve 128
Stilbaai 96
Stofberg House 77
student travel 248
Sudwala Caves 183
Sun City 145
Swakopmund 223
Swartberg 78
Swartkrans 25
Swaziland 216, **219**
Swellendam 83, 94–95

T

Taal Monument 87
Table Mountain and Cableway **62**
Talana Hill 206
Talana Museum 202
Tatham Art Gallery 211

Index/Acknowledgments

Taung "baby" 24
taxis 247
telephones 248–249, 250
television and radio 248
Tembe Reserve 214
Thabo Mofutsanyana 128
Thathe Vondo Forest 180
Thibault, Louis 68, 86, 113, 115
Thohoyandou 180
Thomas Baines Nature Reserve 111
Three Rondavels 182
time differences 244
tipping 255
toilets 255
Tongaat 200
tourist offices 256
tours and safaris 238–240
townships **18–19**, 172–173
Toy and Miniature Museum 90
trains 234–235
Transgariep Museum 130
Transkei 104, **119**
Transport Riders Museum 76
Transvaal **176**, 177
Transvaal Museum 166
travel insurance 243
traveller's cheques 245
tribal groupings 16, 17
Tropical House 116
Tshipise 176
Tsitsikamma Forest National Park 101

Tsonga Kraal Museum 178
Tswaing 171
Tswaing Meteorite Centre 171
Tugela Falls 208
Tulbagh 76–77
Tussen-die-Riviere 129
Tutu, Archbishop 16, **59**
Two Oceans Aquarium 63

U

Uitenhage 118
Ultimatum Tree 200
Ulundi 215
Umgeni River Bird Park 195
Umtata 119
Union Buildings 166–167
University of the Witwatersrand 156–157
Upington 20, **136**
Urquart House 113
uShaka Marineworld 197

V

Vaal River 13, 124
Vaalbos National Park 143
Valley of Desolation 113
Valley of a Thousand Hills 201
van Riebeeck, Jan **28**, 50, 52, 69
Van Ryn Brandy Cellar 93
Van Stadens Wild Flower Reserve 118

Venda 180
Victoria and Alfred Waterfront 63
Victoria Bay 98
Victoria Falls 220
Vilanculos 224
Village Museum 91
visas 216, **243**
visitors with disabilities 254
VOC Kruithuis 90
Voortrekker Monument and Museum (Pretoria) 167
Voortrekker Museum, (Pietermaritzburg) 211
Vryheid 203
Vukani Museum 212

W

Wagon Hill 207
Warmbaths (Bela-Bela) 176–177
Warrior Toy Museum 70
Waterberg 180–181
water sports 199
Waterworld 195
Welkom 130–131
Wellington 87
West Coast Fossil Park 85
West Coast 85
National Park 85
Western Cape 45–101
whales 71,**82**, **95**, 101
White River 183
Wild Coast 103, 105, **119**
Wilderness 98
National Park 99

wildlife, see Safari Guide
Willem Pretorius Game Reserve 131
Willem Prinsloo Agricultural Museum 171
William Fehr Collection of Africana 55, 59
William Humphreys Art Gallery 139
Winburg 131
Windhoek 223
wine 46–47, 68, **88–89**
Winelands 21, **86–87**, 88
wineries tour 92–93
Winterton Museum 208
Witwatersrand 147
Wonder Cave 158
Wonder View 184
Wonderwerk Cave 135
Worcester 77
World of Birds Sanctuary 73
Wyllies Poort 180

X

Xhosa 16, 17, 103, 104, 119, **120–121**

Z

Zimbabwe 216, 217, **220–221**
Zoology Museum 157
Zulu 16, 17, **30–31**, **120–121**
Zululand 212–213
Zululand Historical Museum 212

Author's Acknowledgments

Duncan, for his help in compiling information; South African Airways, Ethos Marketing, Cedarberg Travel, Jembisa, Entabeni, Sabi Sabi, Garonga, the Blue Train and :Legacy Hotels and the many tour guides and tourist offices throughout South Africa who went the extra mile to arrange tours and answer awkward queries.

Photographer's Acknowledgments

Clive Sawyer, photographer, would like to thank the following: Hans van den Berg, Durban Graham Stewart of Dumazulu fame; the manager and staff of the Shamwari Game Reserve; Mr and Mrs Uys, Bloubergstrand, Cape Town; the manager and staff at the Drosdty Hotel, Graaff-Reinet

Publishers' Acknowledgments

The Automobile Association wishes to thank the following photographers and libraries for their assistance in the preparation of this book. 159; DE BEERS 140a, 140c, 141a, 141b; MARY EVANS PICTURE LIBRARY 23, 26b, 27b, 28b, 30, 31, 38, 42c, 144, 160b, 207; GETTY IMAGES 27a, 28a, 29a, 29b, 33b, 34b, 35b, 36/7, 36a, 37b, 38/9, 39b, 40a, 40b, 140b, 199a, 205b; JOHN HOWARD 72; HUMAN AND ROUSSEAU (PTY) LTD 228b, 228c; NATURAL HISTORY MUSEUM 24a, 25; NATURE PHOTOGRAPHERS LTD B. Burbidge 125, Baron Hugo Van Lawick 266 (2), 281 (65), (67), 283 (75); R. Daniel 266 (3), 267 (4), 269 (7), 270 (21), 272 (34) K. J. Carlson, 267 (5), H. Miles 269 (7), P. R. Sterry, 269 (9), 269 (11), (12), (15) (16), 271 (27), (32), 272 (34), 273(45), 274 (46), (48); R. Tidman, 269 (10); 270 (21), 272 (34), 272 (35), 280 (63); E. Janes, 269 (15), 283 (73);P. Craig-Cooper, 269 (13), (17), (18), 270 (25), 271 (26), (28), (29), (30), (31), (32), 272 (36), 273 (37), (38), (39), (41), (42), (43), (44), (45), 274 (48), (49), (52), (53), (54), 277 (55), (56), 279 (60), 280 (64), 281(66), (68), J. Karmali, 269 (19);J. Reynolds, 270 (21), 273 (40); M. Harris 272 (35); E. Janes, 277 (56), 283 (73); M. Gore, 283 (74); J. Sutherland, 284 (77), S. Bisserot, 284 (78), (79); PICTURES COLOUR LIBRARY LTD 141, 160a, 161a, 221, 222b; REX FEATURES LTD 16b (PH Nils Jorgensen), 22a (I. McIlgorm), 41a (M. Peters), 41b 42a 43a (J. Kuus), 42b (S. Bilco), 43b (M. Peters), 44a (Facelly), 111 (J. Witt); MELISSA SHALES 30/1, 198, 212, 239; SOUTH AFRICAN AIRWAYS 242; SOUTH AFRICAN TOURISM 157; SPECTRUM COLOUR LIBRARY 74/5,100/1, 129, 136a, 136b, 161b, 209, 217, 219, 220, 222a, 223; JANE BURTON/WARREN PHOTOGRAPHERS 131:

The remaining photographs are held in the Association's own library (AA PHOTO LIBRARY) and were taken by Clive Sawyer with the exception of pages 15, 49, 153b, 156 which were taken by Malc Birkitt; page 153a taken by Gordon Clemats; pages 2, 4, 5a, 6, 11c, 16a, 32b, 45, 58, 59, 66, 68, 69, 71, 73, 75, 80a, 80b, 81, 84, 93, 95b, 98, 108, 113, 114b, 115a, 115b, 120/1, 120a, 128, 151, 189, 200, 206, 215, 218a, 218b, 225, 227b, 231a, 231b, 232, 233, 237a, 241, 257, 270 (23), 274 (50), 279 (62), 284 (76) taken by Paul Kenward; pages 132a, 148a, 224, 226 taken by Simon McBride.

Contributors

Revision verifier: Melissa Shales
Revision management Apostrophe S Limited